FASCIST MOVEMENTS IN AUSTRIA:
From Schönerer to Hitler

F. L. Carsten

FASCIST MOVEMENTS IN AUSTRIA:
From Schönerer to Hitler

F. L. Carsten

SAGE Studies in 20th Century History   Volume 7

Ⓢ SAGE Publications   London · Beverly Hills

For information address

SAGE Publications Ltd
44 Hatton Garden
London EC1N 8ER

SAGE Publications Inc
275 South Beverly Drive
Beverly Hills, California 90212

International Standard Book Number
0 8039 99925 Cloth
0 8039 98570 Paper

Library of Congress Catalog Card Number
76-22935

First Printing

Typeset by
Wells & Blackwell Ltd., Loughborough

Printed in Great Britain by
Biddles Ltd., Guildford, Surrey

CONTENTS

PREFACE

In view of the vast amount of literature on German National Socialism and Italian Fascism, it seems strange that comparatively little work has been done on the fascist movements of Austria which were intimately connected with both. Indeed, they could hardly have become dangerous to the existing order without the strong backing given to them from Germany and Italy. Yet there are only several Vienna PhD theses (most of them unpublished), a few monographs and some scattered articles dealing with one or the other aspect of the problem, as well as some books on Austro-German relations in the 1930s. There seems to be no comprehensive history of the Austrian fascist movements and the many links between them, no history of the whole *Heimwehr* movement, and none at all of the Austrian National Socialist Party.

This book attempts to fill this gap. It will be seen, I hope, that the Austrian fascist movements differed considerably from their counterparts in Italy and Germany, that Austrian Fascism had important roots and characteristics of its own, and that its study is very much worth while. In many ways, this book is a continuation of the themes discussed in my *Revolution in Central Europe 1918-1919*, for the fascist movements were a reaction to the revolutionary events of that year. Yet they were not simply counter-revolutionary but contained revolutionary elements of their own. This gave them an impetus and a force which a merely reactionary movement would never have possessed. To show this is the purpose of the following pages.

My researches in the Austrian and German archives would have been impossible had I not been granted special permission to use their voluminous files for the years up to 1938. I am most grateful to the Bundeskanzleramt in Vienna for permission to use the Austrian State archives, and particularly so to Hofrat Dr Walter Goldinger. As far as the Austrian provincial archives are concerned, my special thanks are due to the director of the Vorarlberger Landesarchiv, Dr Karl Heinz Burmeister; the director of the Burgenländische Landesarchiv, Dr Ernst; the director of the Steiermärkische Landesarchiv, Hofrat Dr Fritz Posch; the director of the Oberösterreichische Landesarchiv, Hofrat Dr

Hans Sturmberger; and the director of the Tiroler Landesarchiv, Hofrat
Dr Eduard Widmoser. For permission to use the Kärntner Landesarchiv
I have to thank Landeshauptmann Wagner and Hofrat Lobenwein of
the Carinthian Government who made this possible against strong local
opposition. Nikolaus Graf Revertera kindly allowed me to use some of
his father's papers in the Herrschaftsarchiv at Helfenberg, Upper
Austria. For drawing my attention to sources which I might have
missed and for giving me advice on some questions of detail, I am
particularly grateful to Dr Gerhard Botz, of the University of Linz, and
to Dr Anton Staudinger, of the Institut für Zeitgeschichte in Vienna.
Professor Karl Stadler at Linz unfailingly helped me to obtain access to
local archives where this proved difficult.

My many visits to Austrian and German archives would hardly have
been possible without the generous help which I received from the
Council of the School of Slavonic and East European Studies, University of London, as well as from the Institute of Contemporary
History, London, as a part of its general project of the study of
Fascism. Above all, however, my thanks are due to my wife who has
always been ready with her advice and encouragement, and without
whose help my work would have been far more difficult.

F.L.C.
London, February 1976

1

PRELUDE:

Georg von Schönerer and the Pan-Germans

The western parts of the Habsburg Monarchy — the Tyrol, Carinthia, Styria, Upper and Lower Austria, as well as large areas of Bohemia — were inhabited by people who spoke German and considered themselves Germans. In contrast with the Czechs and the Hungarians, the Poles and the southern Slavs, they had no nationality of their own. They were the loyal subjects of the Austrian Emperor and played a leading part in the services of the Monarchy, but they did not feel that they were 'Austrian' by nationality. Before the outbreak of the revolutions of 1848 this did not matter greatly; the German Confederation, founded in 1815, provided what unity there existed among the many German states, and the Austrian Emperor acted as its president. But the events of the revolutionary year gave a strong impulse to German nationalism, inside and outside the Habsburg Monarchy. Although the revolutionary movements were defeated throughout central Europe in 1849 and absolute government was restored in the Monarchy after a short liberal interval, the dream of German unity, called forth by the first nation-wide popular movement and the meetings of the Frankfurt Parliament, remained alive. Black, red and gold had been the flags of the barricades and of the Academic Legions in Vienna and in Prague: black, red and gold remained the colours of the nationalist student corporations and of the sports and gymnastic clubs, although these colours were forbidden by the Austrian government after the defeat of the revolution.

Yet German nationalism within the frontiers of the Habsburg Monarchy, during the second half of the nineteenth century, assumed forms rather different from German nationalism elsewhere; for the Austrian Germans were only a minority among the subjects of the Emperor. They felt threatened by the rising tide of nationalism among the Slavs who together formed the majority of the inhabitants. Indeed, according to the official statistics, the proportion of Germans in the Monarchy (excluding Hungary) was slowly declining: from 36.8 per cent of the total in 1880 to 35.8 per cent in 1900 and to 35.6 per cent in 1910, while the figures for the five major Slav nationalities were slowly increasing.[1] Nowhere else did the Germans find themselves in that position. The fervent nationalism of the Germans of Austria and Bohemia must be seen as a reaction to real or imagined dangers – a reaction which only too often overshot its mark and by its very violence served to increase the dangers which it wanted to prevent.

In 1861 Julius Krickl, who had been an important figure in the revolution of 1848 and a captain in the Academic Legion of Vienna, founded the first Viennese *Turnverein* – henceforth the gymnastic clubs formed an integral part of the nationalist and *völkisch* movement in Austria. The black, red and gold flag of the new club was baptized in the Baltic to symbolize the Prussian and 'Nordic' orientation of the founder members.[2] Only a few years later the defeat of Sadowa expelled Austria from Germany and deprived the Austrian Germans of any backing which they might have received from there. The German nationalists felt isolated and looked with longing eyes at the strong German Empire built by Bismarck on the basis of Prussian hegemony and the exclusion of Austria. The German Empire of 1871 acted as a magnet, and nationalist demonstrations in its honour became the order of the day at the Austrian universities. When a congress of German scientists was held at Graz in 1875, many people put out enormous German flags; the Austrian flag and the national anthem were insulted and the German ones were extolled. There were further incidents at a banquet given in honour of the guests. A few weeks later, at a student celebration at Graz University, the participants loudly whistled at the playing of the Austrian anthem and sang demonstratively *Deutschland über Alles*, the new German anthem, so that the celebration had to be terminated by the authorities.[3]

A few years later another feature of student nationalism made its appearance. The Viennese student corporation 'Libertas' adopted as the first point of its by-laws a rule that it was an association of German students, and that Jews could not be considered Germans, not even when they were baptized. The same rule was soon adopted by other *Burschenschaften* in Vienna, Graz and Prague.[4] Until this time, Jewish students who were assimilated and felt as Germans were freely accepted as members by the Burschenschaften (among them several who later became famous); but this now changed.

Anti-Semitism among the student corporations, where it became rampant in the later decades of the nineteenth century, was to a large extent caused by another fear, that of competition, of being overwhelmed by outsiders. Vienna then had a Jewish population of less than 15 per cent of the total; but in 1880 22.3 per cent of the law students were Jewish, and as many as 38.6 per cent of those reading medicine at the university.[5] In the faculty of medicine 30 per cent of the teaching staff were Jewish in 1869, but as many as 48 per cent in 1889-90; while in the faculty of law the percentage of Jewish teachers rose from 19.8 to 22 per cent in that period.[6] In 1876 a famous professor of medicine expressed his apprehension that so many poor Jewish students from Hungary and Galicia were flocking to Vienna where they were unable to maintain themselves (except by giving badly paid private lessons), and added in a footnote:

> Sometimes one forgets entirely that the Jews form a clearly defined nation and that a Jew is as little able ever to become a German as a Persian is, or a Frenchman, or a New Zealander, or an African; what one calls Jewish Germans are in reality Jews who accidentally speak German and have accidentally been educated in Germany, even if they compose poetry and think more beautifully and better in the German language than many a Teuton of the purest blood . . . .[7]

The professor's apprehensions met with a strong echo among his students. Two years later, in 1878, contact was established between the anti-semitic Burschenschaften and the man who was to become the acknowledged leader of the ultra nationalist Germans of Austria, the man to whom Hitler half a century later paid tribute in *Mein Kampf:* Georg von Schönerer.

Schönerer was born in 1842, the son of a wealthy Austrian railway builder who was ennobled for his services and bought a noble estate and castle as his residence, Schloss Rosenau to the north of Vienna. His son Georg was educated in Germany from the age of 14 to that of 21, and was greatly impressed by German progress and efficiency, which he forever after compared with Austrian *Schlamperei*.[8] In the Germany of the 1850s and 1860s he was no doubt also influenced by the prevailing mood of nationalism and the ardent desire for unification fostered by bourgeois and economic interests. The young Schönerer pursued his studies in two smaller German states which were very strongly affected by the national movement, Saxony and Württemberg. From 1869 onwards he took up residence in Schloss Rosenau, devoted his time and energy to the farming of his estate and founded the local agricultural and forestry society at Zwettl, with himself as the chairman. A few years later Schönerer was elected a deputy of the Austrian parliament for his rural district of Zwettl-Waidhofen by 223 to 197 electors (the franchise was indirect and severely restricted). In the *Reichsrat* he joined the German Progressive Club which was opposed to the *Ausgleich* with Hungary of 1867 and instead of Dualism favoured a loose, purely dynastic union with Hungary. This club also aimed at the separation of the purely Slav provinces of Galicia and Dalmatia from the Austrian half of the Monarchy so as to secure a German majority in 'Cisleithania'.[9] Presumably, the largest Slav nationality in the western half, the Czechs, could then safely be Germanized. In December 1876 Schönerer spoke in parliament in favour of giving up Austria's position as a great power which it was unable to maintain and of a merely personal union with Hungary (to replace the autonomy Hungary had gained in 1867); then closer economic ties with the German Empire could be cemented: 'We German Austrians must never lose sight of our goal, a reunification, i.e. a very close alliance with Germany.'[10]

Two years later, in 1878, Schönerer went considerably further in his desire for German unity and exclaimed in parliament: 'More and more often and louder and louder the call sounds in the German crown lands: if we could only belong to the German Empire, so as to be finally freed from Bosnia and company! ' No taxes should be voted to the government or, if they were voted, they should only be paid if the government forced the people to do so. That evening and during the following night hundreds of students of Vienna University left their cards at Schönerer's house as a sign of their enthusiastic approval.[11] This was the beginning of the close links between him and the nationalist students. It was only now that anti-Semitism was added to Schönerer's armoury. Yet for the time being his utterances remained comparatively free from anti-Semitism and distinctly radical. Early in 1881 he issued a proclamation to his German *Stammesgenossen* ('racial comrades') which listed many of the liberal demands, such as freedom of the press, of association and meeting, the right of coalition, state control over the church, obligatory civil marriage, the granting of their legitimate place in the state to the peasants and the workers, an extension of the rights of the co-operatives and trade unions to the benefit of the productive classes, the creation for them of economic chambers and a central Economic Council, and the nationalization of the railways.[12] In this programme anti-clericalism and radicalism were clearly joined together, as they were in the days of Joseph II, the 'revolutionary Emperor'.

Most of these radical demands were repeated in the famous Linz Programme of the German Liberals, published in September 1882. The intellectual fathers of the programme were, apart from Schönerer, the later leading socialists, Victor Adler and Engelbert Pernerstorfer, the later Christian Social leader Robert Pattai, and the well known historian Heinrich Friedjung; of these two, Adler and Friedjung, were Jewish, if not by religion, at least by origin. In addition to the radical demands, the programme urged that the German language must become the official language of the state, the exclusive language of the army and of the bureaucracy, and the language to be spoken in all representative assemblies; there should be closer cultural and economic cooperation with Germany, culminating in a customs union; Dalmatia, Bosnia and Herzegovina should be incorporated with Hungary; Galicia and Bukovina should share the same fate and in any case be separated from Austria, whose German character would thus be clearly established.[13] Earlier in that year the German Club in parliament decided not to accept Jews or people of partial Jewish origin as members, and this rule was incorporated in its by-laws.[14] This would have excluded two of the fathers of the Linz Programme, but neither was a deputy at that time. But the programme itself was defensive in character, for the German Liberals had lost their positions in the government and felt that their predominance was threatened.

German nationalism, anti-clericalism and anti-Semitism became the main planks of Schönerer's propaganda in the 1880s. In the year of the Linz Programme, 1882, Schönerer submitted to the Reichsrat petitions against the immigration of Russian Jews who were leaving Russia on account of persecution and were causing anxiety among the Viennese. These petitions claimed that responsibility for the persecutions to a large extent rested with the victims themselves; their own behaviour had caused general excitement and disgust — an assumption which allegedly became a certainty through the repeated pronouncements of the Russian government that 'above all the unproductive and obnoxious behaviour of many Russian Jews has brought about their general rejection'. In parliament Schönerer moved that one of the petitions be read out because it no doubt reflected the mood of the Austrian Christian population – 'I mean the Christian population in so far as it has not become infected by the Jews (*verjudet*).'[15]

In 1885 a last point was added to the Linz Programme: 'To carry out the envisaged reforms it is indispensable to eliminate Jewish influence from all spheres of public life.'[16] In 1887 2,206 mass petitions with 37,068 signatures against the immigration of Russian Jews were presented by Schönerer to the Reichsrat. There he strongly emphasized the differences which now separated him from the members of the German Club. He and his adherents, he declared in 1887, did not consider anti-Semitism a regrettable event or a dishonour,

> but on the contrary the very basis of the national idea, the principal means to promote true national convictions, and thus the greatest national achievement of this century. We consider everybody a defector from his people, from his nation who consciously supports Jewry and its agents and abettors... International Jewry preying for booty has struck its claws into the august body of the Germanic people.... Our anti-Semitism is not directed against the religion, but against the racial traits of the Jews which have not been changed either by the earlier pressure or through the freedom that now prevails....[17]

Schönerer proposed that Jews be restricted to certain occupations and be confined in ghettos.[18]

This change from an anti-Semitism based on economic and social motives – a feeling shared by many Austrians – to a racialism, which at the same time emphasized the superiority of the Germanic 'race' above all other races, became Schönerer's characteristic hallmark – a mark that distinguished him from the majority of German nationalists and anti-Semites. In 1886 he wired to the foundation meeting of a gymnastic club: it would be easier to wean a cat from catching mice than to make sportsmen out of members of the Jewish race.[19] Early in 1888, 407 local communes of Schönerer's home district, the Waldviertel, submitted a petition to the governor of Lower Austria which declared:

> ... But we have no intention to exercise cosmopolitan politeness towards immigrating Asiatic foreigners, and we desire of course that in our old German district posts in offices and schools are not entrusted to people who not only have an insufficient command of the German language, but who are totally

ignorant of German ways and customs and German sentiment. . . . They are occupying many influential positions and use and misuse them in the particular interest of their nation. . . . They oppress the peasants, artisans, officials and workers. . . . In truth the Jews are a foreign nation and a foreign race who are not disposed to practise tolerance or humanity towards us, but consider it their tribal right to exploit us by lying and cheating and if possible to subjugate us completely . . . .[20]

To spread the new gospel Schönerer in 1883 founded a journal, the *Unverfälschte Deutsche Worte,* the first issue of which proclaimed that his followers would never consent to accept as German a Jew because he spoke German or behaved like a German nationalist or would agree to a mixing of Jews and Germans:

Adopting the 'brutal racial point of view', we must on the contrary declare that we rather consider possible a mixing . . . with Slavs and Latins than any intimate connexion with the Jews. For the former are related to us as Aryans, while the latter are totally alien to us on account of their origin. . . .

Yet by 1885 the journal had only 1,698 paying subscribers, the large majority of them in Vienna and in Lower Austria.[21]

In Vienna an anti-semitic movement, the Reform Association, sprang up in the 1880s apparently quite independently of Schönerer's propaganda efforts. At a mass meeting held in October 1880, a watchmaker, Josef Buschenhagen, accused the Jewish pedlars of causing the ruin of the tradesman by underselling honest artisans and shopkeepers. In the following year a Society for the Protection of Craftsmen was founded by an anti-semitic leader, and in 1882 it became the Austrian Reform Association. Its journal, the *Volksfreund,* propagated slogans such as 'Do not buy from Jews' and 'Buy only from Christians'; and the movement rapidly grew, leading to boycotts and rioting.[22] In March 1882 Schönerer, although not invited to address a meeting of the Reform Association, nevertheless spoke amidst roars of applause and proclaimed: 'If it ever should be necessary to resort to violence against the capitalists for the good of the workers, I will be the first to do so.'[23] He had found followers among the small people of Vienna and among the people threatened by the advance of big capitalism who found in the Jews a convenient scapegoat. In 1885 the *Deutsche Turnverein* (German Gymnastics Club) was founded in Vienna, which did not accept Jewish members and elected Schönerer an honorary member at its foundation. In 1887 the *Erste Wiener Turnverein* changed its by-laws so that in future only Germans of 'Aryan' descent could become members. Eight local associations of the *Turnerschaft* in Lower Austria then followed this example.[24]

As early as 1884 the socialist leader Karl Kautsky wrote apprehensively: 'We are having great trouble in stopping our people from fraternizing with the anti-Semites. The anti-Semites are . . . much more dangerous [in Austria] than in Germany because their appearance is oppositional and democratic, thus appealing to the workers' instincts.'[25] Thus in Vienna very varied social groups were attracted by anti-semitic propaganda, and even the Social Democratic workers were not immune. Yet in the *Deutscher Schulverein*, which was responsible for maintaining German schools in nationally disputed areas, a motion granting to local wards the right to accept members so that Jews might be excluded, was lost in 1886. In the following year, therefore, the adherents of Schönerer seceded and founded their own *Schulverein für Deutsche* which remained a rather small organization. The Deutscher Schulverein, on the other hand, continued to subsidize even Jewish schools.[26] In 1894 the annual report of the *Deutscher Volksverein* claimed that the anti-semitic movement was steadily gaining adherents among the German nationalists, that the view was gaining ground among them 'that there cannot be a world socialism, but only a national socialism, the precondition of which is anti-Semitism . . . '.[27]

Schönerer's veneration for all things Germanic soon assumed very strange forms. In 1887 two thousand years had passed since the victory of the Germanic tribes of the Cimbri and Teutonici over the Romans at Noreia to the south of the Danube. The anniversary was celebrated by the lighting of solstice fires, and a Germanic calendar was inaugurated with the year One (113 B.C.) that of the great victory.[28] Germanic names were to replace the names of the months, with *Hartung* for January, *Hornung* for February, and so on to *Gilbhart* for October, *Nebelung* for November, and *Julmond* for December. Soon too 'Germanic ornaments' could be bought to decorate ties, shirts and watches, often with Schönerer's image or head; his picture decorated Teutonic beer mugs and pocket knives, pipes and cigarette holders. His more ardent followers sported Jews hanging from the gallows on their watch chains and walking sticks with the head of a Polish Jew. An enterprising tobacconist in Vienna sold cigar holders which showed Schönerer's picture when held against the light, costing 20 *Kreuzer* to anti-Semites, and 25 to the 'aiders and abettors of the Jews and the Jewish press'.[29]

When in a district of the Waldviertel the levying of the excise on wine and meat was farmed out to a Jew for 6,000 fl. Schönerer encouraged the local innkeepers to sell beer instead of wine; strong efforts were made to impede the tax farmer and his employees and such coarse anti-semitic deeds were perpetrated against them that he quickly departed from the district, whereupon the local tradesmen bought the lease of the excise back for 4,700 fl.[30] These activities soon led to conflicts with the police.

Early in 1888 a drinking festivity of the Viennese student corporation 'Teutonia' was declared closed by the supervising official when it assumed a political character. Thereupon Schönerer shouted 'ridiculous' and encouraged the students to remain seated and to sing *The Watch on the Rhine*. When a police platoon of six men appeared to clear the hall, it took them half an hour to do so, while Schönerer was poking fun at their efforts and the students found the proceedings hilarious. Finally the last seven people with Schönerer at their head left slowly and in single file.[31]

Side by side with anti-Semitism there figured attacks on Rome and the Church. In Marburg in Styria Schönerer exclaimed in 1886: 'To be national means to love one's people above everything in the world. Our enemy is clericalism which aims at imposing on us the yoke of an international hierarchy . . . .'[32] At a nationalist mass meeting in Vienna two years later he opposed the appointment of Jewish teachers in 'our schools', but equally the confessional elementary school 'because we German nationalists want the Christian-Germanic, or the Christian-Aryan school' and thus dislike 'a one-sided confessional elementary school system formed according to the wishes of Rome's followers (*Römlinge*)'.[33] Nor were other issues forgotten. With Schönerer as the chairman a mass meeting was organized in the Vienna town hall in 1884 to demand the nationalization of the railway line leading from Vienna to the north: an issue which enabled Schönerer to gain strong popular support. In favour of this demand more than 3,000 petitions were submitted to parliament, among them 1,341 from local communes and associations and 1,334 signed by inviduals with a total of 33,896 signatures; 47,648 individual signatures were appended to petitions desiring a customs union with the German Empire.[34] These mass petitions indeed were a favourite form of propaganda which enabled Schönerer to carry his slogans to the people and to associate them with his demands.

Among the social demands which Schönerer put forward were the introduction of a limited working day, the prohibition of child labour, the limitation of labour for women, and a compulsory rest day on Sundays; otherwise a war was likely to occur 'the like of which has never been waged in Europe so cruelly and destructively'.[35] In a meeting at Marburg Schönerer exclaimed in 1886:

> The workers are our brethren of equal rank; we are obliged to take care of the lowliest and to achieve that the law protects the worker against exploitation of any kind. The workers' leaders thrive on the discontent of the masses, and their role would soon end if the law protected the poor workers against exploitation of any kind.[36]

Schönerer even advocated the introduction of a general and direct franchise, but only as a transition to a more equitable voting system based on nationalities.[37]

There is little doubt that Schönerer found his most enthusiastic followers among the students, or to put it more accurately among the members of the Burschenschaften which were strongly nationalist and anti-semitic even before Schönerer joined forces with them. In 1893, on the day when he recovered his civil rights, no fewer than fourteen student corporations from Vienna and seven from Graz, but only two from Innsbruck sent him congratulations. Schönerer himself once said that his party consisted primarily of students and peasants.[38] Indeed, the movement seems to have been particularly strong in rural areas, especially in Schönerer's native Waldviertel. In the year 1885 the *Unverfälschte Deutsche Worte,* when publishing his electoral address, asked all those supporting it to declare so in writing. There were 3,260 replies, giving the supporters' names, professions and places of residence. Most came from Lower Austria and Vienna, nearly 42 percent of the total; a surprisingly large number were from the small provinces of Silesia, over 20 percent, and a fairly large number from Bohemia, 16 percent – provinces where the Polish and Czech 'threats' to German-hood were particularly felt. Response from all other crown lands was fairly insignificant, and in certain cases minute, for example from Carinthia and the Tyrol which later had very strong nationalist movements.[39]

As to the occupations of the 3,260 respondents, rural ones certainly were strongly represented: 829 of them derived their livelihood directly from agriculture, ranging from peasants to estate owners and estate managers. 606 were local councillors, mayors or village mayors: the majority of them very likely farmers of some kind; and the same may have applied to many of the 159 innkeepers and publicans. Thus almost half the number may have had rural occupations of one kind or another. There was a fair sprinkling of the academic professions, with or without the doctor title, such as doctors, teachers, architects and apothecaries, about 140 or over 4 percent of the total. There were 72 officials, 70 factory owners and five hotelkeepers; 204 or 6 percent were traders or shopkeepers of different kinds. Above all, there was a large number of craftsmen and artisans, with or without the title of 'master', 481 in all, or almost 15 percent of the total.[40] It is almost impossible to distinguish between those who were independent masters and those who were not because many of the latter were probably not wage-earners but working on their own. They represented the lower class of the period, before Austria became industrialized on a larger scale. Entirely absent were not only the students (who were too young to vote), but also the military and the clergy, whether catholic or protestant, which may perhaps be explained by the well known radicalism of Schönerer's appeal.

In general it seems that he attracted above all middle class and lower middle class support. But it has to be remembered that the voting qualification still stood at the payment of 5 fl. in direct taxes, otherwise the percentage from the lower classes might have been higher. What becomes evident is that exactly the same social groups later furnished the National Socialist Party with its early supporters and members: groups which felt particularly threatened by the progress of industrialization and by Jewish competition, or were hostile to the 'establishment' because of financial or economic difficulties. There was not only ideological, but also social continuity between the two movements. Among the leaders of the party in Vienna there was a marked preponderance of professional people, such as lawyers, doctors, teachers and accountants, in addition to a number of business men.[41] A report of the Vienna police to the ministry of the interior from the year 1894 remarked on the lack of success of Schönerer's party among the workers; meetings in the working-class districts were usually badly attended, and the speakers did not come from the working class.[42]

In 1888 Schönerer's political career was rudely interrupted. On 8 March the *Neue Wiener Tagblatt*, somewhat prematurely in a special edition, announced the death of the German Emperor William I (he died on the next day): a report that was specifically withdrawn in a second edition. Thereupon Schönerer accompanied by some thirty adherents full of wrath entered the paper's offices and confronted the editors. Schönerer exclaimed:

> There you see them at work, these infamous newspaper Jews (*Schandblatt-juden*). . . . That they went so far as to use the life, the person, the majesty of

the dying German Emperor for business purposes by the spreading of false
news, must wound us Germans to the utmost. We feel that thus the whole
German nation has been defamed and insulted.

He then demanded that the journalists should kneel down and ask for
forgiveness, and repeated the demand when they merely grinned.[43]
One of them, however, called in the printers because he considered the
situation threatening. A free fight then developed in which the anti-
semites used beer glasses and walking sticks, but after some minutes
were put to flight by the printers. Schönerer was put on trial on a
charge of public violence and forcible entry, after the Reichsrat had
lifted his parliamentary immunity. On 5 May he was found guilty and
sentenced to four months of rigorous imprisonment with two fast days
a month, the loss of his parliamentary seat and of civil rights for five
years, and forfeiture of his noble rank. While the sentence was pronounced thousands assembled outside the court and shouted 'Long live
Schönerer!' A week later about 300 carriages drew up at his door
where 724 visiting cards and 135 bouquets of flowers were delivered.
Thousands of people demonstrated in the streets of Vienna and sang
The Watch on the Rhine in front of the Imperial palace. The demonstrations were repeated on the day when Schönerer went to prison. His
political career seemed to be at an end, and this was also his own
opinion at the time.[44] Among the many visitors to Schönerer's house a
week after his trial was Dr Karl Lueger who, less than ten years later,
was to become Vienna's most popular mayor. There can be little doubt
that Schönerer's popularity had not suffered by his behaviour, nor by
his trial and imprisonment.

Yet without him the movement which he had founded and led
quickly disintegrated. Some of his leading followers retired from political life, others founded new parties or joined another party. 'The most
unedifying conditions' prevailed among the German Nationalists,[45] as
one of Schönerer's most ardent admirers put it, and the party broke up.
One of his followers, Vergani, used Schönerer's absence in prison to
found a daily paper, the *Deutsche Volksblatt,* and to behave as if he
were Schönerer's successor. Vergani held the lucrative post of chief
editor and within a year succeeded in raising its circulation to 19,000.
But Schönerer denounced the enterprise and expelled Vergani from the
party, whereupon he joined Lueger and the nascent Christian Social
Party.[46] Strife also broke out among the few deputies who belonged to
the Schönerer group. In 1889 the deputy Fiegl was expelled, first from
his local ward, and then from the party because 'he had disturbed the

party's harmony and this at a time when the party and its leader were in great difficulties'. In October another deputy, Türk, wrote to the other deputies of his group and threatened to resign from it unless Fiegl was expelled by the end of the month, acting as it seems on Schönerer's instructions. Thus Türk had no choice but to leave the parliamentary group which now ceased to exist.[47] Schönerer, although barred from political activities after his release from prison, tried to assert his control over the party and its deputies, but this met with considerable opposition.

This Schönerer himself had to acknowledge in June 1895: he issued a declaration that the members of the Deutscher Volksverein in Vienna no longer stood solidly behind him, although they had accepted his exclusive leadership on joining the association. On very important matters opinions within it differed widely; hence he retired as chairman and at the same time left the association. He also resigned as leader of the Pan-German party which in his opinion was busy destroying itself. The party's decline he attributed to 'disloyalty, defection, broken promises and treason within its own camp': 'As a German Nationalist and thus an enemy of everything Jewish I must, now as before, always fight against anything that is un-German and corrupt. I thus cannot adopt a friendly attitude towards those party groups which are now led by Dr Lueger . . . .'[48] Indeed, it was the rise of the Christian Social Party, particularly in Vienna, which deprived Schönerer not only of many party leaders but also of his mass following among the small craftsmen and shopkeepers, and to some extent even among the students. Early in 1894 the Viennese police reported to the ministry of the interior that he was losing support in Vienna, Krems and Tulln (in Lower Austria) and among the Burschenschaften. Students shouted down the acting editor of *Unverfälschte Deutsche Worte* in the summer of 1893 when he praised Schönerer and called *pereat* when he mentioned Schönerer's name.[49] In November 1894, at a mass meeting of Catholics, Lueger committed the unforgivable sin of crying 'Praised be Jesus Christ!' and thus, in the opinion of the German Nationalists, destroyed the bridges between them and the Christian Social Party; in their eyes, Lueger had defected to the 'black' camp.[50] Henceforth he became the declared hero and leader of the small people of Vienna.

In 1897 Schönerer, who had regained his civil rights, was reelected to the Reichsrat as a deputy for the rural curia of Eger-Asch-Elbogen in north-western Bohemia by 236 against 141 votes which were split among three opponents. Four of his followers were also elected, all in

Bohemia or Silesia.[51] The party's area of influence shifted to the German-speaking districts of Bohemia where the Germans felt threatened by the rise of Czech nationalism and the penetration of Czechs into German areas. A few months later the outbreak of the Badeni crisis provided Schönerer and his fellow-deputies with the long-awaited chance to stir up trouble not only in parliament but also in the streets — and with a golden opportunity to extend their influence to much wider nationalist circles throughout German Austria. The Prime Minister, Count Badeni, intended to grant equality to the Czech and German languages in the internal administration of Bohemia — a step that was welcomed by the Czechs, most of whom knew German, but aroused violent German fears and protests. In the Reichsrat, the followers of Schönerer aided by many deputies belonging to other German parties resorted to tactics of obstruction, demanded voting by name, separate votes and intervals before voting, and disrupted all orderly parliamentary procedures in a concerted attempt to bring down the government. The deputy Wolf caused pandemonium when he exclaimed that the Slavs were 'culturally deeply inferior' to the Germans and likened Czech culture to that of 'Zulus and Eskimos'. Outside parliament the Burschenschaften and 'national' student corporations paraded to thank Schönerer and Wolf. In July a German People's Congress was to meet at Eger in Bohemia to demonstrate against the Badeni decrees, but the meeting was prohibited by the authorities. The ban was defied by the organizers, among whom were Schönerer and Wolf, and a pitched battle with the mounted police ensued in which hundreds were wounded. During similar riots in Graz in November a student was killed.[52]

On 24 November 1897 there were more violent scenes in parliament where the government in vain attempted to have the vital bill for the Ausgleich arrangements with Hungary passed. Trumpets, whistles, sirens and other 'musical' instruments were blown, desk lids were banged, free fights started, and in the midst of these tumultuous scenes Schönerer demanded to speak and, seizing the president's bell, refused to give way. Another deputy snatched the bell from Schönerer and returned it to the president who finally closed the sitting. On the next day Wolf called the president, Ritter von Abrahamowicz, a 'Polish swindler', while Schönerer again demanded the right to speak. Wolf seconded him crying that no law existed any longer in this state because Badeni had violated it. Parliament became a battlefield; police entered the chamber at the request of the president, and several deputies — among them

Schönerer and Wolf – were forcibly removed. Violent demonstrations took place in the streets of Vienna, Graz and Salzburg, riots broke out in Prague, and martial law had to be proclaimed. Against the crowds which were joined by many highly respectable Austrians and many followers of the moderate parties Badeni was helpless. On the 27th he offered his resignation which was accepted by the Emperor when Lueger declared that he could not guarantee the maintenance of law and order in Vienna.[53] The offensive ordinances which had caused the crisis were withdrawn. The German Nationalists gained an important victory. In June 1898 Schönerer handed in 2,183 petitions bearing together 51,674 signatures which demanded the legal safeguarding of German as the official Austrian language.[54]

The Badeni crisis also produced a spate of meetings in Germany in sympathy with the 'suffering' Austrian Germans. Even before, Schönerer had extended his activities to Germany. In 1892 he was to speak in Hamburg, but the meeting was dissolved by the authorities because it was a public meeting, and not the announced private one; many thousands present hailed Schönerer and marched to near-by Altona in Prussia where Schönerer was able to address them. In 1896 the Austrian Nationalists – travelling to Bismarck's residence at Fried-richsruh – met representatives of sixteen German nationalist organiza-tions in Hamburg to honour Schönerer. After Bismarck's death in 1898 Friedrichsruh became the scene of an annual pilgrimage by Schönerer and his closest followers where they vowed unconditional loyalty to the *Volk*.[55] Veneration for Bismarck and the German Empire remained one of the principal traits of their propaganda. Yet this also impeded the growth of the party in a country where loyalty to the Habsburg dynasty and the reigning monarch was very strong among the German-speaking population. What hindered the party's growth even more was Schönerer's pronounced anti-Catholicism, his efforts to persuade people to leave the Church and to convert to Protestantism, and his fulmina-tions against the 'Jewish' Bible. On 1 December 1898 the *Unverfälschte Deutsche Worte* carried a manifesto 'Break with Rome!': 'the fetters that bind us to a Church hostile to the Germans' must be broken so that the Germanic spirit could prevail. Early in 1899 Schönerer an-nounced that he would leave the Catholic Church as soon as 10,000 conversions to Protestantism had been effected, and this he did a year later. Meanwhile the *Unverfälschte Deutsche Worte* declared: 'The facts cannot be reversed that the Jew Bible is not a German moral and religious book and that the founder of Christianity as the son of a racial

Jewess and a descendant of David is not an Aryan . . . .' But one of his most loyal adherents, the deputy Dr Eisenkolb, warned Schönerer that their cause suffered damage because the *Unverfälschte Deutsche Worte* was constantly writing about the 'Jew Bible'.[56]

Even Schönerer was aware of these facts and declared at the end of 1903:

> The endeavour to form a large party is only possible at the expense of the party's principles! The Pan-Germans too would be able to create a large party if they renounced certain fundamental points of their programme, for example anti-Semitism, the Break-with-Rome movement, non-participation in addresses of loyalty [to the Emperor], etc. This would produce a large party but also the end of the German Volk.[57]

Schönerer himself claimed in 1913 – speaking on the occasion of the centenary of the Battle of Leipzig – that more than '70,000 German men and women have left the darkness of the Roman priests' church'.[58] But this was not an impressive figure in a country of almost 30 million inhabitants, and many of those who left the Church probably did so on account of socialist, not Pan-German propaganda.

In 1901 the Pan-Germans had their greatest electoral success and gained 21 seats in the Reichsrat, mainly in Bohemia and Moravia. But internal rifts continued to mar the party's development. In the same year Wolf, Schönerer's principal lieutenant, renounced his seat but was re-elected, and then accepted the mandate against the wishes of the Pan-Germans. He broke with them and was joined by seven other deputies who were alienated by Schönerer's radicalism and thought that some concessions should be made to the prevailing pro-Austrian sentiment. Wolf then founded the Free Pan-German Party which soon attracted many members from the old and more radical party. Violent quarrels ensued between the two factions. In Carinthia, the Association of Pan-Germans tried to adopt a middle course and sometimes pronounced against Wolf, and sometimes in his favour, 'and thus lost all ground'. The Burschenschaften too demanded that their members should support neither Schönerer nor Wolf, but many students followed the line of their elders and tended towards Wolf.[59]

With the introduction of universal male suffrage in 1907 Schönerer's electoral appeal waned. In the election of that year he received only 909 votes in his old constituency of Eger, against 4,830 for the Social Democrat, 1,623 for the Agrarian and 1,042 votes for the Christian Social candidate. Only three deputies from his party were elected, compared with twelve of the Free Pan-Germans.[60] Schönerer and his followers continued to stress the 'purity' of their movement, but in reality it was split into fragments. There were too many 'traitors' to the cause and almost uninterrupted expulsions, while constant in-fighting took place between various Pan-German and German Radical groups and parties: traits which were to remain characteristic of the völkisch camp in Austria. In 1913 Schönerer himself virtually admitted defeat. Speaking in Germany on the anniversary of the battle of Leipzig he exclaimed: 'Austria is in the process of becoming a Slav state, and later generations will never be able to understand that the Germans and their representatives have consciously helped to create this Slav state . . . . Austria today is under Slav domination . . . .'[61]

The decline of the Pan-Germans and the limited success of Schönerer as a political leader may in the first instance be attributed to his personality. He was too autocratic and dictatorial; he constantly quarrelled with his own most loyal followers and was determined to retain sole control of the party (but so was Hitler a generation later). His violent attacks on Rome and the 'Jew Bible' could only alienate the strongly Catholic population of the Monarchy, as did his veneration for all things German and his hostility to the Habsburg dynasty. The cult of Germanic gods and his Germanic calendar marked him as a sectarian; even in the Germany of the 1920s and 1930s General Ludendorff's attempts to introduce similar cults met with total failure. In the more stable and prosperous society of central Europe before the First World War these traits effectively isolated Schönerer and met with severe criticism even inside his own party. It was characteristic of the movement that one after the other of his deputies and sub-leaders left him – many to join the rising star of the Christian Social Party which was loyal to the Church and the Monarchy. Nor does it seem likely that the fortunes of the Schönerer party would have improved if it had adopted a more democratic and revolutionary course.[62] It seems, on the contrary, to have been Schönerer's right-wing destructive and extremist attitude – apart from his personal qualities – that condemned him to isolation. A more radical mass movement came into being in Austria in the later years of the nineteenth century, but it was left-wing and socialist, led by Schönerer's old associates Adler and Pernerstorfer. Schönerer's extreme nationalism and anti-Semitism had only a limited appeal for the working class, although the socialist movement itself was rent by national conflicts.

Yet the Schönerer movement left a lasting legacy in Austria and in

Bohemia. Countless nationalists and youngsters, especially students, imbibed the ideas of Pan-Germanism and racial anti-Semitism. When they were middle-aged these ideas were apparently realized victoriously in Hitler's Germany. The young Austrian students of the 1930s then became enthusiastic National Socialists, and they often succeeded in winning over their fathers. The latter returned to the ideas of their youth; they felt that they were young once more and could join hands with the younger generation.[63] Many of the later National Socialist leaders had been active members of a Burschenschaft in their younger days. In 1933, when reporting on the local medical officer in Güssing (Burgenland) the *Bezirkshauptmannschaft* simply stated that he was a Burschenschaftler 'and believes that therefore he must be a German Nationalist (*deutschnational*);' the doctor had visited Germany for a few days, and on his return 'was full of praise, even for the Prussian beer' – to the surprise of the beer experts of the district.[64]

In 1938 – a few weeks before the German occupation of Austria – even a personal link of the still underground National Socialists with the days of Schönerer was established. Their Austrian leader Josef Leopold was prevented by the government from visiting Germany for political purposes. He therefore sent Dr Anton Schalk, who had once been Schönerer's deputy and had sat in the Reichsrat for the Pan-Germans, to inform Himmler about the political situation in Austria, with full powers to negotiate with the Germans.[65] As we shall see, the founder members and leaders of the German Workers' Party in Austria and Bohemia were all deeply influenced by Schönerer and hailed him as 'the *Führer* of the German people of the Eastern March'.[66] It was from this party that the Austrian National Socialist Party developed in the 1920s. As a young man in Linz and Vienna another Austrian, Adolf Hitler, came under the influence of Schönerer's Pan-Germanism and anti-Semitism: what Schönerer lacked in Hitler's opinion was political common sense and an understanding of the social question, otherwise his movement might have changed the course of German destiny.[67]

In truth Schönerer also put forward demands for social legislation to improve the position of the working class; this was done to wean workers away from the Social Democrats. In this, as in so much else, Schönerer was following the example of his admired Bismarck. But, like Bismarck, he was too much a man of the upper class ever to become a real rabble rouser, a man aiming at the destruction of the 'system'. Schönerer did his level best to rouse the students and other middle-class groups, to make them aware of the 'threat' to their position emanating from Jews and Slavs. But even that was something very different from the tactics later employed by the National Socialists – not to speak of their methods once they were in power. Schönerer also aimed at the dissolution of the Habsburg Monarchy; yet even this aim was not totally destructive and negative – after all, the revolutionaries of 1848 wanted to create a united Germany including the German-speaking parts of Austria and that too would have meant the end of the Monarchy. The Liberals of 1848 as well as the later Pan-Germans no doubt wanted to include Bohemia and Moravia in this united Germany. One might perhaps say that forty years later this aim was even more unrealistic than it had been in 1848, as Czech nationalism meanwhile became a much stronger force. In general, what Schönerer lacked conspicuously was political realism: on that point Hitler was certainly right. Yet even if he had possessed more political common sense a very different factor was essential to help him to victory: the complete demolition of the comparatively stable and prosperous world of the late nineteenth century. That was achieved by the warring powers of the First World War, and not by the forces at work inside the Monarchy, however bitter their mutual conflicts may have been.

NOTES

1. See the detailed figures given by Robert A. Kann, *Das Nationalitäten-problem der Habsburgermonarchie*, Vol. II (Graz-Cologne, 1964) 390-92.

2. Dirk van Arkel, *Antisemitism in Austria* (Proefschrift, Leiden, 1966) 178.

3. John Christopher Peter Warren, 'The political career and influence of Georg Ritter von Schönerer' (Unpublished London Ph.D. thesis, June 1963) 95-96.

4. Eduard Pichl, *Georg Schönerer*, Vol. II (Oldenburg, 1938) 319-20. The six volumes of this work, by a most ardent admirer of Schönerer, are the standard reference work on the subject, and are a vast collection of material rather than a biography.

5. Berthold Windt, 'Die Juden an den Mittel- und Hochschulen Österreichs seit 1850', *Statistische Monatsschrift*, VII (1881) 442-57; quoted by Warren, op. cit., 140.

6. Friedrich Heer, 'Freud, the Viennese Jew', in Jonathan Miller (ed.), *Freud, The Man, His World, His Influence* (London, 1972) 9.

7. Dr Theodor Billroth, *Über das Lehren und Lernen der medicinischen*

Wissenschaften an den Universitäten der deutschen Nation (Vienna, 1876) 152; 153 n.

8. Pichl, op. cit., Vol. I, 21; Warren, op. cit., 42-44.

9. Pichl, op. cit., Vol. I, 28-29; Warren, op. cit., 58, 66.

10. Pichl, op. cit., Vol. I, 54-55, 118.

11. Ibid., 70-71; Warren, op. cit., 93-95. According to the protocol the speech met with strong opposition in the Reichsrat.

12. Pichl, op. cit., Vol. I, 100-101.

13. Ibid., 112-14; Kann, op. cit., Vol. I, 98-99.

14. Pichl, op. cit., Vol. I, 99.

15. Ibid., 161-63.

16. Ibid., 115.

17. Ibid., 270, 316-17.

18. Andrew Whiteside, 'Austria', in Hans Rogger and Eugen Weber (eds.), *The European Right* (Berkeley-Los Angeles, 1965) 313.

19. Pichl, op. cit., Vol. II, 543. The telegram was couched in poetic form.

20. Ibid., Vol. I, 353-55.

21. Ibid., Vol. II, 59, 66. The journal's name means 'Undiluted German Words'.

22. van Arkel, op. cit., 50-52.

23. Andrew G. Whiteside, *The Socialism of Fools – Georg Ritter von Schönerer and Austrian Pan-Germanism* (Berkeley, 1975) 86.

24. Pichl, op. cit., Vol. II, 381-2; Peter G. J. Pulzer, *The Rise of Political Anti-Semitism in Germany and Austria* (New York, 1964) 223.

25. Quoted by P. G. J. Pulzer, 'The Development of Political Antisemitism in Austria', in J. Fraenkel (ed.), *The Jews of Austria* (London, 1967) 433.

26. Pichl, op. cit., Vol. VI, 155; Vol. II, 274, 277, 288.

27. Ibid., Vol. IV, 204.

28. Ibid., Vol. II, 428-29.

29. Ibid., Vol. II, 31; Vol. IV, 599.

30. Ibid., Vol. IV, 470.

31. Ibid., Vol. II, 376: police report of 29 January 1888. *Die Wacht am Rhein* was the favourite German anti-French song of the time.

32. Pichl, op. cit., Vol. III, 435.

33. Ibid., Vol. I, 190-91.

34. Ibid., Vol. I, 226, 229, 271; Whiteside, *Socialism of Fools,* 109-11.

35. Pichl, op. cit., Vol. III, 112, 117 (1883).

36. Ibid., Vol. III, 426.

37. Ibid., Vol. III, 433 (1884).

38. Ibid., Vol. II, 315; Vol. IV, 421; van Arkel, op. cit., 171. Cp. below, pp. 20-21, for Schönerer's loss and recovery of civil rights.

39. van Arkel, op. cit., 143, gives the detailed geographical distribution.

40. The detailed occupations are listed by van Arkel, op. cit., 136-44, but the additions and percentages are mine. The different occupations given by the respondents are often difficult to interpret, and I am very grateful to Dr Gerhard Botz, Linz, for helping me in this task.

41. Pulzer, *The Rise of Political Anti-Semitism,* 283, from two registers of the Viennese executive committee, s.d.

42. Warren, op. cit., 258-59.

43. The above is Schönerer's own version given to the court: Pichl, op. cit., Vol. II, 436; the version of the public prosecutor is given, ibid., 456.

44. Ibid., Vol. II, 439-41, 470, 484, 497; Warren, op. cit., 211-12, 215-16.

45. Pichl, op. cit., Vol. II, 498.

46. van Arkel, op. cit., 91-92; Warren, op. cit., 237.

47. Warren, op. cit., 231-36, with many quotations from the Türk-Schönerer correspondence of 1889.

48. *Unverfälschte Deutsche Worte*, 16 June 1895, quoted by Pichl, op cit., Vol. IV, 39.

49. Pichl, op. cit., Vol. IV, 407-13; Warren, op. cit., 256 n. 83, 260.

50. Pichl, op. cit., Vol. IV, 58, 204-5, quoting the annual report of the Deutscher Volksverein for 1894.

51. Ibid., 113; Warren, op. cit., 267, 271-72.

52. Pichl, op. cit., Vol. V, 21, 28; Whiteside, *Socialism of Fools*, 168, 174-75, 184-85.

53. Pichl, op. cit., Vol. V, 29-31, with quotations from the protocol; Warren, op. cit., 295-97.

54. Pichl, op. cit., Vol. V, 51.

55. Ibid., Vol. IV, 475, 482, 384.

56. Ibid., Vol. VI, 385-88; Warren, op. cit., 301-2.

57. Pichl, op. cit., Vol. VI, 56: speech in Graz on 28 December 1903.

58. Ibid., 76. Warren, op. cit., 304, estimates that there were some 40,000 converts in the course of twenty years. The figures were much higher in Bohemia than in any other province: Pichl, Vol. VI, 388. In 1902 the figure of conversions began to decline sharply: Whiteside, *Socialism of Fools*, 255.

59. Andrew G. Whiteside, *Austrian National Socialism before 1918* (The Hague, 1962) 81; Pichl, op. cit., Vol. V, 93; Vol. VI, 251, 572; Warren, op. cit., 312-19.

60. Pichl, op. cit., Vol. V, 231, 234; Warren, op. cit., 328.

61. Pichl, op. cit., Vol. VI, 75.

62. This opinion has been put forward by Whiteside, *Austrian National Socialism before 1918*, 84.

63. These points have been made very forcefully from his own experience by Adam Wandruszka, *Österreichs politische Struktur*, in Heinrich Benedikt (ed.), *Geschichte der Republik Österreich* (Vienna, 1954) 405-6.

64. *Bezirkshauptmannschaft* Güssing to *Landesamtsdirektion*, Güssing, 27 October 1933: Burgenländisches Landesarchiv, Landesamtsdirektion, 245/1933.

65. Leopold to Himmler, Vienna, 29 January 1938: Berlin Document Center, Partei-Kanzlei correspondence.

66. Whiteside, *Austrian National Socialism before 1918*, 63, 85.

67. Alan Bullock, *Hitler – a Study in Tyranny* (London, 1973 edn.) 45-46.

2

THE GERMAN WORKERS' UNIONS
AND THE GERMAN WORKERS' PARTY

If Schönerer's Pan-Germans attracted comparatively few workers and
represented above all threatened sections of the middle classes, a similar
but distinctly working-class movement came into being in the German
districts of Bohemia at about the same time. This was caused by the
growing antagonism between Czechs and Germans in the border areas
and above all by the migration of Czech workers into the industrial
towns of northern Bohemia: they had lower living standards than the
German workers and were willing to work for lower wages. The miners
in the lignite fields, the textile workers in old-established industries, the
rural craftsmen, the railwaymen, all felt threatened by the influx of
Czech workmen who were seeking work at almost any price. In 1888 a
German textile worker, Moritz Fleck, at a meeting of the associations
of German workers held at Reichenberg (Liberec) declared that Czech
workers were putting up docilely with living conditions which no
German would accept, that they were frustrating the legitimate demands of German craftsmen and were forcing them to work on a
precarious day-to-day basis. In 1893 the worker Franz Stein from Eger
(Cheb) founded a German National Workers' Association *(Deutschnationaler Arbeiterbund)* in close association with Schönerer. In 1898 a
bookbinder, Ludwig Vogel, and a typesetter, Ferdinand Burschofsky,

31

assembled the representatives of several thousand workers who founded the *Verband der. deutschen Gehilfen und Arbeitervereinigungen in Österreich* (Union of German Assistants and Workers' Associations in Austria); the union was to protect the interests of the German workers and accepted only 'Aryan' members. Burschofsky charged the Social Democrats that, in order to realize their Marxist dreams, they wanted to give jobs and houses to Czechs at the expense of the Germans.[1]

In May 1899 — eighteen months after the Badeni crisis which was the catalyst of nationalist agitation, especially in Bohemia — two or three hundred delegates met at Eger as the first national workers' congress. The majority of the delegates who represented several thousand German workers came from northern Bohemia; others were from Vienna and Graz, even from Munich and Berlin. They demanded equal rights for the workers, the protection of the skilled workers against competition from the unskilled (Czechs), and the nationalization of the large enterprises, the mines and railways. The young weaver, Hans Knirsch, who later became a prominent National Socialist, proposed to send greetings to Schönerer, 'the *Führer* of the German people of the Eastern March', a proposal that was unanimously carried among shouts of *Heil.* By 1901 the Union of German Assistants and Workers' Associations comprised 82 local organizations with about 14,000 members. But soon after it began to run into financial difficulties and declined.[2] The much stronger social-democratic unions were better able to defend their members' interests than the comparatively small nationalist unions. Yet when the First World War broke out in 1914 the latter mustered considerable strength and claimed to have 611 local groups with about 45,000 members.[3]

Based on these workers' associations and unions a political party, the German Workers' Party *(Deutsche Arbeiterpartei),* was founded in 1904 by Burschofsky, Knirsch and other workers; the majority came from the German districts of Bohemia, others from Brno, Graz and Klagenfurt. The party programme repeated many of the demands of the Linz Programme of 1882, national as well as social, and proclaimed: 'We are a liberal and national party which opposes with all its strength the reactionary tendencies, feudal, clerical and capitalist privileges and any influence of alien *völkisch* groups.'[4] Apart from social demands, the programme desired the introduction of the general, equal and direct franchise, rights of free association and assembly, freedom of speech and of the press, a radical extension of political self-government, and the holding of elections every three years — demands which could have been accepted by any democratic party. At the same time the party ascribed the existing social misery to Czech immigration into German areas and stood for a mixture of nationalism and socialism. As it declared in 1910, it was willing to defend the economic and political interests of other German social classes only in so far as they did not clash with the interests of the working class; but as a national and liberal party it was willing to co-operate closely with the other German liberal parties 'in purely *völkisch* and liberal matters which concern the vital interests of our severely threatened people in Austria'.[5]

In the elections of 1907 the party obtained only 3,500 votes in the whole of Bohemia. But in 1911 it polled more than 26,000 and gained three seats in the central Reichsrat against social-democratic rivals, all in industrial districts of northern Bohemia. One of the new deputies was Hans Knirsch. The party did not aim at the dissolution of the Habsburg Monarchy, nor did it adopt Schönerer's radical anti-Semitism and anti-Catholicism; in the eyes of the Pan-Germans it was black-yellow and pro-Habsburg.[6] But this changed to some extent when it gained an important recruit in the person of the lawyer Dr Walter Riehl from Reichenberg. Riehl's grandfather had been a radical deputy in the Frankfurt Parliament of 1848; his father had close associations with leading Social Democrats who strongly influenced the young man. As a student, he was an active socialist, addressed workers' meetings and worked for the socialist trade unions. As late as 1908 he aimed at the transformation of Social Democracy into a party 'class-conscious as well as nationally conscious', combining socialism with nationalism. But in the following year Riehl joined the German Workers' Party and soon became one of its most successful propagandists.[7] Riehl organized numerous mass meetings to instil national consciousness in the German workers and to prevail upon German employers to employ Germans rather than Czechs. He emphasized that the conflict between bourgeoisie and workers must be healed; and in 1909 he boasted that his agitation had been successful and that German workers were taken on in the place of Czechs. These meetings often led to clashes between the hostile nationalities. On one occasion Riehl led twenty young workmen under the German flag into a Czech trade union meeting where they sang *The Watch on the Rhine* and fought with the Czechs until the police closed the meeting. Riehl also organized national youth groups and creches, as well as labour exchanges so that any vacancies could be filled with Germans.[8]

Under Riehl's influence the party, at its congress of September

1913, adopted a new programme in the preamble of which he proclaimed:

> His [Marx's] teaching on internationalism is false and has done enormous
> damage to the Germandom of central Europe. The working class has a very
> special interest in the power position, preservation and expansion of the living
> space *(Lebensraum)* of their people . . . Austrian Social Democracy is a child
> of the German party, and its internationalist principles were to undergo their
> decisive test here. Under the impact of the facts the whole edifice collapsed
> ignominiously. Only the poor comrades of the 'German tongue' adhere faith-
> fully to them – to their own disadvantage . . . The German entrepreneur took
> on the cheaper Slav workmen, but the red organization denied to its old
> German veterans the required protection. Thereupon finally a healthy instinct
> of self-preservation began to stir in the German workers' heads. Inspired by
> the great German national bourgeois movement of the 1890s in German
> Austria, they founded in the various towns German *völkisch* associations of
> workers and journeymen. They recognized the pernicious results of the inter-
> nationalist teachings for their own nation and the duplicity of Social Demo-
> cracy, led by Jews and interlinked with the mobile big capital . . .

The programme itself demanded the socialization of monopolies, the
banning of any income without labour, the formation of a hard
national front against aliens, clericalism and Jews, capitalism and
Marxism; in the Austrian state with its many nationalities the German
people must stand together to protect their soil and work.[9] Although
the programme contained anti-semitic phrases, they did not occupy a
central position. A more aggressive nationalism and anti-Marxism had
taken the place of the radical democratic demands of the first programme.

The outbreak of war in 1914 in practice brought to an end the
political activities of all parties, and many members were called to the
colours. But the German Workers' Party continued to be active in the
interest of its members. At a meeting of party representatives in April
1918 it was suggested for the first time to change its name to 'German
National Socialist Workers' Party' (DNSAP) to facilitate propaganda;
the word 'national socialist' had informally designated its activities
before. But the motion was rejected by a large majority. Only a few
weeks later, however, the party leaders reversed this decision and
accepted the new name. It was approved in August 1918 at a party
conference held in Vienna. This conference also adopted a new party
programme which rejected 'as unnatural a union on the basis of super-
nationalism *(auf allvölkischer Grundlage)*. An improvement of the
economic and social conditions can on the contrary only be achieved

by a combination of all producers on the basis of individual nationalities . . .' The party declared itself to be 'liberal and strictly völkisch and opposed to all reactionary tendencies, capitalist, noble and clerical privileges, and all alien influences, but above all to the parasitic power of the Jewish trading spirit in all spheres of public life.' In the political field the programme demanded the 'combination of the whole area settled by Germans in Europe (!) in a democratic and social German Empire'. In the economic field the demands became considerably more radical and included the 'transfer of all capitalist large-scale enterprises in which private management is obnoxious to the commen weal' to public ownership. This was to apply in particular to transport undertakings, mines, water power, insurance companies and advertising. The predominance of the Jewish banks in economic life should be eliminated, and people's national banks be created with democratic forms of self-government.[10] The programme was mainly drafted by Rudolf Jung, a railwayman from Bohemia; it was strongly socialist and anti-semitic.

The first German National Socialist Party which thus came into being was, in its origins and composition, considerably more working class than its later Austrian or German namesakes. It was also democratic in its structure. The delegates to party conferences were elected and decisions taken by a majority of votes; it had no recognized Leader. What it had in common with the later National Socialist parties was the mixture of radical national with socialist demands, the bitter hostility to anything non-German, the demand for *Lebensraum,* and the general völkisch ideology. When the Habsburg Monarchy broke up in 1918 Knirsch and Jung became the leaders of the party's major branch in what was now Czechoslovakia, the leaders of the German National Socialist Party in the 'Sudeten' districts. Riehl in his turn moved to Vienna and became the party's leader in the Austrian Republic. There was also an offshoot of the party in the part of Silesia which became Polish, the 'German National Socialist Association for Poland' with its headquarters at Bielsko. There was thus a marked continuity of leadership, and there continued to exist fairly close connections between the Sudeten German and the Austrian parties. Even after Hitler had secured his control over the Austrian party he appointed one of the 'Sudeten' leaders, Hans Krebs, as its leader; earlier on, there were frequent conferences at the 'inter-state' level between the several parties concerned. Yet Hitler's opinion of the Austrian party to which he owed a great deal was not a flattering one. At a conference with the Austrian

National Socialists held at Passau in Bavaria in 1926 Hitler classified the Austrian party as 'a party like many others', a party which liked to pass resolutions, and he particularly criticized it because it had never been forbidden in the old Austria. The movement in Germany, on the other hand, he continued, had always been intolerant; it had never accepted a compromise, nor had it ever combined with others.[11] Yet this was hardly a correct version of the events in Munich in 1923, where Hitler joined forces with right-wing leaders and associations such as *Oberland* to carry out his coup. And in later years he was to combine only too often with the German Nationalist Party and other forces of the right, until he was strong enough to destroy them.

How much the German National Socialists owed to their Austrian and Bohemian comrades becomes clear from a book which the engineer Rudolf Jung, one of the Bohemian leaders, published immediately after the defeat of the central powers in the first world war, under the title *Nationaler Sozialismus.* In this defeat and the rise of independent Slav states on the ruins of the Habsburg Monarchy he saw merely the culmination of a long, deadly campaign aiming at the destruction of the German nation. Czechs, Jews and other aliens were held responsible for the difficulties of the German workers; German liberal entrepreneurs and German and Jewish Social Democrats had 'created and furthered the Czech minorities in the areas of German settlement of the Sudeten lands'; the survival of the Germans there did not depend on reaching an agreement with the Czechs, but on removing them and on increasing the German Lebensraum. Jung praised Schönerer as the 'only politician of fame who showed understanding of the situation of his poor co-nationals *(Volksgenossen)*', while the Social Democrats were supporting unnatural and alien powers by linking socialism with internationalism. The forces of 'productive national capital' were juxtaposed to those of 'disintegrating finance capital'; equally rejected by Jung were ground rents and interest. Monopolies, department stores and large estates were to be taken over for the benefit of the community. 'Honest productive work' was extolled together with 'productive' capital, while unproductive finance capital (banking, the taking of interest) was repudiated, exactly as in the later National Socialist propaganda. Jung also coined the slogan *Gemeinnutz geht vor Eigennutz* ('The common weal comes before private interest') which was to figure so prominently in Hitler's Twenty-five Points of 1920. Jung despised mammon and materialism which he considered tools of international Jewry. The true German spirit he saw incorporated in a free peasantry able to bear arms and in artisans working as free partners in a co-operative: an idealized picture of a pre-capitalist society, far removed from the society of cut-throat competition and the class struggle.[12]

If Schönerer's appeal aimed principally at the middle and lower middle classes, that of the German Workers' Party was directed at the working class and did not really embrace other social groups. But before 1914 Austria and Bohemia were only partly industrialized, and the success of the Social Democrats among the working class was so massive that even in Bohemia an appeal to its 'national' interests found only a limited echo. This remained true even in the chaotic conditions of Germany and Austria after the First World War, and was much more the case prior to 1914. For the majority of workers, the class struggle was a reality, not a 'Jewish invention', and they acted accordingly. The German Workers' Party — even more than the Pan-Germans — also lacked a dynamic, 'revolutionary' leader, a man without scruples and hesitations, a man motivated by a desire for power and for nothing else. Its leaders were not all that different from those of the socialist trade unions with which they competed: small, ordinary people, active in the interests of the workers as they saw them, earnest and limited, far removed from the armed coups and military fights for power which became so characteristic of the post-war world. Their historical importance lies in the fact that they planted the seed which germinated after 1918, that the later National Socialists were able to build on older foundations, especially on the völkisch ideology which in one form or the other influenced many thousands.

In Austria, this ideology was kept alive in many different organizations, not only in political parties and trade unions. Prominent among them were the völkisch sports and gymnastic clubs which existed in many small towns and villages. In 1902 the *Deutsche Turnerbund* had 133 local associations and 13,000 members; its motto was that of Schönerer 'Through purity to unity'.[13] The local associations accepted only German men of 'Aryan descent' as active or passive members, so as to preserve their 'purity'.[14] In 1901 the *Deutsche Turnerschaft* in Lower Austria also disaffiliated all Jewish branches and expelled all Jewish members.[15] In 1905, at the second German Students' Congress held in Vienna, the chairman discussed in detail the Jewish question and demanded the removal of Jews from the universities as well as the introduction of a numerus clausus for the academic professions. In the Deutscher Schulverein, which was responsible for the maintenance of German schools in nationally 'endangered' districts, the by-laws were changed in 1899: henceforth its local associations could decide on the admittance of members and thus the expulsion of Jewish members became possible. It was only in 1921 that the term 'Germans' in the by-laws was defined anew so as to include only 'racial' Germans. An old aim of Schönerer had been achieved. In the same year the Austrian Alpinists' Association, 'Austria', also adopted an 'Aryan paragraph' and expelled its Jewish members.[16] Thus racial anti-Semitism remained a pronounced trait in many fields, including those of gymnastics and alpinism, and it infected the younger generation. It was to blossom forth with renewed vigour in the German Austrian Republic which came into being with the collapse of the Habsburg Monarchy, for the Jews could now be blamed not only for the collapse, but for all the ills and upheavals of the post-war period. The threats which had only been feared in the late nineteenth and early twentieth centuries now seemed to have become very real.

Anti-Semitism, of course, was only one component of the völkisch ideology, but a very crucial one. It also contained a veneration for all things German or Germanic, a belief in the superiority of the Germanic 'race' over all others, a conviction that the Germans must gain Lebensraum, a hankering after the lost world of the Middle Ages and the Holy Roman Empire, a rejection of 'modernism' in all its forms, whether in the arts or economics, a worshipping of the 'heroic' deed and martial virtues, as exemplified in the Germanic sagas and the epic of the Nibelungen. It was strongly romantic, but with a special flavour. Its adherents were unable to look at the world realistically, and instead peopled it with gods and demons, with people destined to rule, and with others for ever condemned to slavery. It was a pernicious doctrine, but it exercised a magnetic power. It was a new faith, with the battles of Noreia (113 B.C.) and the Teutoburg Forest (9 A.D.) as the saints' days, and the Germanic nation taking the place of Christianity and the Church. It was a myth, but the myth was to inspire many thousands. To quote one of Schönerer's poems:

> In the great year Seventy
> There sounded 'The Watch on the Rhine':
> Germania has arisen,
> Will never sleep again.
>
> With German blood and iron
> The Reich was strongly built,
> And German will and spirit
> Shall guard it to the hilt . . .

Germania, your summons
Shall be our clarion call,
And then the *Ostmark's* children
Will build their German hall.[17]

NOTES

1. Andrew Gladding Whiteside, *Austrian National Socialism before 1918* (The Hague, 1962) 38, 49, 52, 60-61; Pichl, *Schönerer,* Vol. VI, 219; K. D. Bracher, *Die deutsche Diktatur* (Cologne-Berlin, 1969) 56. The monthly organ of the union was first called *Der deutsche Gehilfe,* changed in 1898 to *Der deutsche Arbeiter.*

2. Whiteside, Austrian National Socialism before 1918, 62-63; Pichl, op. cit., Vol. VI, 219, 226-27; Bracher, op. cit., 56.

3. A. Ciller, *Vorläufer des Nationalsozialismus* (Vienna, 1932) 96.

4. Ciller, op. cit., 43, 135; Andrew G. Whiteside, 'Nationaler Sozialismus in Österreich vor 1918', *Vierteljahrshefte für Zeitgeschichte,* IX (1961) 333-34.

5. Ciller, op. cit., 65, 136; Bracher, op. cit., 56.

6. Ciller, op. cit., 90; Pichl, op. cit., Vol. VI, 228; Bracher, op. cit., 57; Whiteside, loc. cit., 344, with election figures.

7. Whiteside, *Austrian National Socialism before 1918,* 95-96; Bracher, op. cit., 57.

8. Whiteside, op. cit., 97-98; Bracher, op. cit., 57; Whiteside, *Socialism of Fools,* 279.

9. Whiteside, 'Nationaler Sozialismus . . .', 344-46; Bracher, op. cit., 57-58.

10. Rudolf Jung, *Der nationale Sozialismus,* 2nd edn (Munich, 1922) 65; Ciller, op. cit., 108, 140-42; Whiteside, 'Nationaler Sozialismus . . .', 349.

11. Hitler's speech on 12 August 1926: Bundesarchiv Koblenz, NS 26/54, fos. 100-1. Cp. below, pp. 146-47.

12. Whiteside, *Austrian National Socialism before 1918,* 107-14, and 'Nationaler Sozialismus . . .', 350-51. The first edition of Jung's book was published at Troppau in Bohemia, the later ones in Munich.

13. Pichl, op. cit., Vol. VI, 314.

14. Thus the printed by-laws of the *Deutschvölkische Turnvereine,* s.d.: Steiermärk. Landesarchiv, k.k. Statthalterei, depart. vii, no. 18285.

15. Pulzer, *The Rise of political Anti-Semitism . . .,* 223.

16. Pichl, op. cit., Vol. VI, 155, 258, 454; Pulzer, op. cit., 159. These examples could easily be multiplied.

17. Schönerer to the *Burschenschaft* 'Teutonia' on 18 September 1886: Pichl, op. cit., Vol. II, 542. 'Ostmark' was the völkisch name for Austria, later also used by the National Socialists.

3

AGAINST RED REVOLUTION
– THE EARLY 'HEIMWEHREN'

In October 1918 the Habsburg Monarchy collapsed – a collapse caused
not by the efforts of left-wing revolutionaries, but by the overwhelming
military power of the Entente. Indeed, there were no organized revolutionaries in Vienna or any other Austrian town, and the mass party of
the left, the Social Democrats, set its face firmly against any Bolshevik
experiments. The government of the new 'German Austrian Republic'
was from the outset a coalition of all major parties. In Vienna as well as
in the provinces the Social Democrats for the first time participated in
the government but – in contrast with Germany where the new
government was purely socialist – their bourgeois partners curtailed
their freedom of movement and kept the new government on a very
moderate course. This was also made necessary by the utter dependence
of Austria on imports of food and coal which could only be obtained
from the victor states. It is true that under socialist influence workers'
and soldiers' councils were formed in the towns; but their power
outside Vienna was weak, and even in Vienna they did not represent a
serious challenge to the government.

Attempts at communist revolution in Vienna, made in April and
June 1919, were inspired and financed by the Hungarian Soviet Republic, but they were put down firmly and without difficulty by the

new Austrian army, the *Volkswehr,* which was controlled by the Social Democrats.[1] The Austrian Communists, in spite of hunger and turmoil, were and remained a very weak party — again in contrast with Germany where the Communists benefited from the conditions of civil war and the drift to the left among the Independent Social Democrats. But in Austria there was no split in the socialist ranks and no civil war; the more radical and energetic policy of the Social Democrats kept the party together and prevented any growth of Communism. Large parts of Austria were still rural and conservative, with the Catholic Church as the dominant factor. The Social Democrats were only strong in the few industrial areas, and when they left the coalition government in 1920 their influence quickly declined.

Yet this weakness of the left was not realized by the masses of conservative and catholic middle-class people. Whether they were in independent or dependent positions, they felt threatened by the disappearance of the monarchy and the old order in which everybody had known his place, by the rise of a seemingly strong socialist movement, by 'red' Vienna where the Social Democrats were carrying out ambitious social reforms, and by the social and economic changes which destroyed their security. Their savings melted away because of inflation, their incomes shrank, their social position was endangered. Although a left revolution was out of the question after 1919, there was widespread fear of socialism and communism.[2] The new democratic republic was unpopular with many who were unable to understand the workings of democracy, considered political parties unnecessary, and their leaders corrupt or stupid.

Only a year after the outbreak of the revolution, the police directorate of Vienna reported that there was very little political interest but 'a general cry for a strong government which would rally all forces to attend to the needs of the people . . . promote the interests of the *whole* working population of this country, and above all would see to it that the six million inhabitants of this state have enough to eat and to keep warm.'[3] The implication was not only that the Social Democrats, who were still strongly represented in the government, were only promoting the interests of their own followers, but that the government in general was doing too little to procure the necessary food and coal. According to the report, two-thirds of the population shared these critical views; people were remembering the great merits of the pre-war administration of Vienna by Dr Lueger and his Christian Social Party; bitterness against the black-market activities of eastern Jews was grow-

ing from day to day, and so was 'the hatred of the Jewish Communists';
'responsibility for all the misery and all the difficulties are attributed to
the present state and to the Social Democratic Party'.[4]

Added to this disillusionment with the new democratic government
and the parties responsible for it another sentiment began to spread in
the small towns and villages of Austria: dislike of Vienna, of its
never-ending demands for food, its 'parasitic' population, its 'red'
government, its workers' councils which confiscated illicit food stores,
its ever-hungry people who scoured the countryside in search of food.
Feelings such as these grew rapidly and quickly turned into hatred and
contempt. They were the motor behind the formation of the early
home defence units or *Heimwehren* which sprang up like mushrooms in
the Austrian countryside. The first such units came into being in the
early months of the revolution, principally to prevent looting and
forced requisitions by returning soldiers or released prisoners of war.
The units were issued with arms by orders of the government. In the
southern parts of Styria and Carinthia fighting developed with advancing Yugoslav units, and there Heimwehren were organized by army
officers. As the fighting with the Yugoslavs lasted for many months, the
defence formations became well organized and supplied. In February
1919 a complaint reached Graz from Knittelfeld that quantities of
weapons were being sent into the villages on sleighs on the instructions
of a Volkswehr officer. The workers protested against these clandestine
armaments; but the local authority defended them on the grounds that
the Heimwehr was absolutely non-political and only served to 'defend
the rural population against the ever-growing bands of robbers and
other vagrants'; its commanding officer was a major of the general
staff.[5] According to the military police in Graz a fund of about three
million crowns was available for the purchase of arms and ammunition.
In June 1919 the commanding officer of Styria reported to the provincial government that there was considerable misuse of the weapons
allocated to the Heimwehren and that far too many military weapons
remained in the hands of the population.[6]

In May 1919 the same commanding officer informed the government of Styria that Heimwehren existed in about 70 percent of all
communes, their strength varying according to that of the population,
with 15 to 30 men in small communities, and up to 100 in larger ones;
the control of their activities rested with specially appointed officers;
he would be opposed to any reduction of their strength. The Bezirkshauptmannschaft (district government) of Graz reported in July that

the Heimwehren co-operated closely with the police and gendarmerie, were entirely non-political, and composed of all sections of the population: they did not threaten anyone, and all the more surprising were the attacks upon them made by the Volkswehr which demanded their dissolution. This demand was countered by the commandant of the peasant units in Lower Styria. He declared that his men would have achieved their purpose 'if the anarchic conditions of today, with different councils issuing orders, were brought to an end and every citizen participated, with joyful and self-sacrificing delight in work, in the economic reconstruction of our enslaved people [*sic*]'.[7] As these conditions clearly could not be fulfilled he obviously thought that the Heimwehren should continue. His claim that they were non-political was contradicted not only by his attack on the council movement, but equally by his own declaration that he was only pursuing 'purely völkisch aims', such as 'the defence and regaining of German land and soil and the maintenance of law and order'. In his opinion, the attacks on the Heimwehren were due to 'the purity and honesty of our truly völkisch aims' and to 'the power' which his organization was exercising.[8] In Styria this power was solidly based on weapons. As the *Landeshauptmann* of Styria, Dr Rintelen, admitted later, the Heimwehren acquired about 17,000 rifles with the necessary ammunition, 286 machine guns, 12 pieces of artillery, and even aeroplanes, largely by ruse from Volkswehr depots. One of Rintelen's closest co-operators in this work was a son-in-law of Schönerer. In Upper Styria the leader was a local lawyer, Dr Walter Pfrimer, with the engineer Hanns Rauter as his chief of staff.[9] Most of the leaders were former officers.

Apart from the peasantry which provided the bulk of the local Heimwehr members, two social groups were particularly prominent, students and officers; and of course, many students of the early post-war years had served as officers or cadets during the war. In Styria, Dr Pfrimer's position was considerably strengthened when the student battalions of Graz University and Leoben's Mining College put themselves under his command; they were the most radical element among the Heimwehren. Their leader in Graz was Rauter who had been a first lieutenant in the war.[10] As he wrote later, it was due to the students' influence that the Heimwehr flags showed the swastika and the former German colours of black-white-red. Their aims were: 'fight against Marxism and bourgeois democracy, creation of an authoritarian state, and the *Anschluss*'; anti-Semitism figured in their programme from the outset. The members were not permitted to belong to any political party.[11]

In the Tyrol too, the mobile Heimwehr units were formed by the student companies of Innsbruck University which were German Nationalist in their politics and had close connections with Germany.[12] Interestingly enough, student units from the universities of Graz and Innsbruck in 1921, at the time of the Polish uprising, went to Upper Silesia and fought there side by side with German Free Corps, especially Oberland from Bavaria; thus a common nationalism created strong bonds between them. One of those who fought with great enthusiasm in Upper Silesia was Ernst Rüdiger von Starhemberg, the later Austrian Heimwehr leader, as he recounts at length in his autobiography. For people like him soldiering was a life of adventure which embellished the dullness of university studies; many among his comrades had been too young to serve in the war. Many officers and non-commissioned officers of the old army, on the other hand, found it impossible to adjust themselves to civilian life or to find a job corresponding to their social rank. The Heimwehren, and similar organizations like the German Free Corps, provided them with the position which they considered their due, with the atmosphere and mentality to which they were accustomed.[13] There they could continue the struggle against the 'enemy', be that the Yugoslavs or the 'reds' at home.

In June 1920 the British diplomatic representative reported from Vienna: 'There is no doubt that peasants who have all along had arms are being organized into regular formations in the Tyrol and Styria to resist any attack from armed workmen or perhaps to attack them. In short, scene seems to be set rather for a civil war . . .'[14] The Heimwehr units were organized on a local basis and differed widely from each other in their political aims, their ideology, their combat readiness, and the quality of their leaders. They had only local leaders, and no central leadership. Indeed, these were characteristics which the movement never lost entirely, although as we shall see, strenuous efforts were made later to overcome these handicaps, to unify and centralize the Heimwehren, and to provide them with an ideology beyond the simple hostility to anything 'red'.

As early as 1920 very important changes were imported from outside Austria, by a powerful organization that had grown up in neighbouring Bavaria, the *Orgesch,* or Organization Escherich, named after its leader, the forester Georg Escherich. The Orgesch comprised local Bavarian defence units which had sprung up as a reaction to the short-lived Munich Councils Republic of 1919. They were intended to support the regular army in case of unrest and to provide it with trained recruits in case of war or civil war; they were fiercely anti-bolshevik and anti-semitic. In Bavaria, under a right-wing government, they were a power in the land and amply provided with weapons and funds. These partly came from the German government, in spite of all the friction and hostility between Berlin and Munich. In February 1920 a close colleague of Escherich, Dr Kern, visited the Minister of Defence, Noske, in Berlin and achieved that considerable quantities of weapons were sent to Bavaria, from where many of them finally reached Austria,[15] for in the early months of 1920 close links were established between the Orgesch and the Austrian Heimwehren. A special branch of the Orgesch was founded for this purpose, the *Orka,* or Organization Kanzler, named after the man who occupied after Escherich the most important post in his organization. In the Orka an active major of the *Reichswehr,* Hörl, functioned as a liaison officer to the Heimwehren and organized special staff conferences to discuss technical military and organizational questions.[16] According to Escherich's own account his organization possessed about 2,500,000 infantry rifles, 130,000 light machine guns, 3,000 heavy ones, 100 batteries of light artillery, in addition to heavy cannon and 30 aeroplanes.[17] It was thus well able to divert some of these to Austria.

Kanzler, according to his own testimony, considered the intervention of the Bavarians in Austria as 'a protective action in favour of those districts which rejected the misery inflicted upon them by the Bolshevism of Vienna'. In the negotiations with the Austrians he and his collaborators emphasized the necessity to build a common anti-bolshevik front with Austrian organizations of similar persuasion, to support the movement for the *Anschluss* with Germany, and to render strong opposition to all legitimist pro-Habsburg tendencies. In February 1920 Kanzler held a conference with leading members of the Christian Social Party in Salzburg where a defence formation of 1,200 men already existed; it was planned to create mobile units from the younger men who were to receive intensive military training.[18] A second conference in Salzburg in March was attended by representatives of sixteen communes, where the Heimwehren had 2,000 men, and by several local deputies and notables. To them Kanzler explained:

> The old militarism has been overthrown; paid Jewish villains have stabbed the armies at the front in the back because all the armies assembled against us were unable to defeat us militarily. Jewish charlatans made the revolution; they promised us peace and bread, work and order; none of the promises has been kept. On the contrary, bribery, corruption, black marketeering have spread to such an extent that it is high time to put matters right. We must do

everything to put a stop to the Jew government, that is the international Jewish black marketeers ... Therefore we must combine on a *völkisch* basis and eliminate the international Jewish rabble which is sucking the last drop of blood from our veins. The Bolsheviks are advancing against us from all sides so as to unite with the misled brethren of our own race, who are paid by Jewish money, and to impose upon us their well known salvation ....

One of the Salzburg deputies present replied that, in the interest of the people, all must stand together as one man; because many had forgotten these terms, rejuvenation must come from the peasantry; the latter must never forget that it was the mainstay of the whole nation and that all would be lost 'if it were swept away by the current of black marketeers and Jews'. At the end of the meeting a Captain for the *Gau* Salzburg was elected.[19]

The first contacts between Munich and the Tyrol were established during the same month, March 1920, when a conference with Orka representatives was held at Kufstein, but against the wishes of the head of the provincial government, the Tyrolese Landeshauptmann Josef Schraffl. In April Kanzler went to Innsbruck where he met leading local politicians, such as Dr Steidle, Dr Stumpf and Professor Schullern. It was decided to form, after the Bavarian example, a Tyrolese 'Block of Order', with Schullern as the chairman; and the first steps were taken to organize the Heimwehren.[20] A further meeting took place at Innsbruck in May under the chairmanship of Steidle, this time also attended by Landeshauptmann Schraffl and many local dignitaries. The Orka representative, Professor Stempfle from Munich, reported on the political situation in Bavaria, where the Orgesch mustered 300,000 men who formed a strong bulwark against Bolshevism:

If the whole of Germany was to be saved a united front of all bourgeois forces must be formed. This can only be done from the south because the north is entirely orientated towards the left, not only the workers, but also the government. The Bavarians need above all support in their rear by the Tyrolese and the Salzburgers if they should be forced to march to the north ....

A Lieutenant Krazer from Bavaria supported Stempfle and stressed that a new great struggle was starting in central Europe: the fight of Asiatic hordes, in the form of Bolshevism under Jewish leadership, against Germanic culture.[21] Thus not only Germanic völkisch ideology, but even the plan of marching to the north to overthrow the Berlin left-wing government was put to the Tyrolese leaders who apparently accepted it without a murmur.

Even Landeshauptmann Schraffl, who was not a wild extremist, concurred with the general tenor of the Bavarian proposals. He pointed out that the men of the Tyrol for centuries had been entitled to bear arms, and that not even the Entente demanded the disarmament of the Tyrolese peasants (thus the Heimwehren could be based on the traditional riflemen's companies).

> Only the parasites [Schraffl continued] who are grouped around the Viennese socialist clique and who are up to 90 per cent non-Tyrolese demand their disarmament. But if Vienna ever attempted to carry this out there would be open resistance in the Tyrol. Then the Tyrolese would appeal to the brotherly help of the Bavarians; in the reverse case the latter would be able to rely on most energetic support from the Tyrol. . . .[22]

Schraffl's motives were anti-socialist and anti-Viennese, and on this basis he was willing to co-operate with the Bavarians. Only two days after the meeting Dr Steidle informed the Tyrolese government that the Heimwehren were being formed, and stressed the Bavarian connection by enclosing two decrees of the Bavarian government from the year 1919 on the formation of local defence units. Appeals to join the units were published in the press, and the local authorities too were active in the good cause. Thus the Bezirkshauptmann of Landeck reported that the mayor of Landeck had invited about thirty people to a conference, which was attended by most local officials and dignitaries, to take the desired action. The speaker declared that, in the struggle against Bolshevism, all must unite who were interested in order and reconstruction, without any party political tendency; only the most rigorous methods were sufficient to secure success against a party which was well organized, possessed ample means and all weapons and knew no scruples; the backbone of the Block of Order must thus be formed by a well organized and equipped Heimatwehr; the military side need not be discussed, for in the local valleys successful propaganda had started and the armaments were taken care of.[23]

In the much smaller Vorarlberg, close to Bavaria, the Heimwehren by August 1920 had a strength of 3,350 men and possessed 3,600 rifles and 16 machine guns, most of them smuggled from Bavaria. As their report for September 1920 pointed out, the receipt of the weapons had given a strong impulse to their organization; they had thus been able to arm the peasants in the villages of the Bregenzerwald and to the south of Bregenz; in Bregenz itself a machine gun company was being formed from the members of the local rowing club.[24] The political committee for Vorarlberg consisted of three local dignitaries, one of whom was classified as *grossdeutsch,* and the two others as Christian Social partisans, but the military leader reporting this to Munich added that two of the three were 'unconditionally loyal to the Orgesch'.[25] By the end of 1920 he was able to report that a conference had taken place at the invitation of the government of Vorarlberg to discuss measures against strikes. It was attended by the Bezirkshauptleute, the mayors of the towns, representatives of the railways and the gendarmerie, and the leaders of the Heimwehr; their ideas gained a victory, and the Vorarlberg government was solidly behind them; the organization would make great strides in the future.[26] Indeed, in Vorarlberg even more than in the Tyrol, the Heimwehren developed under the protective umbrella of the provincial government; they considered themselves a semi-official organization, responsible to the Landeshauptmann, who appointed or at least confirmed the local leaders.[27] But it does not seem that the Heimwehr strength grew beyond about 3,500 men.

In June 1920 Stempfle and associates also visited Graz and Klagenfurt to establish contacts with the local Heimwehr units. In Klagenfurt they saw the commanding officer, Colonel Hülgerth, and his deputy, Colonel Klimann, but criticized that both officers were 'black-yellow', i.e. monarchists. Hülgerth nevertheless made a very good impression upon the visitors and 'was for ever active as leader of the Heimwehr organization'.[28] Thus in Carinthia, where there had been bitter fighting with the Yugoslavs, leadership of the Heimwehren was combined with that of the army: here too the Heimwehren had an official character. The political information, however, was incorrect, for Klimann was an active Grossdeutscher who was opposed to the Christian Social influence and intrigued against their party, which did not prevent them from supporting the Heimwehren so as to win them over.[29] In Styria, however, the original unity of the bourgeois parties in support of the Heimwehren broke down in 1920, so that they split into two organizations, the one grossdeutsch, and the other Christian Social. The latter was also supported by the local Peasant League and was thus stronger in the rural districts. The combined strength was very considerable: Graz alone claimed 13,000 armed men, central Styria 5,000 with 40 machine guns, and Upper Styria about 2,000 armed men; in the south there were another 8-9,000 men; apart from small arms, they possessed ten lorries, two wireless stations and two aeroplanes.[30] In 1920 the Styrians as well as the Salzburgers received direct subsidies from Munich, the latter 12,000 marks a month.[31]

The Orka was principally active in the Austrian provinces bordering on Bavaria, but its interests also extended to Vienna. In August-September 1920 it established contacts there with two leading völkisch organizations, the 'national' student corporations and the Deutsche Turnerbund 1919. At a conference in August its leader, *Regierungsrat* Klaudius Kupka, declared that his league was 'Aryan and grossdeutsch' and had 50,000 members, among them 15,000 trained soldiers. At another meeting with the Turnerbund in September the speaker, Professor Holtey, declared his absolute confidence in the leadership of the Orgesch, especially its 'aim of uniting all Germans in a Greater Germany'; it was unanimously decided to recommend to the Turner to join the Orgesch.[32] Agreement was quickly reached with the student corporations: in the same month not only the Burschenschaften, but also the corps, singers, academic Turner, etc. declared their support for the Orgesch.[33] The founding meeting of the Orka in Vienna was held in December and attended by about 400 people, mainly officers and students. Among other speakers Dr Riehl, the National Socialist leader, welcomed the new organization 'which would fight against the red International and the terror emanating from it'. Major Hörl, who was deputizing for Kanzler, pointed to the success of the Orgesch in Germany where it helped to suppress the uprising in the Ruhr after the Kapp Putsch.[34]

In November 1920 the first open clashes occurred in the Tyrol between the Heimwehren and the Social Democrats. The former announced that they would hold a large Shooting Festival *(Landesschiessen)* which would be joined by many units from Bavaria. The Viennese government opposed the plan because it feared Allied intervention and the outbreak of unrest. The Social Democrats called a strike and distributed arms to their followers. Armed workers occupied the gas and electricity works of Innsbruck, and the engine drivers removed vital parts from the engines so that these could not be used by strike-breakers. No trains were running, and the Bavarian units were prevented from crossing the frontier. But, in spite of the wishes of the central government, the festival took place, and the leading members of the Tyrolese government were present at the celebrations. Steidle declared that the defence formations only wanted to maintain law and order and to protect 'honest work'; anyone breaking the peace was their enemy. His speech ended in a Heil to the German nation and the singing of the German national anthem. Landeshauptmann Schraffl informed Vienna that, in view of the great importance of the Bavarian

Heimwehren for the restoration of law and order, the bourgeois circles of the Tyrol had decided to create an organization which aimed at combining their forces so as to maintain law and order and to prevent any attack on the constitution, either from the right or from the left. The Tyrolese government had to reject the Social Democratic demand for a prohibition of the festival, for the men had enjoyed the right to carry arms for centuries; 'the use of rifles is a holy right of which no one can deprive the Tyrolese . . .'.[35]

When Schraffl retired as Landeshauptmann and was replaced by Dr Franz Stumpf the close connections between the Tyrolese government and the Heimwehren continued. At a conference held in July 1921 Dr Steidle thanked Stumpf for the help he had promised and assured him that the Heimwehren did not intend to set themselves up as rivals to the government; the population must realize that they were an organization which co-operated with the authorities, and close co-operation with the gendarmerie was equally desirable; in the first instance, the provincial government and the Bezirkshauptmannschaften would be entitled to call out the Heimwehren; only in a case of emergency would the district leaders have the right to act independently of the authorities; exactly as the Landeshauptmann sided with the Heimwehren, they would support him wholeheartedly, and would provide a strong backing for the authorities and police.[36] A few months later Stumpf instructed the Bezirkshauptleute that there was a clear difference between the Heim-wehren and the workers' units of the Social Democrats. In his opinion, the latter were the instrument of a political party, aiming to achieve one-sided party goals, and hidden from the authorities as an instrument of the class struggle. He had been informed that the Social Democrats put the workers' units at the disposal of the Bezirkshauptleute and that one of them was envisaging a direct co-operation of workers' units and Heimwehr: this was contrary to his intentions and would endanger the whole structure of the Heimwehren which did not permit a connection with such 'radical elements'.[37]

In December 1921 Steidle admitted in an interview that the Tyrolese Heimwehr was pursuing the same aims as the Orgesch, that there were 'relations of a comradely kind' between the two, and that sometimes bigger, sometimes smaller help was received from Bavaria. The Tyrolese Social Democrat Gruener, on the other hand, told the same questioner that the Heimwehren were organized on a completely military basis, with German money and German arms, possessed 20 cannon in add-ition to rifles and machine guns, and that there were shock troops of officers and students. He even admitted the impotence of his own side in view of these extensive military preparations: the trade unions would not be able to persevere with their demands in view of the Heimwehr strength.[38] According to a German diplomatic report of the same month German officers were active in Innsbruck in the central Heimwehr command; they had close connections with the student battalions which included a 'terror company'; supplies from Bavaria had now ceased as none were required any longer: 'one is complete'.[39] The Heimwehr itself returned a strength of 12,008 men for the Tyrol, armed with 8,446 rifles, 140 machine guns and 22 pieces of artillery plus the necessary ammunition. The men were divided into five districts, among which Innsbruck was by far the strongest, with 5,229 men, followed by the lower Inn valley with 3,014 and the district of Reutte with 1,724 while East Tyrol had 1,343 and Landeck 698 men.[40]

Of the other Austrian provinces only Upper Austria reported a considerably greater strength at a meeting held at Klagenfurt in August 1921, namely 23,000 men. The small Land Salzburg had 8,000, Carinthia 9,000, Lower Austria around Vienna 12,600 men, Vorarlberg only 2,200. Professor Stempfle from Munich advocated the creation of youthful 'terror groups', with the students as the leading element. On the other hand, he was opposed to the clandestine activities of former members of the Upper Silesian Free Corps; the secret goal of all their efforts must be the preparation of a national uprising *(Vorbereitung zur nationalen Erhebung)*. The Bavarian Lieutenant-Colonel Hörl complained about the lack of funds, for the industrialists were still hesitating, and the banks negative; only the owners of large estates were paying. For Austria too the aim must be 'to create a strong bourgeois government and to break the red power'; a 'secret organization' was being built up, and even its leaders would remain unknown. The reports from the different provinces were, above all, concerned with the formation of mobile or shock troops. The Upper Austrians complained that the German Major von Wandesleben conspired behind their backs and asked on whose instructions he was acting; in their opinion, he disregarded 'the sovereignty of the Länder' (meaning the separate rights of the local leaders). The Styrian representative was able to report that the Heimwehren had successfully broken strikes of the woodworkers in the Enns valley and of the agricultural workers in the Hungertal.[41] Indeed, in many of the provinces this became one of the major fields of activity for the Heimwehren, especially as the anticipated 'red' revolution failed to materialize. There were questions too whether Escherich and Kanzler were still the leaders in Bavaria and, if not, who the new leaders were; for, under strong pressure from the Entente, the Orgesch formations in Bavaria were officially disbanded. But they were immediately replaced by a new para-military organization, *Bayern und Reich,* led by a medical officer, Dr Otto Pittinger, who claimed the old Orka rights in Austria. But these rights were disputed by German officers and certain Austrians who suspected him of particularist Bavarian leanings, of being 'white-blue' and not grossdeutsch.

In Austria too, in the course of 1921, open differences emerged between the followers of the two parties supporting the Heimwehren, the Grossdeutsche and the Christian Social Party, by far the larger of the two. In October 1921 its followers within the Heimwehr held a separate conference at Salzburg to discuss this state of affairs. The Styrian leader Dr Ahrer reported on the open split between the two rival camps and claimed that his side comprised the majority, especially in the rural areas; they refused to have any connections with the Orka or with Hörl, they had never asked them for money and did not need any. After the murder of Erzberger in Germany (26 August 1921) the radical German circles gained the upper hand within the Orka, and they were responsible for the bitterness of the conflict in Styria; this resulted even in thefts of weapons by the partisans of the Grossdeutsche from their Christian Social rivals. In Carinthia, the Heimwehren were dominated by the Grossdeutsche who were trying to misinform and exclude their rivals; particularly active in this sense was the chief of staff, Colonel Klimann, but in spite of this the Christian Social side claimed that it was slowly gaining ground. In Salzburg the state of the Heimwehren was considered more satisfactory and the understanding between the Grossdeutsche and the Christian Socials continued; but among the latter there was not sufficient understanding for the importance of the movement, and the units were thus weak in the city of Salzburg itself — in case of emergency this would have to be evacuated and to be reconquered from the countryside; there the district of Zell am See was the best organized.[42]

Most confused was the state of affairs in Upper Austria, largely on account of the passivity or worse of the Christian Social Party and its leaders. For this the representative blamed above all the Upper Austrian Landeshauptmann, Prelate Hauser, who wanted to co-operate in everything with the Social Democrats, and was opposed to any links with Bavaria and Germany. Hence the local initiative rested often with the

Grossdeutsche, especially their representative in the government, Franz Langoth; they were 'reasonable' and opposed to any radicalism, while in the Orka the radicals had gained much ground and wanted to push the Heimwehren into an activist pro-Anschluss policy. The complaints were above all directed against German officers: Major von Wandesleben (who now worked in Vienna) and Captain von Obwurzer who was seconded to Upper Austria. The latter, it was claimed, sent secret reports to Wandesleben about internal Heimwehr matters and had to be removed when this was discovered; these activities were directed against the 'legitimists', the adherents of the Habsburgs, and aimed at splitting the Heimwehren; but the worst of the German officers was Colonel Hörl, the 'evil spirit', 'who made in nothing but radicalism and thus caused all the confusion'. The Upper Austrian Heimwehren were supported by the banks and the industrialists and did not receive any funds from Bavaria. At the end of the meeting Dr Ramek, the secretary of the Christian Social Party in Salzburg, expressed his opposition to the Anschluss policy; in his opinion, it would only result in a dismemberment of Austria among the neighbours, who were non-German. When Dr Ramek also defended Vienna and emphasized its importance, he met with the united condemnation of the representatives of the Länder who all held the opposite point of view.[43]

The differences within the Austrian Heimwehren were exacerbated and complicated by conflicts on the German side and the intervention of rival German organizations, all centred in Munich, the Mecca of the German extreme nationalists and para-military *Verbände*. Their leaders violently disagreed on most issues, disagreements which were embittered by strong personal rivalries. After the failure of the Kapp Putsch in Berlin, several German officers involved became active in Austria, among them Ludendorff's right-hand man, Colonel Max Bauer, Captain Hermann Ehrhardt (whose Brigade had led the mutiny in Berlin), Captain Waldemar Pabst (who was implicated in the murder of Liebknecht and Luxemburg); and with them came many of their men. Major Max von Wandesleben founded in Vienna a 'Storm Brigade Ehrhardt' from officers and men of the dissolved Ehrhardt Brigade, which continued underground under the name 'Organization Consul' and was strongly anti-semitic and völkisch. Their weapons came from the Orka, but their orders they took only from Ehrhardt.[44] Among the members were students and former officers; one of them was Carl Tillessen, a formal naval officer implicated in the murder of Erzberger. The Free Corps Oberland also formed groups in Austria, especially from students of Vienna and Innsbruck universities. From Vienna links were established with cognate right-wing organizations in Hungary. Colonel Bauer stayed for a considerable time in Budapest and, according to the Vienna police, even received a passport from the Hungarian foreign office. Another Free Corps officer, Captain Herbert von Obwurzer, was transferred by the Orka, first to the staff of the Heimwehren in Innsbruck, then to Linz, and finally to Vienna. In Linz he drafted a plan to find jobs in Upper Austria for former officers and men of the Baltic Free Corps and was apparently successful in placing some of them as 'agricultural workers' on big estates. The police also reported rumours that common actions of the Bavarian, Austrian and Hungarian defence formations were planned to establish a new order in central Europe, but that evidence was still lacking, apart from regular visits by right-wing German officers to Budapest.[45]

The activities of these German officers with their ambitious political plans, aiming at an axis Munich-Budapest, were centred on Vienna, which of course was of vital importance to any such scheme. Colonel Bauer was responsible to General Ludendorff in Munich who saw himself as the future right-wing dictator of Germany. The officers of the Ehrhardt Brigade were strongly opposed to any Bavarian or Austrian particularism which they considered catholic and reactionary. The Orka on the other hand, was above all Bavarian and interested in the Austrian provinces bordering on Bavaria, i.e. Vorarlberg, Tyrol, Salzburg and Upper Austria; it had little interest in Vienna and its 'Bolsheviks'. In October 1922 two officers complained to Bauer about these tendencies. Obwurzer wrote that only the Länder close to Bavaria were being amply supplied with funds, weapons and personnel, while the others received nothing but promises; to his criticisms Colonel Hörl always replied that Vienna was prone to fall to Bolshevism, and that would serve the Viennese right as they were doing nothing against it. The western Länder, on the other hand, could withstand 'the red peril' and would combine with Bavaria; in Upper Austria only the Inn Quarter close to Bavaria was well supplied with arms, and he could not obtain weapons for the other parts. Wandesleben received a similar reply from Hörl when he asked him for arms; he should approach Ehrhardt to whom he was responsible, for the Orgesch was not interested in the 'hydrocephalus Vienna' or in Lower Austria. Hörl implied that his only interests were Bavarian and warned Wandesleben repeatedly against Ehrhardt. In Vienna an open clash occurred between the Orka and the Viennese leader, Fieldmarshal Lieutenant von Metzger; the 'national' groups — students, Turner and nationalist officers — left Metzger and founded their own *Deutscher Wehrbund.*[46]

These internal quarrels — partly German, partly Austrian — soon affected the whole movement. In Austria, the Christian Social partisans separated from the 'nationalists'. Strangely enough, however, the 'nationalists' maintained their good relations with Dr Pittinger in Munich, who was a strong defender of the (Bavarian) monarchist cause; while the Christian Social side looked to Ludendorff, and his Austrian representative Colonel Bauer. According to the latter, Pittinger was aiming at a partition of Austria and the Anschluss of the western provinces to Bavaria; but the Ludendorff side was led by men who escaped from Germany after the Kapp Putsch, could not return there and hence wanted to overthrow the German government by another Putsch. In Austria, the rival military leaders were 'fighting furiously with each other' and did 'not divulge their real aims'. The Deutsche Wehrbund, which owed allegiance to Pittinger, claimed that it had the students and Turner behind it; but the students declared that they had no such ties and did not accept any political orders. For the Turner, their leader Kupka denied that they were members of the Wehrbund. The funds for the defence units largely came from the Austrian industrialists — to the tune of a hundred million paper crowns per month, according to Dr Hans Schürff of the Grossdeutsch Party who debated the issue in October 1922. 'It is a pity', he stated, 'that Austrian industry supplies such colossal sums, for in a case of emergency it could not rely on these defence units.' More recently, however, he continued, the industrialists had made it a condition that the formations would support the government and that representatives of the political parties would have the decisive voice. The following representatives were then elected to the committee which was to adjudicate between the factions: for the Tyrol Dr Steidle, for Styria Dr Rintelen or Professor Hartmann, for Carinthia Colonel Klimann, but no one for Vienna and Lower Austria (apparently because conditions were chaotic there). The speaker added that he was pleased not to have been elected, he had met the representatives of the industrialists and 'completely enlightened them about the state of affairs'. He thought that it was 'ridiculous that we in Austria let ourselves be ordered about by these gentlemen [the German officers.] We must take over the leadership ourselves.'[47]

Only three weeks later, however, Wandesleben reported that Colonel Klimann had sharply attacked the leaders of the defence units in Vienna and Lower Austria because of their attitude towards the

Deutsche Wehrbund. In Wandesleben's opinion the whole 'unity action' was seriously endangered and was likely to become a 'disunity action'. On account of Klimann's connections with the industrialists, Wandesleben continued, his attack was bound to exercise a considerable influence on the financial circles, especially those of Carinthia and large sections of the Styrian industry.[48] Bauer reported to Ludendorff that there was a complete breach with Pittinger because the latter had repeatedly broken his word, his behaviour constituted 'a mixture of untruthfulness, secretiveness and well-aimed villainy'; his policy was Bavarian separatism designed 'to use us North Germans . . . as long as possible and to deceive us'.[49] Pittinger in his turn sent Colonel Hörl to Vienna to force Wandesleben to 'a clear discussion' and to give him notice. But when he went to the restaurant where the officers of the Ehrhardt Brigade usually met he was informed that Wandesleben had again gone to Budapest, without informing the leaders of the Deutsche Wehrbund. In Hörl's opinion, these journeys (meaning Wandesleben's contacts with Hungarian right-wingers) were 'catastrophic' on account of the unsolved question of West Hungary (the Burgenland): if the students heard of them, Wandesleben would be 'finished'. Victor Pietschmann, the deputy leader of the Deutsche Wehrbund, was equally indignant; hence Hörl decided that Wandesleben must be immediately replaced as the latter's chief of staff.[50] Following the result of the plebiscite held in the Burgenland in December 1921 the disputed territory was divided between Austria and Hungary, but the extremists of both countries refused to accept the verdict and passions remained very much alive on both sides.

Such minor issues, however, could not curtail the far-flung political schemes of Colonel Bauer. In his opinion, the preservation of German Austria was essential, so as to avoid the establishment of a Czech-Yugoslav corridor which would cut off Germany from the East and the Balkans and give 'an extraordinary stimulus to the Pan-Slav idea'; only after the dismemberment of Czechoslovakia would it be feasible to unite all Germans. The Anschluss would have to await this development, otherwise a disintegration of Czechoslovakia could not be expected; a large German Empire including all Germans living within the German pale of settlement would need a clear-cut, short frontier towards the East, from Vienna northwards along the river March towards Upper Silesia (thus including Bohemia and Moravia): 'to sacrifice Vienna and Lower Austria to Pan-Slavism would be a crime that could never be expiated'.[51] Bauer's other great scheme was a Bavarian-

Austrian-Hungarian Union under a Wittelsbach or Habsburg king, necessitating the separation of Southern Germany from Germany. To win Hungarian support for this plan it would be necessary for Austria to renounce the Burgenland just acquired from Hungary. In the opinion of the former Austrian General Alfred Krauss, Bauer was thus willing 'to sacrifice völkisch demands so as to gain questionable help'; Bauer's connections reached from the White Russian General Biskupski to Mussolini and the Austrian Clericals and Monarchists; he was, Krauss wrote to Berlin, 'the greatest enemy of the German people and of Austria'.[52]

In March 1923 Bauer reported from Vienna that the Deutsche Wehrbund had achieved very little, although it had received more than a million paper marks from Dr Pittinger since its foundation at the end of 1921. In the area around Vienna it had at most 1,500 members won over from the nationalist associations which formed its natural recruiting ground; its leaders' main activity was to fight against everybody who did not recognize their leadership and did not completely agree with them.[53] But, according to its own testimony, the Deutsche Wehrbund had at least one other task, to break the strikes of agricultural workers: 'It will always be possible to find among the members a corresponding number of people who are willing . . . to go to the country for one to two weeks and there . . . to take on the protection of those willing to work'; the affiliated organizations should form for this purpose groups of twenty volunteers under energetic leaders.[54] The Viennese leader of the Deutsche Wehrbund was General Alfred Krauss, who was grossdeutsch, but that did not prevent him from accepting the over-all control of Pittinger. This at least to some extent explains the bitter hostility of Bauer, Wandesleben and the Ehrhardt men to the Wehrbund.[55]

This hostility also affected the relations between Christian Social partisans and the Grossdeutsche in the Tyrol, a Christian Social stronghold. Hence that party looked at the Heimwehren almost as a party fief, and when the Landeshauptmann negotiated with Orka representatives he failed to admit a representative of the Grossdeutsche. The latter could not accept the Bavarian separatist tendencies, especially those aiming at the foundation of an Alpine state, be that under a Habsburg or a Wittelsbach ruler. They had equally strong reservations about the Heimwehr collaboration with the Bavarian Free Corps Oberland which possessed a strong group in Innsbruck. But they decided in spite of all misgivings, that it was 'absolutely necessary to remain within the

Heimatwehr'.[56] Meanwhile the Tyrolese leader Steidle tried to mediate between the warring factions and at the same time to reduce their financial dependence on Munich. In August 1922 representatives of all para-military formations met at Innsbruck. Those of Carinthia, Salzburg, Upper Austria, Tyrol and Vorarlberg as well as one Styrian organization favoured the continuation of the link with Dr Pittinger, while Vienna and Lower Austria and the majority of Styria demanded a break with him.[57]

In the previous month Steidle himself visited Munich to see the former prime minister, Dr von Kahr, as well as Pittinger and the Bavarian generals von Möhl and von Epp. As Steidle told Colonel Bauer, he intended to offer his thanks in Munich for the help rendered hitherto, but to declare that the Austrian defence units were now forced to take their fate into their own hands and to create a military force which would enable the government to preserve the state: he would request the Bavarians not to disturb 'the united front' in Austria which was supported by the bourgeois parties.[58] For this purpose a close associate of Steidle, the German Captain Waldemar Pabst who, after his escape from Germany, had found refuge in Innsbruck, drafted a 'Working Programme' so as to 'forge a sword for the inevitable final battle of all conservative elements without party distinction . . . against the subversive tendencies of the red International of all shades'. In the political field the programme envisaged the issue of oral directives by the Austrian chancellor to all authorities that they should use the administrative machinery unofficially to promote the cause of the defence formations and the preparation of emergency measures in case of a general strike or riots, after the example of the Tyrolese preparations. Furthermore, the programme asked, should the government remain in Vienna in case of serious unrest, and if not, where should it go?[59]

Colonel Bauer too visited Munich in July 1922 and at army headquarters saw Captain Röhm who had very close connections with Hitler. Röhm told his visitor that the Bavarian Reichswehr formed the true centre of all nationalist organizations and that this co-operation was working well; Pittinger merely provided the money, and even that not alone. If the Bavarian government became weak-kneed those men would have to take the lead who were willing to fight against Berlin; then the black-white-red flag would be hoisted in Munich and the call would go out to the comrades in Germany's north and east.[60] Thus sixteen months before the attempt was made by Hitler the plans for the march to the north were drawn up at army headquarters. On Bauer it made the impression of 'a military authority at the moment of a threatening war'.

In the same month, July 1922, Steidle also went to Vienna to negotiate with the Austrian government about support for the Heimwehren, but found that others had preceded him; as these were declared monarchists Steidle considered them too pronounced politically and 'totally unsuitable to play a leading part in the Austrian Heimatwehr movement.' He also warned Bauer to channel all his efforts with regard to official and financial circles through the Heimwehr executive committee which was in the process of formation, otherwise the efforts were bound to fail.[61] In this respect Steidle was successful, at least for the time being. The chairman of the industrialists' association *(Industriellenverband)*, Urban, early in 1922 promised large subsidies to the Heimwehren of Carinthia, Salzburg, Upper Austria, Tyrol and Vorarlberg, and also to those of Styria and Vienna provided that agreement were reached between the Orka and the rival local organizations. In July the industrialists, after lengthy negotiations, declared themselves willing to pay 50 million paper crowns a month. In September the negotiations were concluded with a promise that, on account of the continuing inflation, 150 million would be paid a month, but that these sums would be channelled to the individual formations through the office of the Austrian chancellor, Dr Ignaz Seipel, the leader of the Christian Social Party. Thus Dr Seipel was given a very effective instrument to achieve the unification of the right-wing movement which was his goal. According to his programme, the provincial Heimwehr formations, the anti-semitic and other right-wing organizations were all to combine, to be financed by the industrialists and to be at the disposal of the government as its strong arm against internal 'anarchy' and foreign threats. Under Seipel's influence an executive committee was formed, with Dr Steidle as the guiding spirit, to promote this unification; 'a reliable instrument of power' was to be formed, to serve as a kind of auxiliary police, if the army proved too weak or unreliable. Steidle in his turn aimed at making the Heimwehren into a 'power factor above the political parties' which in the long run would make the 'talkative parliaments' superfluous – a concept that went much further than Seipel's intentions.[62]

But it was not so much Seipel's hesitation or his fear to get too much involved with Heimwehr politics that ruined Steidle's efforts, but the disunity within his own camp. Especially the radical völkisch units in Carinthia, Vienna and parts of Styria were openly hostile to Seipel's plan and to any alliance with the Christian Social Party which they considered reactionary and monarchist. They preferred their links with Munich and with the Pan-German Association in Berlin. The Pan-German groups in Graz believed that Seipel was the exponent of a clerical anti-German policy; to them he was of the same hue as the German catholic politicians 'Erzberger, Wirth and company'. Steidle, on the other hand, favoured looser connections with Munich and rejected any orders coming from there unless they coincided with his own aims. As he wrote to Pittinger in November 1922, only the executive committee elected by the Austrians should be responsible for internal Austrian affairs; its consent was to be required for any generally valid directives in Austrian matters issued by the supreme command *(Oberleitung)* in Munich. Any decision whether the policy of the Munich organization was to the advantage of the Austrian Germans or not must remain with the Austrians; Munich could not possibly conduct an Austrian national policy, as little as Vienna could take decisions in Bavarian or all-German affairs. But Steidle's more Austrian line met with strong opposition within the Heimwehren and had to be abandoned.[63]

Above all, the industrialists themselves became suspicious that their large subsidies were not properly used by a movement that was so disunited. They wanted to see a united front of all defence organizations established, as well as a unified command in those provinces where none existed, i.e. Styria and Vienna-Lower Austria. To them, the political differences were unimportant: they wanted purely military formations under a 'unified command'; unless these conditions were met the subsidies would cease, and the Austrian government would simply stop all transfers. In this sense the addressee was informed from the Tyrol in November 1922. The Innsbruck writer did not fail to add that, after all, there was unity in the Tyrol, and he expressed the hope that the same would be achieved elsewhere, 'in the great German interest — not that of the Grossdeutsche'.[64] In January 1923 Steidle wrote to Chancellor Seipel that he had undertaken the task of unification on two conditions: sufficient financial resources and the unconditional co-operation of the entire state apparatus with the defence formations, as it already existed in the Tyrol. The promise had been given but was not kept in practice, and the executive committee was writing and writing but did not achieve anything. Seipel, however, refused to receive it and ordered the subsidies to be stopped on account of the chaotic situation within the Heimwehr camp.[65]

In the same month, January 1923, Steidle wrote once more to the chancellor that he had continued 'the ungrateful and laborious task of unification' in spite of all the difficulties which seemed 'insurmountable, especially in Styria and in Vienna'. He must now consider the whole action condemned to failure; neither he nor the Tyrolese Heimwehren had 'any time or energy left for things which have become totally pointless'.[66] But in spite of his forebodings Steidle, only four weeks later, undertook another attempt at mediation at a meeting called to Salzburg. Colonel Bauer, who was present, believed that all the attempts of the past six months had only one purpose: to drum up support for Pittinger so that he could play a role in Munich, and to force Bauer and his adherents to 'co-operate with the people around that old fool Krauss', the Austrial general. At Salzburg, the representatives of Carinthia, Salzburg, Upper Austria, Tyrol and Vorarlberg founded an 'Alpine Club' which remained loyal to Pittinger. According to Bauer, Colonel Hörl was once more the moving spirit and achieved this success by distributing large bundles of bank notes; but the loudest advocate of the 'Club' was Colonel Klimann from Carinthia who was always ready to change sides. Klimann did not see why he should suddenly desert his old friends, expressed his full confidence in the Bavarian State Commissar von Kahr, and refused to agree to Ludendorff's demand that he must break with Pittinger.[67]

During that month, February 1923, Ludendorff himself visited Vienna where some Free Corps units took an oath to him. The students who declined to do so were 'expelled' from the movement, and then continued their connections with the Viennese policy director Schober and leading industrialists.[68] But the industrialists themselves were now deeply divided. As Bauer informed Captain Pabst in Innsbruck, the 'nationalist' industrialists were only willing to pay for the 'nationalist' formations, and the Jewish ones refused to continue their payments to formations which were anti-semitic and völkisch *('hakenkreuzlerisch')*; 'but that applies to nearly all, and it is a rather bad dilemma'.[69]

In April 1923 the five provincial organizations which had united in the 'Alpine Club' reconvened at Salzburg. Steidle was elected the leader of the association; the Tyrolese were also successful with their demand that some distance should be kept from Munich and its political aspirations. The principle was adopted that 'agreements with foreign organizations should only be entered into with the unanimous consent of all the member associations'. The opposition was defeated with ease.

But the Heimwehr movement was now split into three hostile camps. Apart from the members of the 'Alpine Club', there were the formations in Vienna, Lower Austria and Styria which sided with Ludendorff and his Austrian representatives. There were finally some minority groups, such as the League of Germans in Styria (which was expelled from the 'Alpine Club') and the students' and ex-officers' organizations in Vienna, which were strongly pro-German and looked at the two other groups as traitors to the German cause and semi-monarchist.[70] With the failure of the Hitler Putsch in Munich, however, the various German links lost their importance, Ludendorff's influence was eclipsed, and Bauer had to leave Vienna. Yet, as we shall see later, the grossdeutsch idea remained very much alive in the Heimwehr movement, and so did certain völkisch and anti-parliamentarian ideologies.

Already in 1923 the influence of another foreign ideology was beginning to be felt in Austria. In the Tyrol strong words were used, not only against 'red' Vienna, but against the Tyrolese government which nurtured and protected the Heimwehren. At a meeting of the local leaders of central and western Tyrol, 'vigorous words were uttered against bureaucracy and the never-ending compromises and concessions towards Vienna and the Social Democrats . . . If the Land government cannot muster the courage to create order . . . the Heimatwehr itself will do so', and in particular cleanse the Tyrol 'from the foreign Jewish rabble'. One of the central demands put forward at the meeting was 'the complete subjugation of the marxist parties in the Tyrol. These must be reduced to the same unimportance which has been forced upon them by the Fascists in Italy. (Great spring cleaning in Tyrol.)' If the Heimwehren cleaned out the Tyrol, it was claimed, this would set an example to the other Länder which would follow it sooner or later. Another point brought up at the meeting was 'the consolidation of the Heimatwehr in a fascist direction' so as to carry out their programme in its original extension.[71]

Yet at that time the Heimwehren were far from strong and vigorous in the very area from which these demands came, as their own reports to the Tyrolese command proved. In January 1923 it was reported that only few new members could be recruited. Because of a lack of weapons (what had happened to all those smuggled from Bavaria?), no new local groups could be founded, and even existing ones could only accept recruits in so far as they had weapons for them. The group at Flirsch was disintegrating for the third time because they had no weapons; the group at Hall was making very slow progress on account

of the indifference of the local business people, and the other groups of
the Hall district could not be commended either.[72] From at least two
places – Landeck and Zams on the Upper Inn – it was related that the
National Socialists were making 'further progress' among the workers,
who clearly found a more radical posture more to their liking than the
more cautious Heimwehr policy. In a later report it was stated that the
Heimwehr members were often too passive: they had originally joined
because they saw in the Heimwehr 'a protection for their shop
windows', or because their boss had suggested it; these reasons were no
longer valid, and thus the movement had to carry a large amount of
ballast which caused obstruction and damage.[73] The friction and
bickering among the leaders must have been a further cause which
prevented the growth of the movement – at a time when economic
difficulties were growing and the inflation of the currency deprived so
many people of their security. As the same report stressed, 'the economic distress presses down on everybody, whether he is employed or
in business'.

Although outside Vienna and a few industrial centres the Social
Democrats were much weaker than their political rivals, their reply to
the large-scale armaments and military preparations of the right was the
foundation of the 'Republican Defence Corps', a para-military socialist
organization established in 1923 in the place of older workers' units
and party stewards. The result – as might have been expected – were
constant clashes between left and right, years before the tragic events of
1927 and 1934. Two such clashes between armed or semi-armed groups
occurred in the area of Klagenfurt in October 1923, and the details may
be recounted here by way of example. On 1 October a worker was
beaten up by Heimwehr members in the village of Waidmannsdorf
(probably because he was a socialist), whereupon forty men of the
Republican Defence Corps marched there from St Ruprecht but found
their adversaries had left. On the following day, however, an armed
Heimwehr unit encircled Waidmannsdorf in military formation, apparently to conduct a search in the village or, as they claimed, to
protect its houses. Thereupon the leader of the Republican Defence
Corps of St Ruprecht mobilized his men, as he declared unarmed, and
marched to Waidmannsdorf. On arrival there he suggested to the major
commanding the Heimwehr unit that both sides should withdraw, but
the offer was rejected. The members of the Republican Defence Corps,
clearly superior in numbers, then surrounded their adversaries and took
away some of their rifles, and finally the latter left, or as their enemies

claimed, fled. The whole affair aroused the Carinthian Heimwehr leader, Colonel Klimann, to take action. He assembled his men in front of the government house and declared that he would no longer suffer any such 'provocation'; if the Landeshauptmann did not act, his men would resort 'to self-defence'. He submitted the following demands: disarmament of all who had taken part in the events, arrest and punishment of the ring-leaders. He further declared that the Heim-wehren were strong enough to enforce law and order, but would first try to achieve their object in a legal fashion. The provincial government had to promise that those found guilty would be duly punished and those who carried arms would be disarmed. It added that the demon-stration of the Republican Defence Corps planned for 7 October would only pass peacefully if the Heinwehren too abstained from any provoca-tion.[74]

On 20 October 1923 the men of the first district of the Klagenfurt Heimwehr were ordered to assemble in a local inn on account of the impending elections. One of them stood in front of the house when a crowd of workers approached. From the crowd a voice called: 'Now we will go and buy some wine!'; but the man in front of the inn replied that because of the election no alcohol was permitted to be sold. The crowd now assumed a threatening attitude (presumably recognizing him as a Heimwehr member) and he ran inside. Even before he heard that in the courtyard rifles were loaded, and then two shots were fired. The Heim-wehr men shut the gates of the inn, but they were pushed open again, and then the crowd saw the armed Heimwehr men inside. Excitement increased quickly on both sides. The Heimwehr advanced from the inn in military formation and closed the neighbouring streets; shots were fired into the air, and the crowd retreated. When the gendarmerie arrived on the scene they demanded from the Heimwehr men 'in the name of the law' they should put down their rifles, but in vain. On the contrary, for reasons unknown at least one of them fired three shots at the advancing gendarmes, but without hitting his target. Thereupon the police surrounded the inn, searched it and found 23 loaded rifles and about a hundred cartridges hidden under the roof and in the cellar. There was enormous excitement among the workers, and a workers' unit was summoned by tocsin. But the police report praised the workers of Klagenfurt for not arming themselves and not replying to the Heimwehr in their own fashion.[75] The report did not mention any arrest carried out among the Heimwehr members.

When General Ludendorff visited Klagenfurt in the same year he was given a hero's welcome by the Heimwehr which saluted him at every station where his train stopped and lined the streets of Klagenfurt. The Carinthian government claimed somewhat ingenuously that the visit had nothing whatever to do with the National Socialist movement, but that the general came as the owner of an estate in Bavaria and a member of the Bavarian Peasant League, and thus at the invitation of his fellow-agrarians.[76]

In Styria the first severe clashes between Heimwehren and Social Democrats took place in November 1922 in the small town of Judenburg. There socialist workers searched the houses of Heimwehr men and confiscated their weapons. The Landeshauptmann, Dr Rintelen, who strongly sympathized with the Heimwehren and was violently anti-socialist, allowed the Styrian Heimwehr leader Dr Pfrimer to use his men as an auxiliary police, allegedly because he assumed that the gendarmerie would not be able to cope with the Social Democrats. Their leaders were arrested in Judenburg, whereupon 3,000 steel workers at Waltersdorf came out on strike. But they were forced to break off the strike by a large-scale mobilization of the Styrian Heimwehren. Thanks to the support of the authorities, their superiority was clearly established in an area where socialist influence was weak.[77]

Even in Styria, however, there were two rival Heimwehr organizations, of which that led by Dr Pfrimer was the stronger and more independent one. In general, the Heimwehr movement presented a fantastic picture of in-fighting, personal and political intrigue and inability to take any decisive action. The movement disposed of large funds and accumulated vast stores of weapons, but did not gain any great political success. Its leaders liked to make blustering speeches, but were unable to bury their differences. These were exacerbated by rival political influences emanating from Bavaria, and the Bavarian military leaders only succeeded in exporting their mutual animosities to Austria. The Heimwehr ideology was above all grossdeutsch and sharply anti-marxist, but partly it was strongly conservative and catholic. Indeed, throughout its history a major weakness of the movement was that it did not possess a common ideology. The following years were to see strenuous efforts to create such an ideology and a unified command, but — as we shall see — the efforts failed.

NOTES

1. For all details, see F. L. Carsten, *Revolution in Central Europe 1918-1919* (London, 1972) 78ff., 223ff.

2. Fritz Fellner, 'The Background of Austrian Fascism' in Peter F. Sugar (ed.), *Native Fascism in the Successor States* (Santa Barbara, 1971) 22; Rudolf G. Ardelt, *Zwischen Demokratie und Faschismus* (Vienna-Salzburg, 1972) 10.

3. Police report of 17 November 1919: Verwaltungsarchiv Wien, Staatsamt des Innern, 22/gen., box 4860. Italics in original.

4. Police report of 17 November 1919, ibid.

5. Reports of 14 February and 15 March 1919: Steiermärk. Landesarchiv, Akten der k.k. Statthalterei – Präsidium, E. 91, 1919.

6. Reports of 22 July, 23 June 1919: ibid., E. 91, 1918 (ii).

7. Reports of 26 May, 15 July, 16 September 1919: ibid., Präsidialakten 1919, 289 J 204, 443 J 204.

8. Order issued by Dr Brodmann, *Untersteirisches Bauernkommando,* 14 June 1919: ibid., Akten der k.k. Statthalterei – Präsidium, E.91, 1918 (ii).

9. Anton Rintelen, *Erinnerungen an Österreichs Weg* (Munich, 1941) 126-27, 130.

10. Bruce S. Pauley, *Hahnenschwanz und Hakenkreuz* (Vienna, 1972) 41-42.

11. Lebenslauf Hanns Rauter, 15 February 1935: Institut für Zeitgeschichte, Munich, 2108/57. Rauter later became a high SS leader.

12. 'Notiz', s.d.: Polizeiarchiv Wien, Nachlass Schober, box 46/1.

13. Fellner, op. cit., 21.

14. F. O. Lindley to Foreign Office, Vienna, 11 June 1920: Publ. Record Office, FO 371, File 5445, vol. 3538, no. 203366.

15. Ludger Rape, 'Die österreichische Heimwehr und ihre Beziehungen zur bayerischen Rechten zwischen 1920 und 1923' (Unpublished Ph.D. thesis, Vienna 1968) 52, 111.

16. Rape, op. cit., 59-60.

17. Horst G. W. Nusser, *Konservative Wehrverbände in Bayern, Preussen und Österreich 1918-1933* (Munich, 1973) 131.

18. Rape, op. cit., 48, 76, 83.

19. 'Bericht über die Vertrauensmännerversammlung am 7 März 1920 im Mödelhammerbräu zu Salzburg': Bundesarchiv Koblenz, NS 26, vorl. 649.

20. Rape, op. cit., 108, 111.

21. 'Protokoll der Sitzung am 13 Mai 1920': Bundesarchiv Koblenz, NS 26, vorl. 649.

22. Ibid.

23. Steidle to *Landesregierung,* 15 May; Bezirkshauptmann Landeck to same, 20 May 1920: Tiroler Landesarchiv, Präsidialakten 1932, 303 III 10, 'Bildung der Heimatwehren in Tirol'.

24. *Lagebericht* Nr. I, Bregenz, 23 September 1920: Bundesarchiv Koblenz, NS 26, vorl. 648.

25. Captain Matt to Orka, Bregenz, 28 October 1920: ibid., vorl. 647.

26. Same to same, Bregenz, 3 December 1920: ibid., vorl. 648.

27. *Heimatschutz in Österreich* (Vienna, 1934) 294.

28. Report of 26 June 1920: Bundesarchiv Koblenz, NS 26, vorl. 649.

29. Report about a conference in Salzburg on 29 October 1921: Tiroler Landesarchiv, Präsidialakten 1932, 303 III 10.

30. Report about a meeting in Salzburg on 4 July 1920: Bundesarchiv Koblenz, NS 26, vorl. 649.

31. Rape, op. cit., 247.

32. Ibid., 217-18, 234; report about the negotiations in Vienna on 12 September 1920: Bundesarchiv Koblenz, NS 26, vorl. 649.

33. Report about a conference with the student associations in Vienna on 12 September 1920, ibid.

34. Police report of 8 December 1920: Polizeiarchiv Wien, Polizeiberichte 1919-1921.

35. Schraffl to Ministry of Interior, 23 November and 2 December 1920: Tiroler Landesarchiv, Präsidialakten 1922, II 11 g, 165 II 11 g; report of Gendarmerieposten Kufstein of 19 November 1920, ibid., II 11 g.

36. 'Protokoll über die Besprechung des Landeshauptmannes mit den Leitern der pol. Bezirksbehörden und dem Vorstande der Heimwehr', 18 July 1921: ibid., Präsidialakten 1932, 303 III 10.

37. Stumpf to the Tiroler Bezirkshauptmannschaften, 2 November 1921, ibid.

38. The German Consul at Innsbruck to _Auswärtiges Amt,_ 1 December 1921: Bundesarchiv Koblenz, Reichskanzlei, Akten betr. Österreich, R 43 I 105.

39. von Stockhammern to _Reichskanzlei,_ 2 December 1921, ibid.

40. Map of 1922: Landesarchiv Tirol, Präsidialakten 1932, 303 III 10.

41. 'Protokoll der Stabsleitersitzung in Klagenfurth', 13 August 1921: ibid.

42. 'Bericht über eine zwischen christl.-sozial. Heimatwehrführern stattgefundene Besprechung in Salzburg', 29 October 1921 (11 pp.): ibid.

43. Ibid.

44. Rape, op. cit., 338-44; report of 16 August 1922: Bundesarchiv Koblenz, Nachlass Bauer, Nr. 30a.

45. Information for Police President Schober, Vienna, 1 and 6 July 1922: Polizeiarchiv Wien, Nachlass Schober, box 37. Partly confirmed by Obwurzer's report, 17 October 1922: Bundesarchiv Koblenz, Nachlass Max Bauer, no. 30a.

46. Reports by Obwurzer, Vienna, 17 October and by Wandesleben, Vienna, 18 October 1922: ibid.

47. The above according to '159. Sitzung des Verbandes der Grossdeutschen Volkspartei am 18. Oktober 1922': Verwaltungsarchiv Wien, Grossdeutsche Volkspartei, box 3. Rintelen and Steidle belonged to the Christian Social Party, Hartmann and Klimann were grossdeutsch.

48. W. to Bauer, Innsbruck, 8 November 1922: Bundesarchiv Koblenz, Nachlass Bauer, Nr. 30a.

49. Nusser, op. cit., 227.

50. Report by Hörl, 13 March 1922: Nachlass Bauer, Nr. 30a.

51. Report by Bauer, Vienna, 6 March 1923: ibid., Nr. 30b.

52. General Krauss to _Nationalverband deutscher Offiziere,_ s.d.: Friedrich Berg, _Die weisse Pest – Beiträge zur völkischen Bewegung in Österreich_ (Vienna, 1926) 17-18.

53. Report by Bauer, Vienna, 6 March 1923, pp. 16, 21: Bundesarchiv Koblenz, Nachlass Bauer, Nr. 30b.

54. Deutscher Wehrbund to Brigade von Wandesleben, etc., Vienna, 29 April 1922: ibid., Nr. 30a.

55. Report by Commander Missuweit and Captain Obwurzer, Vienna, 16 August 1922: ibid.

56. 'Verhandlungsschrift über die Landesparteileitungs-Sitzung', 4 February 1922: Verwaltungsarchiv Wien, Grossdeutsche Volkspartei, box 29.

57. Report by Bauer, Vienna, 6 March 1923: Bundesarchiv Koblenz, Nachlass Bauer, Nr. 30b.

58. Report by Bauer, Vienna, 15 July 1922: ibid., Nr. 30a.

59. 'Entwurf eines Arbeitsprogramms', s.d. (July 1922): ibid.

60. Report by Bauer, Vienna, 15 July 1922, about his conversations in Innsbruck and Munich: ibid.

61. Steidle to Bauer (?), Innsbruck, 10 July 1922: ibid.

62. Rape, op. cit., 406, 413-14, 423-25, 435-37, 500; Nusser, op. cit., 230.

63. Rape, op. cit., 433-34, 483-84, 517.

64. *Landesleitung Tirol* to Bauer (?), Innsbruck, 3 November 1922: Bundesarchiv Koblenz, Nachlass Bauer, Nr. 30a.

65. Rape, op. cit., 500-2.

66. Steidle to Seipel, 29 January 1923: Bundesarchiv Koblenz, Nachlass Bauer, Nr. 30a.

67. Bauer to Count Revertera, 26 February 1923, and Klimann's remarks at Salzburg on same day: ibid.

68. Rape, op. cit., 585-86.

69. Bauer to Pabst, 12 March 1923: Nachlass Bauer, Nr. 30b. The Swastika was the emblem not only of the National Socialists, but also of many völkisch organizations and Heimwehr units.

70. Rape, op. cit., 547-55; Nusser, op. cit., 231.

71. Report by *Gauleitung* Mittel- und Westtirol on the Gau leaders' assembly of 17 March, Innsbruck, 26 April 1923: Tiroler Landesarchiv, Präsidialakten 1932, 303 III 10.

72. Report by the same Gauleitung, Innsbruck, 16 January 1923: ibid.

73. Reports by the same Gauleitung, Innsbruck, 21 March 1923, 20 November 1924: ibid.

74. Protocol about the negotiations with the Carinthian government, 2 October 1923: Kärntner Landesarchiv, Präs. 7-1/1038, 1923, fasz. 672.

75. Police reports of 22 October and 2 November 1923, ibid.

76. Carinthian government to Ministry of Interior in Vienna, 7 February 1923: ibid.

77. Pauley, *Hahnenschwanz und Hakenkreuz,* 43-44.

4

THE EARLY YEARS OF
NATIONAL SOCIALISM

Through the break-up of the Habsburg Monarchy the Austrian National Socialists were separated from their principal area of influence, northern Bohemia, and the party's activities were conducted on a very minor scale in the immediate post-war years. Its leaders, such as Dr Walter Riehl in Vienna, often appeared on common platforms with other right-wingers to fan the strong anti-Semitism caused by the large influx of eastern Jews from Galicia and Bukovina at the end of the war. This produced strong popular resentment at a time of enormous scarcity of food, coal and living accommodation. Mass meetings and demonstrations were organized to demand the expulsion of the undesired newcomers and the curtailment of their activities. In June 1919 an 'Anti-Semitic League' was founded 'to free our people from Jewish rule'.[1] The National Socialist leaders who joined in this agitation were no more radical or violent than other speakers, nor was their appeal in any way different. They found a cause which they could exploit and a mass audience receptive to their propaganda. Their own meetings were much less well attended than the anti-semitic mass rallies in the Viennese town hall, rallies which often overspilled into the street.

Thus a National Socialist meeting held in August 1919 in central Vienna was only attended by about 600 people, among them many railwaymen who had marched to the meeting hall with a placard 'Out with the Jews!' The meeting was addressed by the Viennese Gauleiter Karl Schulz, by a spokesman of the railwaymen from Znaim in Moravia, and by Riehl. The speakers pictured the misery of the railway employees in the areas occupied by the Czechs; those who were forced to leave their homes in Bohemia and Moravia were put into barracks in Vienna, while 'the Galician Jews in Vienna live in palaces'; the government was doing nothing for the refugees who would be forced to resort to self-help. The speeches were received with thunderous applause and many anti-semitic outbursts by the audience. After the meeting, the participants marched, among much shouting against Czechs and Jews, to the Ballhausplatz where Riehl and others were received by the undersecretary of state in the Foreign Office. Then the crowd was once more addressed by Riehl who exclaimed that they demanded action, not against the Viennese Jews, but against the immigrants from Poland. Afterwards the demonstrators attempted to break into cafés frequented by Jews, but were prevented from doing so by the police.[2] Apparently Riehl tried to control his followers and made a clear distinction between Jews domiciled in Vienna and recent immigrants: other anti-semitic agitators were less cautious. Twelve months later the National Socialists held another meeting in Vienna to demand the expulsion of the eastern Jews, which was attended by 800 to 1,000 people. Riehl again emphasized that the popular movement was directed in the first instance against the eastern Jews; but if that question were not solved very soon it would attack all the Jews. A resolution was adopted which demanded the removal of eastern Jewish pupils from the secondary schools and ended: 'We native Viennese declare that we will no longer starve, freeze and remain homeless while tens of thousands of eastern Jews engage here in black marketeering. Out with the eastern Jews! If the legal way proves impossible force will be used.'[3]

The National Socialist programme for the elections in Vienna and Lower Austria in 1919 demanded: foreigners were not to be given any ration books and not to be protected as tenants any longer, in particular not the 'Eastern Jewish plague', and all non-Germans to be dismissed from any public or private service; water power, railways and banks were to be nationalized, and the administration was to be reformed. But it was only in Salzburg that two National Socialists were elected to the Diet in that year.[4] That the party was comparatively weak in Austria also emerged at the conference of National Socialists of 'Greater Germany' held at the end of 1919. At the 'all-German representatives' meeting' the Bohemian party, represented by Jung, Knirsch and other leaders, was allocated four votes, compared with two for the Austrians, and only one each for the representatives from Germany and from Polish Silesia. Vienna was more strongly represented than any other area at the meeting of Austrian delegates: there were six from Vienna and five from Lower Austria, three from Styria, two each from Salzburg and Upper Austria, and one each from Carinthia and Tyrol. As there is no evidence of how many members the party had at that time, this gives some indication of its distribution in the country as a whole.

Among twenty-six Austrians present, six were academics, with the title of Dr or Prof., and two engineers with the title of Ing. in front of their names; three represented nationalist trade unions, and one of the items on the agenda was 'party and trade union', to be introduced by two trade union secretaries.[5] To some extent the party had preserved its working-class character from pre-war days and its strong interest in trade union matters − a character very different from that of Hitler's party in Munich. The same is indicated by a scrap of information from the small Upper Austrian town of Neumarkt. There a local group of a few members was founded in 1919, which 'was a pure working-class party and a counterweight to the Social Democrats'. But it was unable to develop beyond a figure of at most twenty members.[6] Yet the large number of academics among the leaders − almost a third of the named delegates at the party conference − indicates the presence of a very different social group; and a third important component was formed by white-collar workers and small officials, especially of the railways, groups particularly conscious of their status distinct from the working-class. In contrast with the Heimwehren, the National Socialists during these early years were a purely urban movement and their propaganda was limited to the towns.

The party group at Innsbruck was founded in the autumn of 1919 and had 48 members by the end of the year. The police reported that among them were members 'of all social groups, such as intelligentsia and salaried employees, people working in commerce, railway officials and servants etc'. The speaker at the meeting defined as

the task of the National Socialist Party the creation of a people's party with the simultaneous organization of the employees of all trades in a trade union ... on an economic basis, repudiation of the class struggle and temporary postponement of the confessional issues; [the party was] as it were a middle party between the Liberal, Christian Social and Social Democratic parties....[7]

What seems curious in this report is that the Innsbruck National Socialists were considered a 'middle party', between the bourgeois and socialist parties, and not a party of the extreme right. How small the National Socialist Party was emerged clearly when it put up its own candidates in the general election of October 1920. Riehl, probably realizing his party's weakness, suggested an electoral combination with the Grossdeutsche on the basis of their common all-German and anti-semitic ideology, but the latter declined. In the election the National Socialists altogether polled a mere 33,898 votes, compared with over 1.2 million for the Christian Social and over one million votes for the Social Democratic parties; even the Grossdeutsche received more than half a million votes. Riehl himself gained only 4,876 votes in two Viennese constituencies, and the party not a single seat in parliament — a bitterly resented defeat which it attributed to the behaviour of the Grossdeutsche.[8] At that time the party was hardly more than a small sect on the extreme right wing of the political spectrum; but so was Hitler's National Socialist German Workers' Party in Munich when he began his activities there. The National Socialists considered themselves the party of a 'national socialism which would break the rule of money', but the Grossdeutsche a 'bourgeois party, based on mammonism'.[9]

In August 1920 there took place at Salzburg the second meeting of representatives of the National Socialists of 'Greater Germany', this time attended by 235 delegates, among them about one hundred from outside Austria. Among the latter there appeared for the first time Anton Drexler, the founder of the Munich German Workers' Party, and Adolf Hitler. The meeting adopted a resolution in favour of close cooperation of all National Socialists. Riehl, as a kind of elder statesman, tried to mediate between the Munich National Socialists and their rivals in northern Germany, the German-Socialists, by arranging a partition of Germany between them, but without much success. He went to Germany to speak there and, recognizing Hitler's oratorical gifts, invited him to address meetings in several Austrian towns. Yet at the Salzburg conference the Munich National Socialists were only accorded one vote, compared with two for their German-Socialist rivals, three for the Austrian, and four for the Bohemian National Socialists, and single votes for several other völkisch organizations.[10]

In 1921, at the following 'inter-state representative meeting of the National Socialist Party', however, the Munich party was allocated two votes, as many as the North German National Socialists, but fewer than the Austrians or the Bohemians, who retained their representation of the previous year.[11] The Munich National Socialist, Gottfried Feder, was asked to speak on his pet subject, 'the Breaking of the Shackles of Interest', but several others were permitted to voice their criticisms and divergent opinions on the subject. A debate was also arranged on the decision of the Bohemian National Socialists to call themselves a 'class party of productive labour' — a decision that ran counter to the repudiation of the class struggle. It was planned to adopt 'common directives for a unified National Socialist policy for the entire German people', and the invitation even spoke of *one* 'National Socialist Party of the German people';[12] but in reality there were half a dozen separate parties in four different countries. They did not recognize a common leadership, and differed considerably in their politics. In Austria, at any rate, the local groups still elected their delegates to the party conference, and the delegates in their turn the party leadership — in no way different from the mode in force in any democratic party. But in Munich by this time Hitler had assumed 'dictatorial power' with himself as the party's first chairman, and relegated its founder, Drexler, to a role of very minor importance. Hitler's aim was achieved by a successful coup and a party purge which removed his critics; in future he alone had the power to take important decisions.[13]

When the fourth 'inter-state representatives' meeting' convened in Vienna in 1922 it was attended by six National Socialists from Munich, among them Hitler, Drexler, Esser and Rosenberg; there the party now had 6,000 members and was larger than any other similar group. Riehl recognized this fact and hailed Hitler in a public meeting as 'our Reich German *Führer!* '[14] Hitler's expected presence was also announced for an international meeting of leading anti-Semites which took place in Vienna in March 1921; it was attended by about 150 people and thirty-nine Austrian organizations, among them many local catholic, Christian Social, and German nationalist groups. Hitler, however, did not appear, but instead his close associate Hermann Esser. He spoke in favour of a united struggle against Jewry; in Munich, as in Vienna, well-fed Jews gorged themselves in the restaurants and places of entertainment, while the starving natives stood outside; but in Munich things had changed and the Jews were thrown out; 'when the first Jew would be thrown into the Isar Jews must swim also in Budapest and Vienna'. The writer Anton Orel, a follower of Schönerer, spoke on Germanic culture: already the Germanic tribes had produced a culture higher than that of any other heathen people and, in the Middle Ages under the influence of Christianity, they became the leading cultural group. The Jews, he claimed, were aiming at world power and a world order in which they would have no duties; free masonry, liberalism, and democracy were products of a Jewish culture which was bound to lead to communism.

A speaker from Budapest, Professor Kmosko, told the meeting that it was the purpose of the revolution of 1918 to subject the whole of Hungary to Jewish domination, but thanks to the work of the 'Awakening Hungarians' things had changed; he proposed the foundation of a 'League of all Christian nations'. Another Hungarian speaker, Dr von Palosi, praised the achievements of the anti-semitic organizations in Hungary: no Jew could any longer adopt a Hungarian name; the Jewish names were entered in the passports; Jews were no longer admitted to the civil service and the municipal service of Budapest; the aim was to eliminate them entirely from Hungary's political life. A public meeting in the town hall was attended by about 8,000 people. Among the speakers was the National Socialist Gattermayer who described the world war as an enterprise of Jewish money bags; while the Jews remained at home the German youths bled in the trenches. He demanded separate Jewish schools, a numerus clausus for the universities, the dismissal of Jewish teachers and professors, and threatened violence if the government did not concede these demands. A speaker from Graz, Colonel Zborowski, demanded a conscription of the Jews by the state; against the Jews, he stated, the German people acted in self-defence and were entitled to employ any means, even pogroms – a remark which met with general approval.[15]

In the general election of 1920 the Grossdeutsche had declined Riehl's offer of a combined list. At the end of the year the National Socialists of Klagenfurt turned down a similar offer from the Grossdeutsche, although the latter promised them two to three seats on their list. They pointed out to the National Socialists that the city administration of Klagenfurt had always been in German nationalist hands, and that many of their voters would be deterred if there were two or more völkisch lists. In spite of this, the National Socialists were confident that they alone would get five to six seats on the city council, while a combined list would damage them badly, and declined the offer. In spite of 'feverish electioneering' they only obtained one seat – a result they found bitterly disappointing; even in Villach, their main bastion, their strength declined.[16] In the Tyrol, the National Socialists put up their own candidates for the first time in the Diet election of

May 1921, but gained only 1,226 votes in the whole country, 691 of them in Innsbruck itself, and not a single seat. The party's membership consisted mainly of students, but it had a certain working-class following.[17] At a meeting of representatives of völkisch organizations to discuss the question of a united front, the National Socialist speaker admitted that the working class accepted the concept of the class struggle; hence it was necessary for his party to make 'some concessions' to the workers 'so as to win them over slowly'. If the National Socialists gave up their independence they 'would destroy the national workers' movement itself'.[18]

Developments in 1923 seemed to justify this independent stance: thanks to the continuing inflation and economic crisis and the government's stringent measures of economy, the membership of the National Socialist Party trebled, and by the summer it had, according to its own figures, 34,000 members. Within a year, its weekly organ, the *Deutsche Arbeiterpresse*, could raise its circulation from 4,000 to 22,000.[19] To some extent this growth also took place in the provinces. In the Tyrol, the local paper, *Der Nationalsozialist*, had 1,900 subscribers, and many members of the Grossdeutsche went over to the National Socialists, especially in Landeck and Kufstein. The German Consul reported from Innsbruck that the local National Socialists had not yet established a direct link with Hitler in Munich, and Hitler declared that he could not do anything with the Tyrolese party because it lacked good organizers.[20] The meetings organized by the National Socialists in Graz in the spring of 1923 were attended by 150 and 350 persons, respectively, and the speeches were principally anti-semitic. The first speaker pointed to the growth of the party, blamed the Jews for causing the world war and fratricidal strife within the German nation; the nation must rid itself of these blood-suckers and, if that could not be achieved legally, a pogrom must be organized; only when some Jews were strung up on the lamp posts in Vienna would the masses of Jews flee back where they had come from. The other speaker attacked the Jews who held important posts in the municipal administration of Vienna and those who were the 'leaders of the international social-democratic proletariat': the class spirit created by the Jews among the masses must be eliminated, so that the German nation could be reborn.[21]

In Vienna too, the numbers attracted by National Socialist propaganda increased quickly. In January 1923 Hermann Esser from Munich spoke to meetings attended by 1,200 and 2,000 people. The posters inviting to the meetings proclaimed: 'Danger of a Putsch in Bavaria!

Mass flight of Jews from Munich!' Esser declared that, if only the people realized that they had to sacrifice three-quarters of their income to the exploiting Jewish banks, they would take vengeance on those responsible for their misery; three-quarters of all large flats were in Jewish hands. Dr Riehl announced that the National Socialists would soon demonstrate in the streets of Vienna, especially in front of the University, but the time for the real attack had not yet come, and he warned against any piecemeal action.[22] The anti-Semitism of Esser and others was far outdone by Julius Streicher who addressed audiences of about 300 and about 1,500 in Vienna in August 1923. According to Streicher the Jews were the carriers of all bad racial traits; he pointed in particular to the German chancellors Dr Wirth and Dr Stresemann, who had both married Jewish women, and warned all women present against having sexual intercourse with Jews; if they saw a girl together with a Jew they should box her ears. He claimed that thousands of children had been the victims of Jewish ritual murder: it was only necessary to read the Talmud to understand this. After these speeches it was decided by the authorities to expel Streicher from Vienna and to start a court case against him, but he left Austria before he could be notified.[23]

Within the National Socialist Party a military formation was organized which grew quickly — variously called a Storm Detachment (*Sturmabteilung* like the SA in Munich) or *Ordnertruppe* (Party Stewards) or *Vaterländischer Schutzbund* (Patriotic Defence League). In April 1923 Colonel Bauer sent its commander, a German lieutenant called Lechner, to Hitler with a message that, as Vienna contained the best organized social-democratic workers' battalions, it was essential to create there units of equal value which could provide flank protection for Hitler's Bavarian movement.[24] But the principal purpose of the SA was to deal with political opponents, and the men were at least partly armed. In November 1923 the National Socialists held a public meeting in Voitsberg in Styria; an SA unit of forty men appeared from Graz to protect the meeting. But this was principally attended by Social Democrats who demanded a vote to decide who was to act as the chairman. One of them was elected by a majority and he then allowed the National Socialist speaker, Professor Suchenwirth from Vienna, ten minutes for his speech. His anti-socialist remarks were drowned by noise, and he was followed by a Social Democrat who finally demanded that the meeting be closed. The National Socialists then ordered their storm troopers to attack, and a general melée ensued in which beer mugs and table legs were freely used by both sides, but in which the SA slowly gained the upper hand. A workers' unit of 120 men then appeared on the scene, and the National Socialists demanded the right to leave unhindered; but the Social Democrats were only willing to grant this if their enemies were first disarmed by the police. The latter found 15 revolvers, 20 truncheons and other weapons, but handed back the revolvers to their owners because they possessed licences! Apparently there were no casualties.[25]

A far more serious incident occurred in July 1923 near Vienna when two young National Socialists murdered in the woods one of their comrades who was suspected of being a Communist. Within the Viennese SA a secret formation, called *Trutztruppe*, was formed. One of its detachments had the task of killing political enemies if ordered to do so by their leader who claimed to be a German lieutenant and an emissary of the 'Organization Consul' in Munich. The members had to take an oath to carry out these orders without questioning them. A similar secret organization called itself the 'Schlageter Brigade', after a German National Socialist who was arrested and sentenced to death for sabotage by the French in the Ruhr; the unit counted about forty members, also recruited from the SA of Vienna.[26]

In April 1923 Bauer expressed his worries about the Viennese National Socialists to General Ludendorff. He considered it impossible that the SA formations should be subordinate to Captain Göring, their Munich leader, which seemed to be Hitler's intention. In Bauer's opinion, any such scheme was bound to cause a complete failure, for neither the government, nor the police, nor the political parties would countenance any military formations which received their orders from Munich. Bauer suggested that Munich should confine its activity to the provision of arms and funds and to the issuing of directives 'on German questions', as in the case of the Free Corps Oberland — provided that they recognized Ludendorff's supreme leadership. For German issues too, such directives must go through him, Bauer (as the representative of Ludendorff in Vienna). He was worried that Hitler and Göring were lusting for power, not only in Germany, but he could only advise that they should leave Austria alone.[27] Bauer apparently also wrote along the same lines to his old comrade in arms, Pabst, in Innsbruck. But the latter reassured him. So far, he replied, the National Socialist storm troops in the Tyrol were extraordinarily weak and unimportant; the local National Socialist leaders were co-operating 'with us' and were accepting military orders from him; but within the party some radical elements were opposed to this and to the 'moderate tactics' of the local leaders.[28] Apparently, Pabst did not know of any close links between the Munich National Socialist leaders and the Tyrol.

Bauer was above all interested in preserving his own influence and in preventing any poaching from Munich. As he wrote to Hitler in April, he was willing to co-operate closely with him and had no desire to create any competition; but he was subordinate to Ludendorff and could only accept orders from him. He had been informed by a visitor from Munich that there his (Bauer's) anti-semitic attitude had been questioned, but he could prove that he had 'taken up the fight [against the Jews] earlier than most of your friends'.[29] Such remarks and his more independent attitude were unlikely to endear Bauer to Hitler; all Bauer's doubts were confirmed when he visited the National Socialist Party congress at Salzburg in August 1923.

On his return to Vienna Bauer reported to Ludendorff that his impressions had been anything but favourable: 'A lot of people were there, but most of them youngsters of 17 to 19 years, most of them lively boys and more or less disciplined. But what I have missed altogether are older, reasonable people and politicians.' It was decided at Salzburg to submit Austria to the 'military dictatorial leadership of Hitler'. He, Bauer, had discussed the matter at length with Captain Göring, Hitler's SA leader, but he must doubt very strongly whether Göring or any of his subordinates would be capable of organizing a militarily useful formation, and they over-estimated the strength of their own movement enormously. It would have to be made absolutely clear that the Austrian National Socialists in all purely Austrian matters came under Austrian orders; for German interests, they would of course be available, but Bauer would have to be informed whether they recognized Ludendorff's military command. As far as he, Bauer, was concerned he had no intention of accepting orders from Hitler or Göring.[30] In September Bauer sent another messenger to Munich to see Hitler. He repeated his advice not to unite the Austrian National Socialists with the Bavarian movement; it would be a cardinal mistake to intervene in the complex Austrian affairs from Munich, but he was still willing to recognize its leadership 'in all German affairs'; a great deal could be made out of the Austrian movement, but for that cleverly thought-out tactics were essential[31] (clearly, he implied, such clever tactics could be mastered by Bauer, but not by Hitler or Göring).

The most important issue to be decided at Salzburg was that of participation in the forthcoming general election. Once more, the Grossdeutsche suggested a combination of lists and offered to the

National Socialists four or five safe places on that list. Riehl, Gattermayer and other leaders were in favour of acceptance. But the opposition proved very strong, and was supported by the Munich leaders
present.[32] Then Hitler appeared to decide the controversial question
and came out 'in favour of abstention, according to the party's programme which rejected all parliamentarianism'.[33] Hitler's recommenda-
tion was accepted by the conference. Formally the decision was left to
a committee of five under the chairmanship of Esser on which only two
Austrians sat; and it was taken 'in view of the catastrophic situation in
the Reich', in other words, because the German National Socialists
believed that a revolution would break out there in the near future. As
the Grossdeutsche were quick to point out, it was based on the
assumption that conditions in the two countries were very similar and
that the establishment of a dictatorship would solve all problems.[34]
Bauer took a more cynical attitude and attributed it to the facts that
the youngsters who predominated at Salzburg had no vote, hence the
party could not expect any seats, and that it had no money to conduct
an election campaign.[35]

The Salzburg conference also appointed an executive committee
under Riehl's chairmanship, either to keep the situation under review,
or as Suchenwirth put it, to take a final decision; but this seems
unlikely as the conference had already decided in favour of abstention.
The committee met a few days later. Riehl declared that he could not
accept the decision because the Austrian party needed representation in
parliament and the 'Bavarian tactics of an extra-parliamentary struggle
are not applicable to Austria'. He demanded the convening of an
extraordinary party conference in September to revise the Salzburg
decision. But he remained isolated; the other seven members of the
committee voted against his motion. Thereupon Riehl resigned his
office as party chairman, but not his party membership. Of the
Austrian Länder, all the important ones — Vienna, Lower Austria,
Upper Austria, Carinthia, Styria, Tyrol — favoured abstention.[36] But at
least at one party meeting in Graz the three speakers all spoke against
the Salzburg decision. One of them declared that 90 per cent of the
members could not accept it because many of them were trade
unionists, hence they would be forced to vote for a bourgeois party.
Another speaker pleaded for a separate National Socialist list 'because
the bourgeois parties have never defended the interests of the manual or
non-manual workers . . . . First capitalism must be fought because it has
never stood for any social improvements, and only the socialists have

defended the demands of the manual and non-manual workers in parliament . . . .' A motion was then carried by a majority to urge the party's leadership to absolve the members from the obligation to abstain and to put up its own candidates for the election.[37]

At the beginning of September Lieutenant Lechner reported to Munich that efforts were still being made to revise the Salzburg decision, that therefore the sums reserved for the election campaign were not paid out to him, although it had been decided at Salzburg to make them available to his SA; hence he was unfortunately unable to appoint full-time paid officers to the SA, unless Munich was willing to pay for them. Lechner also voiced his criticism of the appointment of Lieutenant Rudolf Schalek as the commandant of the Austrian SA by Göring and asked for information whether Schalek had been appointed definitely or not, as he had not been informed.[38] There was thus still considerable uncertainty how far the power of Munich went and who was entitled to appoint SA leaders in Austria.

Dr Riehl steadfastly adhered to his own opinions. In October he wrote to Munich that the election result had confirmed his view, for the Grossdeutsche collapsed as a party — they obtained only 420,000 votes and ten parliamentary seats — and 'our principal enemy, the Marxists, have the advantage. There was no question of abstention, for the participation was higher than ever before, with up to 95 per cent in workers' districts.' Parliament in Austria could not be mechanically compared with its German counterpart, and it would have been in the interest of the German National Socialists to preserve some influence on political developments in Austria through a combined list with the Grossdeutsche; that party's ministers would now be forced to resign, and to whom 'are our Sudeten German fraternal party, and finally also the Bavarians to address their appeals for help in future?' Riehl added that the party's new leaders were 'continuously steering the party ship in the wrong direction, or to put it more correctly, not steering it at all'.[39]

After the failure of the Hitler Putsch Bauer added his own postscript to the affair. At Salzburg Göring had explained to him that, at the right moment, the National Socialists intended to force the Bavarian State Commissar von Kahr to join hands with them (this is exactly what Hitler attempted to do on 8 November); he, Bauer, had warned long ago that Kahr would never combine with the völkisch circles but would try and find an opportunity to get rid of Hitler, as Bauer had then written to the unfortunate Scheubner-Richter (who was killed on 9

November).[40] After the Munich Putsch in which many Austrian National Socialists actively participated, Ludendorff and Bauer departed from the Austrian scene, the first to worship Wotan, the second for China to serve Generalissimo Chiang Kai-shek. Riehl was expelled from the National Socialist Party because he had aired his differing views in non-party papers. He could have appealed against the expulsion but chose not to do so. In August 1924 he founded a new organization, the 'German Social Association for Austria' (*Deutschsozialer Verein für Österreich*) which remained a political sect.[41] The departure of those who were critical of Hitler and his ambitions and could stand up to him to some extent left the scene clear for those who could not. But the failure in Munich further meant that the Austrian National Socialists too went into political eclipse for the time being. The currency was stablized and more normal economic conditions returned to Austria, so that political extremism declined. Furthermore, after the drying up of the subsidies from Munich the Austrian National Socialists lacked the funds to conduct any effective propaganda,[42] this and the defection of Riehl and his adherents contributed to the party's decline.

NOTES

1. *Reichspost,* 29 June 1919.

2. Police report, 20 August 1919: Verwaltungsarchiv Wien, Pol. Dir. Wien, Berichte 1919.

3. Police report, 1 September 1920: ibid., Berichte 1920.

4. Rudolf Brandstötter, 'Dr Walter Riehl und die Geschichte der nationalsozialistischen Bewegung in Österreich' (Unpublished Ph.D. thesis, Vienna, 1969) 150.

5. *Deutsche Arbeiter-Presse – Nationalsozialistisches Wochenblatt,* no. 49, 6 December 1919.

6. Ferd. Raab, 'Geschichte der nationalsozialistischen Bewegung in Neumarkt', MS. in Oberösterreichisches Landesarchiv, p. 1.

7. Police report, 3 January 1920: Tiroler Landesarchiv, Präsidialakten 1920, XII 77.

8. Brandstötter, op. cit., 171, 175.

9. Walter Gattermayer, a National Socialist trade unionist, quoted in Pichl, *Schönerer,* Vol. V, 283 (Jan. 1920).

10. Brandstötter, op. cit., 162-64, 170.

11. *Deutsche Arbeiterpresse – Nationalsozialistisches Wochenblatt,* no. 26, 23 July 1921, with an invitation to the *second* inter-state representatives' meeting of the National Socialist Party. It clearly was the third such meeting, not the second.

12. Ibid.

13. Bullock, op. cit., 74-76; F. L. Carsten, *The Rise of Fascism* (London, 1967) 104-5.

14. Brandstötter, op. cit., 184-87.

15. Schober to Ministry of Interior, Vienna, 8 March; police reports of 12-13 March 1921: Polizeiarchiv Wien, Nachlass Theodor Reimer, box 7, and Verwaltungsarchiv Wien, Bundeskanzleramt, 22/gen., box 4862.

16. *Grossdeutsche Volkspartei* of Carinthia to *Reichsparteileitung,* Klagenfurt, 25 February 1921: Verwaltungsarchiv Wien, Grossdeutsche Volkspartei, box 29.

17. German Consul in Innsbruck to *Auswärt. Amt,* 20 April 1923: Bundesarchiv Koblenz, Reichskanzlei, R 43 I/106.

18. 'Sitzung der Vertreter der deutschvölkischen Landes- und Parteiorganisationen am 12. Mai 1920': Verwaltungsarchiv Wien, Grossdeutsche Volkspartei, box 1.

19. Brandstötter, op. cit., 194.

20. German Consul in Innsbruck to *Auswärt. Amt,* 20 April 1923: Bundesarchiv Koblenz, Reichskanzlei, R 43 I/106.

21. *Polizeidirektion* Graz to Styrian government, 22 March and 26 April 1923: Steiermärkisches Landesarchiv, Präsidialakten, E.91, 1921-1925 'Polizeiberichte'.

22. Police report, Vienna, 10 January 1923: Haus-, Hof- u. Staatsarchiv, Liasse Österreich 2/21, fasz. 302.

23. Police report, Vienna, 1 September 1923: ibid.

24. Bauer to Hitler, Vienna, 14 April 1923: Bundesarchiv Koblenz, Nachlass Bauer, Nr. 30b.

25. *Bezirkshauptmannschaft* Voitsberg to Styrian government, 2 November 1923: Steiermärk. Landesarchiv, Präsidialakten, E. 91, 1921-1925.

26. Report by Schober, 5 July 1923: Haus-, Hof- u. Staatsarchiv, Liasse Österreich 2/3, fasz. 275.

27. Bauer to Ludendorff, Vienna, 26 April 1923: Bundesarchiv Koblenz, Nachlass Bauer, Nr. 30b.

28. Pabst to Bauer, Innsbruck, 2 May 1923: ibid.

29. Bauer to Hitler, Vienna, 25 April 1923: ibid.

30. Bauer to Ludendorff, Vienna, 20 August 1923: ibid.

31. Bauer to Scheubner-Richter, Vienna, 30 September 1923: ibid.

32. 'Die Geschichte der Bestrebungen nach Herstellung einer nationalen Einheitsfront', p. 12: Verwaltungsarchiv Wien, Grossdeutsche Volkspartei, box 28.

33. Thus the leading National Socialist Prof. Suchenwirth on 16 August 1923: Polizeiarchiv Wien, Nachlass Schober, box 49 (report of 17 August).

34. Brandstötter, op. cit., 197-98; 'Verhandlungsschrift über die Sitzung der Landesparteileitung Wien', 20 August 1923: Verwaltungsarchiv Wien, Grossdeutsche Volkspartei, box 16.

35. Bauer to Ludendorff, 20 August 1923: Bundesarchiv Koblenz, Nachlass Bauer, Nr. 30b.

36. Lechner to Munich, 29 August 1923: Polizeiarchiv Wien, Nachlass Schober, box 49.

37. Police report, Graz, 6 September 1923: Steiermärk. Landesarchiv, Präsidialakten, E. 91, 1921-1925.

38. Lechner to Munich, Vienna, 1 September 1923: Polizeiarchiv Wien, Nachlass Schober, box 49.

39. Riehl to Lauböck in Munich, Vienna, 23 October 1923: Institut für Zeitgeschichte, Munich, Microfilm MA 731.

40. Bauer to Ludendorff, Vienna, 20 November 1923: Bundesarchiv Koblenz, Nachlass Bauer, Nr. 30b.

41. Brandstötter, op. cit., 214, 218.

42. Schober to *Bundeskanzleramt*, Vienna, 17 March 1925: Haus-, Hof- und Staatsarchiv, Liasse Österreich, 2/21, fasz. 302.

5

THE 'VÖLKISCH' CAMP

The völkisch camp in Austria consisted of a multitude of small and not so small parties and organizations which provided a fruitful recruiting ground for the Heimwehren as well as for the National Socialist Party. Pride of place among these belonged to the Grossdeutsch Party — the successor to the German Liberals as well as the German Nationalists of the old monarchy — hence often also called *deutschfreiheitlich* or *deutchnational.* It corresponded to the German Nationalist Party of Weimar Germany, but it considered itself a völkisch party; it was often ready to combine with the National Socialists, and some of its provincial organizations — Carinthia, for example — adopted the swastika as their emblem. Its importance was recognized by the two major parties of Republican Austria — the Social Democratic and Christian Social parties — and it received several portfolios in the coalition government formed at the birth of the Austrian Republic in late October 1918. In the general election of February 1919 it polled 545,000 votes, and still more than half a million in October 1920, 18 and 17 per cent, respectively, of the votes cast.[1] In later years the party's strength declined; thus the 17 or 18 per cent of the early years of the Republic give an indication of the strength of the völkisch, non-catholic camp in the post-war period, when the National Socialist vote was still very small.

The *Grossdeutsche Volkspartei*, as it was called officially, was an amalgamation of several older and smaller organizations, such as the Pan-German Association, the German Nationalist Association, and the German People's League – all of which had been much influenced by Schönerer in his day. In October 1919 they combined and adopted common guidelines which were accepted unanimously. These pronounced strongly against any restoration of the Habsburg Monarchy and accepted the democratic republic because 'the form of the state is at the moment not the principle issue'. They declared in favour of private property, but also of a 'fight against capitalist excesses' and of a land reform. As to the Jewish question, the party stood for the 'casting off of the Jewish yoke' and declared: 'The Jewish question can only be approached from a racialist point of view.'[2] At a meeting of the party's parliamentary deputies held at the end of 1919 Dr Josef Ursin reported that the work of unification had largely succeeded: the guidelines had been adopted and the three associations had decided to dissolve themselves and to unite in one party.

From Upper Austria the party chairman, Dr Franz Dinghofer, added that there the unification had taken place in the form of a Party of Freedom and Order which was spreading its propaganda into the smallest villages; 'all who are German and libertarian must stand together against Black and Red', i.e. the two largest political parties. Significantly he also mentioned that the party was founding everywhere new gymnastic and sports clubs: 'that looks non-political and yet creates the best and most loyal troops (*beste Kerntruppe*)'. Dr Ursin mentioned that not even the National Socialists were in principle opposed to unification; Dr Riehl was against the class struggle, but others were adopting a class position (clearly meaning the völkisch trade unionists); a *Grossdeutscher Bund* should unite workers, peasants and burghers. Dr Dinghofer emphasized the difficulties as these groups differed widely in their economic, social and even cultural interests: 'it is really a work of art to bring about the unification and to give it a punch. It is most difficult for the bourgeois representatives. The interests of the civil servants are strongly opposed to the interests of business people. Everywhere there are dangers of a split. . . .'[3] Dr Ursin represented the old followers of Schönerer. He liked to stress his veneration for Bismarck and the principle that 'the interests of the whole nation have always precedence over any other interest'; in other words those of 'the great German fatherland' came before Austria.[4] He also was a strong anti-Semite.

A further attempt to achieve greater unity on the extreme right was made in May 1920 when representatives of more than a dozen völkisch parties and groups assembled in Vienna, including the National Socialists, a number of peasant leagues from Carinthia, Salzburg and Styria, and various German Liberal and German Nationalist parties. Dr Ursin, in opening the proceedings, urged those present to put aside all party vanities and minor matters: 'We are all grossdeutsch by conviction, we all put the interests of the entire nation above everything, we are all anti-semitic, liberal and social in our views.' But the peasant representatives were against a united party, and so were the National Socialists. A representative of the Independent Peasant League explained that his party stood only for the peasants' interests; if they abandoned their own party their followers would return to the Christian Social camp; only as a separate peasant party could they hope for success in an election. Several other peasant leagues made similar declarations. The National Socialist representative, who also represented a union of railwaymen, did not consider this a question of principle but of tactics; his party favoured a tri-partition, separate parties for workers, peasants and middle classes. Although his party rejected the class struggle, it had to make certain concessions to the workers, who were in favour of the class struggle. The second National Socialist present declared that, if they joined a united party, they would have to support 'a decidedly capitalist policy'; no *Volksgemeinschaft* was possible in the present conditions, but a united front for the elections would make possible 'a powerful demonstration of the nationalists'. Dr Dinghofer in summing up had to admit that a united party was out of the question, and only 'a unified approach' feasible. A motion was then put to the meeting to create an all-Austrian party and to elect a committee to draft a common programme and to discuss the matter further. But the representatives of the peasant leagues voted against the motion and the National Socialists abstained. The committee was elected, with representatives from all Austrian Länder, but without the peasants and the National Socialists, who only accepted seats on another, larger coordinating committee. In concluding, the chairman had to acknowledge that the deliberations had only brought them 'a small step forward'.[5] The election of the committee only masked the continuation of disunity.

The programme adopted by the first all-Austrian party congress of the Grossdeutsche Volkspartei in August 1920 affirmed:

The idea of the *Volksgemeinschaft* (national community) includes the fight against Red as well as Black internationalism and the struggle against the pernicious influence of Jewry. The party adheres to democracy, it will oppose with all its might any attempted return of the Habsburgs, it will ... provide enlightenment about the pernicious influence of the Jewish spirit and the necessity of racial anti-Semitism caused by it. It will oppose the Jewish influence in all spheres of public and private life; the immigration of foreign Jews is to be curtailed; the eastern Jews are to be expelled.[6]

In the same year Dr Dinghofer once more emphasized the importance of gymnastic and sports clubs for the nationalist cause. In Upper Austria, a number of gym teachers were trained by them, a matter of real urgency for the villages and small market towns; in every place of some size a club must exist, and this club must promote a völkisch education. In Linz a training course was organized for eighty gym teachers, with an enormous success. He hoped that within a few weeks it would be possible to raise one to two million crowns through one of their friends, and then financial support could also be given to the other Länder; if the Turner saw that the party could help them financially it would be able 'to gather a rich political harvest'.[7]

In January 1921 the party celebrated the fiftieth anniversary of the foundation of the German Empire by Bismarck 'full of heartfelt thanks towards the creators of the German Reich'. The speaker declared it was the duty of every single member to work towards the completion of the unification of the Germans that had been started by Bismarck, 'the greatest leader of our people', and a telegram to this effect was despatched to the German President, Friedrich Ebert,[8] although Ebert was the butt of constant attacks from the German right. At the same meeting, one deputy reported that the party leadership was receiving letters from almost all the Austrian Länder which criticized in the sharpest form the collaboration of the deputies with Jewish newspapers, and threatened a break-up of the party if this continued. Dr Ursin agreed: he too had received such letters, and he moved that the publication of articles in the Jewish papers be prohibited — a motion which had been accepted once before by the Grossdeutsche. Dr Dinghofer, however, disagreed: in his opinion, the Jewish press could be used in the party's interest as it possessed no large papers of its own; one could not speak of 'collaboration' if the *Wiener Tagblatt* published an occasional article by him. If Ursin's motion were carried, he, Dinghofer, would have to leave the party; such 'a hurried dictate is impossible'. Surprisingly, Ursin withdrew his motion and was content to have the matter transferred to a committee where it could effectively be buried. It was a very old complaint of the party that it did not possess an influential daily paper; only six months before exactly the same discussion had taken place among the deputies in which both Ursin and Dinghofer put forward exactly the same arguments.[9] But to many members the fees offered by the large daily papers, however 'Jewish' they might be, proved more attractive than the purest ideology.

Disunity also reigned in another question of great practical importance — whether the party should continue as a 'pure' opposition party, or whether it should combine with the Christian Social Party in a common anti-Marxist front. Once more Ursin advocated a course of sharp opposition: a coalition would not further the aims of the Grossdeutsche and would bury the idea of the Anschluss; the Christian Social policy aimed at an Austria without Germany and in a coalition they would have to accept this aim. The deputy Angerer from Carinthia, on the other hand, declared that they would not change the parliamentary system if they retired sulking into a corner. The majority of their followers demanded that they should not quietly look at a further expansion of Marxism; they must conduct an active anti-Marxist policy, and that they could only do by participating in the government. Dinghofer acknowledged that there were at least three different tendencies within the party because even the adherents of a coalition differed on the conditions. In his opinion, the Austrian population was only interested in economic questions, hence did not understand an opposition policy — in contrast with the Bohemian Germans who were willing to remain in opposition even if their economic interests suffered; if they left the government to the Christian Social Party it would be 'entirely reactionary, and without us the idea of Anschluss will not be stressed'.[10] As many of the Grossdeutsche, on grounds of principle, were unwilling to enter into any combination with either the 'Reds' or the 'Blacks', the party was unable to solve the dilemma. But some of its leaders served in various coalition governments in the later 1920s; on occasion, the party even entered into electoral alliances with the Christian Social Party, so as to prevent a 'marxist' victory. It thus provided its political adversaries, principally the National Socialists, with plenty of opportunities to accuse it of 'inconsistency'.

Similar difficulties occurred in the relations of the Grossdeutsche with the völkisch trade unions which possessed influence among white-collar workers and railwaymen. In 1923 the representatives of the *Deutschnationaler Handlungsgehilfenverband* (DHV), a white-collar union, approached a grossdeutsch member of the government, Dr

Schürff, with the request not to be excluded from negotiations between the industrialists and the unions, in which the government too participated. The socialist unions, however, refused to negotiate in the presence of adherents of the swastika, and surprisingly the industrialists' representatives also objected to the presence of the DHV because otherwise 'their own words might be misconstrued'. The DHV representatives then withdrew and demanded from the Grossdeutsche an urgent interpellation in parliament, but the latter considered this 'very clumsy tactics'. One of their deputies remarked that the DHV was not a National Socialist, but a general 'non-political' and völkisch organization which also had many grossdeutsch members: the party should use every opportunity to support it and to bring it over to its side.[11]

In the following year the Grossdeutsche felt even more embarrassed when, during a strike of the railwaymen, the völkisch trade union, *Deutsche Verkehrsgewerkschaft*, under the influence of radical elements put forward very far-reaching demands. Thus the much stronger socialist unions, with more realistic demands, emerged easily as the leaders of the strike; in the opinion of the Grossdeutsche they were likely to achieve success. Another deputy, Dr Angerer, added that quite impossible demands had been put forward by the völkisch union because liaison with their party was insufficient; the world was turned upside down 'when the anti-marxist elements make a marxist policy'; the 'reasonable' followers of the party ought to form their own union, for the influence of the National Socialists was 'disastrous' and 'endangering the community'. Another deputy, however, replied that this was unrealistic because they would not find any followers to join their own trade union. But Angerer was undeterred. He repeated his attacks upon the activities of the National Socialists: it was essential for the party to gain influence among the trade unions. If National Socialists in consequence resigned so much the better; the strike was irresponsible, and the government's economy measures were essential to preserve the state. He was even in favour of the Grossdeutsche again entering the government.[12]

In spite of all misgivings, the party established a trade union section in Vienna which developed into a 'non-political trade union', the *Gewerkschaft deutscher Arbeiter*. Similar organizations were later founded in Carinthia, Styria and Upper Austria. These were opposed to the party-political unions controlled by the National Socialists, but they never prospered. With the foundation of 'independent trade unions' by the Heimwehren in the later 1920s which were strongly supported by the industrialists, most of the unions organized by the Grossdeutsche merged with those of the Heimwehren which were considerably stronger.[13] The workers obviously considered the Gross-deutsche too bourgeois a party, and it had some influence only among white-collar workers and state employees. Even the more radical National Socialist unions drew their support principally from the same social groups. It is significant that in 1927 the *Deutscher Gewerk-schaftsbund* in Austria consisted of ten trade unions, but that only one of them was a working-class union and the others unions of white-collar workers, state officials and employees, and people working in public transport, social insurance and local government.[14] Early in 1930 a leading National Socialist gave their combined membership as 'more than 50,000', not a very impressive figure.[15]

Considerably more important than the völkisch trade unions were the gymnastic and sports clubs which had supported the German nationalist cause since the later decades of the nineteenth century. They were founded on the Prussian model and venerated the *Turnvater* Jahn, who inspired the youth of Prussia in the fight against Napoleon and tried to steel them for the national task; he was their hero and example in the coming struggle for national liberation. Indeed, many local Austrian clubs took their names from Jahn or another leader of the wars of liberation of 1813-14. They accepted only 'Aryans' as members and provided a fruitful recruiting ground first for the Heim-wehren and later for the National Socialist stormtroopers. To them, the formation of such armed units was a mere act of self-defence, to counter the 'terror' emanating from the 'Reds'. As the *Bundesturn-zeitung* wrote in 1920: 'While the workers' councils, the communist and social-democratic organizations arm themselves to the teeth, the middle classes look at the movement . . . with folded arms, instead of taking up new positions to counter the threat of revolution head-on. . . .'[16] It was therefore necessary to found new völkisch sports clubs. The strength of the Deutsche Turnerbund 1919 was given by its chairman, Kupka, as 50,000 in discussions which he had with the Orgesch in the summer of 1920,[17] but the figure is difficult to check. Kupka classified his organization as 'Aryan and grossdeutsch', and this was confirmed by Colonel Bauer in 1922. But the latter criticized the leaders for 'their exaggerated völkisch views and their wishy-washy aims'. They also disagreed among themselves, partly tending towards Ludendorff and the Pan-German leader Class, partly towards Pittinger in Munich, while most of the members were indifferent towards all the bickering and not strongly influenced by their leaders.[18]

There was, however, little that was 'wishy-washy' in the writing of the *Bundesturnzeitung,* the organ of the Deutscher Turnerbund 1919. Its comments and articles were strictly racialist and violently anti-semitic. In 1920 its readers were treated to a racialist interpretation of European history. As to France, they were informed, 'the remnants of Aryan-Germanic blood have disappeared quickly from the body politic since the great revolution of the 18th century, and the Frenchman of today racially is a mixture of Alpine and Mediterranean people with Celtic, Semitic and Negroid blood. The national character is steadily deteriorating . . . .'[19] As to Britain, things were hardly better. As the same author averred:

> Since the days of the Puritans much Semitic blood has penetrated into the English people, and even Mongoloid and Negroid blood, and this has made it possible that a large part of the English of today consider it praiseworthy to be the descendants of the ten tribes of Israel. The purely Germanic section of the people has strongly declined, with the peasants ruined by industry and the nobility killed in the wars, and only the top of the social 'pyramid' still shows the Nordic type . . . In the industrial towns, on the other hand, there jostle more and more from one year to the next a dark, short type of people, among which the old aristocracy and the gentry stand out like isolated blond warriors . . . .[20]

At home, the *Bundesturnzeitung,* again on racialist grounds, bitterly attacked clerical as well as socialist influence, influences encouraged by the Jews to secure their goal of world domination:

> Not the worker, peasant and burgher shall together govern the state, but the proletarian, often without any education, shall rule, that is the worker who has no will of his own but is a tool of the party, who sees his greatest enemy in the burgher or peasant of his own race . . . Like the clerical priest of German race, the social-democratic 'comrade' of German race has been separated from his people so as to realize the slogan 'Proletarians of all countries, unite', which was coined by the Jewish leaders . . . Thus the non-semitic part of Social Democracy forms the wall behind which the Jew works with the racial cleverness that has made him the demon of the decline of humanity . . . . It lies in the interest of the Jewish lust for world power not to raise the moral level of the masses, but to demoralize and to pauperize them . . . .[21]

In the best style of Julius Streicher, German girls were warned not to let themselves be seduced by Jews, for there would be dire con-sequences:

In a weak hour there came the seducer. He had much money and they succumbed. He bought her clothes and shoes, and she gave herself to him. He left her sick and ill. Unable ever to bear German children to a German man, our people have thus suffered enormous damage. And there are thousands of such seducers. Jewish shop assistants and clerks, stock exchange swindlers and bon viveurs of all kinds every year seduce innumerable German girls and make them unfit for a healthy marriage. Jews drive them from their jobs so that the Jewish white slave trade may flourish. And you blond ones are those who those of foreign race have marked out for themselves! They who feel that they are foreign [the Jews] think full of hatred of everything non-Jewish; it gives them the highest pleasure and the greatest joy to subjugate you, you blond girls! . . .[22]

Hatred was equally meted out to those 'Aryans' who supported Jews or sympathized with them. They were accused of 'accepting an ideology totally alien to us, of furthering a degeneration of the Aryan by promoting the Jewish spirit'; their way of life and their thinking were declared 'especially pernicious to the preservation of our Nordic-Germanic race'.[23] The collapse of the 'power and glory of the German Empire' was attributed to the stab in the back. The outbreak of the world war and the war of starvation waged against women and children was the 'work of the World Jewish press, in the framework of which the German Jewish papers have amply contributed their own share'. After the end of the war the same papers favoured economic exploitation and black-marketeering and promoted moral decadence through the 'fanning of the class struggle' and their opposition to 'any true *Volksgemeinschaft'*.[24]

It is therefore hardly surprising that, brought up on this heady diet, the Turner often combined with the National Socialists and similar völkisch organizations in demonstrations, even before the party became a major force in right-wing politics. Thus, in September 1923 many thousands demonstrated in the streets of Vienna to show 'their sympathies with the hard-pressed racial comrades (*Stammesgenossen*) of the German Reich' and to protest against the peace treaty of St Germain. The procession was headed by the Turner, followed by the nationalist singers, the students and school children, the National Socialists, the Grossdeutsche, and finally the *Frontkämpfer*.[25] The demonstration was repeated twelve months later, again as a protest against the peace treaties of St Germain and Versailles, and this time the police noted the exact numbers of the participants. The contingent of the Turner was by far the strongest, 5,208 men, followed by the Frontkämpfer with 3,048. All other groups were much smaller: the *Hackenkreuzler* (*sic*:

National Socialists) mustered 1,496 and the völkisch union of railway-men 1,368 men. All other groups were very small: 560 students, 528 singers, 208 of the Free Corps Oberland, 108 Grossdeutsche, 84 Sudeten Germans, etc. making a total of over 13,000.[26] Thus on this occasion the Turner represented about 40 per cent of the combined strength of the völkisch associations, and the National Socialists only about 11 per cent.

In 1925 the Deutsche Turnerbund 1919, the National Socialists, the Pan-German and Anti-Semitic Leagues and many similar organizations combined to form the 'völkisch-anti-semitic action committee'; its aim was to prevent the meeting of the Zionist Congress which was to open in Vienna on 17 August. The director of police declined to give way to pressure and ordered sharp measures against the riotous crowds, which numbered many thousands. Even the Grossdeutsche who debated the issue soon after were severely critical of 'the undermining tactics' of the National Socialists. According to their speaker, Dr Waber, the Zionist point of view ought to be supported, emigration to and colonization in Palestine ought to be encouraged, for it would alleviate the situation in Austria. But he added that he did not dare to say so publicly, 'so as not to be called a protector of the Zionists in the end'.[27] But another deputy stated that the permission to hold the congress and the police measures caused grave disquiet among the party's followers, who apparently criticized it for its too conciliatory attitude.

The *Frontkämpfer* Association, which participated in the general völkisch demonstrations of the early 1920s, consisted largely of ex-servicemen of the First World War, above all ex-officers. Its leader was Colonel Hermann Hiltl, and it was particularly strong in Vienna. In its composition and aims it resembled the German *Stahlhelm,* which also was a large organization of ex-servicemen with a nationalist and völk-isch ideology. In May 1920 the Frontkämpfer Association proclaimed that it was 'Aryan in character', stood outside party politics, and would have 'no truck with international, subversive elements, such as Social Democrats and Communists'. It aimed at 'the unification of the entire German Volk' and was opposed to 'petty party politics'. It provided para-military training for its members and held secret courses for youngsters who were to become its 'iron kernel', 'the sword of the leader'. An instruction sheet of this Iron Kernel declared: 'The Iron Kernel does not itself lead; it is the executive organ of the Leader and carries out every task that is necessary in the interests of the Associa-tion. The Iron Kernel is the soul of the organization – a soul imbued with the spirit and the will of the Leader. . . .' At a conference held in 1926 the Frontkämpfer Association adopted a programme which declared its opposition to Marxism, demanded a strengthening of the powers of the president of the republic and a change in the electoral law in the direction of a corporate system. Although Colonel Hiltl denied that he was attached to fascist ideology – mainly on account of the treatment of the South Tyrolese by the Italian Fascists – it seems clear that his association borrowed ideas of the role of the leader and the corporate system from them.[28] But the Tyrolese Heimwehr leader Dr Steidle was not impressed with the achievements of the Frontkämpfer in Vienna. In his opinion, all they had done was to create 'a colossal apparatus with expensive trimmings', and what they achieved was 'bullshit' (*Bockmist*). He hoped that some day they would be forced to give up 'their knickknacks' and do some 'reasonable work'.[29]

However disunited the völkisch camp might be and however much its rival leaders might quarrel there was one issue that united them – anti-Semitism. This was no doubt partly so because anti-Semitism was a popular cause, especially in Vienna with its great economic and social stresses and its large Jewish population, where the völkisch associations could always pack large halls with people eager to applaud strongly anti-semitic speeches, and molest individual Jews after the end of the meeting. In September 1919 the 'German People's Council for Vienna and Lower Austria' organized a meeting in the town hall to demand the immediate expulsion of all eastern Jews who had arrived since 1914. The meeting was attended by about 5,000 people so that many had to remain outside. The principal speaker, the grossdeutsch deputy Dr Ursin, developed the Pan-German programme with special emphasis on anti-Semitism and declared that all nations were now tributary to the Jews who had gained colossal power; even the reparation payments of the defeated nations accrued to 'Jewish-American billionaires'; all völkisch Germans considered the Habsburgs traitors to the national cause and an obstacle to the achievement of German unity, and no true German would desire their return. He demanded the dissolution of the Jewish banks, their replacement by a völkisch national bank, and the expropriation of all Jewish property. Outside the town hall numerous speakers addressed those who had been unable to gain admittance. A resolution demanding the expulsion of the eastern Jews within ten days was carried unanimously.[30]

A second meeting at the same place organized by the Anti-Semitic League in October was attended by about 2,500 people, while another

3,000 stood outside. Several speakers again demanded the expulsion of the eastern Jews who exercised 'an intolerable pressure on the German-Aryan population'; 'for hygienic reasons alone a liberation of Vienna from the eastern Jews' must be achieved; the Jews were 'active in the black market, had acquired riches and bought palaces while the native population was starving'; fat Jews sat in the restaurants and coffee houses, and the Communist movement too was led by Jews who wore well-pressed trousers and gold rings and used the term 'We proletarians'. The audience then vehemently demanded to be addressed by the journalist Anton Orel, who declared that not only the eastern Jews but 'all Jews must be removed from Vienna to prevent at the last hour the threatening destruction of Vienna'. He was followed by a National Socialist who echoed the same demand: all who were consciously German must agitate among the workers against the Jewish leaders, 'so that the German workers would finally realize that their true advantage must be sought within the German nation and not under the red Jewish leaders'. A resolution demanding the removal of the eastern Jews within two weeks was carried.[31]

A similar meeting organized by the Anti-Semitic League in June 1920 mobilized about 8,000 people so that several parallel meetings had to be held in the square outside the town hall. Some Jewish-looking people were removed from the hall. Several speakers, among them once more Dr Ursin and Dr Riehl, but also the Christian Social deputy Leopold Kunschak, demanded the expulsion of the eastern Jews. After the end a large demonstration preceded by two bands marched along the Ring amidst much shouting against the Jews. Riehl asked the participants to disperse quietly and under no circumstances to continue into the Jewish district of the Leopoldstadt; but about 4,000 demonstrators did not heed his warning, tried to penetrate there, and had to be dispersed by the police.[32] Another meeting called by the Anti-Semitic League to the town hall in November 1920 was only attended by about 3,000 people. Again Kunschak, Orel, Riehl and others spoke to the crowd, among them also a captain as the representative of the Frontkämpfer Association; but this time the audience, taking up a remark of one speaker about the former dynasty, for several minutes shouted: 'Long live the House of Habsburg!' A resolution was adopted demanding the expulsion of all Jews who had come to Vienna after 1 August 1914, the introduction of a numerus clausus for students and professors, and the removal of Jewish civil servants.[33]

Meanwhile the anti-semitic propaganda spread to the provinces. In

Innsbruck a Tyrolese Anti-Semitic League was founded in 1919 by three deputies of the Diet, among them the Heimwehr leader Dr Steidle. In November it organized a mass meeting in the town hall, where the students and the Turner served as stewards. The demands adopted by the meeting went considerably further than those carried by the Viennese meetings. The Jews were to be declared a nation, including all who had only one Jewish great-grandfather or great-grandmother, going further even than the later Nuremberg Laws of Adolf Hitler. Jews were to be excluded from the army, from the professions of journalist, judge, public prosecutor, civil servant, university teacher, school teacher, apothecary; they were not to be allowed to buy property or houses in the Tyrol, to trade in timber or cattle, or to acquire mining or hunting licences; text books written by Jews were to be banned from schools and universities, and the admission of students was to be regulated by a numerus clausus; the same was to apply to Jewish doctors and lawyers. Strong opposition was voiced to the minister of defence, Julius Deutsch, as 'a member of that race which during the war was not to be seen at the front but was active in the rear filling its pockets'[34] (though Deutsch himself had served for years at the front as an artillery officer).

Although the number of Jews in the Tyrol was very small, the Anti-Semitic League demanded early in 1920 that all Jews not domiciled in the Tyrol and all those who had acquired domicile after 1 August 1914 were to be expelled: to which the Tyrolese government replied that this demand was in accordance with decisions taken by the Diet, and that the steps necessary to carry it out were being taken.[35] To the other demands of the League the government returned a more non-committal answer: the League could rest assured that the government was closely observing the situation and would use all legal means to prevent or lessen any damage which the community might suffer, but many of the League's demands were contrary to the principle of legal equality in public life; if the demands were met a group of citizens would be treated as standing outside the law. But the Tyrolese government was convinced that the existing abuses could be dealt with without violating the law, and 'in this sense, it welcomes the cooperation of the Anti-Semitic League most heartily', in particular in the fight against the black market.[36]

The elections of 1919 were fought in the Tyrol on a sharp anti-socialist and anti-semitic line, the two being usually lumped together. As the *Neue Tiroler Stimmen,* which supported the Christian Social

Party, wrote: 'The best answer will be given to Social Democracy on 16 February with the ballot paper. Not a vote to the alien red party which intends to barter away our freedom to the Viennese Jews and Berlin Bolsheviks, so that we Tyrolese would become slaves working like niggers for foreign exploiters, paying taxes to them and starving.'[37] In an election meeting of the *Deutschfreiheitliche* at Hall the Engineer Hans Reinl appealed to the middle classes to participate actively in the political fight 'at a time when the German nation is ruled by Polish and other Jews and every Jewboy is posing as a political leader'. He then attacked the attitude of the *Innsbrucker Nachrichten,* in which not a word could be found against the Jews but all the more Jewish advertisements, in spite of the allegedly anti-semitic policy of the Deutschfreiheitliche Party. In Reinl's opinion, only the Christian Social and conservative papers were fighting against Jewry, 'the greatest danger to the German nation', and therefore he, who had always voted *freiheitlich* in the past, would vote Christian Social in future.[38] In another election meeting at Inzing to which the invitations had been sent out by the local priest, another priest, Pfarrer Köll, attacked the aims of Social Democracy, in particular its attitude towards the peasants, 'and stigmatized in sharp words the behaviour of the Viennese Jew Government in the question of the catholic marriage'. The meeting then protested in particular against the appointment of a Jew as a rapporteur 'in this purely Christian matter and declares this an impudent and malevolent provocation of the Christian people'.[39]

In September 1921 demonstrations were organized outside the Vienna stock exchange, mainly by members of Christian Social trade unions, to protest against the continuing inflation and the price increases resulting from it. Suddenly some demonstrators entered a Jewish bank and maltreated people inside, while others surrounded Jewish-looking members of the stock exchange and used their fists and sticks on them. A few days later the Frontkämpfer tried to occupy the stock exchange. At a given signal some demonstrators were lifted high so that they could reach the balustrade, but they only succeeded in smashing two windows. Later the demonstrators, whose number had increased to about 2,000, tried to storm banks and coffee houses in the neighbourhood, but were prevented from doing so by the police, who had been informed about the plans in advance.[40] In November another rally was organized by the Anti-Semitic League, but the attendance dropped to about 2,000, and the chairman had to express his regret about the poor attendance. A National Socialist demanded the confiscation of Jewish property and the closure of the stock exchange — demands which were echoed by other speakers. It was claimed that 'the patience of the Aryans in this state was exhausted and that the floral decorations on the lamp posts would soon be replaced by a different decoration'. If the government continued to do nothing the Christian population would take action; the days of a 'closed season for the Jews' were over.[41] Yet when Anton Orel went to Graz to address a meeting on 'cultural revival and Judaism' he found among the audience of about 900 two oppositional groups, Social Democrats and Grossdeutsche. Although he avoided all attacks on a political party and spoke 'in very moderate terms', in particular on Christian teaching, he was interrupted by constant noise and had to stop after about an hour.[42]

In January 1923, after the occupation of the Ruhr by France, a monster demonstration was organized in front of the Vienna town hall by the 'völkisch-anti-semitic action committee', not only to protest against the occupation, but also to demand the introduction of a numerus clausus at the universities and an end to 'preference shown to the Jews'. The principal organizations participating were the two para-military formations of the Deutsche Wehrbund and the Frontkämpfer with about 3,000 men each, followed by the National Socialists and the students with about 2,000 each. Apart from them, there were the adherents of the grossdeutsch and Christian Social parties, the Turner, the members of the Anti-Semitic League, the nationalist former officers and NCOs, and several other like-minded organizations, altogether — according to the police — about 15,000 people. Schönerer's old colleague Karl Hermann Wolf urged the Viennese to adopt a practical anti-Semitism, instead of a merely theoretical one. Dr Riehl declared that the numerus clausus at the universities was an issue, not of a party, but of the whole German nation. Dr Ursin, General Krauss and a Frontkämpfer spokesman were among the other speakers.[43] But only three weeks later two meetings of the Anti-Semitic League drew much smaller crowds: that in the town hall only about 2,000, where Wolf spoke again and demanded the dismissal of Jewish officials, and a parallel meeting in Meidling only about 800 people; while the Social Democrats prevented the holding of yet another meeting in the third district (Landstrasse).[44] With the end of the political and economic crisis, however, these mass demonstrations against the Jews and for German nationalist causes came to an end for the time being, and the Anti-Semitic League faded out of the picture. Yet the völkisch cause remained alive among smaller sections of the people, ready to be revived when an opportunity should arise.

Even in the relatively quiet year 1924 the combined völkisch associations of Vienna were able to mobilize — according to the police — 13,133 people for a demonstration against the peace treaties of St Germain and Versailles:[45] a surprisingly high figure, but the day chosen was a Sunday, and probably members were brought into Vienna from Lower Austria. In these years the activities of the Heimwehren as well as the National Socialists declined considerably, but other organizations, such as the Frontkämpfer, remained very active and founded many new local groups. When the völkisch associations put forward their own candidates in local elections they were only very moderately successful. Thus in Eisenstadt, the capital of the Burgenland, only one völkisch town councillor was elected, compared with twelve Social Democrats and eight Christian Social councillors, although there the National Socialists made common cause with the Völkische. They considered that the Social Democrats were partisans of internationalism and the Christian Social Party protectors of the Magyars, and tried to pass themselves off as the only party 'that openly and honestly defends the cause of our people', while the others were lining up with Jews for electoral purposes. The slogan used was Hitler's Munich slogan: 'The common weal comes before private interest!'[46] Although the National Socialists supported the Völkische on this occasion and there was no competition from any German nationalist party, the völkisch success was a very limited one in this sleepy capital of the smallest Austrian Land.

In general it might be said that the *völkisch* appeal was mainly successful among the students and certain disgruntled and dissatisfied urban groups, above all in Vienna and a few other towns. Elsewhere the influence of the Church and of the Christian Social Party proved too strong a barrier — exactly as it had been during the pre-war period. Only during a major economic and political crisis would it be possible to overcome these obstacles; then the feeling of a common German nationalism would powerfully reassert itself, this time against the existence of a separate Austrian state.

NOTES

1. Detailed figures may be found in C. A. Gulick, *Austria from Habsburg to Hitler*, Vol. I (Berkeley and Los Angeles, 1948) 690.

2. Pichl, *Schönerer*, Vol. V, 275, quoting the *Alldeutsche Tagblatt*.

3. 'Die Einigung der nationalen Parteien': Verwaltungsarchiv Wien, Verhandlungsschriften der 'Grossdeutschen Vereinigung', 16 December 1919.

4. Ursin's declaration of 26 February 1919: ibid., '1. Sitzung der deutschnationalen Nationalräte'.

5. 'Sitzung der Vertreter der deutschvölkischen Landes- und Parteiorganisationen am 12. Mai 1920': Verwaltungsarchiv Wien, Grossdeutsche Volkspartei, box 1. The terms 'deutschfreiheitlich' and 'deutschnational' are almost impossible to translate; the connexion with Liberalism is a very tenuous one.

6. Pichl, op. cit., Vol. V, 289-90.

7. '13. Sitzung des Verb. d. Abg. der Grossdeutschen Volkspartei', 16 December 1920: Verwaltungsarchiv Wien, Grossdeutsche Volkspartei, box 1.

8. '18. Sitzung des Verb. d. Abgeordneten der Grossdeutschen Volkspartei', 25 January 1921: ibid. (speech of the deputy Zeidler).

9. Meeting of 25 January 1921, ibid.; meeting of 8 June 1920: Verwaltungsarchiv Wien, Verhandlungsschriften der 'Grossdeutschen Vereinigung'.

10. '106. Sitzung des Verbandes der Abg. der Grossdeutschen Volkspartei', 21 February 1922: ibid., Grossdeutsche Volkspartei, box 3.

11. '4. Sitzung des Abgeordnetenverbandes der Grossdeutschen Volkspartei', 21 November 1923: ibid., box 4.

12. '46. Sitzung des Abgeordnetenverbandes der Grossdeutschen Volkspartei', 11 November 1924: ibid., box 5.

13. *Grossdeutsche Volkspartei* to *Geschäftsführer* Ibounig in Klagenfurt, Vienna, 9 July 1929 (copy): ibid., box 29.

14. 'Verband deutschvölkischer Vereine Deutschösterreichs', signed Max Kilhof, Vienna, s.d.: Verwaltungsarchiv Wien, Grossdeutsche Volkspartei, box 10.

15. Hans Krebs to Gregor Strasser, Aussig, 18 March 1930: Bundesarchiv Koblenz, Sammlung Schumacher, Nr. 305 I.

16. *Bundesturnzeitung*, 11 March 1920, quoted by R. G. Ardelt, *Zwischen Demokratie und Faschismus – Deutschnationales Gedankengut in Österreich 1919-1930* (Vienna-Salzburg, 1972) 43.

17. Rape, op. cit., 217-18.

18. Bauer to Ludendorff, 10 December 1922: Bundesarchiv Koblenz, Nachlass Bauer, Nr. 30a.

19. Ferdinand Khull-Kholwald, 'Rassenfragen', in *Bundesturnzeitung*, 15 September 1920, quoted by Ardelt, op. cit., 65.

20. The same, in *Bundesturnzeitung*, 1 December 1920, quoted ibid., 66.

21. 'Unsere Leitsätze', in *Bundesturnzeitung*, 15 May 1920, quoted ibid., 93-94.

22. 'Hüte dich, deutsches Mädchen', in *Bundesturnzeitung*, 1 October 1924, quoted ibid., 105.

23. 'Der verjudete Arier', in *Bundesturnzeitung*, 15 January 1925, quoted ibid., 63.

24. 'Hinaus mit der Judenpresse', in *Bundesturnzeitung,* 15 January 1925, quoted ibid., 83. The same article also recommended the reading of *The Protocols of the Elders of Zion.*

25. Police report, Vienna, 30 September 1923: Polizeiarchiv Wien, Nachlass Schober, box 49.

26. Police report, Vienna, 28 September 1924: ibid., box 50.

27. '97. Sitzung des Abgeordnetenverbandes der Grossdeutschen Volkspartei': Verwaltungsarchiv Wien, Grossdeutsche Volkspartei, box 5; Brandstötter, op. cit., 226-27; Friedrich Berg, *Die weisse Pest* (Vienna, 1926) 69.

28. Ludwig Jedlicka, 'The Austrian Heimwehr', *Journal of Contemporary History,* I (1) (1966) 130-32. For the *Stahlhelm* see Volker R. Berghahn, *Der Stahlhelm, Bund der Frontsoldaten* (Düsseldorf, 1966).

29. Steidle to Schober, Innsbruck, 27 June 1925: Polizeiarchiv Wien, Nachlass Schober, box 27/4.

30. Police report Vienna, 25 September 1919: Verwaltungsarchiv Wien, Pol. Dir. Wien, Berichte 1919, Pr.Z. 13814. Dr Ursin was an old follower of Schönerer and an active Burschenschaftler.

31. Police Report, Vienna, 5 October 1919, Pr. 13909/4: ibid.

32. Police report, Vienna, 7 June 1920, Pr.Z. 5248/1: ibid., Berichte 1920.

33. Police report, Vienna, 7 November 1920, Pr. 9780: ibid.

34. Leaflet with the demands in Tiroler Landesarchiv, Präsidialakten 1919, XII 76 e.

35. Letters of the 'Tiroler Antisemitenbund' to the government, 21 January and 22 February 1920, with government reply of 25 February: ibid., Präsidialakten 1921, XII 76 e.

36. Tyrolese government to the Anti-Semitic League, Innsbruck, 13 February 1920 (draft): ibid.

37. *Neue Tiroler Stimmen,* evening edn, 9 January 1919.

38. Ibid., midday edn, 13 February 1919.

39. Ibid., evening edn, 21 January 1919.

40. Police reports, Vienna, 20 and 22 September 1921: Polizeiarchiv Wien, Nachlass Reimer, box 7.

41. Police report, Vienna, 6 November 1921: Verwaltungsarchiv Wien, Bundeskanzleramt, 22/gen., box 4862.

42. Police report, Graz, 6 April 1921: Steiermärk. Landesarchiv, Präsidialakten, E. 91, 1921-25, 'Polizeiberichte'.

43. Police report, Vienna, 20 January 1923: Polizeiarchiv Wien, Nachlass Schober, box 49. Perhaps the mass attendance was due to the fact that it was a Sunday.

44. Police report, Vienna, 14 February 1923: ibid., box 38/1.

45. Police report, Vienna, 28 September 1924: Polizeiarchiv Wien, Nachlass Schober, box 50.

46. *Polizeikommissariat* Eisenstadt to *burgenländ. Landesregierung,* 14 November 1924 and 12 February 1925, and *völkisch* leaflet, s.d.: Burgenländisches Landesarchiv, Regierungsarchiv, 4-11/1924; V-8/1925. For the slogan cp. above, p. 36.

6

THE 'HEIMWEHREN' IN THE ASCENDANT

The years 1924 to 1926 saw a decline of the *Heimwehr* movement as the danger of 'red revolution' subsided, prosperity slowly returned to Austria, and more stable political conditions prevailed under conservative governments dominated by the Christian Social Party. This mood was expressed by the Heimwehr Gauleitung of the Lower Inn Valley in 1925: the general opinion was that 'there was quiet anyhow' and 'no danger exists', that 'nothing was to be feared from the Reds'. But, they added, 'nearly everywhere the opinion prevails that this only applies to the Tyrol and the Alpine lands'; hence it was still considered necessary to preserve the Heimwehr organization, even in those local groups where passivity predominated. This indolence the Gauleitung attributed to the lack of initiative and drive on the part of the elected local leaders.[1] From the town of Hall near Innsbruck it was reported in 1926 that most members of the local Oberland group had joined the Heimwehr and that the local Turnverein was forming a para-military group of its own, which in a case of emergency would come under Heimwehr command.[2] But this did not mean an accretion of new strength, only a transfer of activity from the one to the other organization. From Innsbruck too a lack of interest was reported.[3]

In any case, the Tyrolese Heimwehr leader Dr Steidle was indefatigable in promoting the Heimwehr cause and in trying to secure funds for it, for he was convinced that — unless money could be raised — 'some of the co-operative and usable self-defence formations in the Alpine lands will wither away'.[4] But there were grave difficulties which emanated partly from the government, and partly from the industrialists. In June 1925 Steidle was asked to confer with the finance minister, Dr Jakob Ahrer, about the subsidy question and told him that for years all the money had gone to the formations in Vienna without producing any result, and none to those in the Alpine provinces. Ahrer then waxed indignant because he knew from his own experience that, for example, the units in Salzburg were withering away for lack of funds. He demanded from his visitor a detailed account how much government money or funds allocated through government channels had been used and how much had gone to the individual Länder. He declined to do anything more for the time being and threatened to revoke earlier measures.

Steidle then wrote to the industrialist and ex-officer Baron Bernhard Ehrenfels, who had been instrumental in obtaining earlier subsidies, in an attempt to secure the desired information for the finance minister. But Ehrenfels replied that, after the central payment of subsidies came to an end in 1923, payments were only made to individual Länder. He had seen to this in Vienna, but in the agreement nothing was mentioned about participation of other Länder; as he was in no way obliged to give information to 'outsiders' he must decline Steidle's request. It was now Steidle's turn to become indignant about Ehrenfels' 'arrogant letter', which he forwarded to the Viennese police director Dr Schober in an attempt to mobilize support. In Steidle's opinion, an 'enormous apparatus' had been created in Vienna by the various defence formations, but the results stood in no relation to the means used. He was particularly vexed that Ehrenfels had gained the help of the chancellor and the finance minister for his purposes — a support which Steidle himself clearly did not enjoy.[5] Nor did he succeed in modifying the attitude of the government which seemed to have paid out vast sums without any proper accounting system.

Because of the bad financial situation Steidle and his chief of staff, the German Captain Pabst, in 1926 made renewed efforts to secure German funds. But there too they were disappointed. As the German Consul reported from Innnsbruck, only two of the organizations approached were willing to co-operate. Once more Pabst used 'his old personal connections to the German reactionary para-military associations', and a conference was arranged in Munich in January 1927 of the chiefs of staff of the Austrian Heimwehren and German representatives. According to the Consul, 'the financial situation of the Heimatwehren is very bad'.[6] It may well have been these disappointments which induced Steidle to adopt a more radical stance, not so much against the 'Reds' and Jews, but against the parliamentary system and the political parties as such; or it may have been the influence of Italian Fascism to which he was to subscribe openly some years later. He used the unveiling of a warriors' monument at Brixlegg on the Inn in August 1926 to declare that 'a wave of discontent and disgust is sweeping through the ranks of men loyal to home and nation'; he attacked 'the strait jacket of party uniforms' and the narrowness of party thought; he claimed that

> not the majority of the people and its more or less freely elected representatives rule today, but a minority which has known how ... to create a party power organized in a military fashion – this puts the necessary pressure behind the will of the minority, has made it the real ruler in the state, and has scornfully shoved against the wall the majority and its pusillanimous deputies who are busy bickering about trifles.

He then appealed to the Heimwehren to be ready for action. A second speaker, the Christian Social minister Thaler, equally sharply attacked the Viennese party caucus: if need be the Heimwehren would one day march against Vienna.[7]

Two months later at Innsbruck Steidle organized a rally of all the Austrian para-military associations, including the Frontkämpfer, Oberland and völkisch formations. In the presence of Landeshauptmann Dr Stumpf he fulminated once more against Austrian Social Democracy, 'the representative of the most radical socialism of a marxist colour outside Soviet Russia', which was planning to conquer power by revolution and to erect a 'dictatorship of the marxist revolution'. This threat must be met by force of arms and by 'the national revolution'. After Steidle the Landeshauptmann expressed the thanks of the Tyrol to the men of the Heimatwehr: a critical period had begun and soon the question decisive for the future would have to be tackled; he hoped that, if a man was required, that man would be there.[8] The term 'national revolution' was widely used in Bavaria, especially by Hitler and his followers in 1923, but it was new in Steidle's vocabulary. Was Steidle casting himself for the role of its leader, 'the man' of whom Dr Stumpf had spoken? The words used by him seem to indicate that he was no longer thinking of a merely defensive action against 'red revolution', but that his ambitions had grown.

At the same time military preparations were also made in the neighbouring Vorarlberg. There the *Heimatdienst* was directly subordinate to the Landeshauptmann, Dr Otto Ender, and the military leader was a former professional officer, Major Moriz von Matt. Difficulties arose, however, when it was suggested to Dr Ender that the post occupied by another former officer, Lieutenant-Colonel Kunze, should be preserved, otherwise 'the enemy' would be able to prevent any military action by eliminating Major Matt; for it was essential to have a trained reserve. Dr Ender replied to the industrialist in question, Julius Rhomberg, that there was not enough work for the second officer, but this he could disregard because he did not pay his salary: yet he found it more difficult to overcome the criticisms directed against the employment of two professional officers as leaders because several important people had declared that in that case they would have to resign their functions. He therefore suggested to employ the second officer as the district leader for Bregenz; his salary should no longer be paid by the Land government but directly by the industrialists who would be free to deduct that amount from their monthly contributions. The suggestion about the district of Bregenz was accepted by Rhomberg, but not the suggested mode of payment: 'that must be done by the Heimatdienst because it is out of the question that industrialists should pay as it were for their own military man'. He repeated that an organization which did not possess good military leaders was valueless, for the adversary would be led by officers, 'and then we would play a lamentable role and be annihilated!' He also voiced his general criticism of the political system: 'Without any doubt we are going to have a very critical year; the *Herren* politicians in parliament will continue their game until the whole economy has been ruined.'[9] The majority parties of the Vorarlberg Diet, the Christian Socials and the Grossdeutsche, meanwhile passed a law according to which the Land was responsible for any compensation to be paid to the members of the Heimatdienst when called up, for any damages suffered by them, and for all payments to their dependents in case of death or fatal accident.[10] In this small Land the Heimwehren clearly enjoyed official status.

By-laws of the Styrian *Heimatschutz* for the same year, 1927, on the other hand, emphasized that the association was 'an independent, private, non-military institution'. Among its aims were: the preservation of the legally established form of government, support for the authorities if law and order were seriously endangered, the struggle against corruption and disintegration in public life, 'assistance to all those circles which favour the creation of a strong and neutral state power', fight against all tendencies which aim at 'the curtailment of the liberty of the citizen in favour of a single class and at the establishment of the rule of one class', in other words the fight against socialism. The by-laws emphasized that the national heritage, the culture and the economy of the Alpine lands could only be preserved 'by the union of all German tribes in a great German fatherland'; the slogan was: 'for homeland, people and fatherland! '[11] Presumably it was in the pursuance of these aims that Dr Pfrimer, accompanied by two of his leading officers, twice – in August 1926 and in May 1927 – met Adolf Hitler in Germany. 'From that day onwards there were good relations between the German NSDAP and the Styrian Heimatschutz', one of the participants wrote later.[12] From their foundation there had been a strong völkisch tendency among the Styrian formations many of which wore the swastika as their emblem. Their leader, Dr Pfrimer, was an old follower of Schönerer and member of a Burschenschaft.[13] During the following years the links to Hitler were to become much closer.

Hitherto no para-military formations were established in the small Burgenland which was acquired from Hungary in the early 1920s. Indeed, in 1923 the Social Democratic and Christian Social parties agreed not to extend their military activities to this area and this was more or less observed until 1926.[14] In that year, however, the Frontkämpfer Association – which had been no party to the agreement – began to form local groups in the Burgenland, some of them in places where the Social Democrats were very strong. The latter reacted angrily and founded groups of the Republican Defence Corps. Considerable friction resulted, and soon there were local skirmishes and clashes, especially as both sides received reinforcements from outside. In May Colonel Hiltl, the Frontkämpfer leader, spoke in Wissen; when his followers returned by train in the evening there were clashes with socialist workers in the course of which a shot was fired by one of them. In Rohrbach the Frontkämpfer group was largely pro-Hungarian and monarchist – an additional cause of friction. The Bezirkshauptmann of Mattersburg reported in June that 'the situation was dominated' by the foundation of local groups of the two rival para-military organizations. Several reports expressed the apprehension of the authorities which feared further clashes; and the Bezirkshauptmann of

Mattersburg in June prohibited a planned meeting of the Frontkämpfer at Schattendorf because the workers of the surrounding villages decided to prevent the assembly by force. When the meeting finally took place in August it was attended by only thirty people and was completely orderly, but afterwards a serious fight broke out in a local inn.[15]

At the end of 1926 the Bezirkshauptmann of Mattersburg once more reported that both para-military formations were concentrating their activities on his district; meetings were held on every Sunday and holiday and there were almost daily clashes between the rival parties; the Frontkämpfer succeeded in establishing local groups in Rohrbach and Schattendorf, and further groups were in process of formation.[16]
For the 30 January 1927 both organizations announced meetings in Schattendorf which were not prohibited by the authorities in spite of their earlier apprehensions. Both sides received strong reinforcements from outside, and the Republican Defence Corps tried to prevent the arrival of further Frontkämpfer units by blocking the entrance to the station and closing the road leading from the station to the village. Finally an agreement was reached that both sides should leave in opposite directions, and the Republican Defence Corps marched from the station to Schattendorf where a social-democratic meeting was nearing its end. Then shots were fired from an inn into their ranks: one man marching at the end of the column was killed, and four others wounded; a small child was also killed by the shots and another severely wounded. From eye-witness accounts it seems that the column was marching along peacefully when it was fired upon; as they had no arms they could not retaliate.[17] Only after these events did the authorities prohibit all further political meetings for the time being and reinforced the local gendarmerie by five men.[18] Friction between the political adversaries continued, but during the summer it subsided – as the Bezirkshauptmann surmised, the members were now occupied by work in the fields.[19]

Three men who had fired from the inn were arrested and tried in Vienna in July 1927; but they were acquitted by the jury who had doubts about their guilt, or were influenced by the strong political passions aroused by the case. On the next day, 15 July, there were tumultuous left-wing demonstrations in Vienna to protest against the acquittal which quickly got out of hand. The Palace of Justice was set on fire as an act of protest against the legal system. The popular social-democratic mayor, Karl Seitz, in vain tried to calm the crowd which prevented the fire brigade from reaching the building. Policemen were attacked and the police, armed with rifles, retaliated. After two days of rioting the result was seven policeman and 77 demonstrators killed and many more wounded.[20] The socialist trade unions proclaimed a general strike which brought public transport to a standstill in many parts of Austria. But the government of Chancellor Seipel did not resign and remained in control of the situation.

This was at least partly due to the mobilization of the Heimwehren. Their hour had arrived; 'red revolution' could finally be fought by energetic counter-measures. The 15 July 1927 was their 'great stroke of luck',[21] for it seemed to confirm all the stark prophecies of days past. It brought about a mobilization of the middle classes and the peasantry against the threat of 'Marxism', the threat of 'red' Vienna, which they so wholeheartedly disliked. It is true that in Vienna and Lower Austria the para-military formations were unable to act in July because they were immobilized by the strike.[22] But in the other Länder they were able to force the unions to call off the strike after a few days, and their formations proved highly superior to those of the Republican Defence Corps. On 17 July the Heimwehren put their demands in an ultimative form to the Landeshauptmann of Upper Austria, Dr Schlegel: if the railways did not run by the following day they would run them themselves, and the trade unions gave way.[23]

In the Tyrol and Vorarlberg the Heimwehren were mobilized as an auxiliary police, and the general strike was nipped in the bud; in both provinces the Heimwehren had enjoyed the support of the Land government from their foundation, and their employment as auxiliary police had always been envisaged. The Landeshauptmann simply ordered Dr Steidle 'to have the required forces ready and to make them take an oath to fulfil their duties'. The whole operation cost the Tyrolese government the sum of 19,000 Schilling.[24] Afterwards the government strongly recommended the precision and speed with which the units were mobilized and concentrated around Innsbruck, to occupy the city in case of need. It thought that the Social Democrats were bitterly disappointed because 'without any doubt they reckoned with the indifference of the peasant population towards the Heimatwehr idea', as one of their leaders pointed out to the Landeshauptmann in the critical days.[25] In Upper Austria, on the other hand, the Heimwehren objected in particular to the fact that the Republican Defence Corps was blocking certain roads and controlling passengers, so that the population believed that the legal government was 'powerless and only able to transact official business under the red terror', and they demanded the immediate cessation of any such activities.[26] There the Heimwehren were highly critical of the passivity of the government which obviously had no intention of using them as an auxiliary police or to grant them any official status.

The most forceful action was taken in Upper Styria by Dr Pfrimer. In an area with considerable industry and strong socialist influence, he repeated on a larger scale what he had achieved at Judenburg in 1922.[27] In Styria too the unions proclaimed a general strike and the Republican Defence Corps was mobilized to protect the workmen. Pfrimer countered by concentrating his much stronger forces around the industrial area and ordering them to cut off the industrial towns from food and other supplies. He issued an ultimatum to the Social Democrats to clear the streets, to call off the strike and to demobilize their units: if not, he himself would restore order. The socialists, who after all were the weaker side and could not possibly risk a military conflict, had to retract. On 19 July work was resumed in all enterprises, and public communications were restored. During the previous days the representatives of the two rival para-military associations negotiated at Judenburg, and finally reached an agreement with the help of the Styrian government. Pfrimer agreed to withdraw his forces on the 19th if his conditions were met and not to order an advance into the industrial area unless grave unrest broke out there; no member of either organization should be victimized because of his participation in the action. The agreement was signed by the Bezirkshauptmann of Judenburg and seven representatives from each side.[28] This agreement, apparently drawn up between equals, seemed to give to the Social Democrats the chance of an honourable retreat. But it was a retreat, and the Heimwehren were able to claim with some justification that 'it was the first time in the new republic that the Social Democratic Party was forced to a complete capitulation'.[29] Over Austria as a whole its forces were distributed very unevenly; it was strong only in Vienna and a few industrial areas and was completely surprised by the riotous mass action in Vienna which it was unable to control. Henceforth its strength was undermined, its only weapon – the general strike – was blunted.

Hitherto the Heimwehren had not been considered a very serious force by many conservative politicians who were irritated by the never-ending personal rivalries. These doubts were forcefully expressed by the Vienna police director Schober to a Hungarian visitor only two days before the events of July. Schober declared that he had been very sceptical about all Heimwehr plans, but recently he received information that they had established a firmer basis and that the co-ordination of the Heimwehr units in the different Länder was making progress.[30] After the events of July the credit for the breaking of the strike went to the Heimwehren, and soon there was a mass influx of new members from very varied social backgrounds, from great aristocrats to humble peasants and workmen. The Frontkämpfer, on the other hand, whom Steidle had always despised, remained completely passive during the decisive days. Their principal strength was in Vienna and around Vienna where socialist power was overwhelming, and this they were unable to overcome.[31]

According to a German expert opinion of the same month, July 1927, the Heimwehren were well organized and possessed a strong following only in the Alpine provinces, principally among students and peasants. Their leadership, especially in the lower eschelons, was vastly superior to that of the Republican Defence Corps because it consisted of officers, while the latter was mainly led by former NCOs. In Vienna and the industrial areas the Heimwehren were much less important; as a military force they were only usable in combination with the army and police and would be unable to take action if the Left were in the possession of state power.[32] After July 1927, however, the Heimwehren also expanded very considerably in areas where they had been weak, and at least some progress was made in the creation of a central leadership for the whole of Austria, with Dr Steidle in Innsbruck as the leader, and the German Captain Waldemar Pabst as his ever-active chief of staff. Their old ambitions now came close to fulfilment. Twelve months after the events of July the assembled leaders of the Heimwehren appointed Steidle as their all-Austrian leader, with Pfrimer as his second in command.[33]

The considerable growth in Heimwehr strength and influence also increased Steidle's political ambitions. In May 1928 he emphasized in a memorandum destined for the Hungarian Prime Minister, Count István Bethlen,[34] that the Heimwehr was no longer a purely military organization; it was being transformed into a political one

which will and must force the so-called bourgeois parties through the weight of its men with their anti-marxist views to change the constitution, which is half-bolshevik and was adopted under the pressure of the Red Viennese street.... The 150,000 men organized in the ranks of the *Heimwehr*, ready to risk everything for the victory of their *Weltanschauung*, will not be content with the role of a threatening watchdog who has to keep quiet until his master, in this case the bourgeois parties, for once lets him loose, as on 15 July 1927, and as soon as the thief has been chased away put him again on his chain, but they want to participate in the forming of the state . . ..

Steidle continued that, in drawing the lesson from the events of July, the leadership had begun to select the most active men from the large mass of members and to form storm troops from them. The strongest, best equipped and most mobile formations existed in Styria, Tyrol and Vorarlberg, followed by Carinthia and Salzburg, while Lower Austria and Burgenland came last. Many of the Länder had enough men — Upper Austria had 20,000, Lower Austria 32,000 members — but they lacked funds and equipment, and these Steidle now hoped to obtain from Hungary.[35]

The idea to use the Heimwehren to achieve a right-wing take-over in Austria was mentioned by the Hungarians for the first time in conversations between Bethlen and Mussolini in Milan in April 1928: a right-wing Austria would form the bridge between fascist Italy and revisionist Hungary. Bethlen noted that the Heimwehr organization had been strengthened and that they had close links to the head of the Viennese police (Schober) and to army leaders. In his opinion, they needed 300,000 Schilling and some weapons which should be supplied by Italy, with Hungary acting as a go-between. Mussolini replied that he would do so provided the Heimwehren undertook to seize power within a given period; after they had done so he was willing to negotiate with them about an improvement of the situation of the German population in the South Tyrol. When Mussolini received from Budapest Steidle's memorandum quoted above, his foreign minister Grandi informed the Hungarian envoy that his government approved of the Heimwehr aims and was willing to grant the sums requested, but that it insisted on a written declaration of its leaders that they would not raise the question of the South Tyrol after their seizure of power. The required declaration was sent by Steidle to Budapest at the beginning of July. Steidle promised that the new Austrian government would give a written undertaking not to raise the South Tyrol issue in public and not to permit any propaganda in this respect; if the issue were raised independently the government would declare that this was an internal Italian question. Two weeks later the Italian government put the sum of 1,620,000 Lire at the disposal of the Hungarians for transfer to the Heimwehr leaders.[36]

Steidle simultaneously revived his old German contacts, especially those to Escherich in Bavaria. In the summer of 1928 Escherich visited Steidle to urge him to a more speedy action. He now conceived the grandiose scheme of starting the national rising against the Republic in Innsbruck, and to carry it from there to Munich, and finally to Berlin.

In Berlin the Councillor of Legation Redlhammer in the Foreign Office was the liaison man to Steidle and Pabst; he was in favour of reviving the old Orgesch ideas of cultural reformation and settlement in the East, and he equally sympathized with fascist ideas of a corporative state. Many letters were exchanged between Steidle and Escherich in which they fondly remembered the times of past glory; and the leaders of the Carinthian Heimwehr too expressed their joy that the 'old comrades-in-arms from the times of the Orgesch' were co-operating once more under the same name.[37]

It is clear, however, that Berlin was now more important for the Heimwehr plans than Munich where Escherich and the Orgesch were a spent force and the plans for a march to the north were buried for good. In Berlin it was above all the influential German Nationalist Party and its new leader, the 'newspaper king' Alfred Hugenberg, and the strong para-military association of the *Stahlhelm*,[38] which pursued aims similar to those of the Heimwehr, with whom connections were established in 1928. At the beginning of 1929 Pabst accepted an invitation of Hugenberg and lectured in Berlin to a closed circle on the development and aims of the Heimwehren. He also negotiated there with Hugenberg and the Stahlhelm leaders Seldte and Duesterberg, who showed strong interest in the Hungarian-Italian connections of the Heimwehr, and asked Pabst to induce the Italians to extend their co-operation northwards so as to include the German Nationalists. · After Pabst's return from Germany, Steidle wrote to Count Bethlen that the Germans wanted to establish closer links with 'the conservative and para-military circles of those countries in which the para-military and anti-marxist elements have seized the leadership of the state'; the Germans looked upon Hungary and Italy as their natural allies and were convinced that the South Tyrolese question must not make them forget 'the great common aims'. As they knew about the Heimwehr connections with Hungary, they had asked him to pave the way for them there and hoped that they could thus also establish links to Rome.

> I am herewith passing on this wish, the result of several, very long discussions in Munich and Berlin, because I believe that *everything* must be done to oppose the strenuously working Red International by a common front of all those who are linked with us by a common *Weltanschauung* and to establish, in spite of all the difficulties, a White International.

He thought rather optimistically that this would lead 'automatically to the real solution . . . of all difficulties in Europe including the minority questions'.[39]

As a result of these links a Heimwehr rally in Vienna in September 1929 was addressed by a Stahlhelm representative, the Württemberg deputy Dr Hölscher from Ulm. He exclaimed that the Stahlhelm would not allow the *Reichsbanner Schwarz-Rot-Gold,* the para-military German republican organization, to come to the aid of their Austrian comrades if they got involved in struggles with the Heimwehr, although such action had recently been threatened by the leader of the *Reichsbanner,* Otto Hörsing.[40] During his stay in Vienna Hölscher also informed a German diplomat that the Stahlhelm leader Seldte had recently visited Steidle at Innsbruck where they agreed to form a common front of the right-wing Verbände in both countries. In the opinion of the German right-wing parties Austria was 'ripe for an Action', because there the middle classes had regained their self-confidence – in Germany this was unfortunately not yet the case – and they hoped that the fight against Social Democracy in Austria would set an example to Germany.[41] On the local level too connections were now established, and uniformed German Stahlhelm units began to participate in Heimwehr parades in Austria,[42] while Heimwehr delegations attended rallies in Germany where their different uniforms caused some surprise.

Yet for Steidle and the Heimwehr leaders the links to Hungary and Italy were more important: there they could lean on groups which controlled the government, while in 1929 the chances of Hugenberg or Seldte forming a German government must have looked pretty slim, and governments had large funds at their disposal. These priorities were clearly indicated by Steidle in his letter to Count Bethlen of March 1929. But those who provided the money and the arms wanted to see deeds, and not words. They thus pressed the Heimwehr leaders to take the promised action. Mussolini in particular was reluctant to commit himself to further aid unless a written promise was given. Therefore Steidle and Pabst in August 1929 signed a declaration in which they undertook 'to carry out the decisive action to change the Austrian constitution not later than during the period 15 February to 15 March 1930'. They also promised to make all efforts to do so already in the autumn of 1929; the earlier they obtained the promised 'co-operation', the sooner would they be able to act. This declaration was also given in the name of Dr Pfrimer who had to leave Vienna for urgent reasons.[43] This curious declaration, in which the Heimwehr leaders promised a foreign government to overthrow the constitution of their own country, was apparently not sufficient for Bethlen. In September he also insisted on a guarantee by Steidle that the city of Vienna must be 'completely smoked out'; the whole Heimwehr movement was value-less, Bethlen averred, if the socialists, such as Seitz and Breitner, remained ensconced in the town hall. He also expressed his grave apprehensions that the movement would be ruined through negotia-tions with the party leaders.[44] Thus the Hungarian government — perhaps pushed by Mussolini — put pressure to adopt a more radical course on the Heimwehren, which these were unable to resist.

In the same month, September 1929, the Hungarian foreign minister, Lajos Walkó, saw Steidle in Vienna. Steidle explained to him that 'it would be best if a provocation of the socialists would create the opportunity for an eruption, . . . but he did not believe that they would provide this chance, so that they [the Heimwehren] would have to use other means to achieve that the police was rendered weak and had to be reinforced by the Heimwehr, and thus power would in fact be trans-ferred to it.' Steidle further assured his visitor that he was opposed to any compromise and was determined to have 'a final settlement of accounts' and to finish his work completely. He expressed doubts about the qualifications of his second in command, Dr Pfrimer, whom he held 'unsuitable for a larger part', but who had the advantage 'that he knew extremely well how to deal with the people of Styria'. As to the subsidies, Walkó informed Steidle that half the sum would be sent within the next few days via the Hungarian councillor of legation in Vienna; the other half would follow later. Pabst also appeared for a short time and impressed upon the visitor that the Heimwehren above all needed automatic weapons and ammunition.[45]

Pabst, ever active in the good cause, also visited Rome to establish direct links between the Heimwehren, the Stahlhelm and the Italian Fascist Party and to negotiate about the thorny question of the South Tyrol. In September the German nationalist leader Hugenberg took part in a conference held at Lugano where the Austrian issues were dis-cussed. But at that time Hugenberg's main interest was the organization of the popular initiative in Germany against the acceptance of the Young Plan (settlement of the reparations issue), and it was only afterwards that he again found time and money for the Heimwehren. Pabst wanted to see the fascist example followed in Austria and Germany, and it was rumoured that, during his stay in Rome, he had concluded an agreement to that effect with the Secretary General of the Fascist Party.[46] What Pabst aimed at becomes clear from his 'Action Programme' of November 1929. According to this, the reform of the constitution was only the beginning which would give the Heimwehr a legal base for further action; Estates were to be organized on a compulsory basis and the existing two houses of parliament replaced by one House of Estates. 'We want a State of Estates or – to put it into good German (!) – the Fascist State! ' There was no question of the Heimwehr making concessions, for the Italian example would be followed. Pabst's final aim was to make Germany again a strong power able to take action against the West. First Vienna must be reduced to obedience in one form or the other, and then the issue of Greater Germany could be tackled from Vienna, for the Stahlhelm would repeat the experiment of the Heimwehr. Meanwhile Austria must join the common front of Italy and Hungary. For the time being, Pabst emphasized, no one in Austria should mention the word 'South Tyrol', and the Tyrolese leaders – presumably including Dr Steidle – accepted this point of view. But opposition came from Munich which exercised pressure on Innsbruck, hence Pabst did not have much to say in favour of Munich.[47]

Pabst's ambitious schemes went far beyond the frontiers of Austria – not surprisingly in view of his German völkisch background. What is not clear is to what extent he was successful in winning over the Heimwehr leaders, especially his chief Dr Steidle, to his wider aims. But a certain influence is indicated by the fact that in May 1930 Steidle and the other leaders were to accept officially a 'fascist' programme. To that extent at least Pabst's policy – and the influence of Italian money – carried the day. Looked at from the point of view of a general fascist ideology, the question of the South Tyrol – which especially among the Tyrolese aroused strong passions – became a minor issue hardly worth mentioning: it is very interesting that at the same time Adolf Hitler adopted exactly the same attitude. But it was difficult to reconcile with German nationalism, in view of Mussolini's strong measures against the South Tyrolese population. As late as December 1932, the Styrian Heimwehr paper, *Der Panther,* which by that time strongly sympathized with National Socialism, published a photograph of a uniformed SS detachment in front of the Italian Victory Monument in Bozen, taken at the celebration of the tenth anniversary of the Fascist march on Rome. The photograph was given the sarcastic headline *'Deutschland erwache! '* (the German Nazi slogan) and underneath was the comment: 'In this place, in the year 1809, Peter Mayr . . . was shot by the French.'[48] The SS detachment was commanded by Theodor Eicke who a few months later became the notorious commandant of the Dachau concentration camp. Even one of Hitler's most faithful henchmen in Austria, the *Landesinspekteur* Theodor Habicht, protested against the appearance of 'a high SS leader with a proper unit as an official representative of the Party' on such an occasion. According to his letter, the SS unit also paraded after the celebration in front of the fascist leaders together with the local fascist militia.[49]

In his public utterances Steidle was more cautious than in his promises to the Hungarians. In a speech made to the general assembly of the Lower Austrian units at the beginning of 1929 he declared:

> Our critics say that we are against representative assemblies *(Volksvertretungen)*. Our movement originated in a Land which is proud to have possessed a representative assembly for six hundred years, from a time when around us everything was still unfree. We are only opposed to a representative assembly that is alien to our race and people *(art- und volksfremd)*, of the kind one wants to force upon us (enthusiastic applause). We want a popular assembly corresponding to our German history and German culture. But we also want a representative assembly which possesses authority and is removed from the influence of unbridled party oligarchies . . . .

At a mass demonstration in July 1928 he proclaimed: 'When the struggle for power in the state will be fought out this state must belong to us.'[51] Dr Pfrimer in his turn, speaking in Vienna to employees of the tramways in July 1929, exclaimed that the aims of the Heimwehr movement were: 'the liberation of the worker from the claws of the Jewish-marxist leaders, the elimination of the party bureaucracies, and the abolition of the parliamentary system in Austria in its present form'[52] — meaning a parliament based on parties and democratic elections.

According to a detailed and well informed memorandum of the Viennese police from that time, the Heimwehren were agreed that 'Marxism' must be totally eradicated, together with the abuses caused by it, such as 'terror' in the factories (the overwhelming influence of the socialist unions) and the socialist trend in the field of education. The Heimwehren further aimed at sweeping changes in the constitution, e.g. changes in the electoral system to secure more influence for them, greater powers of the president, and of the central government vis-à-vis the Länder. The more radical circles wanted a parliament based on Estates; while the moderate members hoped to achieve their demands through pressure on the government and in a parliamentary way, the more radical groups were inclined to use force and to push aside the leaders who favoured moderation. The movement claimed to have

200,000 members, but that figure seemed to be too high. Most of them were manual workers, and there were also many unemployed. The remainder came from all social groups, business circles, officials, employees of the state and of the municipalities, many of whom had joined recently. Most of the members were between 25 and 40 years old. Politically, there were many former Social Democrats, but also many who had belonged to the moderate bourgeois parties and the anti-semitic extreme Right.[53] The social group entirely omitted in this report was the peasantry which furnished the bulk of the membership outside the big towns. But then the report was drawn up by the Viennese police and was probably based on local information. According to another estimate, the peasants constituted about 70 per cent of the total membership, workers about 10 per cent, and the middle and upper classes about 20 percent.[54] There are no more accurate figures; but there is no doubt that the Heimwehren were above all a rural movement — a movement of protest against modernization and urbanization. Their leaders, on the other hand, often came from the middle and upper classes: many had the Dr title, many were former officers, and many came from aristocratic families.

The 'provocation of the socialists', which Steidle mentioned to the Hungarian foreign minister in September 1929, the Heimwehren tried to achieve by organizing mass demonstrations in 'red' strongholds, so as to show their strength, to win over workers, and to prove the weakness or bias of the authorities. In this respect, Lower Austria with its industrial concentration was a favourite target. In 1928 3,500 Heimwehr men marched through Gloggnitz in the south, close to the border with Styria. But this parade was dwarfed by that held in Wiener Neustadt on 7 October where 19,000 Heimwehr men marched through a 'red' centre. The Social Democrats replied by mobilizing their followers and the units of the Republican Defence Corps; and all the authorities could do — unwilling as they were to prohibit these rival marches — was to separate the two demonstrations to prevent a clash.

For this the Heimwehren were fully prepared. Before the event they cleared out the depots of the gendarmerie in Graz and took away 4,200 rifles and several machine guns with ammunition. To the south of Wiener Neustadt shock troops with 700 rifles and ten machine guns were awaiting the signal to attack, but the signal never came. Even so the Heimwehren considered the Day of Wiener Neustadt a great moral success, and their movement received a strong impetus.[55] In addition to the counter-demonstration in Wiener Neustadt, in which 14,800 members of the Republican Defence Corps took part, an almost equal number were assembled at Leoben in Styria 'in case something should happen at Wiener Neustadt'. Allegedly it was planned that in that case Bruck on the Mur was to be occupied 'to protect the population against armed bands'.[56] Thus Austria was divided into two armed camps. The German envoy reported from Vienna that the march in Wiener Neustadt was prepared 'in agreement with the Styrian industrialists who thus wanted to achieve a further expansion of the Heimwehr movement in the metal and mining industries . . .'; he added that Wiener Neustadt was chosen 'to prove its courage and strength'.[57] But it was extremely fortunate that the demonstrations passed without any serious incident.

Only five weeks after Wiener Neustadt the Heimwehren from the whole of Austria converged on Innsbruck to 'celebrate' the tenth anniversary of the existence of the Austrian Republic — the day was an official holiday. Ten thousand men paraded from Carinthia, Salzburg, Styria, Vienna and Lower Austria, and another 8,000 from Tyrol and Vorarlberg. Many units appeared fully armed 'according to that curious interpretation of the Tyrolese right to bear arms', and as the Tyrolese government reported to Vienna, 'they made the best possible impression in view of their equipment and discipline'. After a solemn mass the men paraded for two-and-a-half hours in front of the highest official of the Tyrol, the Landeshauptmann. He felt induced to compare the general mood to that of 'the days of mobilization of the year 1914' and was convinced that 'the organizers of the meeting have rendered an extremely valuable service to the whole state'. But there were serious clashes with the Social Democrats, and the units from Carinthia almost stormed the trade union building if this had not been prevented by Dr Steidle.[58]

A few months later, in February 1929, Vienna was the scene of a similar monster demonstration in which more than 10,000 men of the Heimwehren were joined by the other right-wing para-military units, such as the Frontkämpfer, the Academic Legion, and the Turnerschaft. On that occasion Steidle exclaimed: 'Today we still have the oppressors of Vienna, the Turks of today, sitting in the town hall. And it seems to me almost a slander of the brave Turks if I compare them with these gentlemen who have also come from the Far East . . . .'[59] Twelve months after Innsbruck the Styrian capital, Graz, saw 17,000 uniformed Heimwehr men parading through the streets, and their leader welcomed the Landeshauptmann Dr Rintelen and the numerous representatives of other authorities and of the city. Dr Pfrimer emphasized once more that they would not put down their arms 'until Marxism was destroyed'. Dr Rintelen donned the Heimwehr hat with the cock's feather and declared that they could rely on him during the days to come. According to the same report, Graz 'for two days was transformed into a veritable military camp'. Perhaps that was the reason for the 'enormous enthusiasm' among the population which was reported by the Graz police.[60]

The rising Heimwehr movement also attracted some of the smaller völkisch groups which adopted its symbol, the cock's feather, and co-operated with it. A celebration held in 1929 in honour of the new military leader 'of the Austrian storm battalions of the Free Corps Oberland' was attended by the Heimwehr leaders Steidle and Pabst as well as Heimwehr detachments; while Prince Starhemberg, 'who himself as an Oberland man participated in the Upper Silesian struggle of liberation', apologized for his absence. The new Oberland leader, Captain Enrich from Innsbruck, declared that the Austrian Oberland battalions 'as the first militant organization . . . have joined the ranks of the people's movement and would stand with the Heimatwehr in unswerving loyalty as long as it preserved its purity'.[61]

The frontal attack on 'Marxism' went hand in hand with strenuous attempts to win over workers, and these were at least partially successful. Exactly like the Austrian National Socialists (but not the German ones) the Heimwehren founded trade unions to break the strong influence of the socialist unions in the factories. These were officially called 'independent trade unions', but they were in reality dependent not only on the Heimwehr but also on the employers who promoted them in many ways. They were founded in nearly all the Länder, but became strongest in Styria where they claimed some 15,000 to 20,000 members.[62] There the lead was taken by the directors of the *Alpine Montangesellschaft,* one of the most important Austrian industrial enterprises, where the relations between employers and employees were of a markedly hierarchical order. Using their strong personal power, the directors after July 1927 no longer hired workers organized in the socialist unions and by preference employed members of the Heimwehren. The latter received special premiums. The local offices of the other unions were closed and put at the disposal of the 'independent unions' in which the leading posts were occupied by the works engineers and managers. Thus the near-monopoly which the socialist unions had enjoyed was broken and the employees in their vast majority were made to join the Styrian Heimwehr or at least the 'independent union'. The purpose was to create a 'works patriotism', a 'positive' attitude to the company, and the aim was achieved in so far that strikes were out of the question in future.[63] With a certain justification the Styrian Heimwehren could claim that they had 'won an ever-growing following among the working class'; but this was clearly due to pressure at a time of widespread unemployment, and it proved the helplessness of the socialist unions in an area where the Heimwehren as early as 1922 were able to break their strike weapon.[64] In Vienna, the only working-class group where the Heimwehren gained some influence was that of the tram and public transport workers employed by the 'red' municipal administration.

While the Heimwehren paraded their strength through the streets and staged monster demonstrations to impress the population, they were also busy negotiating with the government and exercising pressure on it to reform the constitution in an authoritarian and corporative sense. These negotiations were facilitated by the fact that the chancellors of the later 1920s sympathized with certain aims of the Heimwehr movement and considered it a valuable counterweight to the Social Democrats, but were nevertheless reluctant to hand over power to it. This applied in particular to the two 'strong' men of the period, the Christian Social leader Dr Ignaz Seipel as well as the head of the Viennese police, Dr Johann Schober, both of whom were chancellors during this critical period. In September 1928 Chancellor Seipel met Steidle and three other Heimwehr leaders who asked him whether he was willing to support the Heimwehren in case of clashes – this was shortly before their mass demonstration in Wiener Neustadt – by armed force and openly to take their side. Again Seipel said yes, but he requested that the Heimwehren should not provoke the clashes.[65] For the same reason – the security preparations for the Wiener Neustadt march – a meeting was held in Schober's office in which an army general and Heimwehr leaders participated. According to a report by the Hungarian General Jánky to Budapest, the meeting proved that the chancellor was 'absolutely for an active attitude. The organs of the state will back and secure it!'[66] But Jánky added that a more radical solution favoured by the Hungarians was simply a Putsch for which the Styrian Heimwehr, according to a memorandum of one of their leaders, was fully prepared. The Republican Defence Corps was to be defeated, the public buildings and utilities were to be occupied, and a Directory consisting of the Heimwehr leaders and Schober was to seize power. According to the memorandum sent to Budapest in the spring of 1928

Schober knew all the details and fully agreed with the plan.[67]

To Seipel the Heimwehren were a welcome buffer that could be used to reduce the influence of the hated socialists; in this good fight the Heimwehren with their mass membership were very useful allies; but apparently he did not want them to become an independent party, nor did he want to entrust power to them.[68] On the contrary he aimed at strengthening the influence of his own Christian Social Party within the Heimwehren, and for that purpose sent his friend, the deputy Julius Raab, into the Heimwehren to keep them in line. At the end of 1928 Seipel himself spoke in Graz in the attempt to lead them into the camp of his party – in a city where the Heimwehren had very different political leanings, more radical and more grossdeutsch.[69] In July 1929 Seipel – no longer chancellor – went to the university of Tübingen to give a lecture on 'Democracy and Critique of Democracy', in which he rejected democracy in the sense of rule by political parties and declared: 'In Austria there exists a strong populist movement which wants to free democracy from party rule! The carriers of this movement are the Heimwehren.' In Seipel's opinion, they did not threaten civil peace; their unruliness sprang from their rejection of 'undemocratic party rule'.[70] The German minister in Vienna, Count Lerchenfeld, commented that Seipel thus hoped to encourage the 'constructive' elements within the Heimwehren and to check the outright fascist forces, but he warned against the 'illusions' of a policy which tried to maintain 'personal influence' over such a movement – thinking of the vain attempt of Kahr and the Bavarian government to control Hitler and his forces in 1923.[71]

Seipel resigned as chancellor in the spring of 1929 and was replaced by another Christian Social politician, Ernst von Streeruwitz, who had close links to the Lower Austrian Peasant League, and through them to the Heimwehr. The formation of his government was strongly influenced by Heimwehr pressure, but during his short term of office his policy disappointed the Heimwehr leaders by its moderation. Indeed, according to a well informed Austrian source, it was their opposition which eliminated several other candidates for the chancellor's post during the government crisis of the spring of 1929. They also torpedoed the candidature of the Landeshauptmann of Vorarlberg, Dr Otto Ender, by leaking the fact that he maintained the local Heimwehren from public funds. The real Heimwehr candidate was the Styrian Landeshauptmann Dr Anton Rintelen, a strong protector of the Heimwehren, but there was too much opposition to him from inside his own

Christian Social Party. As Streeruwitz was a leading member of the Association of Industrialists, which financed the Heimwehren (together with the banks), they did not expect any difficulties from him.[72] But they soon turned against him and, in co-operation with Seipel, brought about Streeruwitz' downfall.[73]

The new chancellor was the 'strong man' of July 1927, Dr Johann Schober, whose government was supported by several conservative and right-wing parties. The Heimwehren gained their immediate end — the toppling of Streeruwitz — and thus considerable prestige. They had confidence in Schober and 'looked to him as the man who would change the structure of Austria and bring the Heimwehren to a position of power or even predominance', the then minister of the interior wrote later.[74] Yet the Tyrolese leader Steidle voiced his criticism of Schober as a 'bureaucrat', who would be unable to 'cope with a difficult political situation', even before he became chancellor.[75] And the Heimwehr leaders were soon disillusioned when Schober failed to take strong measures against the socialists and did not co-operate sufficiently with the Heimwehren on the issue of constitutional reform about which both sides had very different ideas. The reform finally agreed on by the Austrian parliament strengthened to some extent the rights of the president, who in future was to be elected by the people, and envisaged the transformation of the second chamber into a chamber of the Länder and Estates, but this was never carried out. The Heimwehr leaders desired far more radical changes in the constitution and worked out a project which, according to Schober, was 'distinctly fascist in character'; they wanted stronger powers for the central government and talked about the abolition of the separate Länder governments. Such plans aroused the opposition not only of Schober, but also of the political parties which supported him.[76]

Thus the honeymoon of Schober and the Heimwehren did not last long, and slowly there developed 'an ever growing chasm' between them.[77] As a leading Heimwehr member, Dr Neustädter-Stürmer, explained later, in 1929 the Heimwehren were so strong that they could have carried out any change of the constitution without shedding a drop of blood, but they made

the little mistake to grant their confidence to Chancellor Schober, because they believed that he alone was strong enough. But Schober treated with the Social Democrats and considered it an honour to have friendly relations with a Dannenberg [the party secretary] or a Seitz [the Viennese mayor]. The Heimwehren in reality elevated Schober to the chancellor's position, but he misused their confidence. ....[78]

There was a more weighty reason for the breach. Schober was informed from a reliable source that the Heimwehr leaders tried to induce the Italian government to postpone its consent to the Austrian loan which Schober wanted to raise under international guarantees. It was generally known that Steidle's chief of staff, the German ex-officer Pabst, had close personal relations with Eugenio Moreale, the press attaché at the Italian legation in Vienna, and that Moreale possessed great influence in Rome through the Fascist Party. Schober considered Pabst the spiritus rector of these anti-Austrian intrigues, a man who would commit a cold-blooded murder if need be, and he was determined to expel him from Austria.[79] For the Italian government, however, the situation in Austria had changed with Schober's appointment as chancellor: it seemed to open the possibility that he would bring about a turn towards the right, which should be supported by the Heimwehren. Thus their plans to carry out a Putsch should be shelved, and the Italian envoy in Vienna, Auriti, was instructed to admonish Steidle to patience with the government.[80] In general it seems that about this time Mussolini lost confidence in the Heimwehr leaders who always talked but did not *do* much. He was even unwilling to accept the excuse that they did not have enough weapons, because in his opinion no arms were necessary for a coup d'état and he himself had conquered Rome without any weapons, only with sticks.[81]

In September 1929 Dr Pfrimer, speaking at a Heimwehr demonstration, welcomed the new chancellor who had been chosen with their assent 'as a bearer of the people's will'. He assured Schober that, if he met any obstacles, he should 'turn towards the people, represented by the Heimatschutz,' and they would support him. But he added the warning that, if the change of the constitution and the introduction of order in the field of public administration were not carried out in their entirety and were watered down, their attitude to Schober would change.[82] This, however, was exactly what happened. None of the 'essential' changes demanded by the Heimwehren — real power to be given to the president, a parliament based on Estates, the abolition of Vienna's status as a separate Land with its own government — were incorporated in Schober's constitutional reforms. When these were accepted unanimously by the Austrian parliament at the end of 1929 this constituted a defeat for the Heimwehren.[83] And above all, 'red' Vienna was still there, and the Social Democrats had only made some minor concessions, e.g. they agreed to the raising of the age qualifications for voting and for deputies. Yet the Heimwehren did not proceed to any 'deeds'.

This failure of the Heimwehren to take action was also due to the factor which had marred the movement since its foundation: their disunity. Especially the relations between the two most important formations, those of Styria and Tyrol, or rather between their leaders, Pfrimer and Steidle, deteriorated to such an extent that they no longer communicated with each other. Then, in October 1929, a meeting was arranged in Vienna which almost led to an agreement, but at the last moment Pfrimer, offended by the Tyrolese tactics, left the room. He was equally offended by certain reproaches emanating from the Viennese Professor Othmar Spann of which he was not directly informed. Steidle and Pabst were above all interested in preventing an agreement between the Schober government and the Social Democrats and in extracting certain guarantees from Schober which he was reluctant to give.[84]

According to a German report, there were by the end of 1929 at least three different currents within the Heimwehr movement: a moderate one which was satisfied with the changes introduced so far, a central one which wanted to continue the support for the 'anti-marxist' united front and was led by Steidle, and a more radical one under Pfrimer which aimed at fundamental changes. In Carinthia, a local Heimwehr group expelled the former Landeshauptmann and then minister of the interior Schumy from its ranks, and thus caused a conflict with the Peasant League which hitherto supported the Heimwehren. The Völkische were highly critical of the political line of the Heimwehr leaders, especially Steidle, towards the South Tyrol and Italy.[85] The Grossdeutsch Party in its turn criticized that the Heimwehren no longer were 'an organ in favour of law and order' and 'a support for a bourgeois government', but developed into an 'independent factor', except in Vorarlberg where they were firmly controlled by the Landeshauptmann. The speaker considered it necessary that his party spoke openly to the Heimwehr leaders, but his suggestion was opposed by another grossdeutsch deputy.[86] In Lower Austria, the Christian Social deputy Raab stood in opposition to the more radical Heimwehr leadership of Steidle and Pfrimer, who aimed at seizing political power.[87]

Chancellor Schober was well informed about these internal conflicts. During an official visit to Rome in February 1930 he told Mussolini about the antagonism between the various factions and stressed that the movement had many heads but no real leader. He himself, he added, was aiming at bringing about unity between the various competing

right-wing organizations.[88] Thus Mussolini's suspicions of the Heimwehr leaders were reinforced. Schober's opinion was certainly justified
by the facts: it was a weakness which the Heimwehren — in spite of
their numerical strength and the great impetus they received in July
1927 — were not able to overcome.

There is a certain amount of detailed information about the strength
of the Heimwehren in the different Austrian Länder. An apparently
well informed police report of 1929 from Klagenfurt gave for the nine
Kreise into which Carinthia was divided a total strength of 24,460 men.
But the strength of the mobile units was only 11,275 men, consisting of
ten 'storm battalions' and sixteen 'march battalions', and even from
that figure at least 10 per cent should be deducted because 'many
members in case of a military action would not participate on account
of business and other interests'.[89] A contemporary report from Graz
gave for Styria a total strength of 29,300 men, consisting of 10,350
men of mobile units, 6,500 of reserves, and 12,450 of local defence
units, to which should be added another 25,000 supporting members,
together 54,000. In the small Land Salzburg there were about 10,000
members, mainly peasants.[90] In eleven communes of the district of
Linz (without Linz itself) the police counted only 940 men in 1927;
most of the local leaders were peasants.[91] For Lower Austria, the
Christian Social leader Raab in 1930 reported 830 local groups and
52,000 'combatant members'.[92] In Vienna, according to a very detailed
police report of 1929, there was the association *Wiener Heimwehr,*
commanded by the former Major Emil Fey, with about 2,000 active
and about 6,000 supporting members. There was also the *Heimatschutzverband Wien,* which included several völkisch organizations,
such as the para-military sections of the Deutsche Turnerbund, the Free
Corps Oberland, and the Deutsche Wehr; its active members counted
about 3,000, the reserve about 5,000, and the supporting members
about 15,000 men; the Frontkämpfer, on the other hand, only numbered about 2,000: a total of 33,000 plus several minor groups. Among
these there also figured the *Vaterländische Schutzbund* or SA of the
National Socialists, with 300 to 400 members. This, however, was an
organization separate from the Heimwehr movement and only co-
operated with it on occasion.[93] Although these are fragmentary figures
they indicate a very considerable strength.

Detailed reportes about the activity of the Heimwehren are available
from the small Burgenland, close to Hungary. In 1928 the Heimwehren
announced the foundation of local groups in all the 84 communes of

the district of Oberwart, as they did elsewhere, but in fact many of them only existed on paper. In several communes the Social Democrats declared that they would then found groups of the Republican Defence Corps and at least in Pinkafeld the mayor achieved that both sides agreed not to do so unless the other started.[94] Another district reported in 1929 that the Heimwehr groups had been founded but were inactive because of lack of interest;[95] and yet another that the Heimwehr movement was growing, or that local groups were in the process of formation.[96] In the commune of Hornstein, district of Eisenstadt, the foundation of a Heimwehr group was 'in preparation'; but a note was added by hand that it was 'already formed, but had not yet been constituted' *[sic]*.[97] In Rechnitz the issue was debated in the local council where the representatives of the other parties expressed their opposition to the Heimwehren, but the mayor and vice-mayor declared in favour, as it seems on the grounds that the Republican Defence Corps had existed for some time 'in secret'.[98] Only from Eisenstadt itself, the capital of the Burgenland, did the police report that the population followed 'with undisguised interest' the events in Lower Austria and the Heimwehr movement, with which 'a large part of the population' sympathized; many new members were joining and new local groups were founded; in Bruckneudorf even many Social Democrats changed over to the Heimwehr.[99] But this was contradicted during the same month by the local authority which reported lack of interest in the Heimwehr although it had local groups 'in nearly all places'.[100] Only one report mentioned in 1929 that the remarks of Heimwehr leaders relating to support from Hungary met opposition from those friendly to Austria.[101]

Several reports from the district of Eisenstadt indicate that the situation was more or less the same during the early months of 1930, but that friction between the Heimwehren and the Social Democrats was growing once more. The Heimwehren were trying to penetrate into villages inhabited by Croats but met with resistance from the inhabitants, and the same applied to villages where the Peasant League had influence. In the village of Goberling, on the other hand, thirty social-democratic miners welcomed the appearance of the Heimwehr, 'declared that they were fed up with the terror and the "Russian" conditions' and immediately joined the Heimwehr. When a fire broke out in the village of Rechnitz Social Democrats, who offered their help to extinguish it, were rebuffed and threatened by the local Heimwehr men. After the celebration of May Day in the village of Mörbisch the

Heimwehr leaders induced some farmers not to sell any milk to those who took part in the celebration and not to employ Social Democrats any longer.[102] From the district of Neusiedl it was reported at the same time that the Heimwehren were conducting an active propaganda and recruiting many new members, while nothing was said about their opponents.[103] Altogether more than 300 local Heimwehr groups were officially founded in the Burgenland in the years after 1927, i.e. in most of the small communes and villages, but it is impossible to say to what extent they functioned and how strong they were. Several men who were approached to become the leaders of such a group expressly declined or replied that no suitable recruits were available, or that too much unrest would be created in the village.[103]

According to the by-laws of the *Heimatschutzverband Burgenland* of 1927 the aims of the association were: protection of the constitution and resistance to any attempt at changing it by force; protection of labour and property; and support of the authorities in the maintenance of law and order. It was expressly stated that the association did not occupy itself 'with military matters' and that the leaders on each level were elected, e.g. the district leaders by the leaders of the local groups. It is significant, however, that new by-laws for the Gau Nordburgenland passed in 1929 omitted the 'protection of the constitution and resistance to any attempt at changing it by force' and replaced it by 'furthering the creation of a strong and independent state power' and the opposition to 'self-interest, destruction and incitement by alien elements *(volksfremde Verhetzung)*'. Omitted too was the clause about military matters, but it was still stated that all leaders were elected.[104] A new and more völkisch vocabulary was now used, with words such as Gau, Gauleitung, *volksfremd,* and *Volksgemeinschaft* which had not figured in 1927. All this indicated a decisive change in the aims of the Heimatschutz; only that it still possessed a democratic structure, and that even within the Gauleitung all decisions were taken by a majority of votes, in contrast with the practices of the National Socialists.

Less detailed local information is available for the other Austrian Länder. A police report on the Heimwehren of Upper Austria from 1929 stated that circumspect local politicians looked at them 'as a subsidiary force which would be at the disposal of the legal government if the power of the state or the legal executive should prove insufficient'. The Heimwehren of Upper Austria were opposed to a Putsch, but many members were not against a coup carried out by the government aided by 'the state executive which, if need be, would be strengthened by Heimwehr units'. Within the past months the movement had experienced a great development, not only in Linz, but in the whole of the Land, and it was estimated by its own leaders that it now had about 30,000 members; even the 'anxious' members of the middle classes were now joining. It was planned to recruit in all districts so-called *Jäger* battalions as a proper military formation to support the executive effectively. The first battalion with about 550 men was already formed, and twelve others were planned. The völkische Turner were forming their own military unit to support the Jäger battalions. Two events marked the rise of the Upper Austrian Heimwehr movement: the march through Linz in October 1928, where the men were most cordially welcomed by the population, and the election of Prince Ernst Rüdiger von Starhemberg as the Upper Austrian Heimwehr leader in July 1929.[105]

The two events mentioned as inaugurating a new phase in Heimwehr development were closely connected, for it was the young Prince Starhemberg who raised the mobile Jäger battalions, largely by his private means. As he wrote later, he

> wanted to make out of the petit-bourgeois and hardly activist Heimwehr an activist, political fighting movement. My aim was to recruit for the whole of Austria . . . formations like the Free Corps; to select from the amorphous mass of the Heimwehr with its more than 200,000 men 40 to 50,000 men in militarized storm battalions, that was the task which I set myself. If that was achieved the instrument of power would exist to give punch to political ideologies. . . .[106]

Starhemberg, as an Innsbruck student, took an active part in the fighting of German Free Corps against the Poles in Upper Silesia in 1921 and, after his return to Innsbruck, joined the German Free Corps Oberland which was also active in Austria. As a member of Oberland he participated in the Hitler Putsch in Munich, when the Bavarian capital was 'the great hope of the nationalist patriots of Austria and Germany', when there 'prevailed a national mood in the south German capital which carried everything before it and justified the greatest expectations', as he put it himself.[107] There in Munich, Starhemberg continued,

> I met *him* who announced in words which captivated and which unleashed innermost passions what the embittered generation of the trenches and the war-time and post-war youth with its unchecked national radicalism wanted and felt . . . I met Adolf Hitler. . . Like hundreds of thousands I was captivated. He was fascinating as an orator, and irresistible were his words and demands in their naturalness and seemingly compelling logic . . . .[108]

After the failure of the Hitler Putsch, Starhemberg served for a time in the German army as a 'temporary volunteer'. Thus his whole background was nationalist, grossdeutsch and völkisch, and he was an ardent admirer of Hitler. But he was also the young grand seigneur, very conscious of his good looks and aristocratic origin, who lived in style and wanted to make a mark for himself in history, like his illustrious ancestor who had saved Vienna from the Turks in 1683. In the whole of Austria the name of Starhemberg was a household word, and none was better suited to win new recruits for the Heimwehren, not only from the old upper class. Another Upper Austrian aristocratic leader, Peter Count Revertera, gave the composition of the new Jäger battalion as follows: four companies with 200 rifles each, one machine gun detachment per company, with a motorized unit and a medical detachment. In the Upper Austrian Mühlviertel there even existed a whole Jäger Brigade of six battalions, with 48 machine guns, an artillery detachment and a staff company for special purposes.[109] These were fully militarized units which hardly justified the claim that their purpose was merely the support of the executive in case of need.

The elevation of Starhemberg entailed a defeat for the Christian Social Party which had possessed the prevailing influence in the movement in Upper Austria. The moving spirit behind his election was a district leader, Major Friedrich Mayer; but it was contested because the former leader, the Christian Social deputy Baltasar Gierlinger, declared that he alone was entitled to summon the district leaders and that Mayer's move was unconstitutional. Hence another meeting had to be summoned to Linz, this time attended by Steidle, Pfrimer, Pabst and many other leaders. At this second meeting Starhemberg's election was confirmed – which did not terminate the opposition of Gierlinger and his party.[110]

According to notes made later by an active National Socialist, Starhemberg's success was due to 'his nationalist past . . . and his oratorical gifts', so that within one year he gained the confidence of the most active members;

> his popularity rose like a meteor . . . An enthusiastic youth saw in him the leader of their dreams. Sunday after Sunday meetings took place, one demonstration followed upon the other. It seemed that the moment had come when this youthful movement with a drive without parallel would unhinge the whole democratic system of government, and establish a true government of the people with the best man at the helm. . . .

These notes also stress that the former leadership in Upper Austria had been 'democratic', but that Starhemberg was appointed 'with full power of command'; in other words the structure now became hierarchical.[111] Many local officials became anxious to hitch their waggon to the rising star. As one Bezirkshauptmann explained in 1929 to his superiors, his name was mentioned in a local Heimwehr meeting as an alleged opponent of its aims, and therefore (!) he sent a greetings telegram to a Heimwehr festival at Kremsmünster to which he was invited, but which he was unable to attend on account of ill health. He accepted full responsibility for his step.[112]

A police report of 1929 on the Heimwehr in Salzburg mentioned that here the Heimwehren were above all opposed 'to the flaws of the constitution and the present parliamentary system' and aimed at changing them by force if necessary; their hostility to 'Marxism' and the Republican Defence Corps was principally caused by the latter's rejection of any such change. The Heimwehr leaders were particularly active in providing jobs for their members and established an employment exchange for them which was used by many entrepreneurs and hotel owners so that the monopoly enjoyed by the trade unions in this respect was destroyed. Well-situated burghers and business men supported the Heimwehren financially, and they possessed an extensive intelligence service which disposed of large funds. In the city of Salzburg the Heimwehr had about 1,500 members, and in the Land about 10,000, mainly peasants, and a peasant was also the Land leader, with a lawyer as his second in command (Dr Franz Hueber, brother-in-law of Hermann Göring). The military leaders were two former colonels.[113]

In Graz, the Styrian capital, the Heimwehren were well organized and possessed a staff company, a sharp shooters detachment, and a student battalion apart from the other units, while the völkische and the Christian Turner and the Free Corps Oberland formed separate detachments within the Heimwehr organization.[114] A serious incident occurred in the small Styrian commune of Andritz in 1929; a Heimwehr unit halted its march in front of a factory canteen and shouted Heil, whereupon the workmen replied with the social-democratic greeting *Freundschaft*. The Heimwehr men retaliated by throwing stones through the windows and attacking the workers, but the latter were at first successful in defeating the attackers. Then these received massive reinforcements which quickly demolished everything inside the canteen and beat up the men and women present. When the mayor appeared on the scene the commandant of the Heimwehr unit informed him that he held him responsible for every man wounded and that he would not leave the place until all were bandaged, even if he must wait until the next morning.[115] In spite of these events, the authorities permitted a large-scale Heimwehr demonstration in Andritz only a few weeks later at which Dr Pfrimer and his chief of staff, Rauter, spoke.[116] It seems to have passed peacefully.

Not much of interest was reported from the Tyrol during this period. Curiously enough, Dr Steidle complained to the Tyrolese government about a lack of rifles for the local Heimwehren. The leaders 'are unable to fulfil numerous demands and even have to register some difficulty in the further expansion of the whole organization'. He hoped that the government would make good this defect from the depots of the financial administration or 'the black stocks of the brigade' of the Austrian army.[117] Clearly there were 'black' weapon depots in the Tyrol on which Steidle would have liked to lay his hands; but what happened to the vast quantities supplied from Bavaria and Italy during the past years? Had they all gone up in smoke? There is no reply of the Tyrolese government to Steidle's curious request in the file, and perhaps none was given.

To some Austrians, the great aristocratic names, which became prominent in the Heimwehren about this time, simply looked like a revival of noble and dynastic claims. According to a report sent by the German legation in Vienna to Berlin, these circles were now thinking of a come-back: 'The Starhembergs and Czernins, the Hohenbergs and Morseys scent the new air; they even form cavalry detachments, the horses of which they keep and feed. One thinks the Middle Ages have returned. . . .'[118] But this was a very much over-simplified picture. All fascist movements contained an element of protest against modernism and industrialism; many aimed at a return to 'blood and soil', at the restoration of a 'healthy' peasantry; many rejected modern trends in art and literature. Yet they were also modern mass movements, using highly modern propaganda techniques and aiming at sweeping constitutional changes. It could be argued, however, that the Heimwehren, if they had ever succeeded in seizing power in Austria, on account of their predominantly rural composition could not have introduced the radical social changes which became characteristic of Hitler's Germany. The Heimwehren seem to have possessed comparatively little social dynamism, and in this respect they corresponded more to the German para-military Stahlhelm and to the Finnish Lapua Movement than to the National Socialists. In all three cases — Stahlhelm, Lapua and

Heimwehren — the bulk of the members came from the peasantry and the more conservative countryside, rather than from the large industrial towns, and none of them developed into a political party proper. Nor did any of them produce a charismatic leader; but this was also true of the Austrian National Socialists.

NOTES

1. Gauleitung Unterinntal to *Landesleitung,* Melans, Absam, 30 September 1925: Tiroler Landesarchiv, Präsidialakten 1932, 303 III 10.

2. Gauleitung Mittel- und Westtirol to *Landesleitung,* Innsbruck, 17 April 1926: ibid.

3. Same to same, Innsbruck, 20 November 1924: ibid.

4. Steidle to Schober, 14 July 1925: see following note.

5. The above according to the correspondence in the Schober Nachlass, box 27/4 (Polizeiarchiv Wien): Steidle to Baron Ehrenfels, Innsbruck, 27 June 1925; Ehrenfels to Steidle, Vienna, 10 July; Steidle to Schober, Innsbruck, 27 June and 14 July 1925, with copies of the other letters.

6. German Consul at Innsbruck to *Auswärt. Amt,* 13 January 1927: Auswärt. Amt, Abt. II, Akten betr. Heimwehr-Organisationen, 6080 H, E450990.

7. Same to same, 9 August 1926: Bundesarchiv Koblenz, Reichskanzlei, R 43 I/108.

8. Same to same, Innsbruck, 27 October 1926: ibid.

9. Kommerzialrat Rhomberg to Dr Ender, Dornbirn, 29 December 1926; Ender to Rhomberg, 10 January, Rhomberg to Ender, 11 January 1927: Vorarlberger Landesarchiv, Präsidialakten 900, 1928; *Vorarlberger Volksblatt,* 31 December 1926, with the by-laws of the Heimatdienst.

10. The chairman of the Heimatdienst to Major Matt, 30 May 1927: ibid.

11. Steiermärk. Landesarchiv, Bezirkshauptmannschaft Graz 1927, Gruppe 14.

12. Lebenslauf Hanns Rauter, 15 February 1935: Institut für Zeitgeschichte, 2108/57.

13. Josef Hofmann, *Der Pfrimer-Putsch* (Vienna-Graz, 1965) 8-9.

14. '50 Jahre Burgenland', *Burgenländisches Leben,* XXII (11-12), Nov-Dec. 1971, 21.

15. Reports of Bezirkshauptmannschaft Mattersburg to Landesregierung, 1 May, 1 June, 1 July, 1 August 1926: Burgenländ. Landesarchiv, Regierungsarchiv, III-6/1926; Polizeikommissariat Eisenstadt to *Polizeiabteilung der Landesregierung,* 14 June 1926, ibid. The file contains many similar reports, showing the serious tension in the area caused by the para-military formations.

16. Bezirkshauptmannschaft Mattersburg to Landesregierung, 31 December 1926: ibid., III-16/1927.

17. *Burgenländische Freiheit*, Sauerbrunn, 4 February; *Bauernstimmen* (Burgenländische Ausgabe), Graz, 5 February 1927.

18. Bezirkshauptmannschaft Mattersburg to Landesregierung, 1 February 1927: Burgenländ. Landesarchiv, Regierungsarchiv, III-16/1927.

19. Same to same, 1 July 1927: ibid.

20. Police reports Vienna, 18 and 21 July 1927: Polizeiarchiv Wien, Nachlass Schober, box 87 (which contains all details about the events).

21. Franz Schweiger, 'Geschichte der niederösterreichischen Heimwehr von 1928 bis 1930' (Unpublished Ph.D. thesis, Vienna, 1964) 3.

22. Ibid., 5.

23. *Heimatschutz in Österreich* (Vienna, 1934) 75.

24. Dr Stumpf to Dr Steidle, Innsbruck, 17 July 1927, and account, s.d. (Sept. 1927): Tiroler Landesarchiv, Präsidialakten 1929, 1709 XII 57.

25. Tyrolese government to *Bundeskanzleramt*, Innsbruck, 4 August 1927: ibid.

26. Upper Austrian Hcimatwehr to Landeshauptmann Dr Schlegel, Linz, 17 July 1927: Oberösterreich. Landesarchiv, Nachlass Theodor Berger, Nr. 26.

27. See above, p. 66.

28. 'Vereinbarung, Judenburg, 18.7.1927': copy in Steiermärk. Landesarchiv, Bezirkshauptmannschaft Liezen, Gruppe 14; B. F. Pauley, *Hahnenschwanz und Hakenkreuz*, 49.

29. Thus *Der Panther — Steirische Heimatschutzzeitung*, 1. Jahrgang, Folge 13, Graz, 26 July 1930, in an article celebrating the third anniversary of the agreement. Cp. Pauley, op. cit., 49.

30. Report of the Hungarian envoy in Prague, Masirevich, about a conversation with Schober on 13 July, Prague, 16 July 1927: D. Nemes, ' "Die österreichische Aktion" der Bethlen-Regierung', *Acta Historica*, XI (Budapest, 1965) 191.

31. Opinion of the Hungarian army commander Jánky, quoted ibid., 197.

32. *Reichskommissar für die Überwachung der öffentlichen Ordnung*, 'Unruhen in Österreich', Berlin, 22 July 1927, 5: Bundesarchiv Koblenz, Reichskanzlei, R 43 I/109.

33. Schweiger, op. cit., 34.

34. Steidle's first memorandum for the Italians, emphasizing the danger of Bolshevism as well as those emanating from the Republican Defence Corps, is from April 1927: *I Documenti diplomatici Italiani*, 7th series, Vol. V (Rome, 1967) 177.

35. Memorandum for Bethlen, Innsbruck, 23 May 1928: L. Kerekes (ed.), 'Akten zu den geheimen Verbindungen zwischen der Bethlen-Regierung und der österreichischen Heimwehrbewegung', *Acta Historica*, XI (2) (Budapest, 1965) 309-10.

36. Steidle's declaration of 1 July 1928: ibid., no. 8, 317; Lajos Kerekes, 'Italien, Ungarn und die österreichische Heimwehrbewegung', *Österreich in Geschichte und Literatur*, IX (1) (1965) 2-6.

37. L. Kerekes, *Abenddämmerung einer Demokratie* (Vienna-Frankfurt-Zürich, 1966) 23; Nusser, *Konservative Wehrverbände* . . . 303-5.

38. For the Stahlhelm see: Volker R. Berghahn, *Der Stahlhelm, Bund der Frontsoldaten, 1918-1935* (Düsseldorf, 1966).

39. Steidle to Bethlen, Innsbruck, 4 March 1929: Kerekes, 'Akten zu den geheimen Verbindungen . . .', no. 13, 319-20; Kerekes, *Abenddämmerung einer Demokratie,* 32-3, on Pabst's visit to Berlin.

40. Schweiger, op. cit., 134, with a misspelling of Hölscher's name.

41. Note without signature, Vienna, 10 September 1929: Auswärt. Amt, Akten betr. Heimwehr-Organisationen, 6080H, E451059.

42. Front page photograph of *Stahlhelmer* parading in Salzburg on 6 July: *Der Panther,* 1. Jahrgang, Folge 12, Graz, 19 July 1930.

43. Kerekes, 'Akten zu den geheimen Verbindungen . . .', no. 16, 324.

44. Bethlen's message for Steidle, 27 September 1929: Kerekes, *Abenddämmerung einer Demokratie, 52.*

45. Walkó's conversation with Steidle, 20 September 1929: Kerekes, 'Akten zu den geheimen Verbindungen . . .', no. 21, 329-30.

46. Unsigned notes, 'Die Rolle Italiens in der österreichischen Heimwehrpolitik, Wien, 14. November 1929': Oberösterreich. Landesarchiv, Nachlass Theodor Berger, Nr. 27; they seem well informed.

47. 'Major Pabst über sein Aktionsprogramm, Wien, 1. November 1929': ibid. These seem to be notes written by someone present at Pabst's talk.

48. *Der Panther,* 3. Jahrgang, Folge 49, Graz, 10 December 1932.

49. Habicht to Hitler, Linz, 4 November 1932: Bundesarchiv Koblenz, Sammlung Schumacher, Nr. 305 I.

50. *Die Heimwehr,* Nr. 2, 11 January 1929, quoted by Schweiger, op. cit., Vol. II, 104.

51. Steidle in Amstetten on 1 July 1928: ibid., 25.

52. Police report, Vienna, 20 July 1929: Polizeiarchiv Wien, Nachlass Schober, box 31.

53. Detailed report by Schober, Vienna, 31 August 1929: ibid. (12 pp.).

54. Pauley, *Hahnenschwanz und Hakenkreuz,* 60, referring to the year 1928.

55. Schweiger, 'Geschichte der niederösterreichischen Heimwehr . . .', 11, 29, 53-59.

56. *Gendarmeriepostenkommando* Bruck to *Bezirkshauptmannschaft* Bruck an der Mur, 6 October 1928: Steiermärk. Landesarchiv, Bezirkshauptmannschaft Bruck, Gruppe Vrst.

57. Count Lerchenfeld to Auswärtiges Amt, Vienna, 20 September 1928: Bundesarchiv Koblenz, Reichskanzlei, R 43 I/110.

58. Tyrolese government to Bundeskanzleramt, Innsbruck, 13 November 1928: Verwaltungsarchiv Wien, Bundeskanzleramt, 22/gen., box 4865.

59. Schweiger, op. cit., 89-90.

60. Polizeidirektion Graz to Bundeskanzleramt, 13 November 1929: Verwaltungsarchiv Wien, Bundeskanzleramt, 22/gen., box 4865; Austrian report of 16 November 1929: Bundesarchiv Koblenz, Reichskanzlei, R 43 I/110.

61. *Deutschösterreichische Tageszeitung,* 3 December 1929: Verwaltungsarchiv Wien, Bundeskanzleramt, 22/gen., box 4866. For Starhemberg and Oberland see below, p. 131.

62. Pauley, op. cit., 52.

63. 'Zusammenfassender Bericht über die auftragsgemäss bei den Werks-

betrieben der österr. Alpine Montangesellschaft durchgeführten Erhebungen',
Graz, 30 August 1934: Verwaltungsarchiv Wien, Bundeskanzleramt 22/gen.,
box 4923; Hans Hautmann and Rudolf Kropf, *Die österreichische Arbeiterbewegung
vom Vormärz bis 1945* (Vienna, 1974) 158-59.
64. See above, p. 66.
65. Kerekes, *Abenddämmerung einer Demokratie . . .*, 24.
66. Kerekes, 'Akten zu den geheimen Verbindungen . . .', no. 11, 318.
General Jánky was councillor at the Hungarian legation in Vienna.
67. Memorandum by the Styrian landowner Freiherr Ferdinand Patz, May
1928: Nemes, ' "Die österreichische Aktion" der Bethlen-Regierung', *Acta
Historica*, XI (1965) 200.
68. Walter Goldinger, 'Der geschichtliche Ablauf der Ereignisse in Österreich
von 1918 bis 1945', in H. Benedikt (ed.), *Geschichte der Republik Österreich*
(Vienna, 1954) 158.
69. Schweiger, op. cit., 80, 201.
70. Klemens von Klemperer, *Ignaz Seipel* (Princeton, 1972) 289; Peter
Huemer, 'Sektionschef Robert Hecht und die Entstehung der ständisch-
autoritären Verfassung' (Unpublished Ph.D. thesis, Vienna, 1968) 580.
71. Klemperer, op. cit., 356.
72. German Legation Vienna to von Bülow, 23 August 1929: Auswärt. Amt,
Abt. II, Akten betr. Heimwehr, 6080H, E451042-43.
73. Klemperer, op. cit., 357.
74. Thus Vinzenz Schumy, leader of Peasant League, in MS. on Heimwehr
written in 1938, pp. 30, 35: Institut für Zeitgeschichte, Vienna.
75. Thus Steidle to the Hungarian foreign minister on 20 September 1929:
Kerekes, 'Akten zu den geheimen Verbindungen . . .', no. 21, 330.
76. 'Gedächtnisstütze über den Bericht des Landeshauptmannstellvertreters
Langoth an Landeshauptmann Dr Schlegel über Unterredung mit Schober im
September 1929': Oberösterr. Landesarchiv, Nachlass Dr Schlegel, Nr. 1/Fasz. 2.
77. Thus MS. by Schumy, p. 46: Institut für Zeitgeschichte, Vienna.
78. Police report, Graz, 9 May 1931, on meeting of Styrian Heimwehr:
Steiermärk. Landesarchiv, Landesamtsdirektion 1932, 384 He 2.
79. Thus MS. by Schumy, p. 46, on conversation with Schober about the
middle of November 1929: loc cit.
80. Kerekes, introduction to 'Akten zu den geheimen Verbindungen . . .',
304.
81. Secret instructions for Auriti, 1 December 1930: Oberösterr. Landesarchiv, Nachlass Th. Berger, Nr. 27. The claim was of course incorrect.
82. *Heimwehr*, Nr. 40, 4 October 1929, quoted by Schweiger, op. cit., Vol.
II, 160.
83. Thus a confidential report from Vienna sent to the *Reichskanzlei* on 17
January 1930: Bundesarchiv Koblenz, Reichskanzlei, R 43 I/111.
84. 'Aktionsplan der Heimwehrführung', Vienna, 14 October 1929: Oberösterr. Landesarchiv, Nachlass Th. Berger, Nr. 27.
85. Confidential report from Austria sent to Reichskanzlei on 17 January
1930: Bundesarchiv Koblenz, Reichskanzlei, R 43 I/111.
86. '123. Sitzung des Verbandes der Abgeordneten der Grossdeutschen
Volkspartei am 14. Mai 1929': Verwaltungsarchiv Wien, Grossdeutsche Volkspartei, box 6. The speaker was Dr Straffner, the opponent Fahrner.

87. Schweiger, op. cit., Vol. I, 150.

88. Kerekes, *Abenddämmerung einer Demokratie,* 66.

89. Bundespolizeikommissariat Klagenfurt to Bundeskanzleramt, 22 August 1929: Verwaltungsarchiv Wien, Bundeskanzleramt, 22/gen., box 4865.

90. Report from Graz, 4 September 1929, and from Salzburg, 10 September: ibid.

91. Report of Upper Austrian Landesgendarmeriekommando, Linz, 28 November 1927: Oberösterr. Landesarchiv, Politische Akten, Nr. 18.

92. Schweiger, op. cit., 187.

93. Report by Schober, Vienna, 31 August 1929: Verwaltungsarchiv Wien, Bundeskanzleramt, 22/gen., box 4865, pp. 3-6.

94. Report of Bezirkshauptmannschaft Oberwart, 12 December 1928: Burgenländ. Landesarchiv, Regierungsarchiv, III-16/1929.

95. Report of Bezirkshauptmannschaft Neusiedl, 2 October 1929: ibid.

96. Reports of Bezirkshauptmannschaft Mattersburg and Güssing, 7 October and 4 November 1929: ibid.

97. Report of Bezirkshauptmannschaft Eisenstadt, 28 December 1928, with note of 9 January 1929: ibid., III-3/1928.

98. Report of Polizeikommissariat Eisenstadt, 17 December 1928: ibid.

99. Report of Bundespolizeikommissariat Eisenstadt, 8 October 1929: ibid., III-16/1929.

100. Report of Bezirkshauptmannschaft Eisenstadt, 31 October 1929: ibid.

101. Report of Bezirkshauptmannschaft Neusiedl, 31 May 1929: ibid.

102. Reports of Bundespolizeikommissariat Eisenstadt, 11 February, 30 April and 28 May 1930: ibid., III-31/1930.

103. Reports of Bezirkshauptmannschaft Neusiedl, 26 February and 1 April 1930: ibid.

104. Satzungen des 'Heimatschutzverbandes Burgenland', Mattersburg, 17 August 1927, and Satzungen des Heimatschutzgaues 'Nordburgenland', 28 October 1929: ibid, Burgenländ. Vereinsakten, A/IV-14, Nr. 1098, 1041.

105. Bundespolizeidirektion Linz to *Bundeskanzleramt,* 24 September 1929: Verwaltungsarchiv Wien, Bundeskanzleramt, 22/gen., box 4865.

106. 'Aufzeichnungen des Fürsten Ernst Rüdiger Starhemberg bis zum Jahre 1938 verfasst während des zweiten Weltkrieges in London', MS. in Institut für Zeitgeschichte, Vienna, p. 29.

108. 'Lebenserinnerungen des Fürsten Ernst Rüdiger von Starhemberg von ihm selbst verfasst im Winter 1938/39 in Saint Gervais', MS. ibid. This is the earlier version which in some ways is much more revealing than the other.

109. Lecture by Peter Graf Revertera on 'Heimwehr' on 9 March 1961: Herrschaftsarchiv Helfenberg, Upper Austria.

110. Report by Bundespolizeidirektion Wien, 21 July 1929: Polizeiarchiv Wien, Nachlass Schober, box 31.

111. 'Heimatwehr in Oberösterreich' by Pg. [sic!´] Gustav Wurm jun., s.d. Oberösterr. Landesarchiv, Nachlass Theodor Berger, Nr. 31. These admissions are the more remarkable coming from a political opponent of Starhemberg. The notes seem to have been written after 1938.

112. Dr Strasnicky, Bezirkshauptmann of Steyr, to Upper Austrian government, 7 September 1929: Oberösterr. Landesarchiv, Landesregierungsarchiv, Nr. 7.

113. Bundespolizeidirektion Salzburg to Bundeskanzleramt, 10 September 1929: Verwaltungsarchiv Wien, Bundeskanzleramt, 22/gen., box 4865.

114. Polizeidirektion Graz to Landeshauptmann Dr Rintelen, 9 October 1928: Steiermärk. Landesarchiv, Landesamtsdirektion 1928, 384 W 26. This report concerns the return of the Heimwehr from the demonstration in Wiener Neustadt, above, p. 120.

115. Gemeindeamt Andritz to Styrian government, 28 March 1929: ibid., Bezirkshauptmannschaft Graz 1929, Gruppe 14.

116. Rauter to Bezirkshauptmannschaft Graz-Umgebung, 21 March 1929: ibid.

117. Steidle to Tyrolese government, Innsbruck, 9 January 1928: Tiroler Landesarchiv, Präsidialakten 1929, 1709 XII 57.

118. German Legation Vienna to von Bülow, 23 August 1929: Auswärt. Amt, Abt. II, Akten betr. Heimwehr, 6080H, E451049.

7

HITLER STAKES HIS CLAIM IN AUSTRIA

The years following upon the great crisis of 1923 saw in Austria —
exactly as in Germany — a sharp decline in the strength and influence
of the National Socialists. The burning of the Palace of Justice in
Vienna and the riots and strikes accompanying it benefited the Heimwehren, but not the National Socialists who played no part in these
events. The economic situation was improving, and for the time being
the National Socialists became a small sect on the fringes of the
extreme right. This was also due to their internal dissensions and the
fact that — after the expulsion of Dr Riehl — they lacked a leader of
sufficient stature to rally the faithful. Indeed, at least in Vienna, many
of them joined Riehl's 'German Social Association' founded in 1924. In
August 1924, at a meeting to discuss its foundation, Riehl sharply
attacked the leaders of the National Socialist Party and the developments within it. After him, the chairman of the party in the district of
Leopoldstadt (the Jewish quarter) announced that his group had decided to dissolve itself and to join the new Association. The leaders of
the districts of Brigittenau and Hernals gave assurances to the same
effect. But in reality there was a split: in Hernals, where the party had
about 200 members, 120 joined Riehl's Association, and about 30 to
40 remained faithful to the National Socialists, as the police reported.

They also stated that the party lost 'a not inconsiderable number of members' in the Viennese districts of Leopoldstadt, Brigittenau and Währing.[1] Even so, the 'German Social Association' remained a very small group. Especially outside Vienna it hardly made any impact, and the majority of the members followed Hitler, not Riehl, although his tactics of participating in elections were adopted by Hitler and amply justified by later events.

Even before Hitler was released from his 'honourable imprisonment'. in Landsberg fortress at the end of 1924 the Austrian National Socialists assured him of their undying loyalty. Only three weeks after the Putsch, the commander of the Austrian SA wrote to Hitler that the events in Munich had given them a most severe shock; on this occasion they wanted to give to the Führer 'the most solemn assurances that we remain bound to you in an unbreakable and unshakable faith and are now as before convinced that you alone are entitled to free Germany and the whole German nation from its terrible plight and to lead them to a brighter future'. The SA men, by an oath to Adolf Hitler, confirmed anew that they devoted their lives to him.[2] All SA men were asked to write to Hitler at Landsberg. The National Socialist Party prepared 'an Address of Homage' which was to be presented to Hitler personally on his release. Money for a present was to be sent in not later than 1 May 1924 with the note 'Homage' and the form of the present was to be decided later.[3]

A party conference held in August elected Karl Schulz, a skilled workman, as the party's new chairman. But the party's development was severely hampered by lack of funds. Even for its current expenditure it had to borrow money on a large scale. In mid-1924 the debts accumulated came to more than 400 million crowns (before the stabilization of the currency) and early in 1925 they still stood at more than a 100 million crowns, so that an efficient propaganda became impossible, and the membership continued to decline.[4] When the assorted völkisch organizations of Vienna protested against the peace treaties of St Germain and Versailles in September 1924 the 'swastika' contingent, according to the police, amounted to only 1,496 people, less than a third of that of the Turner and less than half of that of the Front-kämpfer Association.[5]

With Hitler's release there came renewed signs of party activity and close contacts with Munich were re-established. While earlier National Socialist meetings were poorly attended, a public meeting in March 1925, which was to be addressed by Julius Streicher, mobilized more than 1,700 participants, but Streicher was prevented from speaking. A strike of the railwaymen in November 1924 was largely caused by National Socialist demands and gave then an opportunity to recruit new members. A strong National Socialist group was formed at Vienna's Technical University; at the elections to the students' union in February 1925 it emerged as by far the largest group, with 14 out of 30 mandates in the student chamber.[6]

The party congress held in Vienna in August 1925 was attended by about 300 people, partly delegates, partly guests; among the latter were Gottfried Feder from Munich and the deputy Hans Knirsch from Bohemia. A telegram of homage was sent to Hitler, and Karl Schulz was re-elected party chairman, with the engineer Rudolf Zwerina as his second in command. The party treasurer was able to report that the debts had been reduced from 260 million crowns to a mere 25 million; but it is not clear whether this was due to contributions from Bohemia or Munich.[7] During the same month the National Socialists, allied with several other völkisch groups, organized severe riots in Vienna on the occasion of the opening of the international Zionist Congress — riots that were sharply criticized by the Grossdeutsche who accused the National Socialists of fomenting them.[8] In Vienna, the issue of anti-Semitism was clearly still very much alive and provided the National Socialists with ready propaganda material. Relations between the National Socialists and the Grossdeutsche were not improved by the fact that the former — revising their decision of 1923 to boycott the elections — put up their own candidates in local elections and thus prevented the election of Grossdeutsche as mayors in many communes.[9]

In 1925 too, strikes occupied the attention of the party. In September 4,000 workers went on strike for better wages at the Donawitz works of the *Alpine Montangesellschaft*. Only 600 of them belonged to the socialist unions and there was very little money for strike pay. Hence the Styrian party leaders addressed an urgent appeal to Munich for help: 'If they were deprived of this pitiful support our party comrades would be driven back to work and the strike would be broken. You will be able to imagine the effects on our movement. The most dreadful is hardly conceivable' [*sic*]; and the Munich Party was asked to collect 'a large sum' among its members, without any delay. But the reply was bitterly disappointing: in Munich too, the financial situation was so difficult that there was no hope of collecting any 'special funds'.[10] Even this reply was only sent after a delay of three weeks when the strike was presumably over. What it did not say was whether the Munich leaders approved or disapproved of the more radical Austrian tactics.

In October the party itself was hit by a strike — an almost unparallelled event in the party's history. The editor and the administrative 'officials' of the party paper, *Deutsche Arbeiterpresse,* demanded higher salaries which were refused by the leaders, although the party secretary and some SA leaders were in favour. The leaders split into two groups, for and against, which fought each other bitterly; but those opposed to the demands carried the day on account of the party's bad financial situation. Thereupon the 'officials' went on strike because 'their most modest salary demands were not met', while other party functionaries were paid large amounts by way of 'expenses' every month, among them the second chairman Zwerina and the treasurer. Early in November the leaders of the local Viennese groups were summoned to discuss the issue and decided, after a lengthy debate, to dismiss the strikers, who had meanwhile aired their grievances in public. But that was not the end of the matter. Many members strongly disapproved of the behaviour of the party leaders, there were accusations and counter-accusations, and the second chairman and the treasurer resigned their offices and left the party. Another meeting of the local leaders decided to appoint a committee of investigation under a non-party chairman which was to report to an extraordinary party conference. As a result, the activity of the party suffered badly and far fewer meetings were held. Even the *Deutsche Arbeiterpresse* did not appear regularly. Its new editor, Walter Gattermayer, was sharply criticized by party members for his dealings with an allegedly 'Jewish' bank (he was not the only leader so accused) and in his turn resigned all party offices at the end of 1925.[11]

The conflict was to some extent a clash between the party leaders and the activists organized in the Vaterländische Schutzbund (SA) who objected to 'corruption' in higher circles, but the SA was still very small at this time. In the summer of 1924 the Vienna police counted only 516 men in the whole city, including 36 in the reserve and 75 older men, and another few hundred in Lower Austria. In Vienna itself, they were organized in four companies and two separate detachments.[12]

The conflict erupted at the extraordinary party conference at Linz in February 1926 which was attended by 110 delegates. Even before it started a representative of the SA demanded that its members should be allowed to watch proceedings from the gallery; but this was refused, probably out of fear of noisy interruptions and cat-calls. Then Schulz reported in detail on the inter-party clashes, especially those between the leaders and the 'opposition' to which he reckoned 'numerous members of the Vaterländische Schutzbund'. He was followed by the chairman of the committee of investigation, the old Schönerianer Dr Ursin, who listed 'the incorrectness committed by several party functionaries'. Then numerous delegates from both sides spoke; their speeches were interrupted by much 'noisy uproar which frequently threatened to degenerate into blows'. The main 'culprit', Zwerina, had not appeared and left the party, while the former treasurer resigned. Of the leaders criticized, only Gattermayer was present and tried to refute the attacks upon him, pointing in particular to his long services to the party, but this did not pacify the opposition. In the end the party leaders were victorious and Schulz was re-elected chairman, with Leo Haubenberger, a railway official, as his deputy. But the opposition continued its activities after the conference and was successful in gaining many new adherents, not only in Vienna, but also in Lower and Upper Austria.[13]

Indeed, in April 1926 Vienna was treated to two separate celebrations of Hitler's 37th birthday. In that organized by the 'opposition' on the day before the great event about 500 people participated. They were addressed by Professor Richard Suchenwirth who could claim that he had seen the Leader in person in Munich on Good Friday. In that organized by the party chairman Schulz about 800 took part. Schulz described in detail Hitler's life and the development of his party and vowed that the party would always act in Hitler's spirit, but was also willing to work in parliament 'if that were to the advantage of the German nation' — the latter clearly a concession on Schulz's part. He expelled from the party the local groups of Josephstadt, Hernals and Währing, as well as Suchenwirth, Ernst Graber, the former party secretary, and several others because they refused to recognize him as the party leader. Thereupon Suchenwirth called together the adherents of the opposition, about 150 people, and attacked the party leaders, in particular on account of their financial maladministration which had resulted in the accumulation of heavy debts, and because they did not promote the National Socialist ideas as energetically as Hitler desired it. It was then decided to leave the National Socialist Party and to found a new party with the name of 'National Socialist German Workers' Association of Austria (Hitler Movement)', with Suchenwirth and the former Major Leopold Eder as the leaders.[14] There were now in Austria two organizations which both recognized Hitler as their supreme leader but were openly hostile to each other.

It seems that during the months following Suchenwirth and Eder were the more successful of the rivals in winning over Hitler to their side. They had, after all, added the words 'Hitler Movement' to the party's name which it was to preserve during the following years. In any case, when the factions reassembled in August 1926 it was under Hitler's chairmanship at Passau, in Germany. Hitler addressed them for two hours. Above all, he emphasized the differences between the German and the Austrian parties: the old Austrian party was in his opinion a party like many others; it had never been dissolved by the authorities, while the German party was the victim of constant prohibitions by its adversaries. In Austria, Hitler claimed, they had considered the failure of 8-9 November 1923 'as the end of the movement in Germany', but because of it the German party gained two million votes (in the general election of May 1924 the party obtained 1,918,000 votes); this could not have been achieved 'through a resolution as was the custom in Austria'. The German movement from the day of its foundation was intolerant, opposed to compromises or unions with others; it had always been convinced that in a long struggle the stronger would win through. Italian Fascism, which once counted only a few thousand men, had not united with the organizations of ex-servicemen with their hundreds of thousands of members, but alone it fought on and gained victory; such methods were necessary in Austria too.

His own party once had sixty members and now it polled two million votes (this was not correct, for in the second general election of 1924 the party's vote was reduced to 907,000). The National Socialist Party Congress at Weimar had decided in favour of the formation of *one* party for Germany and Austria. This was considered 'worthy of consideration' by the Austrian National Socialists under Schulz, who wanted the decision to be taken by a proper party conference. In Hitler's opinion, however, such a discussion was of no importance, 'for the Anschluss will come in any case', and surely the party congress 'of the whole German Reich was more competent' than a mere Austrian one. It was essential that the Gau Austria of the National Socialist Party of Greater Germany be led by a man who possessed the confidence of all those who until now had opposed each other, who was capable of acting without summoning first endless conferences, who would assert the Leadership Principle down to the last local group. He must strongly

reject the opinion that the Austrian district had a weight different from
that of Cologne, Rhineland, Thuringia or East Prussia, for the difference between these districts and Bavaria was certainly not greater
than that between Bavaria and Austria. Essential too was the 'uni-
formity of the programmatic basis which must not be shaken by
anyone'. According to the police report, Hitler also demanded that 'the
Austrian party comrades' accept unconditionally his leadership and
become an Austrian Gau of the all-German party.[15]

Apparently there was no discussion because Hitler insisted on a
simple declaration whether those present accepted him as the Leader or
not. Schulz did not return to the meeting but sent in a note that he
must adhere to his party's previous decision, i.e. a party conference
should be summoned, and that he must have time for reflection. Major
Eder, on the other hand, once more emphasized that he, for his
association, accepted 'complete co-ordination' with the German party
and 'subordination without reservation to the leadership of the NSDAP
of Greater Germany'. This declaration was also given by the representatives of the party from Carinthia (Ferdinand Scherian), Styria (Heinrich
Schmidt), Upper Austria (Alfred Proksch) and the Waldviertel district
of Lower Austria. The representative of Vorarlberg declared that they
had not received a letter from Munich, hence were unable to contact
their members and would decide later. No representative appeared from
the Tyrol, but it was said that they too would conform to the decision
of the other Länder representatives.

The only dissent came from Salzburg. Its representative, Nikolaus
Schlamm, stated that they too were willing to recognize Hitler, but
were unwilling to acknowledge some members of the 'opposition' as
leaders; the question of personnel was the decisive one; in Austria, the
trade union issue (Schlamm was a union official) was far more important than it was for Germany because the position of the workers
was much worse in Austria, and anyone who achieved a better wage for
the worker was looked at as a saint; idealism alone would not catch any
worker. The trade union issue was also one of the questions on which
Schulz differed from Hitler: it indicated a social composition of the
Austrian party somewhat different from the German one. At the end of
the meeting it was agreed to hold a conference of the Gau Austria in
Munich after about two weeks, where the details of the complete
incorporation of the Austrian party were to be settled. The result
clearly was 'a great success' for Hitler.[16] It was above all due to the fact
that the Austrian National Socialists had not produced a man able to

unite the party and to overcome the never-ending splits and rivalries.

Schulz and Gattermayer, however, refused to give way and to make their submission to Hitler. They declared that they held different views on 'the political tactics of the party'. Both were old trade unionists with strong roots in the völkisch unions, while the leaders approved by Hitler who now took the helm in Austria were largely of middle-class origin. These social differences may well have been important in causing the new split. But the two were soon deserted by many of their followers. Hitler's oratory and willpower, the vast self-confidence he exuded, his prestige as the acknowledged leader of a considerably larger party – however phoney the claim of two million voters was – carried the day. The fact that he too was an Austrian may also have had some influence: the Austrians had no leader of their own and so they acclaimed the Austrian from Munich, the man who had suffered imprisonment for his deed of 1923, the man who would unite the warring factions. He accomplished a mini-Anschluss – a foretaste of bigger things to come. His praise of Italian Fascism and of fascist methods appeled to the activists who formed the core of the Austrian party and who disliked the 'soft' tactics of Riehl and Schulz. Only a few weeks after the Passau meeting the Vienna police reported that many members of the National Socialist Party left Schulz and adhered to the National Socialist Workers' Association, including significantly the members of the SA, 'in fact, if not officially'. The leaders of the Association announced their sharpest opposition to the Schulz party, which 'already has lost all significant influence in the National Socialist movement'; its meetings were interrupted and broken up by its adversaries.[17] In Styria only 4 out of 41 local groups remained loyal to Schulz.[18]

In the eyes of the Grossdeutsche, the various factions tried to

> court the favour of the Party Pope Hitler who finally concluded that the proper National Socialists in Austria were the Suchenwirth people. . . . Schulz now, exactly as before the year 1923, stands for the old National Socialist programme. He accepts the basis of existing realities. The Hitler people . . . want to be a movement, they preach against interest capitalism, against parliament and want to obtain their demands through a national revolution. They reject the democratic structure of the party . . . .[19]

When Schulz assembled his followers at a party conference at the end of October 1926 only about 25 delegates appeared. They were informed that the party had already approached the Grossdeutsche, the

Frontkämpfer and Dr Riehl with the plan of forming a united völkisch front for the impending elections, and the delegates expressed their consent to this approach. Significantly, however, the representatives of Carinthia and Tyrol demanded that the party should do everything to bring about a reunification with the Hitler Movement and should once more accept Hitler as the leader.[20] Even among the minority loyal to Schulz Hitler's name cast its spell. He may have been the 'Party Pope', but apparently there was no alternative leader.

It had been announced at Passau that within a few weeks Hitler would appoint a Gauführer for Austria. For reasons unknown, the choice fell on a retired army colonel, Friedrich Jankovic, who was fifty-five years old and had not played a prominent part in the party so far. All that the police were able to report about him was that he spoke several times in meetings in eastern Styria; 'his speeches always had a sharp anti-semitic character'.[21] Perhaps Hitler hoped that an older man with a military background who had not been involved in the faction fights would be more respected as his new Gauleiter; perhaps he wanted to remove the party leadership from Vienna where the faction fights were particularly bitter. If so, Hitler's hopes were quickly disappointed. The personal conflicts among the new leaders continued, and so did the party's financial difficulties. According to the Upper Austrian leader Alfred Proksch, Jankovic 'was a complete failure'; according to the police, he had bitter conflicts with other party leaders. In Upper Austria, heavy debts accumulated and the party paper had only 680 subscribers; the activists numbered a mere 200, and the party had no credit whatsoever; 'it was hopeless'.[22] Jankovic was particularly criticized by Proksch for having mismanaged the party's tactics in the elections of April 1927 'so that no one knew what is to happen'.

While Schulz joined a block not only with the Grossdeutsche, but locally also with the Christian Social Party, the Hitler Movement went it alone; but in some areas it adhered to its old tactics of boycotting the elections, and in still others it supported the 'national' block. In the end it received 27,000 votes — a shattering defeat. But the National Socialists at least gained one seat each in the diets of Carinthia and Styria in the provincial elections.[23] In the opinion of the Grossdeutsche, the disunity in the 'national' camp only benefited the Social Democrats. They praised the Turnerbund and the Union of völkisch organizations for supporting the grossdeutsch policy of an anti-marxist united front, while the National Socialists had too many different opinions. Even the Schulz group was divided among itself, above all on the question whether the united front should also include the Christian Social Party. For Vienna with its strong Social Democracy Schulz favoured unity, but he was much more doubtful for the other Länder.[24] In spite of the united front tactics, neither Schulz nor Riehl was elected in Vienna.

Even before the elections Jankovic handed in his resignation as Gauführer of the Hitler Movement because he was 'no longer in agreement with the general direction which our movement in Austria has taken on account of different influences'[25] — a veiled hint at the faction fights and at Munich's interference. A few days later Hitler accepted with alacrity and decreed, apparently without any prior consultations with the Austrians: for the time being there would be no successor to Jankovic, but the Austrian Gaue would be directly subordinate to the Party Leadership in Munich. Two Austrian leaders were specifically mentioned by Hitler: the Styrian leader Heinrich Schmidt was appointed the legal representative or *Obmann* of the Austrian movement; and Major Eder at Krems, the faithful follower of Passau, was put in charge of the Gau Vienna, which had been dissolved 'on account of severe breaches of discipline', but only on a provisional basis, 'until the Gau had been internally strengthened and could be readmitted as an independent link of the movement'. Eder was also to investigate whether the party paper, *Österreichischer Nationalsozialist*, could survive economically.[26]

How bad things were in general, not only in Vienna but in the whole of Austria, emerged from another circular emanating from Munich only a few weeks later, in May 1927. The following tasks for the current year were stipulated: the party organization in Austria must be strengthened by training all members to the punctual payment of their membership dues and the punctual transfer of the agreed proportion of these to the Gau, and from there to the central office for Austria; by the settlement of all existing debts; and by the 'unconditional subordination of all party comrades to the appointed leaders'. The leaders were enjoined 'to remain at their post until they are relieved from it', and the members 'to earnest co-operation . . . without receiving a special invitation': clearly, many had not even carried out these duties. A handwritten note on a copy signed by Hitler further prescribed the compilation of proper membership lists and card indices.[27] The opinion in Munich on the conduct of party affairs in Austria must have been extremely low if even such elementary tasks had to be stressed. The Austrians must first be taught the most primitive rules of party management — and there was no objection from the Austrian side.

As a result of these internal conflicts the activities of the National Socialists became very muted. In Vienna, in contrast with earlier times, there were few public meetings, and even these were badly attended. The membership also declined, in particular that of the SA among whose leaders there were 'serious clashes of opinion'. At an assembly of its men in June 1927 which should have been attended by 600 members hardly 90 appeared. The financial difficulties facing the paper, *Österreichischer Nationalsozialist,* increased, and the party's daily paper, *Deutschösterreichische Tageszeitung,* also lost many subscribers.[28]

What did not abate was the vitriolic anti-semitic propaganda of National Socialist speakers. At a meeting held in Graz in 1926 the principal speaker, Walther Rentmeister from Klagenfurt, declared that 'the Jew looks upon the Aryan as a slave and upon his children as cattle'; Jewish exploitation and enrichment at the expense of the workers was made easy

> because unfortunately the majority of the working people . . . are organized internationally and the leadership of this organization is exclusively in Jewish hands. The whole essence of Jewry, which aims at completely enslaving, exploiting, looting and robbing the Aryan proletariat, is supported not only by this organization, but also by the Christian Social and German Nationalist parties as well as by the whole government.

Therefore all efforts must be made to carry out the National Socialist programme, above all the abolition of the parliamentary system, closure of the stock exchange, confiscation of the fraudulently acquired Jewish money and of 'the so powerful lending and banking capital'. The next speaker, the Graz Obmann of the völkisch white-collar trade union, discussed especially the Jewish influence on the bureaucracy which was evident in Graz too.[29]

Only eleven months after the memorable meeting at Passau another meeting of Hitler and the Austrian National Socialists was organized, this time at Freilassing in Bavaria, just across the Austrian frontier, so that 190 Austrians could get there on foot, and another 50 or so by train. First there was a private meeting to discuss the possible unification of the several National Socialist groups. For this the Schulz party suggested the formation of one National Socialist Party of 'Greater Germany' under Hitler as the Leader, including Austria as well as German Bohemia. The Austrian groups were to be united by a committee of leaders on which each group was to be represented by an equal number and which was to decide unanimously; after unification a special conference of all Austrian National Socialists was to elect an Austrian Leader in agreement with Munich. This suggested revival of a democratic procedure can hardly have recommended itself to Hitler; it was an open challenge to his position gained at Passau.

Hitler's reaction was unequivocal. At a public meeting following upon the internal one he once more exclaimed that 'a strong movement could never win through by way of a compromise or by an amalgamation of currents of different kinds. He therefore must repudiate any negotiations about questions of principle because only that current would prevail which conducted the fight in the most intensive manner.' To conquer in this struggle he could only use men willing to keep strict discipline and to carry out his orders. Once more Hitler sharply criticized the old Austrian National Socialism, which 'was a more or less marxist phenomenon that did not differ in principle from Marxism and was only a little more national than the former. Within its own ranks, it adhered to the majority principle' – a cardinal sin in Hitler's eyes. The public meeting was followed by another private one in which Hitler again categorically refused to appoint an Austrian leader of the Hitler Movement because none of the Austrians had given proof that he was qualified to occupy such a post. Instead the organizations in the individual Länder were to be subordinate directly to Munich. He added that he had no hope that a proper party organization could be created in Vienna, but in the other Länder an intensive propaganda activity had good prospects and would lead to a revival of the movement. A delegation of the Styrian Heimwehren under Dr Pfrimer was also present at Freilassing and reached an agreement with Hitler about friendly co-operation.[30]

All that the Austrians were able to achieve was the election for Austria of a party Obmann, Wilhelm Gruchol from Graz, with two deputies and one party secretary, Alfred Proksch from Linz.[31] But this election was probably carried out on account of legal requirements, and not because Hitler approved of it, and there is no sign of any great political activity of the new Obmann. Another circular, issued in Munich in September 1927, decreed that every party member had to pay four Schillings as a 'press sacrifice' to pay off the press debts. The *Österreichische Nationalsozialist*, which had caused a large part of the debts, was transferred to Linz and transformed into a subsidiary of the Linz *Volksstimme*. Any joint action or close co-operation with völkisch or anti-semitic organizations was prohibited; but local agreements with the Heimwehren were permitted, provided that the National Socialists would march separately as a unit in any demonstration.[32] In spite of the agreed friendly co-operation the Styrian National Socialists and Heimwehren remained quite separate organizations.

It seems very doubtful, however, whether Hitler's personal interventions and the decrees sent from Munich had much effect in Austria where things continued much as before. Between the summer of 1927 and that of 1928 most of the Austrian Gauleiter were replaced by new men, but this did not significantly improve the party's fortunes. The membership figures remained pitifully low. In June 1928 only Lower Austria had a figure above a thousand members followed by Styria and Vienna with over 900 each, and Upper Austria and Carinthia with fewer than 700 and fewer than 500, respectively. Salzburg had a mere 120 and Tyrol only 112 members. For the whole of Austria the figure was 4,466.[33] During the following year there was a slight increase to 5,002;[34] but this was insignificant at a time when the German party was growing rapidly: it had 108,000 paying members in 1928 and 178,000 in 1929.[35] Indeed, on account of the very small membership it was decided in 1928 to combine the three western Gaue, Salzburg, Tyrol and Vorarlberg, into one *Westgau*, under Heinrich Suske as Gauleiter.[36] The Schulz party on the other hand, had 6,274 paying members in November 1928 and was thus somewhat stronger than the Hitler Movement,[37] a very surprising fact which might be explained by its winning new members from various völkisch organisations. But the membership of both parties was so small that neither made any impact in Austria, at a time when the Heimwehren became a mass organization.

In May 1928 the Grossdeutsche noted that the Hitler Movement was receiving new encouragement from Germany (where the party had just polled 810,000 votes in a general election − not a very impressive figure). At the Turner festival at Krems in Lower Austria the National Socialists demonstratively appeared in green shirts and used the fascist salute with outstretched right arm, although it was previously agreed not to engage in party propaganda.[38] The Grossdeutsche were irritated by the 'fascist salute' which evoked memories of the fascist measures against the South Tyrolese, but their's was an impression from outside the Hitler Movement. How matters looked inside only a few months later emerges from a letter sent to all Austrian Gauleiter by the SA leader for Austria, the teacher Hermann Reschny, a former lieutenant and party member since 1921.[39] Reschny tried to organize an SA meeting at Bruck in Styria for his units for which purpose a special train was ordered. But until ten days before the envisaged date only 126 men signed on for the train, and of these only 43 paid the fare. To pay for the train a minimum of 300 paying passengers was necessary, and the SA did not dare to order the train definitely 'because no one is willing to take on responsibility for paying for the non-used tickets'. To escape a public disgrace, Reschny believed it would be best if the meeting were 'prohibited' by the authorities. The party administration's comment was more than scathing. They considered it 'incredible and intolerable that a responsible SA leader should make fantastic statements which then collapse in this way, instead of sober, hard facts'; now they would have to request a prohibition through an intermediary from the Landeshauptmann Dr Rintelen to save their face. But they could not force him to do this because they had neither time nor money for the necessary propaganda and because they had exercised pressure on him so that the meeting would *not* be prohibited: 'a fine situation!'[40]

Yet the Viennese SA could always be used to organize an anti-semitic brawl, especially at the university with its many Jewish students. There a group of the National Socialist Students was founded in 1926; it had only a dozen members, hence was unable to disrupt republican or socialist meetings. A good beginning, however, was made in 1927 on the occasion of the Republic's anniversary which was celebrated by the socialist students' association. The National Socialist students brought some thirty SA men through a back door into the university and broke up the meeting. As they claimed, the whole university was cleared by them within ten minutes and eight Jews had to receive medical treatment. This success inspired the National Socialist students to further deeds by which they wrecked the property of Jewish students' groups, broke up the lectures of Jewish professors, held university beadles prisoner, put forward ultimative demands and laid siege to the vice-chancellor's office. Through these 'actions' they could mobilize thousands of students, although their own group had only 120 or 130 members, thirty of whom were organized in a special SA detachment. After a 'struggle' lasting two years, they claimed, they were 'the masters of the university'; the *Deutsche Studentenschaft,* the official students' union, had to accept their demands, while the academic authorities entrusted the preservation of 'order' to them. Their own motives in organizing these fights were:

A large percentage of the students does not possess the racial and biological preconditions which are necessary to absorb the Hitler Idea; an equally large

percentage is exposed to the pressure of the bourgeois parties (Corporations!). Therefore a conquest of the university with the support of the
student masses was out of the question. There was thus only one way: to weld
together a minority into a fighting community and through this to subject the
university to the terror of the swastika – until the day when the *Führer* will
stand at the helm of the nation. That we have done: God and the Jewish press
are our witnesses.[41]

Meanwhile the National Socialist Students' group was growing, and
as its leaders claimed, among the new members there were many who
were 'less radical and revolutionary, trying to brake whenever there was
an action'. In other words, they favoured arguments rather than
physical force and terror. From these dissatisfied members, the two
sons of Professor Spann, who wielded enormous influence among the
Viennese students with his élitist theories,[42] built up a 'secret organization' (similar to the *Kameradschaftsbund* active on the extreme right in
German Bohemia). They let it be understood that this organization
existed wherever Germans lived and had the full approval of Adolf
Hitler. The organization called itself 'Order of the Third Reich' and was
subdivided into 'rings', 'things' and 'cells'. Apparently one of its aims
was to improve relations between the National Socialist and the Heimwehr student organizations. The Spann brothers had belonged to the
Heimwehr and allegedly carried on propaganda for it among the
National Socialists. One of the brothers declared that 'Hitler, by-passing
the Austrian party leaders, co-operated only with Pfrimer', with whom
he established close relations at Freilassing.[43] But the Heimwehr
students wanted the main attack to be directed at 'Marxism', not at the
Jews, while to the National Socialists anti-Semitism was the crucial
issue. As a result of these developments two factions came into being
inside the National Socialist Students' group. The older members, who
were also SA men, were pushed into opposition, and the new leaders no
longer attacked the Jews and the Heimwehr, favoured academic discussions and criticized the party tactics. In 1929 the conflict became an
open 'mutiny', members and leaders openly attacked each other, and
debates deteriorated into fisticuffs. Finally, the members of the 'secret
organization' were expelled, after they had tried to expel their opponents. From the students' organization the conflict spread to the 'Hitler
Youth' because some of its leaders had allegedly been recruited for the
'secret organization'. Intervention in the affair by the 'Leader' of the
German National Socialist Students, Baldur von Schirach, only exacerbated matters, and both sides addressed endless appeals and counter-

appeals to the party headquarters in Munich,[44] apparently without a decisive result.

The relations between the National Socialist Party, the SA, the Hitler Youth and the students' organization became very strained, and so did those between the different Gauleiter. Munich attempted to find a solution to the never-ending Austrian faction fights by the appointment of an outsider, the Sudeten German National Socialist Hans Krebs, as Landesleiter for Austria in 1929. But Krebs was a deputy in the Prague parliament and a leader of his party in Czechoslovakia and could not devote much of his time to Austrian affairs. Soon there were complaints that Krebs could never be found in Austria. There he attempted to bring about a reconciliation between the Schulz group and the Hitler Movement; apparently he hoped thus to overcome the stagnation and in-fighting in the party. But he met with the determined opposition of many Gauleiter who feared for their positions. In some Gaue there was a veritable revolt of the lower eschelons against any such compromise.

Thus the party group at Salzburg declared its determined opposition to any concessions demanded by Schulz's adherents; in Salzburg the latter were in favour of a united Austrian National Socialist Party with its seat in Vienna, which was to be democratically organized and whose leadership, to be drawn from both sides, was to be supreme, thus not bound to recognize Hitler as supreme Leader. If such a 'unification at any price' had been decided on in Vienna, the Salzburg National Socialists must ask:

> Why did we separate three years ago from the democrats and parliamentarians around Schulz? . . . Are we political children or blockheads who can be deceived by any renegade? Can we push aside Hitler like old iron so as to avoid out of indolence to engage in an ugly fight? . . . Where are all the vows of loyalty to this unique German Leader of tremendous greatness? Can all this suddenly be forgotten? *Never!* [45]

These feelings were echoed by the Salzburg Gauleiter Koller who directly attacked Krebs' policy of compromise which would only lead to another split; Krebs should remain in Bohemia, 'the traditional soil for compromise politics'; now Schulz's followers were to become Gauleiter of Lower Austria, Salzburg, Vienna and Vorarlberg, and a former follower of Schulz even the leader for Austria; but in reality Schulz 'had no longer any useful man behind him': any such solution must be rejected.[46]

The Kreisleiter of Vorarlberg (his post was also at stake) reported on negotiations with the local representative of Schulz, a man by the name of Rüscher. When he was told that the Tyrolese Gauleiter Suske wanted to take part in the negotiations he replied that he did not know any Gauleiter and the Tyrolese should look after their own affairs. When the Vorarlberg Kreisleiter mentioned 'the glorious rise of the movement in the Reich' the other laughed and talked about an article by Otto Strasser which admitted that the German National Socialists were unable to make inroads on the working class. In the Kreisleiter's opinion, 'Rüscher is completely democratic in his views. On what basis are we supposed to cooperate with him? As a political leader he is to preside over us, *lead!* us, the followers of Hitler! ! ! ! How can we justify this to our people, how can we accept the responsibility towards our movement. . . .'[47]

The former Carinthian Gauleiter wrote directly to Hitler to express his worries about 'the sudden "unification" of the Austrian National Socialists'. He refused to accept that this was done with Hitler's consent, 'that the past four years of Austrian party history are simply to be wiped out and that, on receipt of orders, we are to flourish in the democratic parliamentarian current on which, thank God, we then turned our backs'. Now all those were on top who, half pulled by the trade unions, half by the Heimwehr, were wavering for ever and 'seem predestined by their racial predisposition to stand aloof from any revolutionary upheaval'. SA men came to him crying because they could not understand this development, and no one was able to understand it. 'Although I am an Austrian, I hate this mixture of smugness and cowardice of which this Austriandom is composed in reality, and I must confess that the last SA man . . . instils more respect in me than the present leaders of the party in Austria. . .' Even the word *Hauptleitung* (instead of leader) made him feel sick, and the list of its members indicated that the Schulz group were in fact the victors.[48]

From Innsbruck the Tyrolese Gauleiter Suske also protested, in his turn against the plan to separate Salzburg and Vorarlberg from his Tyrol and to appoint two followers of Schulz as Gauleiter there. Both, he claimed, were bitter enemies of Hitler and 'unteachable democrats' who had only one ambition, to become deputies. Suske (whose party had a mere 180 members in the whole of Tyrol) was unable to understand 'that Krebs in the negotiations on unification was cheated to such an extent by the Schulz people'; it must be prevented at all cost that Schulz's men became Gauführer.[49] Apparently Krebs was unable to overcome the opposition of the Gauleiter to his cherished scheme of reunification; or it was vetoed by Hitler, who by his own statements was opposed to any compromise of this kind and who could not very well antagonize his most loyal Austrian followers. In any case, Krebs early in 1930 resigned as Austrian Landesleiter and returned to Bohemia.

In Austria he principally relied on the Upper Austrian leader, Alfred Proksch, but against Proksch too there was very strong opposition. Proksch was given wide powers by Krebs which he used to strengthen his own position and to expel critics. In large circles of the Hitler Youth and of the SA he was looked at 'as the grave digger of the movement', and at least one leading Hitler Youth functionary resigned his office in protest.[50] In Munich a special meeting of the central leadership was held at the beginning of 1930 which was attended by Hitler, Hess, Walther Buch (the arbiter in internal party affairs) and Captain Pfeffer von Salomon, the SA leader. There the Austrian representative attacked 'the System Proksch in the sharpest manner' and equally the Viennese Gauleiter Sacher as a traitor and coward; von Pfeffer remarked that Proksch was well known to them 'as the man who in Austria has killed all active forces'. The Austrian representative stressed that the mood among the SA, Hitler Youth and students was so critical that a collapse would occur if the present conditions were allowed to continue: the leadership in Austria must be entrusted to 'the young active forces'.[51]

Yet no decision was taken in Munich who was to succeed Krebs, and not even a provisional Landesleiter was appointed. When the Austrian leaders assembled at Linz in March 1930 and Krebs took his leave from them, Gregor Strasser who was expected there simply did not turn up. He had asked the chairman of the *Deutsche Gewerkschaftsbund* and an old National Socialist, Leo Haubenberger, to meet him at Linz to discuss matters, but Haubenberger waited in vain. Krebs expressed his irritation to Strasser 'because once again no decision has been taken and the poor German Austria is left to manage somehow without the creation of any firm leadership conditions. . . .'[52] Haubenberger in his turn also criticized the absence of any uniform political leadership:

> Every Gauleiter behaves like a little German princeling of pre-war days ('I am the National Socialist Emperor of Styria!), everyone makes his own policy. There is opposition to the policy of [Chancellor] Schober in one Gau, but approval in another. . . . The relations between party, youth organization, students' organization and SA are today intolerable. . . . The leadership in Linz [i.e. Proksch] is opposed by many which justifies the conclusion that it has not fully stood the test. . . .

In Haubenberger's opinion a very important reason for the ever-changing leadership was 'that whoever wrote to Munich . . . or appeared in person in Munich was often heard and believed there. . . .' Thus leaders were removed wholesale: no other Austrian party used up its leaders at such a rate.[53] In the same month Proksch reported to Munich that, according to the Schulz group, the negotiations for reunification had failed finally.[54]

In February 1930 Alfred Frauenfeld, a bank official who had only joined the party a few months before,[55] reported from Vienna that he had taken over the Gau in place of Gauleiter Sacher who had gone on leave for private reasons and was unlikely to return. The Gau then had fewer than a thousand members who paid their dues, and in December the number of resignations because of non-payment was nearly as large as the number of new recruits; but in January, thanks to several mass meetings, there were eighty new members compared with over thirty resignations.[56] He was clearly proud of this record, but he was not yet the appointed Gauleiter. Soon after 37 named functionaries of the Viennese party wrote to Munich that, as they had heard from there, the former Hitler Youth Leader Rolf West, who had resigned from the party for personal reasons, was a serious candidate for the post of Gauleiter. They were aware that such collective steps by 'whole parts of the organization' were unusual 'in our movement'; 'but the hopeless situation in Austria on the one hand, and the never ending visits of individual party comrades to Munich where they posed as "saviours" on the other hand, induce the undersigned local leaders . . . to make the following request': in their opinion, West was not a man suitable to lead the Viennese Gau with any promise of success, in view of the present state of affairs in the Hitler Youth and the way in which he had given up his post for personal and material reasons. They therefore begged the Reichsleitung to appoint the provisional Gauleiter Frauenfeld definitively and thus not to interrupt the promising development that occurred in the Gau during the past weeks.[57]

Curiously enough, this 'democratic' initiative was not rebuked by Munich and Frauenfeld became the Viennese Gauleiter, which he remained during the following years. But this did not mean the end of difficulties within the Viennese party. His authoritarian ways were resented by many members, and friction also developed between him and the leaders of the Hitler Youth. Even before he was appointed Gauleiter he removed the district leader of Ottakring, Sopper, from his post because he declined to break off relations with the Hitler Youth and the students' organization at the orders of Frauenfeld. Sopper then protested against his removal by issuing a circular to all section leaders of Vienna in which he declared that he rejected 'this piece of folly, for if we lose our youth, our movement will be lost . . .'. But he was sharply rebuked by Gregor Strasser to whom such a method was 'almost unbelievable according to our Reich German organizational principles'. Sopper's circular made it clear to Strasser 'why our movement in Austria has been unable to develop for years'; in his opinion, too, a number of Herren of the Hitler Youth and the students' leaders were using 'the word "activism" as a cloak for behaving like a Soldiers' Council'.[58] This comparison, coming from Hitler's second in command, was a particularly harsh condemnation of the state of the party and its subordinate organizations. It also indicated that Munich was backing the new Gauleiter of Vienna.

In the spring of 1930 Frauenfeld several times complained to Munich about the continuing activities of the secret 'Order of the Third Reich', which allegedly conspired against him and was led by non-members of the party, but, as he claimed, also included the former Hitler Youth Leader West and leading members of the students' organization. The Viennese Hitler Youth in particular did not inform him of its meetings and demonstrations and did not participate as was its duty in party propaganda. There were constant rumours, slanders and insinuations about party members, especially about Proksch in Linz: 'If the Reichsleitung does not decide to support me in the smoking out of this hornets' nest then within a short time National Socialism in Austria, which is developing so well, will again present the old picture of a hord of Bolsheviks fighting each other. . . .' And again: 'How long are we going to be disturbed in our work by a few ambitious young men without a following? All steps against them are in vain as long as the Reichsleitung time and again shields these disturbers of the peace. . . .'[59] We do not know whether the Reichsleitung in Munich replied and whether it took any steps to help Frauenfeld.

New difficulties developed when Proksch tried to persuade the expelled former leader Dr Riehl to rejoin the party. Riehl did not claim any official position within it and was even willing to acknowledge the 'Leadership Principle', but suggested the formation of a 'great council' on the model of the Italian Fascists which was to debate important issues. It was to be composed of the principal Gauleiter and, of course, Riehl himself.[60] His suggestions aroused the fury of the Tyrolese Gauleiter Suske who asked:

Who is Dr Riehl? Is he more than the princes and hundreds of thousands of ordinary mortals who, if they want to join our party, have to sign a declaration to that effect? ... I have told Dr Riehl that, if he wants to join us, we have no objection because we do not have a surfeit of intelligent people. But we make no exception for anyone. Everybody has to start at the bottom. ...[61]

Sharper still was the reaction of the local National Socialist dignitaries in the small town of Klosterneuburg near Vienna. They greeted the announcement that Riehl and Frauenfeld would address a mass meeting in Vienna in September 1930 with open derision. Any newcomer was welcome to them, they wrote, provided that 'he without any reservation subordinates himself to our Leader Adolf *Hitler*. ... For us, there do not exist any "special Austrian conditions", for us there exists no Austria and not even a German Austria. For us our Austrian homeland is a part of the great German Reich like any other German state. ... If we need any advice we will ask for it in *Munich*.' They announced that they would appear in full strength, with the forces of SA and Hitler Youth, at the meeting; if these principles were departed from in the slightest degree, they would take their decisions accordingly and immediately.[62] But Frauenfeld rejected this letter 'as an unheard of presumption and breach of discipline', and the threat at the end as an 'open mutiny'. Only his true estimate of their 'ridiculous bragging' prevented him from using the SS to remove the signatories from the meeting hall, but a second time he would show less forbearance.[63]

In the autumn of 1930 Frauenfeld — as it seems without any consultation with other Gauleiter or with Proksch who was in charge of the Landesleitung's office — decreed that National Socialists must leave the Heimwehr, otherwise they would be expelled from the party. Immediately the Gauleiter of Styria and Upper Austria protested to Proksch who first heard of Frauenfeld's decree when he read it in the press. He wrote sharply to Vienna that he would report to Munich about the 'repeated arbitrary actions in questions which do not exclusively concern one Gau' and demand a change: 'If we work like that we will make ourselves ridiculous in the eyes of the public and the organization will be decried as an even greater shambles *(Sauhaufen)* than we can observe to our horror in the other political parties. ...'[64] Proksch in his turn was sharply criticized by Gauleiter Suske for allowing Dr Riehl to put forward conditions at his readmission to the party; this confirmed 'finally' Suske's opinion that Proksch was unsuitable to become the Austrian *Landesführer*.[65]

The Gauleiter of Upper Austria, Andreas Bolek, complained about difficulties with the SA, especially its leader, *Standartenführer* Zellner. He accused the latter of seeing it as his 'principal task to create friction between SA and party', while his own men objected to Zellner as their leader. These conditions took away all joy from Bolek's work; he considered that Zellner had 'morbid ambitions' and was totally incapable, but nevertheless enjoyed the support of the SA leadership in Munich. He asked the latter to suspend Zellner from his post until matters were cleared up; yet he was disappointed, for the Munich SA leader Pfeffer von Salomon decreed that Zellner should retain his position. Thereupon Bolek asked Munich to be relieved from his duties as Gauleiter because he could not accept the responsibility for a progressive development of the Gau in such conditions. But his resignation was not accepted by Gregor Strasser,[66] and matters seem to have continued as before. In his letters to Munich Bolek touched upon the real cause of his troubles: 'the false interpretation of blind obedience and of the Leadership Principle would cause here unheard-of damage'.[67]

It was precisely this blind obedience and the Leadership Principle which the Munich leaders tried to instil in the Austrian party; and it was this factor above all that prevented a reunification with the Schulz group, the 'unteachable democrats' who objected to a completely hierarchical party structure. The Schulz group too was more willing to co-operate with the other völkisch associations than was the Hitler Movement. Thus in the Viennese district of Brigittenau both the Schulz group and Riehl's association were represented on a joint committee of the völkisch associations, together with the Turner, the völkisch trade unions, the Grossdeutsche and several others, but not the Hitler Movement.[68]

The years 1924 to 1930 saw an enormous growth in the strength and influence of the German National Socialist Party, which in the elections of September 1930 was able to poll more than six million votes, 18.3 per cent of the total. In Austria elections were held two months later than the German ones; but the Hitler Movement only obtained 108,000 votes, less than 3 per cent of the total vote.[69] And that was the first year of the great economic crisis which was engulfing Europe and the world. It was in reality another shattering defeat, the result of the virtual isolation of the party and its constant internal conflicts. Indeed, it seems inconceivable that a party so divided and led so incompetently could ever have come into power through its own efforts, without help from outside, even during the greatest economic crisis that Europe had ever seen. It was now led from Munich, but that had not made any impact on the Austrian scene and rather increased internal friction. From the surviving correspondence the impression emerges that Hitler — preoccupied with German affairs — lost interest in Austria after his successful coup of 1926. Munich often avoided the taking of decisions on Austrian matters, or it adopted a solution which was clearly provisional — such as the appointment of Colonel Jankovic or of Hans Krebs as the Austrian Landesleiter, neither of whom was suitable for the post. Indeed, Gregor Strasser on one occasion informed the assembled Austrian leaders that, if there was no leader in an authoritarian state, 'there is nothing else to be done but to replace him by a leaders' council',[70] a solution similar to that advocated by Dr Riehl but clearly in conflict with National Socialist principles. And how were any decisions to be taken by such a council? If by a majority, that surely was a lapse into the hated democratic procedures and a clear deviation from Hitler's most cherished ideas. In 1930 the future did not look bright for the Austrian National Socialists. It turned out, however, that their future — and that of Austria — was in the hands of the man whom they had with such alacrity accepted as their 'glorious leader'.

NOTES

1. Police reports, Vienna, 24 August 1924 and 17 March 1925: Polizeiarchiv Wien, Nachlass Schober, box 50; Haus-, Hof- u. Staatsarchiv, Liasse Österreich 2/21, fasz. 302.

2. SA order no. 21, Vienna, 30 November 1923, signed Ekkehard Czedron; Friedrich Berg, *Die weisse Pest* (Vienna, 1926) 25.

3. Circular of the party chairman for Carinthia, Klagenfurt, 19 April 1924: Bundesarchiv Koblenz, NS 26, vorl. 143.

4. Report by Schober, Vienna, 17 March 1925: Haus-, Hof- u. Staatsarchiv, Liasse Österreich 2/21, fasz. 302. Schulz was a *Werkmeister* (foreman).

5. Police report, Vienna, 28 September 1924: Polizeiarchiv Wien, Nachlass Schober, box 50.

6. Same report as note 4, above. For the railwaymen's strike, cp. above, p. 92, the attitude of the Grossdeutsche Party.

7. Police report, Vienna, 19 August 1925: Polizeiarchiv Wien, Nachlass Schober, box 27/4.

8. Brandstötter, 'Dr Walter Riehl...', 226-27. For the attitude of the Grossdeutsche, see above p. 96.

9. 'Die Geschichte der Bestrebungen nach Herstellung einer nationalen Einheitsfront', MS. p. 17: Verwaltungsarchiv Wien, Grossdeutsche Volkspartei, box 28.

10. Landesparteileitung for Styria to NSDAP in Munich, Graz, 10 October 1925, and Munich reply, 2 November (by Bouhler?): Bundesarchiv Koblenz, Sammlung Schumacher, Nr. 305 I.

11. Police report, Vienna, 22 January 1926: Polizeiarchiv Wien, Nachlass Schober, box 28.

12. Confidential police report, Vienna, 15 August 1924: ibid., box 50, and Haus-, Hof- u. Staatsarchiv, Liasse Österreich 19, fasz. 401: detailed figures for 30 June 1924, also stating that the SA command was in Munich under Captain von [sic] Goering who was on leave, and during his absence under General [sic] Röhm.

13. Confidential police report, Vienna, 21 March 1926: Haus-, Hof- u. Staatsarchiv, Liasse Österreich 2/21, fasz. 302; Polizeiarchiv, Nachlass Schober, box 28.

14. Police reports, Vienna, 1 and 6 May 1926: Polizeiarchiv Wien, Nachlass Schober, box 28. Professor Suchenwirth was not a university teacher, but a secondary school teacher with the title of 'professor'.

15. Hitler's speech only exists in the form of an abbreviated transcript from shorthand notes: Bundesarchiv Koblenz, NS 26/54, fos. 99-107. A police report clearly written by someone present is in Haus-, Hof- u. Staatsarchiv, Liasse Österreich 2/21, fasz. 302. By Anschluss Hitler seems to have meant the Anschluss of the Austrian party, not that of Austria.

16. The above according to the transcript from shorthand in the party archives: Bundesarchiv, NS 26/54, fos. 104-6; ibid., fo. 112 the names of the various representatives in the shorthand notes. For Schulz's differences with Hitler, see Brandstötter, op. cit., 235-37, apparently from a different source.

17. Police report, Vienna, 31 August 1926: Haus-, Hof- u. Staatsarchiv, Liasse Österreich 2/21, fasz. 302; Polizeiarchiv, Nachlass Schober, box 28.

18. Pauley, op. cit., 94.

19. 'Die Geschichte der Bestrebungen nach Herstellung einer nationalen Einheitsfront', s.d., p. 18: Verwaltungsarchiv Wien, Grossdeutsche Volkspartei, box 28.

20. Police report, Vienna, 6 November 1926: Polizeiarchiv, Nachlass Schober, box 28.

21. Police report, Vienna, 3 October 1926: Haus-, Hof- u. Staatsarchiv, Liasse Österreich 2/21, fasz. 302.

22. Police report, Vienna, 27 June 1927, ibid.; A. Proksch to Untersuchungs-u. Schlichtungsausschuss of NSDAP, Linz, 10 March 1931: Berlin Document Center, Proksch file. Although written four years later, Proksch's testimony seems fairly reliable. Interestingly enough, the two men whom Hitler later appointed Austrian Landesleiter, Leopold and Klausner, were also ex-officers.

23. Proksch's letter of 10 March 1931, loc. cit.; Brandstötter, op. cit., 246, 251-52.

24. 'Verhandlungsschrift über die Sitzung der Landesparteileitung am 12. März 1927': Verwaltungsarchiv Wien, Grossdeutsche Volkspartei, box 16. This was a meeting of the Viennese leaders.

25. Jankovic to Hitler, Munich, 1 April 1927: Bundesarchiv Koblenz, Sammlung Schumacher, Nr. 305 II.

26. Circular of NSDAP Parteileitung, Munich, 7 April 1927: ibid., Nr. 305 I.

27. Circular no. 2 of NSDAP Reichsleitung, Munich, 31 May 1927, ibid. This copy is signed by Hitler and has a stamp 'Propagandaabteilung' with the signature of H. Himmler, in addition. The copy in Bundesarchiv, NS 26, vorl. 642, is unsigned.

28. Police report, Vienna, 27 June 1927: Haus-, Hof- u. Staatsarchiv, Liasse Österreich 2/21, fasz. 302.

29. Police report, Graz, 11 March 1926: Steiermärk. Landesarchiv, Landesamtsdirektion 1926, 384 V 1.

30. Brandstötter, op. cit., 260; Police report, Vienna, 9 July 1927: Polizeiarchiv, Nachlass Schober, box 29; telegram from Salzburg, 3 July: ibid., box 1. I have been unable to find this speech in the Party archives.

31. Circular no. 3 of NSDAP Reichsleitung, Munich, 7 July 1927: Bundesarchiv Koblenz, Sammlung Schumacher, Nr. 305 I.

32. Circular no. 4, 5 September 1927: ibid.

33. 'Notizen anlässlich der am 9.VI.28 in Wien stattgefundenen Führertagung', with the names of the Gauleiter and the figures: ibid. Both Brandstötter, op. cit., 268, and Pauley, op. cit., 96, give the membership for 1928 as 7,000 — an over-estimate.

34. Proksch to NSDAP Reichsleitung, Linz, 22 May 1929: ibid.

35. Figures according to Bullock, *Hitler,* 141.

36. Organisationsabteilung to Suske, Munich, 20 June 1928: Bundesarchiv Koblenz, Sammlung Schumacher, Nr. 305 I.

37. Brandstötter, op. cit., 268.

38. 'Verhandlungsschrift über die Sitzung der Landesparteileitung Wien am 29. Mai 1928': Verwaltungsarchiv Wien, Grossdeutsche Volkspartei, box 16.

39. SA Personalakte H. Reschny, Berlin Document Center.

40. NSDAP Landesgeschäftsführung to the Austrian Gauleiter, Graz, 7 September 1928, with quotations from Reschny's letter of 5 September: Bundesarchiv Koblenz, Sammlung Schumacher, Nr. 305 I. Reschny's title then was 'Gausaf "O" ' (SA leader East).

41. The above according to letter by law student and SA leader Leopold Teimel to Gauleiter Frauenfeld, Vienna, 23 April 1930: Verwaltungsarchiv Wien, NS-Parteistellen, box 5.

42. See Chapter 8, below, pp. 168-69.

43. In April 1929 Rafael Spann was sent to Rome by Pfrimer to negotiate with the Italians and to request intervention in case of a Bolshevik takeover in Austria: *I Documenti diplomatici Italiani,* 7th series, Vol. VII (Rome, 1970) 403.

44. Lengthy material on this in Verwaltungsarchiv, NS-Parteistellen, box 20, in particular letters to the NSDAP Untersuchungs- u. Schlichtungsausschuss in Munich and to the NSDStB Reichsleitung there, as well as reports on the 'Geheimorganisation "Spann"'; also letter by L. Teimel to Frauenfeld of 23 April 1930: ibid., box 5. For the Kameradschaftsbund, see John Haag, ' "Knights of the Spirit", the Kameradschaftsbund', *Journal of Contemporary History,* VIII (3) (1973) 133-53.

45. NSDAP Kreis and Ortsgruppe Salzburg to NSDAP Gauleitung, Salzburg, 20 October 1929: Bunchesarchiv Koblenz, Sammlung Schumacher, Nr. 305 II.

46. Sepp Koller to Gregor Strasser, Salzburg, 23 January 1930: ibid.
47. Josef Kielwein to NSDAP Reichsleitung, Rankweil, 10 February 1930: ibid.
48. Walther Rentmeister to Hitler, Vienna, 4 October 1929: ibid. He had been Gauleiter of Carinthia and was transferred to Vienna in 1927, but at this time the Viennese Gauleiter was Josef Sacher.
49. Heinrich Suske to Gregor Strasser, Innsbruck, 21 January 1930; Proksch to Reichsleitung, Linz, 22 May 1929: ibid., Nr. 305 I.
50. X. Hudelmayer to HJ Reichsleitung, 23 October 1929: ibid.
51. 'Gedächtnisprotokoll Wemmer', Munich, 18 January 1930: Verwaltungsarchiv Wien, Nachlass Walter Lohmann, box 7. Wemmer was the Austrian representative at this meeting; his notes were written on the same day.
52. Hans Krebs to Gregor Strasser, Aussig, 18 March 1930: Bundesarchiv Koblenz, Sammlung Schumacher, Nr. 305 I.
53. Exposé by Haubenberger, Vienna, 30 March 1930: ibid., Nr. 305 II.
54. Alfred Proksch to NSDAP Reichsleitung, Linz, 22 March 1930: ibid., Nr. 305 I.
55. The N.S. Kartei, Berlin Document Center, gives 25 November 1929 as the date when Frauenfeld joined the party.
56. Frauenfeld to NSDAP Reichsleitung, Vienna, 12 February 1930: Sammlung Schumacher, Nr. 305 II.
57. 37 Viennese NSDAP officials to NSDAP Reichsleitung, s.d. (February 1930): ibid. (with functions and signatures).
58. Circular of NSDAP Section Ottakring, 22 March; Gregor Strasser to Ernst Sopper, Munich, 24 March 1930: ibid.
59. Frauenfeld to Reichsleitung, 22 March, 11 April 1930: ibid. Cp. above, p. 155.
60. Riehl to Proksch, Vienna, 30 September 1930: Verwaltungsarchiv Wien, NS-Parteistellen, box 6 (using the familiar *Du* towards Proksch).
61. Suske to NSDAP Reichsleitung, Innsbruck, 27 September 1930: ibid., box 5.
62. NSDAP Ortsgruppe Klosterneuburg to Frauenfeld, 23 September 1930: ibid. (italics in original).
63. Frauenfeld to Ortsgruppe Klosterneuburg, 30 September 1930: ibid.
64. NSDAP Landesleitung Österreich to Frauenfeld, Linz, 30 November 1930: ibid., box 6.
65. Suske to NSDAP Reichsleitung, Innsbruck, 27 September 1930: ibid., box 5.
66. Bolek to NSDAP Reichsleitung, Linz, 18 July and 26 August, Strasser to Bolek, Munich, 6 September 1930: Bundesarchiv Koblenz, Sammlung Schumacher, Nr. 305 I.
67. Bolek to NSDAP Reichsleitung, Linz, 18 July 1930: ibid.
68. Circular of 1 May 1930: Verwaltungsarchiv Wien, Grossdeutsche Volkspartei, box 10.
69. Figures in Klemperer, *Ignaz Seipel*, 379, n. 118.
70. Thus a leaflet *Hitler oder Proksch* which was circulated in 1932, p. 2: Bundesarchiv Koblenz, Sammlung Schumacher, Nr. 302.

8

THE 'HEIMWEHREN' OPT FOR FASCISM

Ever since their foundation the ideology of the Heimwehren was fiercely 'anti-marxist' and rejected modern democracy and the role of political parties within it. They aimed at the creation of a strong state, at centralization and certain constitutional reforms. But they did not possess a positive ideology, any clear idea what they wanted to put into the place of the existing democratic institutions. They did not even possess a programme comparable to that of the old German Workers' Party or to Hitler's Twentyfive Points. As they were supported by the Christian Social as well as the Grossdeutsch parties, which differed widely on ideological issues, there was no common denominator to unite them. This weakness was recognized by the Heimwehr leaders who — from the mid-1920s onwards — also came under the spell of Italian Fascism, most strongly in Carinthia and Tyrol. Some Heimwehr leaders even learned Italian and visited Italy to study Fascism on the spot.[1]

There was, however, a home-grown ideology which was in many ways close to Fascism but put a strong emphasis on German national characteristics: there was thus no need to borrow from Italy and to incur the opprobrium of all good nationalists. This was the teaching of the Viennese Professor Othmar Spann on state and society which he expounded to enthusiastic students ever since 1920. Spann's lectures on 'The true State' were published in 1921 and exercised a lasting influence on 'almost the entire non-marxist, politically interested younger generation', whether it was German nationalist or catholic-conservative; by the beginning of the 1930s it completely predominated among the students with 'national' convictions, as one member of this student generation described it.[2] During the winter of 1928-29 a series of lectures was arranged in the German Club in Vienna to work out a unified programme for the Heimwehr movement where Dr Steidle as well as Spann spoke. His pupils Walter Heinrich and Hans Riehl frequently lectured to the Heimwehren and assiduously made propaganda for Spann's ideas, in Austria as well as in German Bohemia.[3]

If one reads today Spann's once famous book, *The true State,* it is difficult to understand the influence exercised by it fifty years ago. It is severely elitist in character and shows a strong imprint of Plato's *Republic.*

> The best form of state is that which brings the best to power . . . . The best must rule over the good; the good must . . . rule over the less good; the less good must . . . rule over the best among the bad; the best among the bad must rule over the bad etc. . . . It therefore follows that rule according to its nature can only be exercised by steps from the top downwards, . . . but never directly from the top circle to the bottom circle, only through the mediation of the intermediate steps.[4]

But the real message of the book was its plea for a society based on Estates or Corporations, sometimes also called Gilds, which were to replace the institutions of the modern state. The lowest Estate envisaged were the manual workers, the producers of goods. One step higher were the 'higher workers', the producers of intellectual goods and productive intellectual workers. One higher still came the leaders of economic organizations and entrepreneurs. On top of them stood the leaders of public organizations, of the state, the army and the churches. To crown the pyramid there was the Estate of teachers and educators, 'the intellectual heroes'.[5] It may have been this last point which won over the students who saw themselves as 'intellectual heroes' and leaders of the nation of the future, students who took refuge from the grim reality of the day in an imaginary society which they would lead.

In the society of Estates political parties as they then existed would be superfluous; they would be replaced by functional parties which would only debate fundamental ideas and cultural issues as well as the great interests of the various Corporations.[6] Employers and employees would form more or less independent subsections of the all-embracing Gild; the trade unions and the cartels of employers would be linked by a collective work agreement; and thus the conflict between capital and labour would lose its bitterness 'because the worker is no longer isolated and left to himself but forms part of one whole. The subordination of the individual to a whole is the most fundamental social change brought about by the state of Estates.'[7] The affinity of Spann's ideas with those of Italian Fascism emerges clearly, especially in the replacement of parties and trade unions by Corporations as the compulsory organizations of employers and employees alike to overcome the class struggle. What is less clear is how it was possible to foist this child of a German professorial brain on to the Heimwehren most of whose members could not have made any sense out of Spann's complicated and highfaluting theory of 'universalism',[8] or could even have been expected to read his turgid prose. But it should perhaps be borne in mind that the idea of Estates as an ancient German institution, quite different from 'western' democracy, was very much in the air and was given a strong impetus by the hated workers' and soldiers' councils of the 'red' revolution.

From the Tyrol, for example, we are told that as early as 1919 the deputies of the majority party 'gave their serious consideration to the idea of an order and organization of the Tyrolese population by Estates' and that they got in touch with representatives of the German Liberal Party who promised their 'energetic support'. A discussion between leading members of the two parties was also attended by 'representatives of economic organizations', and they resolved 'that in view of the deceptive phantom of the workers', peasants' and soldiers' council a genuine order of our people based on Estates was to be created,' above all party politics.[9] A pamphlet that seems to have resulted from these discussions, *The Estates,* stressed the necessity of opposing

> the plutocracy of the rich by the democracy of the peasants and artisans: not, however, a democracy in the vulgar sense as it was created by the French Republic which basically was plutocratic and ideological, but a genuinely Germanic democracy, that is a democracy permeated through and through by an aristocratic consciousness of rank. For truly, our genuine peasant or artisan is a prouder aristocrat than many a prince or count who does not disdain to protect with his coat of arms the doubtful manipulations of some Jewish profiteering company....

The pamphlet advocated the creation of three Estates — for agriculture, industrial production, and trade – each of which was to be subdivided into small and large enterprises – to overcome the division of powers by liberalism, which separated what belonged together, e.g. the church from the state, and the judicial from the administrative power.[10]

In more radical Heimwehr circles the idea gained ground to replace the existing, democratically elected parliament by a parliament based on Estates,[11] and thus to dispense with 'western' democracy which was allegedly corrupt and un-German. This would at the same time do away with 'Marxism' and Liberalism, with the bickering and 'horse-trading' of the political parties, with the class struggle and all the ills of modern society, with capitalist exploitation and with political demagogy. It would restore the social and political harmony that had allegedly existed in the Germanic past.[12] Yet a man who stood politically very much on the right, the then minister of the interior Dr Schürff, clearly noticed the flaws in this idea: 'If it were really possible to create the Estates, this would mean a sharpening of the class struggle, and not an approximation to the principle of the *Volksgemeinschaft* stipulated in our programme. A state based on Estates would further atomization. The conflicts between the Estates would prevent the development of a common feeling of citizenship and of patriotism.'[13] The minister could have added an historical argument. Wherever there had been representative assemblies based on Estates in the past – and there had been hundreds of them in Germany in early modern times – the different Estates had not lived in biblical harmony with each other, but had clashed often and bitterly. But history was not the forte of the Heimwehr ideologues.

Spann in his turn went on record to make known the Heimwehren to a larger audience. In 1929 he wrote an article for a widely read German paper in which he stated that they could not possibly have developed within two years 'to such greatness' had they not enjoyed the full support of all who thought quietly in Austria. The social-democratic papers day after day accused them of being 'Fascists'; but whoever knew the Austrian mentality would just smile. Unfortunately, a section of the world press was deceived by the noise and believed this fairy-tale. In reality the Heimwehren were 'the last ray of hope', not merely of a few politicians, but the leading industrialists saw in them the last possibility to liberate Austria 'from creeping Bolshevism'. Only when this had been achieved could the great economic reserves be tapped which Austria possessed.[14] It is a pity that the professor did not explain what he meant by 'creeping Bolshevism', but presumably it was once again 'red' Vienna which aroused his wrath.

The National Socialists strongly objected to Spann's theories and to the elitist groups which his pupils and sons tried to build up inside the right-wing organizations. Above all, they severely criticized that Spann did not attach sufficient importance to race and to anti-Semitism. Indeed, *The true State* hardly mentioned these issues which were all-important to the National Socialists. To Spann the people were a 'spiritual' community, not conditioned by race and blood. He accorded to the German-speaking national groups in Europe an organic status of their own, conditioned by historical and political developments and tribal and religious traits, and thus implicitly denied a claim to leadership of the German state, which had to be accepted by all Germans outside the state.[15] In 1931 Spann's name was removed from the membership list of a National Socialist front organization, the *Kampfbund für deutsche Kultur,* because he declined to pay for a parcel sent to him c.o.d. from Munich. But even before there had been objections to Spann's membership 'from several sides', and the Viennese leaders of the organization were delighted that the matter was now 'finally cleared up'.[16] Spann never played a prominent political part, but he provided the tools for ambitious political leaders and he inspired the young with his ideas, however weird these may have been.

It was probably more the attraction of Italian Fascism (and of its subsidies) than that of Spann's ideas which inspired the Heimwehr leader Dr Steidle to the famous vow of Korneuburg of 18 May 1930. Above all, he aimed at a unification of the movement, at excluding from it the influence of political leaders, in particular those of the Christian Social Party, such as the Lower Austrian leader Raab. Thus Steidle exclaimed at Korneuburg to the assembled Heimwehr leaders:

> Because we have seen that none of the parties really has the serious will to create a new foundation of the state we must take our political aims into our own hands and no longer be the mere whips of the parties, but must ourselves conduct an active state policy. This is the decisive question for the Heimwehren: do you want as hitherto to adopt the view that the Heimwehr movement is nothing but a whip for the parties, or do you want, to use a slogan, to declare yourselves for the fascist system? That is the clear and simple formula. If Landesführer Raab today stands up and says: I am willing to do that, we will continue to march together. But if he adopts the point of view that we must be the servants of the parties, our ways will part. . . . Until now we have had one aim: to confront Marxism, to wrest the workers from it. . . . But we have gone further and say: it is unsufficient to fulfil only this one task and to let the parties rule in parliament. That role is not enough for us. . . .[17]

Steidle's speech was followed by the reading out of the solemn vow which the assembled leaders were to take. Its most important parts were:

> We are determined to take over power in the state and to reshape it and the economy in the interests of the whole nation. . . . We reject western democratic parliamentarianism and the party state! We are determined to put into its place the self-government of the Estates and a strong leadership which develops, not from the representatives of the parties, but from the leading personalities of the large Estates. . . . We are fighting against the subversion of our nation by the marxist class struggle and the shaping of the economy by liberal capitalism. We are determined to bring about an independent development of the economy on a corporate basis. We shall overcome the class struggle. . . .[18]

This express avowal of a fascist system was not a spontaneous gesture, but 'was well considered and premeditated', as the police was informed from Steidle's entourage.[19]

After the reading of the oath Raab declared that he had vowed loyalty to the Heimwehr leaders before and was determined to keep his promise. He replied 'yes' when he was expressly asked by Steidle and pledged his approval into Steidle's hand. Raab's subordinates followed suit, and they were echoed by all the delegates who rose from their seats and applauded enthusiastically. The deputy Zippe exclaimed: 'The parliamentary way, the western way will not help us. That can only [be done by] the method which disregards the parties. I am a Fascist.' Dr Pfrimer declared, amidst loud and enthusiastic applause, that only Fascism could save Austria; an attempt must be made to seize power, and then the leaders of the movement would be able to govern; the vow was 'the greatest event which the history of the Austrian Heimwehr movement has seen'.[20] For once there seemed to be complete unity among the leaders, but that unity was not to last. The Korneuburg affair in reality revealed the deep fissures within the Heimwehr movement.

A week after Korneuburg, on 25 May, Steidle spoke at a Heimwehr festival at Feldkirch in Vorarlberg on the subject of 'Fascism': obviously replying to criticisms he now declared that Fascism was specifically Italian and 'not an article for export'.[21] At Innsbruck, a few days before, he exclaimed: 'We want the end of the French Revolution on German soil, if need be a German revolution, through a dictatorship of construction' *[sic]* ; therefore the Heimwehren had cut all their links to the existing system, had severed themselves from the parties and would unite all their forces to achieve the great aim: 'the true German people's state of the productive Estates, based on an old and proven cultural and economic foundation'.[22] Yet Steidle's critics on the right were not taken in by this emphasis on German national aims and the denial of an Italianate policy. The Grossdeutsche in particular were opposed to Steidle's 'coquetry with Fascism, his invention of a "national International", his fight against all parties and parliamentarianism, the ideas of a state of Estates and of the seizure of power', which were crowned by the Korneuburg vow.[23] The leaders of the Peasant League went further. They recognized that the vow was directed against the constitution and could not be reconciled with the holding of a mandate in an elective assembly. The attitude of the Christian Social Party was more ambivalent: it left it to its deputies whether to render the vow or to refuse it because it believed that no conflict of duties would arise if any of them did so.[24]

The clearest refutation of Steidle's policy came from the Landeshauptmann of Vorarlberg, Dr Ender, who spoke after Steidle at the Heimwehr festival of 25 May 1930. He stressed that the Vorarlberg Heimwehren accepted the basis of the constitution; if they departed from it he could not remain at their head for another hour, for he could not as Landeshauptmann vow to observe the constitution and break it as a Heimwehr member: 'Our constitution is democratic and corresponds to the character of our Alemannic people and to the history of Vorarlberg. Voluntarily we will never give up the democratic basis. It would be a black day for our people if it were deprived of the right of democratic self-government, a liberty which we treasure in the communes and the Land.' Allegedly democracy was an import from the West: it certainly did not come from the East, but it had strong roots in the German past.[25] Apparently Dr Ender knew his German history better than the Heimwehr leaders, and during his long speech he provided chapter and verse for his statements. Another leader who dissociated himself from the Korneuburg vow and the acceptance of Fascism, at least privately, was the Upper Austrian leader Prince Starhemberg who let it be known to the Grossdeutsche that he had not been consulted by Steidle.[26]

During the following weeks the leaders of the Grossdeutsche several times debated the Heimwehr issue. At the end of May the deputy Grailer reported that they were invited to meet the Heimwehr leaders who wanted them to disregard party discipline and put themselves under Heimwehr orders; in vital questions they were to put the Heimwehr above their party; but he had told them that he was, in the first instance, responsible to his own conscience and his voters. Dr Waber seconded him: their views and those of the Heimwehr were opposed to each other; the latter wanted to overthrow the Schober government, while they supported it and had to say so in the discussion with the Heimwehr towards which they still had friendly feelings. Dr Straffner was of the opinion that the Heimwehr should keep out of day-to-day politics and remain what it had been when it was founded; they could not accept the Korneuburg vow.[27] At their following meeting the grossdeutsch deputies unanimously voted not to render the vow. Klimann declared that he was a member of the Carinthian Heimwehr (its provincial leader) and the by-laws of the latter were still valid, hence he could not give the pledge. But another deputy remarked that their followers were strongly supporting the Heimwehr, hence they could not adopt an attitude of opposition to it.[28]

At the meeting between the Heimwehr leaders and those of the Christian Social and Grossdeutsch parties, Steidle tried to induce those present to accept the Korneuburg vow. But his move was immediately countered by the Christian Social deputy Dr Salzmann who found it strange that he was invited to a discussion and was now urged to take an oath; he recognized the old principles of the Heimwehr but not the present ones; he had rendered an oath to the constitution which he could not break by a new vow. But Steidle insisted: either they rendered the vow or a separation from the parties would have to take place. Salzmann was supported by another Christian Social deputy, Jerzabek, who also declared that they could not break their oath to the constitution; the issue of Estates should be discussed further, the matter was not yet concluded. The Styrian Heimwehr leader Rauter pointed out that there could be a collision between Heimwehr and party; whoever negotiated with the Social Democrats broke a fundamental law. In the end none of the eight deputies present from the two political parties took the vow demanded: a clear defeat for Steidle's tactics, who now claimed that he would take over power 'by legal means'. In Dr Straffner's opinion, he would try and do so through a disintegration of the parties; if the deputies agreed to take the oath they would have to carry out his orders. For the moment the main aim of the Heimwehr was to overthrow the Schober government; when one deputy asked who would come after Schober, the reply was that it did not matter: 'Schober must go'. Some Christian Social deputies felt that it was not Steidle destroying their party but Schober.[29] At a further meeting between the Grossdeutsche and several Heimwehr leaders the former repated their decision not to render the vow, and a member of the Vienna city council present explained that he would have to resign his seat if he took the oath – a view from which the Heimwehr leaders dissented.[30]

In Carinthia meanwhile the local Heimwehr leaders assembled to render the Korneuburg vow, but several declared that first the members must be asked, and this was accepted by a large majority. Many of those present nevertheless took the oath, but in a form that was considerably watered down and did not mention Fascism or dictatorship.[31] The Carinthian Heimwehr leader Stephan Tauschitz who sat in the Diet for the Peasant League refused to do so and his lead was followed in several meetings organized by him in different parts of Carinthia. In Upper Austria, the Heimwehr leaders who sympathized with the Grossdeutsche were for Schober as chancellor. They were unwilling to pledge their loyalty to Steidle, and only willing to do so to Starhemberg. The deputies who had not rendered the oath then received letters that they were no longer members of the Heimwehr.[32] If it was Steidle's aim to bring about the disintegration of the parliamentary system from within by tying the deputies to his orders,[33] his tactics misfired.

Nor was the Heimwehr more successful in putting pressure on Schober to carry out its demands and to declare the constitution invalid. This was suggested by the Styrian Landeshauptmann Dr Rintelen and he was seconded by the Prince Bishop of Graz, Pawlikowski, who offered to absolve Schober from his oath to the constitution, but Schober declined.[34] He now retaliated and decided to remove from the scene the man whom he considered the evil spirit of the Heimwehr: the German Major Pabst who had taken a prominent part in the Korneuburg ceremony and in the negotiations with the deputies of the parties. Schober informed the German minister, Count Lerchenfeld, that the Austrian government was in full agreement on this issue, unwilling to suffer any longer the Heimwehr interference with the country's government, and that Pabst was 'the most important and most forceful exponent of this counter-government'. As Pabst could be accused of meddling with internal Austrian affairs he was simply expelled from the country by a decision of the minister of the interior,[35] as Schober had already intended to do in 1929.[36] What must have been especially aggravating in his eyes was that, according to reliable information received by the police, Pabst through his close relations with Italy tried to persuade the Italians to make their consent to an Austrian international loan dependent on the Austrian government's acceptance of the Heimwehr demands.[37]

The sharpest reaction to the Korneuburg oath came from the *Landbund* (Peasant League) which hitherto had supported the Heimwehren like the other conservative parties, especially in Carinthia and Styria where it was locally strong. But it was opposed to the Estates' parliament proclaimed by the Heimwehr because it was against any dictatorship and feared to be dictated to by other economic groups, which were stronger and better organized. As the league expected a Heimwehr Putsch it began to organize peasant units, *Bauernwehren,* for the self-defence of the peasantry. These came into being in particular in Carinthia, Styria and Upper Austria and soon were able to show their strength in large demonstrations.[38] But the peasant units aroused the fury of the Heimwehren which rightly considered them 'a hostile act directed against the Heimatwehr', likely to undermine 'the only reliable protective dam against Bolshevism'. It also announced sharp measures against the leaders of the Peasant League whom it accused of 'treason towards the Volksgemeinschaft, . . . treason towards the peasantry which thus is split anew . . .'.[39] In spite of these attacks many peasants left the Heimwehr and joined the new self-defence units.

Pabst left Austria and went to Italy; but his banishment did not last long, for Schober soon resigned as chancellor and the new government allowed Pabst to re-enter Austria. In November 1930 he was able to return triumphantly to Innsbruck, jubilantly received by the local Heimwehr. When Pabst appeared on the Brenner clad in Heimwehr uniform, he was received by the commandant of the fascist frontier police who expressed his hope that Pabst had been well looked after during his stay and concluded with the words: 'Evviva fascisti austriaci! ' — a clear demonstration of fascist solidarity. In the evening there was a great reception in the Innsbruck town hall in the presence of the civil and military authorities: the mayor of Innsbruck, the commandant of the Tyrolese Alpine regiment, and even a real field-marshal as the representative of the old Austrian army. Thanking them Pabst declared that no nation could rise through ballot papers and elections; those methods must be terminated, power must be seized, and that very soon.[40]

The Schober government tried to sound the pope about his attitude towards the Heimwehren. The Austrian minister at the Holy See twice interviewed Cardinal Pacelli endeavouring to obtain some reaction from him. But Pacelli was not to be drawn; he did not show any visible interest in the subject, nor would he say anything negative, 'out of caution in principle', as the minister surmised. Both times Pacelli, from his own Munich reminiscences, compared the Heimwehren with the Bavarian Orgesch, which was dissolved at the demand of the Entente, and then asked rhetorically whether this was not also the case in Austria. The poor minister was reduced to the remark that Pacelli may have meant to indicate the exact opposite of his real opinion.[41] It is indeed difficult to see how he could have adopted an attitude that was not one of extreme caution: after all, the Heimwehren might have been successful in their attempt to seize power. But in spite of Pabst's promptings, the Heimwehren came no nearer to this cherished goal.

After the failure of the Korneuburg coup the differences between their leaders once more came into the open. In June 1930 the Hungarian General Jánky reported that Starhemberg, hitherto one of the most radical, had established relations to Chancellor Schober: 'the young prince has great ambitions, for he seriously dreams of governing Austria'; now he considered the Korneuburg vow too extreme.[42] At a meeting of the Heimwehr leaders in early September Starhemberg, inspired by Schober, sharply attacked the leadership of Steidle and Pfrimer who, he claimed, looked at their task as a sport, while the situation demanded that the leadership should pass to a 'fanatic of the deed'. The result of his impassioned speech was that Starhemberg, with Christian Social support, was elected the Austrian Heimwehr leader in place of Steidle. Previously Schober had arranged that the subsidies paid by the industrialists went to Starhemberg, not to Steidle.[43]

It is doubtful, however, whether Starhemberg was any more successful in his playing at politics than the overthrown leaders. He certainly kept his options open, which in practice meant that he had frequent meetings with National Socialist leaders, in particular Proksch at Linz, who considered this link 'of the greatest importance for the coming elections'.[44] There were also meetings with representatives of the German National Socialist Party, and at least one with Hitler himself. But the envisaged alliance for the election did not materialize because Hitler demanded parity with the Heimwehr, and both sides put up separate lists. This was the first time that the Heimwehren independently took part in an election, and apparently they had high hopes of a great success. But the result was very disappointing. Although in November 1930 the *Heimatblock* gained twice as many votes as the National Socialists, its share of the total was only 6 per cent, or 228,000 votes (the Social Democrats had 41 per cent). It was sufficient to obtain eight seats in parliament, while the National Socialists received none.[45] In Vienna, the Heimwehr leader Major Fey approached Dr Riehl with the request of a joint list, but he too was rebuffed; Riehl simply replied that such a link was out of the question.[46]

Starhemberg himself later described the effect of the very limited election success upon his movement. Those who had exaggerated hopes of a success were disappointed and became restless. Others were so strongly opposed to the parliamentary system that they considered it compromising for the movement to accept seats in parliament. Others still, the largest part, became more and more radical, and these divisions were likely to cause disintegration.[47] How far Starhemberg himself was willing to accept National Socialist clichés he demonstrated in a speech in Vienna in which he exclaimed: 'To me *Volksgenossen* are only those who share the racial instincts of the Germans, in whose veins there circulates German blood; I do not include among the people those alien, flat-footed parasites from the East who exploit us through an unhealthy economic system. We want to create a people's state that is German and Christian!'[48] Starhemberg's prestige in nationalist circles was so great that at the end of 1930 he was also elected the first leader (Bundesführer) of the Free Corps Oberland which had groups in Germany as well as in Austria, and had actively participated in the Hitler Putsch in Munich in 1923 (with Starhemberg among its men). But his election was contested: he received only the 36 Austrian votes and one German one, while 36 German votes were cast against him. The German Oberland groups now resumed their contacts with the SA, and several of them transferred their allegiance to the rising star of Hitler.[49]

The new Austrian chancellor after Schober's resignation was the former minister of defence, Carl Vaugoin, who belonged to the Christian Social Party, but also had close relations with the Heimwehr. Starhemberg was appointed minister of the interior, and another Heimwehr leader minister of justice. At a Heimwehr parade in Vienna early in November Vaugoin took the salute together with ex-chancellor Seipel, and both addressed the men afterwards.[50] After the election of the same month Vaugoin had to resign as chancellor, while Starhemberg demanded to remain minister of the interior, 'for reasons of prestige' as he put it.[51] But his ambitions were not fulfilled. Yet the mere fact that he was now the leader of a small parliamentary group deprived his movement of political impetus and made new conflicts inevitable, above all with the National Socialists, the losers of the election. They began to disrupt Starhemberg's meetings, and there were sharp clashes between the rival movements. Starhemberg declared, amid stormy National Socialist interruptions, that no new state could be built by street demonstrations and Hitler slogans: he must state publicly that the Heimwehren had nothing to do with National Socialism (before the election the tune was rather different). In another speech Starhemberg stressed that nothing could be achieved by rising arms in hand against the government; in the resulting violent clash the economy would be destroyed and the whole nation thrust into even greater misery; the idea of using force must be abandoned. But such ideas were treason to the old members of Oberland who accused Starhemberg of wanting to squeeze them into a 'Roman strait jacket', of accepting a 'Christian Social Fascism', and of selling out to the Austrian bourgeoisie and its parliamentary henchmen.[52]

Soon there were also conflicts with the Christian Social representatives within the Heimwehr, especially the deputy Julius Raab, who was re-elected for his party, but not as a member of the Heimatblock. This caused a new split in Lower Austria: Starhemberg declared that Raab was 'unreliable' and only backed the Heimwehr as long as it supported the Christian Social Party, hence he must separate from Raab.[53] Before the end of 1930 the Hungarian Prime Minister, Count Bethlen, held that the most urgent task was to bring about a reconciliation of Starhemberg with Schober, Seipel and Vaugoin and to reunite the Heimwehr movement.[54] In the Tyrol, the Christian Social government tried to revive the original function of the Heimwehren — that of a police force at the disposal of the government in emergencies — and the ideas that inspired the movement at its foundation because the later course had suffered shipwreck. But in the eyes of the local Grossdeutsche, this was only a manoeuvre to lead the men 'slowly but surely into the Christian Social camp', although the Grossdeutsche saw no alternative but to co-operate with the Tyrolese government.[55] In Vorarlberg the same course was guaranteed in the person of Landeshauptmann Dr Ender, who was the new Austrian chancellor.

In the Tyrol, several local Heimwehr leaders declared that they had no longer any confidence in Steidle because he had no ideals and did not make any sacrifices; the new leaders must be elected and must possess the confidence of the peasants and the local units: then the Heimwehr would resume its former character, but it would take a long time to restore the old confidence and enthusiasm.[56] In a letter to Starhemberg the same writer expressed his deep pessimism about this future development. Among large circles which hitherto supported the Heimwehr there was now either no interest or aversion; even their own men did not know what caused the conflicts among the leaders, and many attributed them to personal ambitions; thus there was a crisis of confidence vis-à-vis Steidle as well as the central leaders so that many left the movement. The cause of the Heimatblock in the Tyrol, he continued, was hopelessly lost; no one believed any longer that the Heimwehr stood above party because it had become a party guard of the Heimatblock; the members of Oberland and the Turner were turning towards National Socialism; the Tyrolese wanted a strong, authoritarian state, but not a dictatorship, not even that of the Heimwehren; important issues must be seriously discussed with the leaders, who did not want to be faced with a fait accompli as under Steidle and Pabst who avoided all discussions. The Heimwehr must become truly patriotic, and that precluded any close connections with the Italian Fascists as long as conditions in the South Tyrol did not improve: 'that is a demand of the instinct of self-preservation'.[57] This picture, drawn from inside the movement, clearly reflected all the ills besetting the Heimwehren less than nine months after the Korneuburg vow.

An equally critical picture was drawn by Major Pabst himself at the beginning of 1931 for the benefit of an Hungarian visitor, the deputy of the Hungarian foreign minister, who asked Pabst to try everything to reunify 'this important movement'. But, in Pabst's opinion, such a revival was very doubtful because it lacked any suitable leader. Brigadier General Hülgerth who might be elected leader was an excellent soldier but too soft; it might be that after him Steidle would once more become the leader; he was intelligent and gifted, 'but incredibly lazy and lacking the *feu sacré*, the true enthusiasm'; this Starhemberg possessed in large measure, but he 'lacked a head and thus he muddled up everything and was incapable of keeping any line'. The visitor then enquired what was Pabst's opinion of the National Socialists, Pabst replied that their movement was growing; their leader was 'a very agile man by the name of Frauenfeld who at the first attempt in the elections gained half as many votes as the Heimwehr. He was financially independent, for he did what Pabst always preached in' vain to the Heimwehr: secure financial independence through a collection of membership dues, while the Heimwehren lived from the subsidies of the industrialists. Now Starhemberg had taken the side of the workers of the *Alpine Montangesellschaft* in a conflict with its employees, with the result that the industrialists stopped their subsidies from 1 January and the Heimwehren had no money. Many incapable aristocrats had recently joined and did more damage than their names were worth; in consequence the conflict between black-yellow monarchists and the Grossdeutsche was growing, and the völkisch character of the Heimwehr was endangered in the opinion of many adherents.[58] According to another Hungarian report, the industrialists' association indeed stopped its subventions, not because of the Alpine Montangesellschaft's labour troubles, but because of the disunity and the intrigues inside the movement. The chairman of the association, Baron Erhardt, tried to mediate between Starhemberg and his opponents at the beginning of February, but without success.[59]

The Hungarian and Italian governments also lost confidence in a movement which promised so much and achieved so little. Thus the lack of funds created very serious problems, and the contributions from Austrian aristocrats, who raised their own Heimwehr units on a semi-feudal basis,[60] could not compensate for the loss. In the summer of 1931 representatives of the Heimwehr approached the secretary of the Hungarian legation in Vienna with the request to resume their old connections with the Hungarian government and 'national circles' in Budapest, claiming that they still received arms from Hungary. The legation then enquired in Budapest what they should do about the request and was told to do nothing, as the Hungarian government had good relations with Vienna and there was but a small chance that the Heimwehr movement would recover its strength. The Heimwehren apparently also approached the Italian envoy, but his reply was equally negative: on account of their faulty organization they had, in his opinion, twice missed the 'psychological moment for an unfolding of their ideas', hence they could not reckon with any further support from Italy.[61]

By that time the Heimwehr movement was in complete disarray. Starhemberg retired to his estates the management of which was in disorder, but officially he remained the Heimwehr leader. Pabst left Austria; Major Fey in Vienna was in open opposition to Starhemberg; Pfrimer in Styria moved ever closer to the National Socialists with whom he had maintained good relations ever since 1927.[62] In March 1931 he declared that not the people ruled as alleged in the Constitution, but 'party representatives who were determined to keep their chairs warm even if nation and economy go to the dogs. Truly speaking it is high time to sweep away this illegal form of government by a liberating *coup d'état*....'[63] In August Pfrimer ordered all leaders and speakers of the Heimwehren under no circumstances to attack the National Socialists; if questions were asked about the mutual relations the answer was that both organizations were 'fighting against Marxism and the party state and therefore had many points of contact. Thus the Heimwehren saw in the National Socialist Party a friendly league which they would not attack as long as the National Socialists did the same.'[64]

In September 1931 Pfrimer undertook the long-awaited coup, fed up with waiting and with the inactivity of the other leaders. Locally, the Putsch was entirely successful: many small places in Styria were occupied by heavily armed Heimwehr units and Graz was surrounded by them. The town halls and local offices were occupied. The police, if they were not willing to co-operate, were disarmed, local socialist leaders arrested, vehicles controlled and guards posted. The police were informed that Dr Pfrimer had taken over the government and absolved them from their oath. It was really all very simple. At Kapfenberg there was wild shooting in which two people were killed and four seriously wounded. Apparently there was no resistance although the authorities had ample warning.[65] But the Putsch remained isolated because none of the other Heimwehr leaders supported Pfrimer. Only in Upper Austria were the units mobilized and even there they did not take any action. In the Tyrol Dr Steidle immediately assured the central government of his loyalty and refused to have anything to do with the undertaking. A similar declaration was issued by Brigadier General Hülgerth. The Lower Austrian leader Raab rejected the Putsch out of hand.[66]

Although the Austrian government knew that Starhemberg was implicated in the rising little was done to him; as the chancellor explained to the German foreign minister Curtius, in Austria it was not all that easy to arrest a prince.[67] In general too, the government reacted very gently to the coup. The Styrian units were allowed to disperse peacefully with their weapons – to keep them for a better day. Pfrimer and a few other leaders were put on trial, but were acquitted by the jurymen who then joined with the accused in giving the fascist salute. The failure of the Putsch caused more angry disputes among the different Heimwehr leaders and a further decline of a movement which so blatantly failed to live up to its promises. But, on the side of the Styrian leaders, it also led for the moment to a disenchantment with the National Socialists who failed to render the promised help.[68]

But, at least in Styria, the disenchantment did not last long. Already in October one of the Styrian leaders, at a meeting in Klagenfurt, proposed a fighting alliance of Heimwehren and National Socialists, and two days later a mass meeting of their uniformed followers took place in Graz. The first speaker was the German National Socialist, Theo Habicht, who spoke on behalf of Hitler. He declared that the first condition of an alliance was a recognition by the Heimwehren that there was only one Leader of the German nation, Adolf Hitler. The second was that they must fight against all forces opposed to the foundation of a Greater Germany, including 'the Habsburgs as the exponents of Paris and Rome'; all attempts to find for Austria a solution other than the Great German one must be rejected. After Habicht the Styrian chief of staff Hanns Rauter reminded those present of his own services to the German cause in Upper Silesia. The Heimwehr leaders Steidle and Pfrimer, he continued, were unconditionally in favour of the Anschluss, and this had been the aim of the Styrian Heimwehren from their foundation; in that spirit they many times met Hitler and Strasser and sought close contacts; the question of the monarchy would only become acute after the Anschluss: 'we all want a German dictatorship, our eyes and our hopes are directed towards the German Reich'. But, Rauter went on, their leader was Prince Starhemberg who must join the Harzburg Front of the united German nationalists, of Hugenberg, Hitler and the Stahlhelm leaders. The next speaker, the Heimwehr leader and police officer Meyszner, was a little more cautious. He emphasized the special conditions in the Alpine lands; the Austrians must first look after their own affairs; but 'if Germany brought the solution, the leader of the great brother nation will also be our leader'. Habicht, in winding up, declared that the Heimwehr leaders had on all issues given the answers expected from them: 'National Socialist Party and Heimatschutz will fight shoulder to shoulder against this system and for the great Third German Reich' (storms of applause).[69]

Immediately after the meeting the members of the two organizations enthusiastically fraternized in the inns and coffee houses of Graz. On the next day Habicht and the National Socialist Gauleiter Walter Oberhaidacher met the Heimwehr leaders in the best hotel of Graz and reached an agreement that in future both organizations will 'march shoulder to shoulder against Bolshevism, Marxism and parliamentary democracy', as well as against 'the liberalist-capitalist economic order' and the 'organized lending capital'. They further agreed to oppose by all means at their disposal any 'attempt to decide the question of the form of state in Austria before its unification with the German Reich', any attempt to restore the monarchy in Austria.[70] The National Socialists, however, insisted that they remained an independent organization and opposed any new Putsch, 'which just now would prevent the possibility of a later Anschluss'. Heimwehr members could become members of the National Socialist Party if they gave an undertaking that, in case of a clash between the political lines of the two organizations, they would leave the Heimwehr and that they recognized the leading role of the National Socialist Party.[71] According to a police report, the close co-operation between National Socialists and Heimwehren also extended to large parts of Carinthia, Lower Austria, Upper Austria and Salzburg; the common aim was 'to radicalize the great mass of the discontented in town and country and to incite them against the government and parliament'. Leaders of the Carinthian Heimwehren also met Hitler; they were determined to work together and to conquer the leading positions within the Heimwehr for the nationalist idea.[72]

Thus the result of Steidle's manoeuvres at Korneuburg and of the failure of the Pfrimer Putsch in Styria was a sharp decline in Heimwehr influence and renewed in-fighting between rival leaders and creeds. The movement threatened to disintegrate, and the gainers were the National Socialists who were by now well able to exploit these differences. If the Heimwehren intended to act and to impose their will upon the country they had missed their chance, and the initiative passed to the National Socialists.

NOTES

1. Schweiger, 'Geschichte der niederösterreichischen Heimwehr . . .', 219.

2. Adam Wandruszka, 'Österreichs politische Struktur . . .', in Heinrich Benedikt (ed.), *Geschichte der Republik Österreich* (Vienna, 1954) 335, 413.

3. Schweiger, op. cit., 216; Martin Schneller, *Zwischen Romantik und Faschismus – Der Beitrag Othmar Spanns zum Konservativismus der Weimarer Republik* (Stuttgart, 1970) 107-8.

4. Othmar Spann, *Der wahre Staat – Vorlesungen über Abbruch und Neubau der Gesellschaft gehalten im Sommersemester 1920 an der Universität Wien* (Leipzig, 1921) 204-5.

5. Ibid., 210.
6. Ibid., 274, 289. Spann calls the parties *Sachparteien.*
7. Ibid., 256, 259, 265.
8. One example of Spann's untranslatable prose must suffice here. 'Ganz anders der Universalismus. Er erklärt den Einzelnen in seiner Selbständigkeit ebenso wie in seiner Verhaftung an die anderen. Er betrachtet als Grundtatsache die Anknüpfung des eigenen Geistes an den anderen Geist, des Einzelnen an die Ganzheit. Er erklärt die Gesamtheit als ein selbständiges Reales, er kennt, ja fordert damit von Anbeginn ein selbständiges Überindividuelles! ': ibid., 70.
9. Tiroler Ständerat to Prof. Michael Mayr, Innsbruck, 18 August 1919: Tiroler Landesarchiv, Nachlass Mayr, V/20.
10. An. pamphlet *Die Stände,* 8-9, ibid. (almost certainly from 1919).
11. Thus a Viennese police report of 31 August 1929: Verwaltungsarchiv Wien, Bundeskanzleramt, 22/gen., box 4865.
12. Thus 'Programm der Ständeorganisation Österreichs', May 1931, quoted by Josef Hofmann, *Der Pfrimer-Putsch* (Vienna-Graz, 1965) 55.
13. 'Verhandlungsschrift über die Sitzung der Landesparteileitung, Mittwoch, 22. Jänner 1930': Verwaltungsarchiv Wien, Grossdeutsche Volkspartei, box 16. This was a meeting of the Viennese leaders of the Grossdeutsch Party. The slogan of *Volksgemeinschaft* (people's community) occurred in the programme of both the Grossdeutsche and the National Socialists.
14. Thus the Austrian Bundespressedienst, quoting Spann's article from *Münchener Neueste Nachrichten* of October 1929 and *Grazer Tagespost* of 23 October: Polizeiarchiv Wien, Nachlass Schober, box 2b.
15. Karl Viererbl, 'Werden und Durchbruch des Volksgedankens', *National-sozialistische Monatshefte,* VI (1935) 814, 816: a sharp attack on Spann.
16. *Kampbund für deutsche Kultur,* Ortsgruppe Wien, to Frauenfeld, Vienna, 17 October 1931: Verwaltungsarchiv Wien, NS-Parteistellen, box 5.
17. *Der Panther,* 1. Jahrgang, Folge 4, 24 May 1930; Schweiger, op. cit., 189-90.
18. The text of the oath is given in Schweiger, op. cit., 192; *Heimatschutz in Österreich,* 43; Jedlicka, 'The Austrian Heimwehr', *Journal of Contemporary History,* I (1) (1966) 138-139.
19. Confidential police report, Salzburg, 22 May 1930: Verwaltungsarchiv Wien, Bundeskanzleramt, 22/gen., box 4866.
20. *Der Panther,* 1. Jahrgang, Folge 4, 24 May 1930, under the headline: 'Voller Sieg unserer Richtung in Niederösterreich'; Schweiger, op. cit., 210. The words 'unserer Richtung' are indicative of the different trends within the Heimwehr, Styria defeating Lower Austria.
21. *Vorarlberger Volksblatt,* Bregenz, 26 May 1930.
22. *Die Heimwehr,* 16 May 1930, quoted by Schweiger, op. cit., Vol. II, 198.
23. T. Climann, 'Die Heimwehrfrage', *Pressemitteilungen der Grossdeutschen Volkspartei,* Nr. 881, 19 February 1931: Verwaltungsarchiv Wien, Grossdeutsche Volkspartei, box 14.
24. *Der Panther,* 1. Jahrgang, Folge 6, Graz, 7 June 1930.
25. *Vorarlberger Volksblatt,* 26 May 1930.
26. '174. Sitzung des Verbandes der Abgeordneten der Grossdeutschen Volks-partei am 23. Mai 1930': Verwaltungsarchiv Wien, Grossdeutsche Volkspartei, box 6.

27. '176. Sitzung . . . am 28. Mai 1930': ibid.

28. '178. Sitzung . . . am 3. Juni 1930': ibid. As no similar protocols exist for the Christian Social Party, these are the only detailed reports available on the parties' attitude.

29. '179. Sitzung . . . am 5. Juni 1930': ibid. One of those representing the Heimwehr was Spann's pupil, Walter Heinrich, apart from Steidle, Pfrimer, Rauter, Pabst and Starhemberg.

30. '180. Sitzung . . . am 6. Juni 1930': ibid.

31. '181. Sitzung . . . am 11. Juni 1930': ibid.

32. '184. Sitzung . . . am 17. Juni 1930'; '186. Sitzung . . . am 25. Juni 1930': ibid.

33. This is the opinion of Walter Goldinger, in Heinrich Benedikt (ed.), *Geschichte der Republik Österreich,* 172, who also sees the events of Korneuburg as 'a symptom of the *Heimwehr's* internal crisis'.

34. Franz Langoth, *Kampf um Österreich* (Wels, 1951) 82. L. was a leading *grossdeutsch* politician, and later a prominent National Socialist.

35. German Legation Vienna to Auswärt. Amt, 16 June 1930: Botschaft Wien, Geheimakten 1930, 4938 part 3, E266492. Pabst had been a German captain and was promoted major after his discharge from the army and his flight from Germany in 1920, after the Kapp Putsch.

36. See above, p. 126.

37. Police report, Vienna, 11 October 1930: Polizeiarchiv Wien, Nachlass Schober, box 32.

38. Bezirksgendarmeriekommando Völkermarkt to Bezirkshauptmannschaft Völkermarkt, 10 September 1931: Kärntner Landesarchiv, Präs. 9-2/1411, fasz. 904; report on Bauernwehr meeting in Oftering on 5 May 1930: Oberösterr. Landesarchiv, Nachlass Th. Berger, Nr. 26.

39. Heimwehr leaflet of January 1930 (?), signed by Starhemberg: ibid.

40. German Consulate Innsbruck to Auswärt. Amt, 13 November 1930: Botschaft Wien, Geheimakten 1930, 4938 part 3, E266467-68.

41. Austrian Envoy at Holy See to Schober, Rome, 4 June 1930: Haus-, Hof- u. Staatsarchiv, Liasse Österreich 2/3, fasz. 276.

42. Jánky to Apor, 28 June 1930; Kerekes, *Abenddämmerung einer Demokratie,* 76.

43. Ibid., 78; Schweiger, op. cit., Vol. II, 211, n. 1.

44. Proksch to NSDAP *Reichsleitung,* Linz, 22 March 1930, who also wrote that 'it is valuable that we here have Starhemberg at hand . . .': Bundesarchiv Koblenz, Sammlung Schumacher, Nr. 305 I.

45. *Der Panther,* Folge 29, 15 November 1930; Pauley, op. cit., 82; Kerekes, op. cit., 87; Goldinger, op. cit., 175.

46. Riehl to Proksch, 4 October 1930: Verwaltungsarchiv Wien, NS-Parteistellen, box 6.

47. 'Aufzeichnungen des Fürsten Ernst Rüdiger Starhemberg bis zum Jahre 1938 . . .', MS. in Institut für Zeitgeschichte, Vienna, p. 43.

48. Starhemberg in Vienna on 25 March 1930: *Die Heimwehr,* 4 April 1930, quoted by Schweiger, op. cit., Vol. II, 202; Langoth, *Kampf um Österreich,* 86.

49. F. Zacherl to Starhemberg, Munich, 17 December 1930, and leaflet, s.d. *Oberländer*: Polizeiarchiv Wien, box 1929/1.

50. Police report, Vienna, 2 November 1930: ibid., Nachlass Schober, box 32.

51. Protocol of meeting held on 29 November 1930: Verwaltungsarchiv Wien, Grossdeutsche Volkspartei, box 7.

52. *Münchner Zeitung,* 17 December 1930, and *Oberland* leaflet, s.d., both in 'Freikorps Oberland 1929-1932': Polizeiarchiv Wien, box 1929/1.

53. Schweiger, op. cit., Vol. II, 210, notes 1-2.

54. Kerekes, *Abenddämmerung einer Demokratie,* 89.

55. Grossdeutsche Volkspartei for the Tyrol to Reichsparteileitung, Innsbruck, 13 January 1931: Verwaltungsarchiv Wien, Grossdeutsche Volkspartie, box 29.

56. Regierungsrat Dr Ernst Verdross to 'Präsident' (of the Tyrolese government?), Hall, 3 and 5 February 1931: Landesarchiv Tirol, Präsidialakten 1932, 303 III 10.

57. Verdross to Starhemberg, 5 February 1931, 'Lage in Tirol': ibid.

58. Gábor Apor's notes on conversation with Pabst, Vienna, 25 January 1931: Kerekes, 'Akten zu den geheimen Verbindungen . . .', no. 24, pp. 337-39. Frauenfeld was only the Viennese Gauleiter.

59. Report of the Hungarian envoy in Vienna, Count Ambrózy, February 1931: D. Nemes, ' "Die österreichische Aktion" der Bethlen-Regierung', 255.

60. See above, p. 134.

61. Note by Legationsrat Th. Hornbostel, Vienna, 14 September 1931: Haus-, Hof- u. Staatsarchiv, Liasse Österreich 2/3, fasz. 277.

62. Kerekes, *Abenddämmerung einer Demokratie,* 93.

63. *Der Panther,* 4 April 1931, quoted by Josef Hofmann, *Der Pfrimer-Putsch* (Vienna-Graz, 1965) 37.

64. Heimatschutzverband for Upper Austria to all local leaders, Linz, 25 August 1931: Haus-, Hof- u. Staatsarchiv, Liasse Österreich 2/3, fasz. 277.

65. Police reports from Kapfenberg, Tragöss and Thörl, 13-14 September 1931: Steiermärk. Landesarchiv, Bezirkshauptmannschaft Bruck 1931, Gruppe Vrst.

66. Pauley, op. cit., 114, 117-18; Hofmann, op. cit., passim.

67. Notes by Curtius, Geneva, 16 September 1931: Bundesarchiv Koblenz, Reichskanzlei, R 43 I/112.

68. Bundespolizeikommissariat Klagenfurt to government, 22 April 1932: Kärntner Landesarchiv, Präs. 7-6/450, 1932, fasz. 941.

69. *Der Panther,* 2. Jahrgang, Folge 45, 7 November 1931; police report, Graz, 1 November 1931: Verwaltungsarchiv Wien, Bundeskanzleramt, 22/gen., box 4869: both reports are virtually identical.

70. Bundespolizeidirektion Graz to Bundeskanzleramt, 2 November 1931: ibid.

71. *Steirische Gaunachrichten der NSDAP,* Folge 44 and 47, 2 und 19 November 1931, quoted in police reports of 3 and 21 November to the Bundeskanzleramt: ibid.

72. Bundespolizeikommissariat Villach to Bundeskanzleramt, Villach, 9 November 1931, based on talks with leading Carinthian National Socialists: ibid.

9

THE RISE OF NATIONAL SOCIALISM

The early 1930s were the years of the great economic crisis which engulfed Europe and the world; as far as Germany was concerned, they were the years of the phenomenal rise of the National Socialist Party from rather modest beginnings to the position of by far the strongest political party, polling 18 per cent of the total vote in September 1930 and as much as 37 per cent in July 1932. In the eyes of millions of enthusiastic followers of Hitler, this rise was bound to sweep them into power: instead of the hated 'system' a Third Reich of power and of glory would be established. Then their economic misery would end, their enemies be defeated, and Germany be free, strong and united under their venerated Leader. Austria was so closely linked with Germany economically and politically that the developments in the neighbour state were bound to exercise a magnetic influence there. All Austrian parties, ever since 1918, were at least in theory in favour of the Anschluss. The Austrians felt that they were Germans and that their growing economic difficulties might at least be assuaged if they joined their stronger neighbours. The Austria of the Treaty of St Germain was not considered economically viable and the western powers — beset by their own economic difficulties — were more than reluctant to grant Austria new credits and loans. It is true that unemployment did not reach the colossal German figures; but by 1933 the number had risen to 480,000, and in addition there were several hundred thousand who lost the benefits of unemployment insurance and had to make do with pitiful 'welfare' payments.[1] Apart from the industrial workers the white-collar employees were especially hard hit by unemployment: a group particularly prone to listen to nationalist propaganda. This applied even more strongly to the students of Vienna and other universities who had no prospect of employment and often lived in conditions of acute misery. They became increasingly radical, their eyes riveted on a glorious all-German future.

Even before the German elections of September 1930 which exhilarated the Austrian National Socialists too, the Viennese police noticed a greater activity of the Hitler Movement, 'evidently inspired by the successes of his movement in Germany'; especially listed were street demonstrations accompanied by bands and propaganda drives with lorries through larger areas. Taking their cue allegedly from Berlin, the Viennese National Socialists were organizing cells to win over the workers and were publishing a new monthly, *The Labour Front,* for 'the workers of brain and fist in the factories'.[2] In May 1931 a Gautag of the Viennese National Socialists mobilized about 3,200 followers who were addressed by two speakers from Germany: the SA leader Captain Röhm pictured 'the heroic deeds of the German soldiers in the world war, the base treason by the hinterland and the "bartering away of Germany to international Jewry" by the peace treaties'. The lawyer Hans Frank from Munich described in particular the persecutions of the German National Socialists by the authorities which arrested and imprisoned whoever was 'wearing a brown shirt or trousers; the leaders were prevented from speaking in meetings, deprived of their parliamentary immunity and forbidden to enter certain urban quarters . . .'. After this gruesome description of conditions in Germany the attack of the Bohemian deputy Hans Krebs on the peace treaties, 'which had thrust the Austrian and German people into indescribably misery', was more traditional and almost mild.[3]

By the end of 1931 the Austrian government was obviously worried about 'the considerable growth of the party in the Länder', especially in the Burgenland, Vorarlberg and Upper Austria, where fourteen new local groups were recently founded, and even more rapid increases in Vienna. There were reports too about National Socialist propaganda in the Austrian army: 200 soldiers attended a party meeting at Linz, and fifty at Klagenfurt; the party gained new members in the army school at Enns and in Upper Austrian barracks; three officers were particularly active as party speakers, among them Captain Josef Leopold, the later Austrian National Socialist leader, who had joined the party in 1926.[4] In September 1931 the police estimated that the party had about 15,000 registered members, of whom one-third belonged to the SA; another 3,000 or so were members of the Hitler Youth.[5] Much more accurate figures have survived for the Viennese Gau. In January 1930 this had only 1045 members, and the figures then grew very slowly until the autumn, to 1409 in September. The German election of that month clearly caused a more rapid rise: to 2,282 at the end of October, and to 2,997 by the end of the year. A further quick growth was registered during the early months of 1931: from 3,302 at the end of January to 3,950 at the end of March and 4,198 at the end of April.[6] Thus within fifteen months the membership of the party in Vienna quadrupled. In elections to the students' union at Vienna University in March 1931 the National Socialist list won more than 35 per cent of the votes cast and was allocated 15 out of 40 seats in the student chamber, compared with only two previously. The National Socialist students thus became stronger than the Deutsche Studentenschaft which hitherto had been the leading group and was itself strongly völkisch in its leanings. The chairman of the Deutsche Studentenschaft in Austria as a whole was a National Socialist.[7]

In local elections the National Socialists for the first time were able to poll considerably more than in earlier years. In the spring of 1931 they gained eight seats in the city council of Klagenfurt (compared with three before), and two (instead of one) in the town council of Eisenstadt. In Upper Austria they increased their vote from 11,482 to 15,770 within six months; and in the Land Salzburg they more than doubled it within the same period, from 2,650 to 5,630.[8] For the first time the National Socialist tactics of 'going it alone' and rejecting any electoral combination with other right-wing parties seemed to pay off. What was perhaps even more significant was the fact that in Upper Austria — a stronghold of the Heimwehr movement — the latter lost heavily and received only three thousand votes more than the National Socialists; but neither party gained a seat in the Diet. Yet the deputy Landeshauptmann believed that the increase in the National Socialist vote by 4,000 in such a short time 'must be estimated a defeat in view of their colossal agitation'[9] — a rather dubious view if one considers the rapidly growing influence of the party.

Many local reports confirm these signs of increasing National

Socialist activity, which soon outdistanced that of the other parties. In the Styrian district of Voitsberg, for example, an energetic local leader organized National Socialist meetings even in the smallest communities, altogether 265 between the beginning of 1931 and the summer of 1932.[10] In the Tyrol, too, the National Socialists carried their propaganda into the countryside and were able to found local groups in many small places; 'their largest gains came when in Germany the government of Brüning was overthrown and the taking over of power in the Reich was believed imminent after the meeting at Harzburg' of the German right-wing groups in October 1931. But at the end of 1931 the membership in the Tyrol was still very small: about 450 in Innsbruck, and about 800 in all. The SA at Innsbruck at 96 men, mainly students, and at Hall near Innsbruck 14, and the SS at Innsbruck 30 men.[11] In the neighbouring Vorarlberg, National Socialist meetings at Bregenz organized in the second half of 1931 drew audiences of 80, 140 and 190 people, and one of them had to start belatedly because at 8 p.m. only fifteen people were present. At another meeting the Viennese Gauleiter Frauenfeld violently attacked the Grossdeutsch Party, which was neither great, nor German, nor a party, as well as the former Chancellor Schober whom he dubbed 'John the deceiver or pig's head garnished with parsley'; as long as he wore the red ribbon of the Legion of Honour Schober was 'not a German minister', and his National Economic Block was in reality an 'international pigsty block'.[12]

In another small rural Land, the Burgenland in eastern Austria, the police noticed increased National Socialist activity before the general election of 1930, and considerably larger audiences drawn by these meetings. There too Schober was violently attacked: the international loan of 630 million Schilling contracted by him would have to be repaid more than threefold within twenty-seven years.[13] In the district of Neusiedl several National Socialist meetings in the spring of 1931 were well attended and noticeable for strong anti-semitic propaganda. The local authority also reported on 'the general misery among the population', which attributed their plight generally to the large number of deputies and high officials in Vienna.[14] One local police report in the summer of 1931 stressed that the intelligentsia was showing increased interest in the Hitler Movement and that a party group was founded in July. From the same place it was reported later that the National Socialists reckoned with a disintegration of the Heimwehr after the failure of the Pfrimer Putsch and with new recruits from that side.[15] In October it was said that in one commune, Gols, the Hitler

Movement already attracted the majority of the people, and that especially the young were stirred and causing disturbances of the peace.[16]

In Carinthia — as in Styria — the National Socialists in 1931 organized large common meetings with the Heimwehren with the aim of forming a united front; the meetings attracted the local peasantry which hitherto had followed the lead of the Heimwehr. In November a rally in the small town of Möllbrücken was attended by a thousand people, among them the mayors and peasants of the surrounding villages. The speakers of Heimwehren and National Socialists alike attacked 'among thunderous applause the existing system of the political parties in the sharpest manner and demanded the immediate resignation of the political parties and their deputies', while representatives of the Christian Social Party and the Peasant League 'endeavoured to justify the activities of their parties'.[17] In December there was a similar meeting in Villach in which the National Socialist speaker praised the Harzburg Front in Germany; this in Austria too produced the idea of a common front of National Socialists and Heimwehren, an idea that caused 'storms of joy' in large meetings in Graz and Klagenfurt: the National Socialists were extending their hands to the Heimwehr men. On this occasion the speaker was answered by the deputy Emmerich Angerer who declared that they could not wait until the National Socialists seized power in Germany, perhaps in ten, perhaps in twelve months' time; for in Austria the economy was collapsing, hence the Heimwehren would be forced to seize power, 'so as to protect Austria from a complete collapse and to preserve it until the time came for the Anschluss to a Germany led by Hitler'.[18]

There can be little doubt that the National Socialists in the early 1930s considered the Heimwehr an organization with which they might co-operate if occasion offered, but from which they could win many new recruits: tactics which were only too successful, for the Heimwehren included many disparate tendencies and lacked any unified leadership or direction. When the local Heimwehr leaders of Windischgarsten in Upper Austria, who were implicated in the Pfrimer Putsch, were released from prison in October 1931 a torchlight procession in their honour was joined by the völkisch Turner as well as by the National Socialists.[19] At Krems in Lower Austria a mass meeting decided in the same month to form a common 'front of battle' of the two organizations. At Amstetten, also in Lower Austria, 200 men of the Heimwehren transferred to the National Socialists and formed their own SA unit.[20] When the Tyrolese Heimwehren celebrated their tenth anniversary the National Socialists distributed a special leaflet asking them to join the National Socialists: the men of the Heimwehr had broken 'the marxist terror in the factories, in the streets and in the meetings', they had helped the government to push through the constitutional reform and the law against political terror, but what were the thanks of the government? and how long did they want to be deceived by the bourgeois parties? Marxism could not be defeated with the latter's help: 'The National Socialists are closest to you. The National Socialist German Workers' Party is the party of the anti-Marxists and activists. *Come to us!*'[21]

That these efforts met with considerable success was admitted by the Austrian police. In April 1932 they reported that during the past months the Heimwehren lost numerous followers to the National Socialists whose propaganda was extremely lively in town and country. The relative strength of the two organizations varied considerable in the different districts, but without any doubt there were some where the National Socialists were already the stronger.[22] But the attitude of the National Socialists towards the Heimwehren was by no means uniform. Hence in August 1931 the newly appointed Inspector General of the Austrian National Socialists, the German deputy Theo Habicht, issued the curious order to kill the Heimwehren by silence, not to mention them any longer either in meetings or in the press; if a reply to a Heimwehr attack was necessary, then to criticize their wrong policies, but never any individual leader.[23] Apparently there were hopes that individual leaders might be won over. In reply the Viennese Gauleiter suggested that the National Socialists ought 'to adopt a friendly attitude towards them', and that was also Hitler's view, with whom he had briefly discussed the matter. Frauenfeld thought that soon the Heimwehr would be unmasked 'as a legitimist and Christian Social device for catching völkisch votes'; further developments would force the National Socialists to draw a clear line of division between the two movements, as the Heimwehren were misused by reactionary, legitimist circles.[24] Clearly there were still differences on this issue. In November Frauenfeld, speaking in the Viennese German Club, advocated an alliance of Heimwehren and National Socialists.[25]

By the end of 1931 the National Socialists stated officially that the leadership of the Heimwehren 'must be considered, now as before, our enemy but has to be criticized strictly factually and in a dignified manner'. All party members were reminded that a participation in a

Putsch (by the Heimwehren) was strictly prohibited, and any constitutional coup was 'illegal'. All the völkisch associations, such as Heimwehren, Pan-Germans, Turner, were to be approached to oppose, either together with the National Socialists or on their own, any attempt to establish a Danubian Federation or a Habsburg Monarchy; any such attempt was to be fought by all means, and equally any kind of 'Brüning dictatorship' (as it then existed in Germany); whoever participated in such an unconstitutional form of government, was tainted with all the sins of 'the present system' and would have to accept responsibility for it; these plans emanated from Seipel and his helpers, they came from the enemies of Germany and National Socialism.[26] This paragraph, under the heading 'prospective political developments', foretold fairly exactly what was to happen in Austria two years later, when the semi-dictatorial Dollfuss régime was established. Nor was the comparison with the Brüning government all that far-fetched, for both régimes emasculated the powers of parliament — and both paved the way to the establishment of a totalitarian dictatorship.

Apart from the Heimwehren, which for years had been the most activist organization on the right, there were other völkisch associations which served as a perfect recruiting ground for the National Socialists. These were, above all, the völkisch sports and gymnastic clubs and to a lesser extent all pan-German and grossdeutsch organizations of which Austria had a surfeit ever since the late nineteenth century. For all their members it was but a small step from the one to the other völkisch group: once the National Socialists succeeded in establishing their lead it was only a question of time until the most voracious fish would swallow the others swimming in the same pond. In Germany, the same trend occurred in the 1920s and by the early 1930s nothing much was left of the völkisch camp but a few sects worshipping Germanic gods. As early as March 1930 it was said of the Turner in Upper Austria that 80 percent of them were followers of Hitler.[27] One police report of 1931 mentioned that the forces of the defence associations were disintegrating to such an extent that everywhere groups of youngsters repudiated their own leaders and organized their own 'wild' meetings without informing the police. As an example they referred to an 'exercise' organized by the Turnverein of Völkermarkt, which was joined by about 60 Brownshirts from Klagenfurt, demonstrating the close links between the Turner and the SA.[28]

At the beginning of the same year the Turngau of the Marchfeld, to the east of Vienna, concluded an agreement with the National Socialists according to which the latter should join a Turnverein, and the Turner the National Socialist Party. This pact worried the leaders of the Grossdeutsche to such an extent that they met representatives of the Deutsche Turnerbund to encourage them to adopt a firmer attitude. The chairman of the Turnerbund, Kupka, gave an assurance that he would make it absolutely clear to his associations that they must remain 'above party', that within them 'Grossdeutsche and National Socialists must not bash in each other's skulls'. The Grossdeutsche also negotiated with the National Socialists to impress upon them that they were undermining 'a building that, once destroyed, could not be re-built', that they were 'undertunnelling the last national bulwark that we possess in German Austria'. Yet the Grossdeutsche had to admit that they had members in different places of Lower Austria who did not belong to them any longer but had in practice defected to the National Socialists: they were to be asked whether they still counted themselves as party members.[29]

By March 1932 the Grossdeutsche thought it necessary to say publicly what their attitude was towards the National Socialists and their undermining tactics:

> The National Socialists hitherto have not done any damage to the inter-national parties. Social Democracy and the Christian Social Party have re-mained entirely untouched by National Socialist propaganda. But those organ-izations and associations which pursue *natinonal* aims suffer heavily from the National Socialist agitation. Some examples: . . . The National Socialists en-danger through their factory cells the *national trade unions* which have been built up by strenuous work over decades and show a favourable develop-ment. . . . There is no doubt that, if a barrier is not erected soon, the national trade unions are extremely likely to be split and thus to be *destroyed.* The work of destruction endangers all other national institutions. Even the core of the national movement in Austria, the *Deutsche Turnerbund*, is endangered to the utmost. This organization too the National Socialists try to penetrate and to transform the league, which has always been above party, into a *party* organization. . . . It is clear that a continuation of the agitation inside the Deutsche Turnerbund must finally destroy it. . . . It is further characteristic that the National Socialists impede the propaganda efforts of a group which politically is very close to them, the Heimatschutz. There are continuous clashes between Heimwehr men and National Socialists, fights in meeting halls which are regularly caused by the National Socialists. . . . The National Socialist policy in Austria is limited to the negative, to annihilation and destruction.[30]

Yet there was practically nothing that the Grossdeutsche could do to protect their own organization and those associated with them. The younger and more activist members forsook them and went over to the more 'revolutionary' National Socialists. And why should these stop their burrowing inside the 'national' organizations for the sake of politicians whom they detested as 'bourgeois' and linked to the 'system'? As one National Socialist speaker put it, 'the Grossdeutsche made the big speeches about Germanhood at tables covered with a white cloth, but otherwise did not understand the worker who was perhaps permitted to watch through the window'.[31]

In the early months of 1932 the leaders of the Viennese SA time and again stressed that their co-operation with the Deutsche Turner-bund was close, 'the strongest *activum* in the development of the SA', or 'very good in all districts'. When the Turner gave a gymnastics display in the Viennese stadium the SA provided the stewards.[32] The other völkisch organization with which the SA co-operated closely was the *Deutsche Schulverein Südmark* which was responsible for main-taining German schools in non-German areas.[33] In general it was stated that the 'national' associations were losing members to the SA. This applied in particular to the Frontkämpfer of whom only a 'black-yellow remnant' remained in some districts.[34] As to the Heimwehren, one SA leader reported that in his district 'there is great confusion among the Heimwehr of all shades' and that there were continuous secessions to the National Socialists. And another proudly declared that the Heim-wehr was virtually wiped out; most of its members had transferred to the SA or to the Styrian national association of Dr Pfrimer. In Hietzing the local group of the Starhemberg Jäger was almost destroyed, some of the men going over to the SA and others retiring; only eighteen members remained.[35] These reports may have been coloured, yet they provide a picture of the growth of the SA in Vienna and of its penetration into friendly and rival associations. Indeed, apart from the Deutsche Turnerbund these were all seen as rivals or enemies who must be 'destroyed', 'wiped out', 'smashed up': the vocabulary of these monthly reports is reminiscent of the 'meeting hall battles' in which the SA specialized and which made up its folklore. As the men had to be trained for these battles, a friendly co-operation with the Turnerbund was indicated, and its members could be recruited for the SA.

We do not know what the strength of the Viennese SA was at that time. In May 1933 – that is, after the seizure of power in Germany – the police estimated it at about 3,000, and for the whole of Austria at more than 30,000 men.[36] In the same estimate they gave the figure of 69,000 for party membership in January 1933. That was over 50 per cent more than the real figure, which was 43,129 on 30 January 1933, i.e. the date when Hitler was appointed chancellor. Of these 28,718 or two-thirds were in Vienna and Lower Austria. Of the other Länder only Carinthia and Styria had comparatively high membership figures, 6,592 and 5,453, respectively. The figures for the remaining Länder were still very small: 1,188 for Tyrol and Vorarlberg, 690 for Upper Austria, and 488 for Salzburg.[37] Thus the figure given by the police for the SA seems very much exaggerated and half of their estimate was probably nearer the truth. It is difficult to account for the small membership in the western Länder — Salzburg, Tyrol and Upper Austria — close to the German frontier and in general very much influenced by the developments there. But in 1928 there had only been 112 party members in the Tyrol and the figure therefore represented a tenfold growth in five years. The same very nearly applied to the whole of Austria, which had only 4,466 members in 1928.[38]

It is much more difficult to establish the social composition of the party at that time, as the data available for Germany simply do not exist for Austria. In certain towns, such as Vienna or Innsbruck, the SA had many student members; otherwise its membership was apparently considerably more proletarian than that of the party, with the category of *Hilfsarbeiter* (unskilled labourer) very prominent, while the SA leaders were often former officers or semi-intellectuals. Intellectuals of one kind or another were also mentioned in some local police reports as prominent among the party members, for example in a local report from the Burgenland as early as July 1931.[39] A later report from Gmunden stated boldly that, if the government settled the Jewish question, 'the doctors, lawyers and university professors would no longer have such a strong interest in the National Socialist Party and thus the intellectual head of National Socialism would be cut off to a large extent . . .'.[40]

When the Vorarlberg police in 1933 compiled a list of leading National Socialists, on the other hand, it only included among 159 names five people who might be classified as intellectuals: two lawyers, one architect, one journalist and one Protestant clergyman. There were in addition two leading local entrepreneurs from Dornbirn and two of their sons; in such a small town their influence and the funds provided by them for the party must have played a major role in making National Socialism acceptable and respectable. The same men, interestingly enough, had earlier supplied the funds for the Heimwehren, and the leading Heimwehr officers had also turned National Socialist.

Among the 159 names there was also a proletarian element, but it was not particularly strong, about 10 to 12 per cent of the total. The large majority were small people, such as craftsmen, artisans or 'masters' of a craft, white-collar workers and small officials, innkeepers and farmers; most likely representing a true cross section of the local population, but there was only one woman among them.[41] Vorarlberg in 1933 was still a Land with little industry — most of it in Dornbirn — and preponderant agriculture, a Land of small towns and villages, far from Vienna and its political passions. But in its capital, Bregenz, the leaders of the National Socialist Party were to a large extent intellectuals and former officers.[42] Such people joined the party at an early stage and rose within it to important positions; indeed, without them the later expansion of the party would have been impossible.

After the election success of the party in April 1932 Dr Riehl wrote to Proksch and provided from his intimate knowledge of the Viennese scene an analysis of the National Socialist vote which confirms some of the points made above. He found

> that not only the entire Aryan intelligentsia and a majority of the academically trained and higher civil servants have voted for us, but curiously enough of the people in enterprise and trade especially the architects, master-builders, etc., very many people who are well situated, and not at all the small men and the Christian workers, who strangely enough have remained faithful to the Christian Social Party. . . .

He found that there had been no influx from the true working class, at least not in Vienna (where the Social Democrats maintained their position): 'What we have won of proletarian and semi-proletarian voters, are very small white-collar employees, chauffeurs, railway and tramway men. . . .' Riehl also thought that many of the bourgeois votes were given to the party in error 'because the people do not know the true nature of our movement and favour only the anti-semitic and above all the anti-marxist point of view'; they were disappointed because the Christian Social Party had given up its anti-Semitism, and they were influenced by developments in Germany and by the failure of one of the largest banks, the *Kreditanstalt* in Vienna.[43] This was a shrewd analysis: it stressed the role of the 'Aryan' intelligentsia which felt threatened by Jewish competition, and of anti-Semitism in general which found new nourishment through the economic crisis. It was very similar to the trend prevailing in Germany, only that there the intelligentsia was less prominent, and the movement more pronouncedly lower middle-class in character. But, in Vienna at least, the National Socialists were able to win some real working-class support, e.g. in factory council elections in October 1931; at that time, according to the police, many employees of the state and the public sector joined the party on account of the government's budgetary policy.[44]

In April 1932 the National Socialists succeeded in inflicting a severe defeat on the Christian Social Party in Vienna, winning 13 of the seats held by it in the town hall, and altogether 15 out of a hundred. They now polled 201,000 votes compared with 27,000 eighteen months before, a remarkable success.[45] Prior to the election, the Grossdeutsche once more suggested a combined list, 'so that no völkisch votes would be lost, while in the opposite case a victory for the völkisch cause would be assured'. But this suggestion was rejected by the Inspector General of the National Socialists, Habicht. After the election he could proudly point to his 'collossal success', while the Grossdeutsche no longer held a single seat.[46]

In simultaneous elections in four of the other Austrian Länder, i.e. Carinthia, Styria, Lower Austria and Salzburg, the National Socialists gained something like 20 per cent of the votes, to a large extent at the expense of the Grossdeutsche, Peasant League and Heimatblock — right-wing groups which were comparatively close to them. The so-called 'national camp' became a camp of the swastika. The two major parties, Social Democrats and Christian Socials, on the other hand, suffered comparatively minor losses (like the Social Democrats and the Centre in Germany), caused by the defection of marginal groups, such as 'anti-marxists' and anti-semites who preferred the stronger fare offered by the National Socialists.[47] But the majority of the industrial workers continued to vote Social Democrat, and the majority of the country population and the peasants Christian Social. The real question was whether the two major parties would be able to withstand the onslaught or would be engulfed by it, as they were in Germany in 1933. In the towns many of the unemployed and in Carinthia and Styria large groups of the peasantry voted for the National Socialists.

In May 1932 the Grossdeutsche who were the principal losers discussed the election results. All the speakers were in favour of preserving their own party although it had been deserted by its followers. A co-operation with the National Socialists was considered 'out of the question' on account of the way in which the latter had fought the election. One deputy announced that he could not co-operate with the National Socialists because their methods were not 'objective'.

Another declared that they could not like dogs run after the National Socialists, and yet another that in Germany Hugenberg, after all, maintained his position next to Hitler's (an opinion that was disproved by developments there within twelve months). They then voted to preserve their party organization.[48] Yet only twelve months later the Grossdeutsche decided to form 'a community of battle' with the National Socialists, to oppose by a united 'national' front the Dollfuss government.[49] In practice that meant that the Grossdeutsche disappeared as an independent group and merged with the stronger 'brother', as did the German Nationalist Party and the Stahlhelm in the Third Reich at about the same time. By that time, most of the local councillors and other representatives elected on a grossdeutsch list had become National Socialists without, however, giving up their seats, in spite of all attempts of the party leaders to achieve this. It was in vain that some party leaders declared that, although they were willing to co-operate with the National Socialists in a 'Harzburg Front', they were unwilling to become socialists or to fight under the red flag, even if it incorporated the swastika.[50] Nor did their evocation of military virtues fall on more fertile ground: 'The soldier proves his value only during a retreat. Only those who remain firm in defeat will finally conquer.' Their appeal to black-white-red[50] – the German Imperial colours – no longer evoked the emotions once aroused by Schönerer. In Vorarlberg the local Grossdeutsche simply recommended their members to join the National Socialist Party 'because this movement stands for the principal demands of the Grossdeutsch Party, above all the Anschluss and anti-Semitism'.[51]

Other völkisch organizations too quickly recognized the National Socialist supremacy. Thus the *Deutscher Schulverein Südmark* at the beginning of 1932 humbly apologized because one of its papers, the *Alpenländische Monatshefte*, published an article containing certain criticisms of the National Socialist movement. When the Gauleiter of Vienna protested against this article the leaders of the Deutscher Schulverein not only expressed their sharp disapproval, but declared that they had made arrangements to have the principles of 'non-partisanship' respected in future.[52] In the same year the Deutscher Schulverein Südmark distributed a leaflet sharply attacking the plan to establish a Danubian Federation which 'would make us German Austrians a people of slaves without any rights, who would be ruled and maltreated by the enemies of the Germans'.[53] On this issue too it echoed the line of National Socialist propaganda.

It might have been assumed that the successes of the National Socialists in the years 1931-32 would have assuaged the personal rivalries of the leaders and that the infighting which had bedevilled the party's history would have subsided. Yet strong personal conflicts between the Gauleiter and the Austrian leadership at Linz continued unabated. This applied in particular to the relations between the successful Viennese Gauleiter Frauenfeld and the 'administrative' Austrian leader Proksch. In April 1931 the latter wrote to Frauenfeld: 'I deny you the right to set yourself up as a judge of my decrees as if you were the personfication of National Socialist ideass. . . . I have always known how to defend myself against impertinences and in this case too I will know how to ward them off. This provisionally for your information. Heil Hitler! '[54] A few weeks later Proksch wrote again that Frauenfeld had accused him in Munich of drawing a sizeable income from the National Socialist publishing house, of gaining material advantages and using 'Jewish business methods'; as these allegations were untrue, 'you have in the most careless manner spread a slander and thus damaged my name severely in the organization, undermined the authority of an appointed leader and provided an inducement to a breach of discipline although you know that the authority of the leader and discipline are the very bases of our organization . . .'. Proksch demanded that Frauenfeld retract his offensive utterances, for he was unwilling to let himself be made contemptible in front of the party members.[55] But although the letter was sent by registered post there does not seem to have been a reply.

Frauenfeld in his turn wrote to the Styrian Gauleiter, Oberhaidacher, that he solemnly recognized him 'as Emperor of Styria' and that nothing was further from him than an attempt 'to belittle your power in any way', 'but I must state that it is of no advantage to the movement if every Gauleiter, instead of representing the party's interests, always tries convulsively as his first priority to prevent any healthy cooperation. . .'. He declined to take Oberhaidacher's 'temperamental outbreaks . . . particularly tragically'.[56] Frauenfeld himself clearly had strong ambitions to become the Austrian Landesleiter and thus to supplant the 'administrative' leader Proksch. Therefore in July 1931 Proksch invited all Austrian Gauleiter to Linz, but not Frauenfeld, and told them that there was the possibility of a new Landesleitung being established in Vienna. The assembled Gauleiter did not favour this plan, nor did they want Proksch appointed Landesleiter: after all, any leader for the whole of Austria would only detract from

their own powers. Nevertheless Proksch achieved that he was nominated Austrian Landesleiter by Hitler with a strong say in the financial
affairs of the Gaue which were allocated their shares of subsidies by
him. But apparently Hitler did not have much confidence in the new
Landesleiter, for he also appointed the German National Socialist Theo
Habicht as Inspector General for Austria. As the critics put it, Proksch
was put 'under the tutelage of a political midwife'; within a short time
it turned out that Habicht was the real Landesleiter whose task it was
'to provide Proksch with good ideas'.[57]

In the summer of 1931 Proksch, by using in his orders 'a sergeant's
jargon', succeeded in removing one of his rivals, the Tyrolese Gauleiter
Suske, after internal party proceedings had been taken against him.[58]
His successor in the Tyrol, Riedl, prided himself on his Germanic
looks, while he considered Frauenfeld to be of Jewish origin on account
of 'his habits', and Proksch a Mongoloid of equally doubtful racial
origins.[57] In April 1932 Strasser forwarded some documents to
Habicht which dealt with the conditions in the Tyrolese party. In his
opinion, 'Innsbruck has always been a terrible nest of stinkers', and
Riedl was as little capable of mastering the situation there as Suske had
been; Strasser expected from Habicht 'that you will put matters right
there and if need be create order according to Reich German
customs'.[59] This Habicht apparently did by expelling not only Suske,
but also several of his followers from the party; as long as they were the
leaders in Tyrol, he claimed, the organization there 'was a pigsty'.[60]

In 1932 Proksch also attempted to remove his old enemy Frauenfeld
from the post of Gauleiter of Vienna, but the latter was backed by
Munich — probably because of his drive and brutality — and Proksch
had to climb down. His opponents inside the party considered Proksch
'a servant, revengeful, brutal and vain'.[61] But in the party hierarchy the
opinion of him was not much better. After the Anschluss it was
suggested that he might 'become price commissar for Austria or something like it'; his qualities were thought to be in the economic, and not
in the political sphere. If an Austrian was to be appointed Gauleiter of
Vienna it should be Frauenfeld. A Reich German, however, was considered far better as Frauenfeld was not energetic enough for the post —
and this was accordingly done.[62] In 1932 another conflict developed
between Frauenfeld and the Gauleiter of Lower Austria, Captain
Leopold, because the former wanted to found a new daily paper in
Vienna, while Leopold was part-owner of the existing National Socialist
paper, *Deutschösterreichische Tageszeitung.* This paper which had been

through very difficult years would accordingly suffer from Frauenfeld's scheme.[63] Opposition to Proksch as Landesleiter for Austria also came from the SS in Upper Austria, which refused to take any orders from him because they were directly subordinate to the SS leaders in Munich.[64]

SS units were founded in Austria comparatively late and were subordinate to the SS leader Sepp Dietrich in Munich. Small groups were founded in the capitals of the Austrian Länder in 1931, and by June 1932 they counted about 600 men. Their leader in Austria, a man by the name of Turza, according to the opinion of his superiors, 'entirely lacked organizational talent and the capacity to lead a larger unit' and did not co-operate with his adjutant, Hofmann, because he feared to be supplanted by him. He also quarrelled with the SS leader in Linz, Hollitscher; there the SS was rent by conflicts between various subleaders which Hollitscher was unable to settle. The Salzburg SS leader, Dumböck, was involved in quarrels with the leaders of the party and the SA, 'often for petty reasons'. The Innsbruck leader, Klimesch, was considered 'a capable subleader', but he believed that the SS was 'a kind of moral police' and had leading local National Socialists continuously shadowed. He was therefore expelled from the party and the SS. The SS leader in Graz, Schön, left the leadership of the unit to a subordinate who made the local *Sturm*, 'which had many student members, into a pure terror guard'. At Klagenfurt conflicts erupted between the local SS leaders because one of them was promoted over the heads of the others who then resigned. In the spring of 1932 there was a considerable influx of new members, but this made it all the more obvious how incapable Turza was as a leader. He appointed Hofmann the SS leader for Upper Austria to be rid of him. The only well disciplined unit was in Vienna, and the other units had but loose contacts with Turza. Other party organizations too were unwilling to co-operate with him. He was finally removed by Munich; 'he was not missed anywhere'. His successor, Greschke, then succeeded by intensive propaganda in trebling the membership within a short time.[65] This description, coming from an SS source, clearly mirrors the conditions existing in the National Socialist elite unit in the years 1931-32.

In the years 1932-33 the progress of the National Socialists in the different Austrian Länder was uneven, but everywhere it received a strong impetus when Hitler was appointed German Chancellor in January 1933. In Bregenz, for example, National Socialist meetings held in the spring of 1932 were only attended by 120 or 170 people who listened to strongly anti-semitic speeches; but in 1933 attendance quickly rose to 400 and more.[66] In March 1933 a secondary school teacher compared the new German chancellor with Rudolf of Habsburg, who had created order in Germany after the sad period of the *interregnum* when robber barons looted and fleeced the people; now again a king had been chosen who would deal with the modern robber barons with a firm hand; the marxist leaders in Germany were criminals who must be eliminated.[67]

From the Tyrol it was reported early in 1932 that the National Socialists had some success among the peasantry. But their progress was very slow on account of resistance by patriotic circles who were able to use Hitler's renunciation of the South Tyrol to advantage.[68] In April 1933, however, it was stated that the developments in Germany had given 'an extraordinary impetus' to the Tyrolese National Socialists. Large Heimwehr groups in practice ceased to exist, and strong National Socialist groups came into being in the Upper Inn valley; in almost every place, even remote valleys, small party groups existed which were growing quickly.[69] That this report from a German source was not to fanciful is partly confirmed by a police report from Landeck on the Upper Inn. The National Socialists, it stated, were gaining much ground in the whole district; in Landeck itself there existed an SA unit of about sixty which was well organized and possessed even a machine gun which the members of the Turnverein Jahn brought along when they left the Heimwehr and became National Socialists. A clash between them and the Heimwehr could be expected at any moment, for their mutual hatred was very strong.[70]

In Styria, too, the National Socialists advanced at the expense of the Heimwehren. According to the police, the Heimwehr ranks were thrown into 'great confusion' by the failure of the Pfrimer Putsch and the election successes of the National Socialists, and many men went over to the National Socialists. In November 1932 the whole Heimwehr group at Liezen decided to join the National Socialist Party. In the district of Leoben the dominant features of the situation were the crisis in the industrial area and the rise of the National Socialists, and there was strong opposition to the Heimwehren within their own ranks. At a Heimwehr meeting at Rottenmann the speaker asked those present to vote National Socialist as their programme was identical with that of the Heimwehr.[71] This shift affected above all the works of the Alpine Montangesellschaft at Donawitz near Leoben and other places, which had become strongholds of the Heimwehren after 1927. Now many of the leading engineers and managers, as well as officials of the central management in Vienna, became National Socialists and openly recruited for the party inside the works. One director even went on tours of inspection wearing party uniform. If workers were hired preference was given to National Socialists. In the steel works the leading engineer Panzl was at the same time the leader of the National Socialist factory cell. The firm's *Werkszeitung,* its internal journal, openly showed National Socialist tendencies. It was made clear to the workmen that it would be to their advantage if they joined a movement which so clearly received support from higher quarters.[72] These measures were to a large extent successful and the works were transformed into strongholds of National Socialism.

From Klagenfurt the German Consul reported in June 1933 that 'the progress of the National Socialist movement is astonishing'. It gained a firm footing in the most remote valleys of Upper Carinthia and in the reputedly 'black' (Christian Social) eastern Lavant valley, it made good progress among the socialists, and even won adherents among the Slovenes in the linguistically mixed areas of the south.[73] In Feistritz the majority of Heimwehr members went over to the National Socialists, headed by a local factory owner and his son, who also took along the weapons belonging to the Heimwehr unit which they secreted in their factory.[74] Here, as in Dornbirn, and to a much larger extent at Donawitz, it becomes apparent how vital was the influence of the factory owners and employers in determining the attitude of the employees.

In general it seems that, especially in Carinthia and Styria, National Socialism was making quick progress in this period, not only in the towns, but also in the villages, where once the Peasant League had been influential. From the few data available, it seems that Austrian National Socialism was somewhat more broadly based than the German movement of the 1920s, that it had followers among the peasantry as well as among the workers however unwilling some of the latter may have been at the outset. But in both countries the mass of the followers came from the urban white-collar workers, lower state and municipal officials, students, small independent people such as shopkeepers and craftsmen, and in Austria to a larger extent than in Germany, from intellectuals: the groups which were the main victims of the great economic crisis. A well-known Austrian historian who himself experienced these feelings has described the 'intoxication' not only of the young, but also of the older generation of academics who thus could return to the ideals of their own youth – to ideals which they had long believed unrealizable, but which 'seemed to be gloriously confirmed by the successes of National Socialism in the German Reich'. The same could be observed in the 'national' student corporations in which the radicalism of the students had a strong fascination for the 'old boys', who held important positions, and led them into the camp of National Socialism.[75] Thus the rise of the Austrian National Socialists owed a great deal to the success of the German movement; above all it provided them with a Leader which their own movement did not produce. As even the oppositional National Socialists from Tyrol put it *after* their expulsion: 'In the Reich Adolf Hitler stands at the helm, noble in thought, just in action, magnanimous in aims, a military commander who protects his experienced soldiers even against their own officers.'[76]

NOTES

1. Erich Zöllner, *Geschichte Österreichs* (Vienna, 1961) 557-58.

2. Police report, Vienna, 23 August 1930: Verwaltungsarchiv Wien, Bundeskanzleramt, 22/gen., box 4867.

3. Police report, Vienna, 4 May 1931: Polizeiarchiv Wien, Nachlass Schober, box 33/1.

4. 'Information über die NSDAP (Hitlerbewegung) in Österreich in den Monaten Oktober und November 1931', issued by the Bundeskanzleramt: Verwaltungsarchiv Wien, Bundeskanzleramt, 22/gen., box 4869. The information on Leopold from his obituary in the Berlin Document Center.

5. Police report, Vienna, 18 September 1931: Polizeiarchiv Wien, Nachlass Schober, box 33/1.

6. Figures taken from monthly reports for Gau Wien: Verwaltungsarchiv Wien, NS-Parteistellen, box 20.

7. Confidential police report on 'Aufbau und Organisation der NSDAP (Hitlerbewegung)', 20 May 1931: Vorarlberger Landesarchiv, Bezirkshauptmannschaft Bregenz, Nr. 613, 1931.

8. Confidential police report on 'Aufbau and Organisation der NSDAP (Hitlerbewegung)', 20 May 1931: Vorarlberger Landesarchiv, Bezirkshauptmannschaft Bregenz, Nr. 613, 1931.

9. Franz Langoth to Schober, Linz, 20 April 1931: Polizeiarchiv Wien, Nachlass Schober, box 74.

10. Steiermärk. Landesarchiv, Bezirkshauptmannschaft Voitsberg 1931, Gruppe 14 R-Z; 1932, Gruppe 14.

11. 'Bericht über nationalsozialistische Bewegung für Oktober u. November 31', Innsbruck, 8 December 1931: Tiroler Landesarchiv, Präsidialakten 1933, 181 XII 59.

12. Police reports of 5 August, 1 September, 9 November 1931 (the first in the file): Vorarlberger Landesarchiv, Bezirkshauptmannschaft Bregenz, Nr. 613, 1931.

13. Reports by Bundespolizeikommissariat Eisenstadt, 9 September and 8 November 1930: Burgenländ. Landesarchiv, Regierungsarchiv, III-31/1930.

14. Reports by Bezirkshauptmannschaft Neusiedl, 27 February and 31 March 1931: ibid., I-16/1931.

15. Reports by Gendarmeriepostenkommando Oberschützen, in reports of Landesgendarmeriekommando for Burgenland, 31 August and 30 September 1931: ibid.

16. Report by Landesgendarmeriekommando for Burgenland, 31 October 1931: ibid.

17. Bezirkshauptmann of Spittal on the Drau to Carinthian government, 9 November 1931: Kärntner Landesarchiv, Präs. 9-2/1411, fasz. 904.

18. Report by Bundespolizeikommissariat Villach, 11 December 1931: Verwaltungsarchiv Wien, Bundeskanzleramt, 22/gen., box 4872.

19. Report by Gendarmeriepostenkommando Windischgarsten, 6 October 1931: ibid., box 4871.

20. 'Information über die NSDAP (Hitlerbewegung) in Österreich in den Monaten Dezember 1931 und Jänner 1932': ibid., box 4872.

21. Leaflet signed by Gauleiter Suske, distributed in Innsbruck on 11 May 1930: Tiroler Landesarchiv, Präsidialakten 1930, 956 III 10.

22. Police report, Vienna, 7 April 1932: Polizeiarchiv Wien, Nachlass Schober, box 33/1; Verwaltungsarchiv, Bundeskanzleramt, 22/gen., box 4873.

23. Habicht to Gauleitung Wien, Linz, 8 August 1931: ibid., NS-Parteistellen, box 6.

24. Gauleitung Wien to Landesleitung in Linz, Vienna, 22 September 1931: ibid. Legitimism, as it might prevent the Anschluss, was the bugbear of all good National Socialists and German nationalists.

25. Wolfgang Rosar, *Deutsche Gemeinschaft − Seyss-Inguart und der Anschluss* (Vienna, 1971) 44.

26. *Steirische Gaunachrichten der N.S.D.A.P.*, Folge 51-53, quoted in police report, Graz, 11 December 1931: ibid., Bundeskanzleramt, 22/gen., box 4872.

27. 'Gauführertagung Linz am 16.3.1930': Bundesarchiv Koblenz, Sammlung Schumacher, Nr. 305 I.

28. Report by Bezirksgendarmeriekommando Völkermarkt, 10 September 1931: Kärnter Landesarchiv, Präs. 9-2/1411, fasz. 904.

29. Protocols of grossdeutsch meetings on 24 February and 29 March 1931: Verwaltungsarchiv Wien, Grossdeutsche Volkspartei, boxes 16, 22.

30. Pressemitteilungen der Grossdeutschen Volkspartei, Nr. 968, 23 March 1932: Verwaltungsarchiv Wien, Grossdeutsche Volkspartei, box 14. Italics in original.

31. Thus police report on National Socialist meeting in Bregenz, s.d. (June 1932): Vorarlberger Landesarchiv, Präsidialakten 1932, Nr. 232.

32. Thus reports by the leaders of *Sturmbann* III/4, II/4, I/24, II/24 of 25 March, 1 April, 30 June, 1 July 1932: Verwaltungsarchiv Wien, NS–Parteistellen, box 19: SA.

33. Thus reports by the leader of Sturmbann II/4 of 1 April and 1 July: ibid.

34. Thus reports by the leaders of Sturmbann II/4 and II/24 of 1 April, 1 July 1932: ibid.

35. Thus reports by the leaders of Sturmbann II/4, II/24 and III/24 of 1 April and 1 July 1932: ibid. These monthly or quarterly reports unfortunately do not give the strength of the units in question.

36. Confidential report by the Viennese police, 3 May 1933: ibid., Bundeskanzleramt, 22/gen., box 4875.

37. 'Zusammenstellung bis 19 November 1938', supplied by the party on 14 December 1938: Bundesarchiv Koblenz, Sammlung Schumacher, Nr. 303.

38. See above, p. 153.

39. Report by Landesgendarmeriekommando of the Burgenland, 31 August 1931: Burgenland. Landesarchiv, Regierungsarchiv, I-16/1931.

40. Report by Gendarmerie of Gmunden, 30 March 1934: Oberöster. Landesarchiv, Politische Akten, Nr. 11 (Gmunden).

41. The list was compiled by the Bezirkshauptmannschaften of Bregenz, Feldkirch and Bludenz in September 1933: Vorarlberger Landesarchiv, Präsidialakten 757, 1933.

42. The list was compiled by the Gendarmerie of Bregenz in January 1938 and has two ex-officers, one lawyer, one headmaster, one apothecary, two engineers, etc.: ibid., Bezirkshauptmannschaft Bregenz, Nr. 174, 1938.

43. Riehl to Proksch, Vienna, 26 April 1932: Bundesarchiv Koblenz, Sammlung Schumacher, Nr. 305 II.

44. Police report, Vienna, 15 October 1931, with details: Haus-, Hof- u. Staatsarchiv, Liasse Österreich 2/21, fasz. 302.

45. Peter Huemer, 'Sektionschef Dr Robert Hecht . . .' (Ph.D. thesis, Vienna, 1968) MS., II, 272.

46. Habicht to Gregor Strasser, Linz, 2 June 1932: Bundesarchiv Koblenz, Sammlung Schumacher, Nr. 305 I. H. rejected any co-operation with the Grossdeutsche 'who in fact have nothing any longer behind them'.

47. Wandruszka, 'Österreichs politische Struktur', loc. cit., 409; Zöllner, *Geschichte Österreichs*, 511.

48. 'Verhandlungsschrift über die Sitzung der Landesparteileitung für Niederösterreich am 4. Mai 1932': Verwaltungsarchiv Wien, Grossdeutsche Volkspartei, box 16.

49. The German envoy to Auswärt. Amt, Vienna, 18 May 1933: Bundesarchiv Koblenz, Reichskanzlei, R 43 II/1475.

50. Thus a circular of Dr Herbert Stadler, Kreisführer of the Grossdeutsch Party, Vienna, 15 June 1932: Verwaltungsarchiv Wien, NS-Parteistellen, box 12.

51. *Vorarlberger Tagblatt,* 8 May 1933.

52. Deutscher Schulverein Südmark to Gau Vienna of NSDAP, Vienna, 26 January 1932: Verwaltungsarchiv Wien, NS-Parteistellen, box 5.

53. Leaflet of May 1932: ibid., Nachlass Dr W. Lohmann, box 6.

54. Proksch to Frauenfeld, Linz, 4 April 1931: ibid., NS-Parteistellen, box 6.

55. Same to same, Linz, 30 April 1931: ibid.

56. Frauenfeld to Oberhaidacher, Vienna, 4 April 1931: ibid., box 5.

57. The above according to an interesting pamphlet *Hitler oder Proksch* from 1932: Bundesarchiv Koblenz, Sammlung Schumacher, Nr. 302. P's appointment as Landesleiter, Munich, 13 July 1931: ibid., Nr. 305 I. A second form, Munich, 6 July 1931, is in Verwaltungsarchiv Wien, Nachlass Dr Lohmann, box 7. Both are signed by Hitler.

58. Mitteilungsblatt der Landesleitung Österreich der NSDAP, Folge 11, Linz, 1 September 1932: Bundesarchiv, Sammlung Schumacher, Nr. 302.

59. Strasser to Habicht, Munich, 19 April 1932: ibid., Nr. 305 I.

60. Habicht to Strasser, Linz, June 1932: ibid.

61. Thus the pamphlet *Hitler oder Proksch* of 1932: ibid., Nr. 302.

62. Top secret note for Gauleiter Bürckel, Vienna, s.d. (1938): ibid., Nr. 304.

63. 'Verhandlungsschrift über die Sitzung der Landesparteileitung für Niederösterreich am 23. November 1932': Verwaltungsarchiv Wien, Grossdeutsche Volkspartei, box 16.

64. Police report, Vienna, 18 September 1931: Polizeiarchiv Wien, Nachlass Schober, box 33/1.

65. 'SS Abschnitt VIII, seine Entstehung und Entwicklung bis Herbst 1932', 9 June 1933: Verwaltungsarchiv Wien, Bundeskanzleramt, 22/gen., box 4876. The author of the report is not known.

66. Police reports of 27 May, 27 June 1932, 10 February, 6 March and 10 June 1933: Vorarlberger Landesarchiv, Präsidialakten 232, 1932; Bezirkshauptmannschaft Bregenz, Nr. 1380, 1934.

67. Police report, Bregenz, 7 March 1933: ibid., Präsidialakten 252, 1933.

68. Confidential police information of February 1932: Haus-, Hof- u. Staatsarchiv, Liasse Österreich 2/21, fasz. 302.

69. Report by Felix Kraus, Innsbruck, 4 April 1933: Bundesarchiv Koblenz, Nachlass Dr H. Steinacher, Nr. 45.

70. Police report, Landeck, 13 March 1933: Tiroler Landesarchiv, Präsidialakten 1933, 675 III 10.

71. Reports by Landesgendarmeriekommando for Styria, 13 June, 13 August, 11 November 1932: Steiermärk. Landesarchiv, Landesamtsdirektion 1932, 384 He 2.

72. Report on the *Alpine Montangesellschaft* works, Graz, 30 August 1934, ibid.; report by Generaldirektion für die öffentl. Sicherheit on the same, Vienna, 20 October 1934: Verwaltungsarchiv Wien, Bundeskanzleramt, 22/gen., box 4926, both with many details.

73. German Consul at Klagenfurt to Auswärt. Amt, 10 June 1933: Bundesarchiv Koblenz, Reichskanzlei, R 43 II/1475.

74. Report by Gendarmerie Feistritz, 11 August 1934: Bezirkshauptmannschaft Klagenfurt, 1934, J 1-300.

75. Adam Wandruszka, 'Österreichs politische Struktur', loc. cit., 405-6.

76. *Hitler oder Proksch,* 11, from the year 1932: Bundesarchiv, Sammlung Schumacher, Nr. 302.

10

THE DECLINE OF THE 'HEIMWEHREN' AND THE 'VÖLKISCH' CAMP

The early 1930s brought a sharp decline in the strength of the Heimwehren which was partly due to their old weaknesses — lack of unity, in-fighting among the leaders, dependence on foreign support — and partly to the rise of National Socialism which to a large extent replaced them as the 'activist' movement of the right. Yet another cause was the collapse of the Pfrimer Putsch in Styria which ultimately led the majority of the Styrians to accept Hitler as their Leader: the failure of the Heimwehren in the other Länder to support the Styrians was a further cause of disintegration. Some ten years later Starhemberg ingenuously suggested that the opposite was the case, that the National Socialist line of rejecting any Putsch induced 'innumerable young men' to leave that party and to join the Heimwehren, 'that above all in rural areas, less so in the towns, National Socialist local groups dissolved themselves and transferred to the Heimwehr'. He also claims that 'on the day that the Heimwehr proved its activism it exercised a great attraction on the so-called National Socialists', who were dissatisfied with the existing form of parliamentary government and 'degenerate' democracy.[1] This indeed might have been the case *if* the Heimwehr had 'proved its activism' by a Putsch. But such a Putsch was only attempted in Styria, and its dismal failure there had exactly the opposite effect as

211

will be shown later. How the *non*-support of the Putsch by the other leaders, such as Starhemberg, could possibly attract activist young National Socialists seems a riddle which even his fertile imagination could not solve.

Within the Heimwehr movement Starhemberg tried to restore some unity. In February 1932 he went to Innsbruck to address the Tyrolese Heimwehren. The fact that he stood side by side with their leader Steidle was to convince the audience that 'the unification of the Heimatwehr movement is accomplished, . . . that nothing can separate us any longer'. There was a 'storm of applause' when Starhemberg and Steidle shook hands to demonstrate 'the unity of their wills'.[2] Unfortunately, this unity did not last. Already at the beginning of April the Viennese police reported that the representatives of Styria in the Heimwehr leadership intended to bring about Starhemberg's resignation; if the leaders could not reach agreement on a common policy it was feared that the völkisch wing, above all the Heimwehren of Styria, Carinthia and Salzburg, would form their own front which would then get in touch with the National Socialists. The police also noted that the Heimwehren were suffering from such a lack of funds that they had to give notice to the majority of the employees working in their offices.[3] Yet when the leaders met in Vienna a few days later they expressed their confidence in Starhemberg. The Heimwehren, they decided, should if possible abstain from party politics 'so as to regain the confidence of the broad masses', and they protested in advance against a possible coalition government of the Social Democrats and the Christian Social Party. The lack of unity among them, however, was shown by their attitude towards elections: this was not a question of principle for the movement, but the leaders in each Land should adopt any line they favoured for tactical reasons. The police did not expect 'any violent action in the immediate future' because many of the Heimwehr formations were unable to take any.[4]

The success of the National Socialists in the elections of April 1932 and the lack of success of the Heimatblock lists increased among the leaders a tendency towards abstention from party politics and towards a concentration on their own para-military formations. But those of Styria and Salzburg favoured the adoption of 'a strictly national and anti-semitic course' and a sharp rejection of all monarchist tendencies,[5] in other words a course similar to that of the National Socialists. By the summer of 1932 these clashes of opinion erupted publicly. In August the leaders of the Styrian Heimwehren solemnly declared that they

condemned Starhemberg's policy 'because it runs counter to our principles, in effect upholds the mismanagement of the parties and is
contrary to the public welfare'. They demanded that Starhemberg
should resign as the Austrian leader, and in September they proudly
announced that the same demand was also raised in Upper Austria and
that 172 Heimwehr leaders were opposing Starhemberg's policy.[6]
Meanwhile, however, Starhemberg solved at least one of his problems:
he demanded funds and weapons from Mussolini, who apparently still
hoped that the Heimwehren would seize power in Austria, and was
promised both in large quantities.[7] Vast quantities of rifles and several
hundred automatic rifles, which the Italians had captured from the
Austrian army in 1918, were then sent to Austria for repair and
modernization. Some of the loot was to go to the Heimwehren, and the
rest to be transported to Hungary; the owner of the factory at Hirten-
berg where the work was to be carried out was an intimate friend of
Starhemberg and one of his financiers.[8] The Styrian units, on the other
hand, with their German nationalist and völkisch tendencies, were able
to secure financial help from Berlin: not from the National Socialists
who had to cope with great financial difficulties of their own, but from
the Ministry of Defence, which was ever eager to fish in troubled
waters, yet blandly informed the Auswärtige Amt that no such help had
been rendered.[9]

According to Major Pabst, it was this financial support that made
any reconciliation between Starhemberg and the Styrians extremely
difficult.[9] But the political and ideological differences went much
deeper. In 1932 the majority of the Heimwehren adhered by and large
to their old line of opposing the 'system' of political parties and an
elected parliament and demanded their replacement by a Senate and
Chamber of Estates, the creation of a strong central authority, the
reduction of the overgrown bureaucratic apparatus, a reform of the
administration and of the legal system, which should be 'adapted to the
legal sentiments of the native people'. Another aim emphasized was 'the
creation of a great German people's state', i.e. the Anschluss, but
nothing was said about the form in which this might be achieved.[10]
The 'twelve principles of the Styrian Heimatschutz' adopted about
twelve months later were far more outspoken in their adherence to
völkisch and racialist ideology: 'The Heimatschutz sees in Bolshevism,
Marxism and their handmaid, the democratic-parliamentarian party
system, the causes of the existing corruption and the principal enemies
of völkisch traits, Christian convictions and German ideology.... A

natural precondition of völkisch policy is for the Heimatschutz the cultivation of, and high regard for, a Germanic racial consciousness *(germanisches Rassebewusstsein)....*' To make the meaning absolutely clear it was added that only 'Aryan' Germans could become members and only if they accepted the principles.[11]

Even before these principles were adopted Dr Pfrimer went to Munich in May 1932 to see the German SA leader, Captain Röhm, and offered to put his 30,000 men — most of them in Styria — under Hitler's command. Hitler took notice of the offer but ordered a 'detailed investigation', which was to be conducted on behalf of Röhm by General von Hörauf in close co-operation with the Austrian National Socialists.[12] It was only after Hitler's seizure of power in Germany that a formal agreement was reached between the National Socialists, represented by Proksch and the SA leader Reschny, and the leaders of the Styrian Heimwehren to form a 'close fighting community in all matters and for every case'; by this the Styrians formally recognized Hitler 'as the Leader of the German nation'. They proclaimed their determined opposition to the government of Dollfuss, which was to be replaced by 'a strong government of national concentration', after the dissolution of parliament and the holding of a general election. But the two organizations remained separate, at least formally. Ten days later, on 1 May 1933, Hitler received the Styrian leaders in the chancellery in Berlin, and they solemnly assured him of their loyalty and devotion. In Graz the Heimwehr paper published the agreement under the banner headline 'A Common Völkisch Battle Front!'[13]

At a further meeting, in Venice in November 1933, it was agreed to maintain the two separate organizations because meanwhile both had been dissolved by the Dollfuss government, and in view of their illegality a unification was impractical. But common leaders were to be appointed for the different localities, the Styrian Heimwehr battalions were to become SA units, and their leaders in Upper and Lower Styria the commanders of the SA brigades in these districts — clearly because their units were much stronger than those of the SA proper.[14] In the eyes of the Austrian National Socialists these agreements led to the 'creation of a strong national opposition', which forced the Grossdeutsche and the Peasant League to join it, and which made possible the uprising in Styria in July 1934.[15] For the Styrian Heimwehren, which had always been strongly völkisch with the swastika as their symbol, the National Socialist seizure of power finally tipped the scales. But even if this had not taken place at that time it seems likely that their course would have been a very similar one.

In the other Austrian Länder the relationship of the Heimwehr with the National Socialists was much more complex. By the beginning of 1932 the 'community of battle' which had been formed in many places was dissolved.[16] Yet even then Starhemberg did not give up hope of reaching an accommodation with Hitler whom he visited in Berlin in April. Allegedly he was willing to join the National Socialist Party, but on condition that certain of its Austrian leaders were to be removed: did he see himself as the new Austrian leader? Hitler's Austrian Inspector General warned his chief of Starhemberg's intentions – which of course would have affected Habicht's position in Austria – and declared that the Heimwehren 'are completely finished as a political movement' and could no longer risk to put up their own candidates in an election; wherever they would try to do so, even in combination with other parties, they were certain to 'suffer catastrophic defeats'.[17] But Starhemberg's visit to Berlin was in vain, probably because Hitler had no intention of accepting any demand for a change of personnel in Austria and distrusted the ambitions of the young aristocrat; after all, Habicht was a far more reliable tool from his point of view. The Austrian National Socialists would in any case not have accepted the 'traitor' Starhemberg as a leader.

By March 1933 Starhemberg took a leaf out of the National Socialist book; he attacked their Austrian leaders on 'racial' grounds and claimed: 'The National Socialist Party in Austria is a political party led by a handful of men of Czech ancestry which has no right to call itself a movement of national rejuvenation and gravely endangers Germanhood in Austria by the irresponsible ways in which it conducts politics.' In Germany, on the other hand, the National Socialist Party, whether one accepted its programme or not, was in any case a movement of national rejuvenation and liberation, led by men of German blood. It was out of the question that the Chancellor Adolf Hitler approved of the anti-German policy of the Austrian National Socialists, for it could not be true 'that a national fighter like Adolf Hitler sanctions a policy which provides constant support for Austro-Bolshevism' and splits the front erected against it.[18] Yet on the same day Starhemberg declared in front of the assembled Heimwehr leaders that a common front with the National Socialists was necessary: if his person were an obstacle to 'the National Socialists becoming comrades in a united front' he would gladly resign.[19] In the same month the German Legation in Vienna heard from a reliable source that Starhemberg had asked a friendly industrialist to find out whether there could not be a rapprochement between him and the National Socialists. The precondition of such a link seemed to be that Starhemberg wanted to play the part of von Papen or at least that of the Stahlhelm leaders in Germany; he should withdraw his support from the Dollfuss government and demand, like the National Socialists, a general election, which otherwise was very unlikely to take place. The industrialist in question met the Viennese Gauleiter Frauenfeld, but we do not know what transpired between them.[20]

Later in 1933 Starhemberg's tone became much more strident. Speaking at Bruck in Styria he exclaimed that only those had a right to live in Austria who were born there; 'the others ought to be thrown out'. He now opposed the Anschluss 'because we do not want to be ruled by Berlin and environs. Austria was long German when Slav was still spoken in Berlin. . . . We do want the unification of all German tribes, but under the leadership of Vienna.' The National Socialist ideas and movement were born in the student corporations and there the evil must be attacked at the root. The same applied to the civil servants who were only good Austrians when they collected their salaries on the first and fifteenth of the month. The Heimwehren, he continued, were now a power in the state and would take action if their will was not carried out, for their patience was exhausted.[21]

The idea of the German mission of Austria in opposition to Prussia and the Prussianized Germany, always likely to find an echo in Austria, was also taken up in the official yearbook of the Heimwehren: 'The incredible spectacle of the Prussianization of Germany means the end of the idea of the Reich. The German people cannot fulfil their historical mission of the penetration and colonization of the European East and Southeast from Berlin and through Berlin. The force of historical development must lead the Germans back to Vienna, back to the idea of the old Reich.' It was a true service to the German nation, it was claimed further, to make Austria strong and capable of fulfilling its historical mission.[22] But how could the small Austria of 1933, weak and divided, take up where the Habsburgs and Prince Eugene had left off in the eighteenth century? The 250th anniversary of the liberation of Vienna from the Turks was celebrated by a monster parade of the Heimwehren from all over Austria. Starhemberg claimed that there were 40,000 men — but the money for it had to be provided by Mussolini.[23] One of the leaders of the Styrian Heimatschutz alleged that among them were many 'Croats, Hungarians, Social Democrats,

and even Communists, . . . a shame for the Austrian-German people'.[24]
At several places in Carinthia free fights occurred between National
Socialists and Heimwehr men when the latter entrained for Vienna;
crowds besieged the stations, beer bottles were thrown out of the
carriages, and the National Socialists retaliated with stones. But only a
few people were slightly wounded.[25]

In Carinthia the Heimwehren split into two rival organizations when
their founder and leader, Brigadier General Hülgerth, adopted a critical
attitude towards the Pfrimer Putsch in Styria. Whole districts seceded
and founded a rival German-Austrian Heimatschutz which moved closer
to the National Socialists and finally accepted their leadership. Many
local groups had to be dissolved. Yet there was also strong criticism of
the leading Austrian National Socialists who were considered 'incapable
of carrying out the national revolution'.[26] In the small Burgenland too
the Heimwehren split into two hostile organizations, the Austrian
Heimatschutz, which remained loyal to Starhemberg as the leader, and
the Riflemen's Association which moved closer to the Christian Social
Party. But the local reports by the police stressed time and again that
there was a general lack of interest and virtually no activity; several
local groups simply decided to dissolve themselves.[27]

When the Styrian Heimatschutz in 1933 went over to the National
Socialists the police reported that it had 186 local groups and 15,207
members, but that more than three thousand left the organization on
account of its political course. Of these, 2,898 then joined the Austrian
Heimatschutz under Starhemberg. According to another police report,
more members were recruited in the summer of 1933 and new local
groups founded. Many members of the rival Styrian Heimatschutz who
had only joined it so as not to lose their jobs would have liked to resign
and to join the Austrian Heimatschutz 'if they were not subject to the
pressure of the nationalist engineers and officials of their employers
who are the leaders of the Styrian Heimatschutz. But they dare not
undertake anything against this terror of the leaders.'[28] Thus the
Austrian Heimatschutz was unable to gain any footing in the works of
the Alpine Montangesellschaft at Donawitz and elsewhere.[29]

From the district of Linz in Upper Austria the police reported that
the membership of the Heimwehren was declining and that most of
those who left went over to the National Socialists. At the end of
February 1933 there were 1,285 members left in this district about half
of whom were Starhemberg Jäger, organized in fourteen local groups,
while the SA had only 368 members.[30] In the district of Ried the

Heimwehren in 1934 had 728 members in sixteen groups.[31] These are the only Upper Austrian districts for which figures are available.

From the Tyrol Landeshauptmann Dr Stumpf wrote to the minister of defence in Vienna that the Heimwehr men were fed up with politics and saw it as their only duty to give support to the legal government. In his opinion, they should be used as volunteers to support the army, as was done in Germany, because the Austrian army was too weak; the army should establish contacts with the Heimwehren in this sense; as they were subordinate to him as Landeshauptmann no difficulties could arise on that score.[32] Six months later a pro-German observer drew a very unfavourable picture of the Tyrolese Heimwehren. He claimed that large groups had in practice ceased to exist, and that especially the peasants were leaving; what was left were mainly the adherents of the Christian Social Party; in Innsbruck itself, many units were divided, and many members opposed to Steidle as the leader; there was severe friction between Heimwehr men employed as an emergency police and the regular police forces; in general, the ill-discipline of certain Heimwehr units which consisted of unemployed workmen severely damaged the Heimwehr cause.[33] A local Heimwehr leaflet from the same year declared they did not want to become a 'Prussian colony', nor did they want 'a brown, party dictatorship' or a 'brown Cheka', for the Heimwehren were fighting 'for a free and German Austria'.[34]

A German diplomatic report gave the strength of the Heimwehr units in the autumn of 1933 as about 15,000 in Upper and 12,000 in Lower Austria, another 3,200 in Vienna and about 3,000 in Tyrol (probably an underestimate). 'The Burgenland, Carinthia, Styria and Salzburg are in their majority National Socialist and the number of reliable Heimwehr men in these four Länder has fallen to a minimum.'[35] Yet even 33,200 men in four Länder was still a sizeable figure, and the statement was certainly exaggerated as far as Carinthia and Styria were concerned. At the end of 1933 the Austrian SA leaders were equally negative about the development of the Heimwehren: 'The signs of disintegration in the Heimatschutz grow from month to month. . . . This disintegration proceeds without any special propaganda effort by the National Socialists, and one is often astonished about the lack of any real propaganda on the part of the Heimatschutz leadership.'[36] Statements such as these have to be read with caution, but disintegration there certainly was, and much of it was due to a lack of leadership and to intrigues of the National Socialists with individual Heimwehr leaders.

The centre of these intrigues during the later months of 1933 was the ambitious Viennese Heimwehr leader and vice-chancellor in the Dollfuss government, Major Emil Fey, who approached the Viennese Gauleiter Frauenfeld through his adjutant, Major Lahr, with a plan to bring about a reconciliation of the Heimwehren and the National Socialists. He declared that he was fed up with Christian Social intrigues and was determined to 'create order' in collaboration with the National Socialists. Major Pabst together with another Austrian intermediary sent a similar message to Habicht. Count Alberti, Heimwehr leader in Lower Austria, was of exactly the same opinion: Austria must be ruled by a force which united Heimwehren and National Socialists.[37] It was then arranged that Alberti should meet representatives of Habicht on 5 October at Sopron in western Hungary where Alberti produced a written authorization from Fey who was ready to form a coalition government of the two movements. He also suggested that Habicht should become an Austrian, and the latter informed Hitler who gave his consent to a continuation of the negotiations.[38] In December Habicht told the Auswärtige Amt that not only Fey and Alberti, but also Starhemberg and Steidle were vying with each other in their approaches to the National Socialists and in their endeavours to picture the other leaders as 'impossible'. In Habicht's opinion the rival leaders presented 'a picture of total confusion and loss of their heads!', and all were equally opposed to Chancellor Dollfuss.[39]

In Vienna Alberti resumed his contacts with Frauenfeld. When the police in January 1934 raided Frauenfeld's flat they found there another leading National Socialist, and a German 'diplomat', the Hereditary Prince of Waldeck-Pyrmont, negotiating with Alberti and another Viennese Heimwehr leader and arrested them. Starhemberg declared publicly that those two had acted contrary to his express orders and that he alone was entitled to get in touch with other political groups.[40] In reality, however, he let the National Socialists know through an intermediary that he too was willing to negotiate and that he did not object to Habicht becoming chancellor, while he, Starhemberg, could become the Austrian president, and Dollfuss too should be given a ministerial post.[41]

In July 1934 Fey once more informed the National Socialists that he aimed at 'a reconciliation and cooperation with National Socialism' because to him the only enemy was Marxism. He suggested the formation of a 'national transition cabinet', but insisted on a guarantee that he would retain some influence even after the passing away of the

transitional government. Major Lahr, Fey's intermediary, was determined to put these proposals to Hitler himself; but when he was instead
referred to Habicht, he broke off the negotiations because he did not
consider Habicht suitable 'for work of such responsibility'.[42] It was a
sordid picture of personal rivalries, intrigues, and constant attempts to
insure the personal future of individual leaders in case of a National
Socialist success, while many Heimwehr members became passive or
deserted their movement to join a more 'activist' one. The Dollfuss
government accomplished the elimination of parliament and of the
political parties and was promising the creation of Estates as the basis
of the future social order, but the Heimwehren contributed very little
to these 'achievements'. The days when they could talk about seizing
power and imposing their will upon the country were gone. Their
continuing influence in the government was only insured by the fact
that the government itself was without any solid mass support.

The fate of the Grossdeutsche, who once had enjoyed a comparatively strong representation in parliament and government, was
even worse, as their followers deserted their party. As early as 1932
they were threatened by 'catastrophe' when they tried to raise funds,
especially from the industrialists. Allegedly because of the Christian
Social attitude, they were refused even 'a single button'. They therefore
approached the Brüning government in Germany with a request for
help.[43] Twelve months later their chairman, Professor Foppa, went to
Berlin where he had conversations with Hugenberg, now a nationalist
minister in Hitler's government, and the Stahlhelm leaders. The German
minister in Vienna favoured renewed German support for the Grossdeutsche: 'The representation of the German interests in parliament
and in the country is today almost the sole raison d'être of this party';
as the National Socialists were not represented in parliament, the
Grossdeutsche were still 'a very important factor for us' and should be
supported. They thus received from Germany throughout 1933-34
certain small sums, amounting in all to about 42,000 Schilling.[44] Even
under Hitler as German chancellor these subsidies were continued for a
considerable time although the German Nationalist Party had long
dropped out of the government.

By the time that they were discontinued the Grossdeutsche had
virtually disappeared as a party. From Gmunden in Upper Austria it
was reported in 1934 that especially its younger members had become
National Socialists or at least sympathized with them. According to the
police there were about fifty members left in the district, while the

National Socialists had about 400 to 500, and the Christian Social Party about 3,500.[45] From a small commune, also in Upper Austria, it was said that all local officials elected on the grossdeutsch list had become National Socialists and were openly showing their hostility to Austria and the government.[46] In 1936 it was officially stated by the security organs that the 'Grossdeutsch Party, which has lost virtually all its followers to the National Socialist movement, is condemned to total passivity. The few people who still represent the grossdeutsch views do not dare to make a stand against the National Socialist movement.'[47] The 'fighting community' which the party formed with the National Socialists in May 1933 ended in its demise. The same fate befell the German Nationalist Party, but only *after* Hitler's seizure of power.

Very similar was the fate of the Landbund (Peasant League) and of the Bauernwehren which it had founded to defend the peasants' interests. In his unpublished memoirs one of its former leaders wrote that it 'finally inclined towards the side of the National Socialists'; it always stood for 'the national idea and remained loyal to it to the end'.[48] From a small commune in Upper Austria it was reported in 1933 that the Landbund concluded an alliance with the National Socialists so that the latter were now completely on top and intimidated the rest of the population.[49] From Braunau on the Inn it was stated that the majority of its youth organization, the *Junglandbund,* sympathized with National Socialism, and from a smaller place in the same district that the former Landbund no longer existed because part of it had become National Socialist, and the rest was 'without any activity'.[50] In Carinthia, many members of the Landbund and the Bauernwehren went over to the National Socialists. From two other districts it was reported that the Bauernwehren were strongly 'brown' in colour, and many of the younger members secretly belonged to the SA; many young peasants went to agrarian schools in Bavaria and returned as National Socialists.[51] In other Austrian Länder too the local groups of the Bauernwehren consisted to a large extent of National Socialists, and it became clear that they thus tried to continue a 'legal' existence after the dissolution of their party by the government.[52]

Apart from these old-established organizations on the political right, a new one – or rather three – made a brief appearance in the early 1930s and proclaimed officially that they were 'fascist'. In 1930 a 'Party of Austrian Fascists' was founded by one Leo Rösler who had seceded from the Heimwehr. But the police found that the organization did not develop any noticeable activity and was unable to pay the rent for its premises. In 1931 one Karl Hekl founded a 'National Austrian Fascist Legion' which proclaimed its strict respect for the law and aimed at the elimination of the class struggle. The Legionaries wore a black shirt and black caps with a cockade in the Austrian colours; but the meetings were badly attended. In the same year one Viktor Grien-seihs announced the formation of a 'Fascist Party of Austria', which wanted to establish Fascism through a dictatorship, but its foundation was prohibited by the authorities on the basis of a law of 1867 which forbade the foundation of local groups. In 1936 the police established that the party had dissolved itself in 1933.[53] A National Socialist agent sent to report on its meetings in 1933 found that several had to be abandoned because only two people appeared, and on two occasions he was the only 'enthusiast' attracted by the fascist appeal.[54]

From a similar source comes a report about the National Socialist Schulz group which separated from the Hitler Movement in 1927 and failed to reunite with it in 1930. In March 1933 Schulz held a meeting in the Mariahilf district of Vienna which was attended by only 35 people among whom were ten women. Among the points made by Schulz the most interesting are his comments on Hitler as the new German chancellor, which showed that Schulz remained loyal to the original character of the party as a workers' party. Hitler's 'first deed', Schulz declared, 'has been to put on a top hat and tails for purposes of representation' (actually Hitler had worn a morning coat on the Day of Potsdam a week earlier). 'His achievements', Schulz continued, 'have not benefited the worker so far; workers' leaders have been arrested. . . . The successes gained hitherto are not the achievements of the Leader's genius but those of the brutal and loyal gendarme Göring.' The treatment of the trade unions was contrary to the workers' interests; it was even planned to deprive the German worker entirely of his rights after the Italian pattern, where a workman was not allowed to change his job (this was a remarkably accurate forecast). In Schulz's opinion Hitler had 'no programme', for his Twentyfive Points had nothing in common with the original National Socialist programme; he was doing a lot of talking and would achieve little. The National Socialist observer at the meeting thought that there was no enthusiasm and no drive among Schulz' followers; several of them left before the meeting was over. He classified them as grumblers and people who knew everything better.[55] The National Socialists clearly collected information about all hostile groups and parties, however small they were.

The head organization of all völkisch associations, the *Verband deutschvölkischer Vereine* in Vienna, also suffered a general decline. In April 1930 its chairman, Dr Max Kilhof, informed all member associations that both the last general meeting and the enlarged management committee had been so poorly attended that no decisions could be taken; even the celebration in honour of Bismarck's birthday was badly attended on account of insufficient propaganda for it. If this passivity continued it would have to be considered whether the Verband ought not to be dissolved.[56] A meeting organized in the autumn of 1930 caused such financial difficulties that once more it looked that the continuation of the Verband was in doubt. When it asked the member associations for their financial contributions, only one-third responded. The membership dues for 1931 were equally slow in coming in, so that the Verband was virtually condemned to passivity.[57] Another circular, of April 1932, stated that the district organizations in Vienna had suspended all activity 'for the time being'. At that time twenty-three associations were represented on the management committee of the Verband, among them old völkisch organizations such as the Pan-German League, the Turner, the Aryan League, as well as the Deutsche Studentenschaft and various academic clubs and corporations.[58] In Innsbruck as many as fifty such associations formed a *Deutschvölkische Arbeitsgemeinschaft,* but many of them existed only 'on paper'. Interestingly enough, there the organization was run by the Deutsche Schulverein Südmark, which, at least officially, was a neutral educational organization and enjoyed official support.[59] Although the National Socialists were not mentioned in any of the circulars, it seems clear that they were absorbing the more active elements of the other völkisch organizations: hence their passivity and decline.

The only völkisch organization not affected by this general decline on the right was the Deutsche Turnerbund which closely co-operated with the SA and saw to it that its men reached the required standard of physical fitness. Indeed, in many places the *Wehrzüge* of the Deutsche Turnerbund were hardly distinguishable from SA units. The earlier co-operation with the Heimwehren came to an end and was replaced by agreements with the National Socialists. Early in 1932 the police reported that the *Wehrverbände* of the Deutsche Turnerbund had given up their links with the Heimwehr and moved closer to the National Socialists. The leaders of the Deutsche Turnerbund in Vienna reached an understanding with the SA in Munich that individual Turner could join the SA, but that no Turner groups were to join collectively, and no

SA units were to become Turner groups. The National Socialist Party would not found sports clubs or training sections of its own, and the Turner who were party members were to join an association of the Turnerbund.[60] Thus the National Socialists succeeded in winning over what they themselves described as 'the most unified, the most activist national group' in Austria,[61] and – equally important from their point of view – in driving a wedge between the Turner and the Heimwehren.

At Whitsun 1932 the Deutsche Turnerbund, at a great sports rally in Vienna, reaffirmed that it stood above party politics: 'In its ranks all *Volksgenossen* are welcome who are of German racial origin, follow the principles of racial purity, national unity and spiritual freedom and are ready to live, work and fight for these strictly völkisch principles.' It was symptomatic of the co-operation with the SA that the latter provided the stewards for the gymnastics display at the rally.[62] This resolution was embodied in a pamphlet of 1933 designed to ward off attacks on the Deutsche Turnerbund as a partisan and political organization. Against these attacks the pamphlet reiterated that among the members there had always been 'members and followers of all völkisch and Aryan parties', and that only those of German and Aryan origin were acceptable as members of the individual sports and gymnastics clubs.[63] What it did not admit was that the adoption of such völkisch principles in itself constituted a political act and brought the Turnerbund into close proximity to the National Socialists who by that time were the one major force on the extreme right.

How thin the 'non-political' disguise was also emerged from a resolution adopted unanimously by the Deutsche Turnverein Rudolfsheim in the spring of 1933. It sharply condemned the acceptance of money from 'non-Aryan sources' by the Heimwehren 'which were allegedly völkisch', and equally the 'former close alliance of Turnerbund and Heimatschutz'. It further expressed the association's complete allegiance to the Leadership Principle, but only 'as long as the leaders of the Bund conduct a radically racial anti-semitic policy' and did not expect from the members any support for the Heimwehren, 'because above the leader of the Bund there stands the Leader of the people, *Adolf Hitler,* to whom the members of the association have been pledged in loyalty for many years'. Finally the resolution stressed that every völkisch Turner was obliged to follow the racial and anti-semitic aims stipulated by Turnvater Jahn in the early nineteenth century 'in doctrine and reality, in politics and literature'.[64] It was a clear warning to the leaders of the Turnerbund that loyalty to Hitler and racial anti-Semitism came first, and that to their own leaders second; and it showed the truly 'non-political' attitude of the Turnerbund.

As far as the National Socialists themselves were concerned, there was no longer any need to enter into pacts or agreements with organizations or parties which stood close to them and subscribed to völkisch principles. They felt that they were in the ascendant, that time and the economic crisis were working for them, that the seizure of power in Germany would exercise a magnetic effect on Austria, that the Anschluss was bound to come. But they were willing to use well known names and high sounding titles to further the good cause and to create front organizations with innocuous names led by men who officially were not party members. One of these was the *Deutsche Volksrat für Österreich* under Fieldmarshal-Lieutenant Carl Bardolff, who in 1932 also became the chairman of the German Club in Vienna. The latter provided a forum for National Socialist and other 'national' speakers, for example for the Viennese Gauleiter Frauenfeld.[65] Bardolff's name also figured under a manifesto of the *Kampfbund für deutsche Kultur* signed by prominent writers and other intellectuals which proclaimed that 'the internal enemy forces are busy to destroy the roots of our race, to poison its marrow, to choke its growth. Tribe, people, race are the primeval forms of humanity given by God, from which alone soul and spirit can grow in genuine blood . . .' [*sic*].[66] It was this racialist appeal that found so fertile a soil in Austria and was so eagerly accepted by many who believed in the natural superiority of the German race. Thus they could explain away and compensate for the defeat in the great war, the humiliations of the revolution of 1918 and the Treaty of St Germain. They could feel superior to Jews and Slavs and 'lesser tribes'; they could feel convinced that the future belonged to them.

NOTES

1. 'Aufzeichnungen des Fürsten Ernst Rüdiger Starhemberg bis zum Jahre 1938 verfasst während des zweiten Weltkrieges in London', MS. in Institut für Zeitgeschichte, Vienna, p. 53.

2. *Der Panther*, 3. Jahrgang, Folge 8, Graz, 27 February 1932.

3. Confidential police report, Vienna, 7 April 1932: Polizeiarchiv Wien, Nachlass Schober, box 34.

4. Police report, Vienna, 10 April 1932: ibid. and Haus-, Hof- u. Staatsarchiv, Liasse Österreich 2/21, fasz. 302.

5. Confidential police report, Vienna, 1 May 1932: Polizeiarchiv Wien, Nachlass Schober, box 34, and Haus-, Hof- u. Staatsarchiv, Liasse Österreich 2/21, fasz. 302.

6. *Der Panther,* 3. Jahrgang, Folge 33 and 35, 20 August and 3 September 1932.

7. Walter Goldinger, *Geschichte der Republik Österreich* (Vienna 1962) 169.

8. Auswärt. Amt, Botschaft Wien, Geheimakten 1933, 4938 part 5, E 268013, 268019: reports of 28 and 30 January 1933.

9. Note by Hüffer, Berlin, 17 February 1933: Auswärt. Amt, Abt. II, 6080H, E451075. The note does not give a date when the money was paid but says that Pabst had complained to von Bredow, who succeeded Schleicher as head of the *Ministeramt* in June 1932, and resigned in January 1933.

10. 'Grundsätzliche Einstellung des Heimatschutzes zu staatspolitischen, kulturellen, wirtschafts- und sozialpolitischen Fragen', January 1932: Verwaltungsarchiv Wien, Bundeskanzleramt, 22/gen., box 4872.

11. *Österreichisches Heimatschutz-Jahrbuch 1933,* p. 44, quoted by Schweiger, op. cit., Vol. II, 208.

12. NSDAP Landesleitung to Gauleiter, Linz, 30 May 1932: Verwaltungsarchiv, NS-Parteistellen, box 6.

13. 'Das Abkommen zwischen NSDAP und steirischem Heimatschutz', Liezen, 22 April 1933: Bundesarchiv Koblenz, Sammlung Schumacher, Nr. 277; *Der Panther,* 4. Jahrgang, Folge 17 (text heavily censored).

14. 'Besprechung in Venedig den 23. November 1933': Bundesarchiv, Sammlung Schumacher, Nr. 277.

15. NSDAP Landesleitung Österreich to Reichsleitung, Berlin, 23 January 1935: ibid. For the rising in Styria, see below, pp. 262-63.

16. 'Information über die N.S.D.A.P. in Österreich in den Monaten Dezember 1931 und Jänner 1932': Verwaltungsarchiv Wien, Bundeskanzleramt, 22/gen., box 4872; Pauley, op. cit., 152; police report, Graz, 22 June 1933: Steiermärk. Landesarchiv, Landesamtsdirektion 1932, 384 He 2.

17. Habicht to Hitler, Linz, 18 April 1932: Bundesarchiv Koblenz, Sammlung Schumacher, Nr. 305 I. The visit to Berlin is confirmed by Starhemberg's memoirs.

18. *Offener Brief* to Proksch, Vienna, 10 March 1933: Verwaltungsarchiv Wien, Nachlass Dr Lohmann, box 10.

19. Quoted by Anton Staudinger, 'Christlichsoziale Partei und Errichtung des "Autoritären Ständestaates" in Österreich', *Vom Justizpalast zum Heldenplatz – Studien und Dokumentationen* (Vienna, 1975) 74.

20. 'Die Verfassungskrise', Vienna, 25 March 1933: Botschaft Wien, Geheimakten 1933, 4938 part 5, E268203.

21. Police report, Bruck, 21 November 1933: Steiermärk. Landesarchiv, Bezirkshauptmannschaft Bruck 1933, Gruppe Vrst. 1.

22. *Heimatschutz in Österreich* (Vienna, 1934) 336-37. This was a new form of the grossdeutsch ideology which had always been strong in the Heimwehr movement.

23. 'Lebenserinnerungen des Fürsten Ernst Rüdiger von Starhemberg von ihm selbst verfasst im Winter 1938/39 in Saint Gervais', MS., loc. cit.

24. Police report, Ligist, 11 June 1933: Steiermärk. Landesarchiv, Bezirkshauptmannschaft Voitsberg 1933, Gruppe 14 A-O.

25. Reports by Bezirkshauptmann of Hermagor and St Veit, 15 May 1933: Kärntner Landesarchiv, Präs. 9-2/1411, fasz. 904.

26. Report by Bundespolizeikommissariat Villach, 12 November 1931: Verwaltungsarchiv Wien, Bundeskanzleramt, 22/gen., box 4869; *Heimatschutz in Österreich* (Vienna, 1934) 192, 196.

27. Ibid., p. 278; police reports of 31 January, 29 April, 30 June 1931, 14 March 1932, 30 July 1934: Burgenländ. Landesarchiv, Regierungsarchiv, I-16/1931; nos. 206, 603, 1358 of Burgenländ. Vereinsakten, A/IV-14.

28. Reports by Styrian Landesgendarmeriekommando, Graz, 22 June and 12 July 1933: Steiermärk. Landesarchiv, Landesamtsdirektion 1932, 384 He 2.

29. Police report, Leoben, 31 July 1934: ibid., Landesamtsdirektion 1934, 384 A 114.

30. Reports by Bezirksgendarmeriekommando Linz, 4 March, 5 June, 3 August 1933: Oberösterreich. Landesarchiv, Politische Akten, Nr. 23 (Linz-Land).

31. Police report, Ried, 12 April 1934: ibid., Nr. 31 (Ried am Inn).

32. Dr Stumpf to Vaugoin, Innsbruck, 24 October 1932: Tiroler Landesarchiv, Präsidialakten 1933, 675 III 10.

33. Felix Kraus to Dr Steinacher, Innsbruck, 4 April 1933: Bundesarchiv Koblenz, Nachlass Hans Steinacher, Nr. 45.

34. Heimwehr poster at Landeck, s.d. (1933): Tiroler Landesarchiv, Präsidialakten 1933, 181 XII 59.

35. Report on Austria, 11 October 1933: Auswärt. Amt, Abt. II, Nationalsozialismus, Österreich, Bd. 1, 6111H, E452563.

36. Generaldirektion für die öffentl. Sicherheit, Vienna, 21 December 1933: Oberösterreich. Landesarchiv, Politische Akten, Nr. 1 (Braunau).

37. Langoth, *Kampf um Österreich*, 121: notes on a discussion with Habicht on 27 September 1933.

38. Notes by Councillor Hüffer, Berlin, 13 October 1933: *Akten zur deutschen auswärtigen Politik*, series C, I (1) (Göttingen, 1971) 903, and n. 3.

39. Habicht to Hüffer, Munich, 6 December 1933: op. cit., Vol. II (1) (Göttingen, 1973) 184.

40. *Aufruf des Bundesführers!*, 16 January 1934: Verwaltungsarchiv Wien, Nachlass Dr Lohmann, box 10.

41. Notes by Hüffer, Berlin, 24 January 1934: *Akten zur deutschen auswärtigen Politik*, series C, II (1) 403.

42. Dr Rieth to Secretary of State von Bülow, Vienna, 19 and 23 July 1934: Botschaft Wien, Geheimakten 1934, 4938 part 7, E270049-51, 270058; Major Lahr to National Socialist Party office, s.d.: Berlin Document Center.

43. Hans Steinacher to Minister Treviranus, enclosing a letter from Viktor Miltschinsky, Vienna, 5 February 1932: Bundesarchiv Koblenz, Reichskanzlei, R 43 I/113.

44. *Akten zur deutschen auswärt. Politik*, series C, I (1) 52-55, n. 5.

45. Reports from Gmunden, 30 and 31 March 1934: Oberösterreich. Landesarchiv, Politische Akten, Nr. 11 (Gmunden).

46. Sicherheitsdirektor for Upper Austria to Bezirkshauptmannschaft Braunau, Linz, 6 September 1933: ibid., Politische Akten, Nr. 1.

47. Generaldirektion für die öffentl. Sicherheit, 4 April 1936: Haus-, Hof- u. Staatsarchiv, Liasse Österreich 2/21, fasz. 468.

48. MS. by Vinzenz Schumy, written in 1938, p. 127: Institut für Zeitgeschichte, Vienna.

49. Note on Mettmach, Ried, 3 October 1933: Oberösterreich. Landesarchiv, Politische Akten, Nr. 30 (Ried).

50. Reports of 14 February and 12 August 1934: ibid., Nr. 3 and 4 (Braunau).

51. Report by Sicherheitsdirektor for Carinthia, Klagenfurt, 1 June 1934: Verwaltungsarchiv Wien, Bundeskanzleramt, 22/gen., box 4882.

52. Report by Bundespolizeidirektion Wien, 14 March 1934: ibid.

53. Police reports of 17 April 1930, 30 May, 8 and 18 June 1931, 14 December 1936: ibid., 15/gen., box 2418.

54. Reports by R. Kiffl on meetings of 31 January, 7, 16, 21 and 28 February 1933, Vienna, 11, 19 February and 3 March 1933: Verwaltungsarchiv Wien, NS-Parteistellen, box 12 (Nachrichtendienst).

55. Unsigned report on meeting of 'Deutscher nationalsozialistischer Verein für Österreich' on 28 March 1933: ibid., box 13.

56. 'Einladung zur Sitzung des erweiterten Vorstandes am Mittwoch, den 9. Ostermond 1930': Verwaltungsarchiv Wien, Grossdeutsche Volkspartie, box 10.

57. 'Verband deutschvölkischer Vereine Deutschösterreichs, Wien, am 13. Lenzmond 1931': ibid.

58. Circular of 25 April 1932: ibid.

59. 'Deutscher Schulverein Südmark, Kreisleitung Tirol' to 'Verband deutschvölkischer Vereine Deutschösterreichs', 31 May 1932: ibid.

60. Confidential police report of February 1932, transmitted by Bundespolizeidirektion Wien: Haus-, Hof- u. Staatsarchiv, Liasse Österreich 2/21, fasz. 302; Polizeiarchiv, Nachlass Schober, box 34.

61. Thus the National Socialist speaker at the 'Gauführertagung Linz am 16.3.1930': Bundesarchiv Koblenz, Sammlung Schumacher, Nr. 305 I.

62. Report by SA Sturmbann II/4, Vienna, 1 July 1932: Verwaltungsarchiv Wien, NS-Parteistellen, box 19.

63. *Abwehr der Angriffe auf den Deutschen Turnerbund* (Vienna, 1933) 15-16, sent by Kupka to Steidle on 21 September 1933: Tiroler Landesarchiv, Präsidialakten 1933, 181 XII 59.

64. Resolution of 11 March 1933: Verwaltungsarchiv Wien, NS-Parteistellen, box 13.

65. Rosar, *Deutsche Gemeinschaft,* 61.

66. Leaflet of 1932 in Verwaltungsarchiv Wien, Nachlass Dr Lohmann, box 6.

11

THE DOLLFUSS REGIME

The Austrian chancellor from May 1932 onwards was Engelbert Dollfuss, a prominent Christian Social politician who had been the minister
of agriculture. The government was a coalition of his party with the
small groups of the Heimatblock and the Peasant League, but even so
its parliamentary majority consisted of but one vote because the Social
Democrats as well as the Grossdeutsche were in opposition (the
National Socialists had no seats in parliament). Dollfuss's strongly
anti-socialist outlook prevented any compromise with the Social Democrats, the largest party, and his strong Catholicism made him an equally
determined opponent of the National Socialists, especially after Hitler
became the German chancellor early in 1933. In this struggle against
left and right Dollfuss's support mainly came from his own Christian
Social Party, but he also depended on that of the Heimwehren two of
whose leaders entered the cabinet. But its parliamentary base was so
small and uncertain that the chancellor, like Seipel before him, increasingly inclined to authoritarian solutions, similar to those which
Chancellor Brüning had attempted in Germany, to a rule by emergency
decrees and the emasculation of parliament. In this Dollfuss was backed
by the Church and the bureaucracy — two traditionally very strong
powers in Austria — as well as by Mussolini who for many years had

supported authoritarian movements in Austria, and was equally opposed to the Austrian Social Democrats and the National Socialists as he had no desire of seeing German troops on the Brenner pass. Dollfuss was temperamentally unsuited to play a complicated and uncertain parliamentary game. As he once confided to the Austrian President Wilhelm Miklas: 'I can only govern with one party.'[1]

In retrospect it may seem that the establishment of an authoritarian regime in Austria became a hopeless undertaking with the appointment of Hitler as German chancellor, that it was only a question of time until little Austria would be swallowed up by its far stronger neighbour. But one has to remember that in 1933 it was as yet uncertain how strong the Hitler regime would be, that Mussolini to the south seemed far firmer in the saddle than Hitler to the north, and that the 1930s were the time when dictatorial or semi-dictatorial regimes were established in many European countries, large and small. In any case, Dollfuss's experiences with parliament were very unfortunate; there were bitter debates about the new loan from the League of Nations and about the smuggling of arms from Italy for the benefit of the Heimwehren and Hungary, debates in which the government was barely able to hold its own. Then, in March 1933, accident played into Dollfuss's hands. There was another controversy, this time about the validity of the ballot papers of two deputies in a vote which was lost by the government. In the course of the debate the president of the chamber, the Social Democrat Karl Renner, incautiously resigned, and his example was followed by the two vice-presidents who belonged to different political parties. In the eyes of the chancellor, parliament had simply ceased to function, it put itself out of action by the three resignations, and he was determined to exploit the situation to the full. As the three presidents had resigned they were no longer entitled to summon parliament, and the President of the Republic was prevailed upon not to do so by decree, nor to dissolve parliament which would have necessitated a general election.[2]

On the day after the resignations the leaders of the Christian Social Party met and decided to govern for the time being in an authoritarian fashion, until it was possible to guarantee the functioning of the legislature and the administration through negotiations with the opposition parties, which would have to agree to certain changes of the Constitution and of parliamentary procedures.[3] Apparently this was not envisaged as a permanent solution; parliament was to be suspended but not to be eliminated permanently. A few days later, however, the government published a proclamation to the Austrian people which suspended certain provisions of the Constitution and indicated that parliamentary democracy had ceased to exist, at least for the time being. Henceforth the government ruled by issuing emergency decrees, on the legal basis of a war-time enabling act of 1917 which had never been revoked but in truth only encompassed social and economic measures. When the socialist government of Vienna complained about these procedures to the constitutional court Dollfuss induced its Christian Social members to resign and then declared that the court, having lost its legal composition, was incapable of exercising control over the measures of the government.[4] In a similar situation the German Social Democrats, after the deposition of the Prussian government by Papen's coup d'état in July 1932, took their case to the state court, but its decision proved of no help to the deposed government. Clearly, legal procedures were of little use at a time when constitutional issues were decided by the use of force.

That Dollfuss was determined to prevent a revival of parliamentary government he solemnly indicated at the celebration of the 250th anniversary of the liberation of Vienna from the Turks in May 1933: 'This form of parliament and parliamentarianism which has died will not return. We want to fashion our homeland and the life of our honest German people in Austria in new forms and based on new principles and ideas which in reality are very old ones for a Christian and German people.' And a few months later:

> The time of the liberal capitalist social and economic order has passed. The time of Marxists leading and misleading the people has ended! The time of party rule is over, we are opposed to political streamlining and terror [an allusion to the Third Reich]. We want the social, Christian, German state of Austria on the basis of Estates and under a strong, authoritarian leadership.[5]

The former chancellor and Landeshauptmann of Vorarlberg, Dr Ender, was entrusted with the task of drafting a new constitution based on Estates: the ideas which had inspired the Heimwehr movement for so long were to be carried out at last.[6]

Before he made the second speech quoted above Dollfuss went to Italy to meet Mussolini who demanded from his Austrian visitor a hard course against 'Marxism' and energetic action on the constitutional issue, in other words a more openly fascist course. Dollfuss undertook to press on his with his programme of a new constitution based on Estates which corresponded to his own convictions. Starhemberg informed the Heimwehr leaders shortly after that important constitutional changes were impending: their aim was 'to realize the fascist totality and to influence decisively . . . the fate of all the parties existing in Austria'. It became clear that Mussolini was using the Heimwehr as a pressure group to bring about the desired constitutional changes, for the Social Democratic Party was still legal and its Viennese stronghold, although by no means impregnable, still constituted a formidable obstacle to any dictatorial plans. That the government itself was by no means united emerged when the vice-chancellor and leader of the Peasant League, Franz Winkler, publicly voiced his determined opposition to the Heimwehr demand 'that Austro-Fascism was to be the form of constitution which Austria must accept, that means in good German that the Heimwehren claim the state and its leadership for themselves'.[7]

Only a few days later Dollfuss radically transformed his cabinet. He removed the leaders of political parties, such as Winkler; the Viennese Heimwehr leader Major Fey became the new vice-chancellor and the influence of the Heimwehr leaders grew considerably. So did their appetite, for to them these were but small steps in the direction of an Austrian Fascism which they hoped to realize with the help of Mussolini, or through an arrangement with the National Socialists, in either case by the methods which had been used with such success in Germany and in Italy.[8] It seems that at this time Mussolini thought that a combination Dollfuss-Starhemberg-Fey could bring about the changes desired by him. As a German diplomat reported from Rome, there one did not have a high opinion of either Dollfuss or of Starhemberg, who was considered vain and a turn-coat, but it was believed

> that the chancellor, tenaciously clinging to his ideas would finally succeed in in spite of his limited popularity and would be helped in this by the mass appeal which Starhemberg aroused without any doubt. Thus Mussolini in the final result certainly reckons with a success of the new energetic government on a corporative basis because he believes that – by the creation of a state akin to Fascism and National Socialism – the National Socialist movement in Austria will be induced to accept a compromise and the ground will be prepared for a rapprochement with Germany which is still very close to his heart. . . .[9]

But, if neither of these aims could be achieved by the Dollfuss regime, would Mussolini continue to support his Austrian protégé? That question the diplomat did not attempt to answer.

In any case, Dollfuss and the Heimwehr leaders were by no means united in their political aims, and either side was not averse to an arrangement with the National Socialists, at the expense of their partner. That the Heimwehr leaders were intriguing behind Dollfuss's back we have already seen. But in May 1933 Dollfuss too negotiated with Hitler's Inspector General, the German Theo Habicht, and offered to the National Socialists two seats in the government if for the time being they gave up their demand for a general election. But the latter demanded five ministerial posts, the exclusion of the Heimwehr and the Peasant League from the government, and new elections on which demand the negotiations foundered. But they were renewed in the autumn when Habicht met two leading Grossdeutsche in Bohemia and authorized them to reopen the negotiations. He now demanded 50 per cent of the cabinet seats for his party and for himself the post of vice-chancellor under Dollfuss. Internally, there was to be 'the sharpest fight against Marxism', and externally 'close friendly relations with the German Reich and the recognition of Austria's independence'. According to German sources, Dollfuss was willing to accept the majority of these demands and even to receive Habicht, but the determined opposition of the Heimwehr leaders brought about the suspension of the negotiations.[10] With the example of the rapid transformation of the German cabinet from a coalition between National Socialists and Nationalists to a one-party government before his eyes even Dollfuss must have been aware what the demand for 50 per cent of cabinet seats meant in practice.

At the beginning of 1934 the pressures on Dollfuss to bring about changes in the direction of Fascism increased. At the end of January the Undersecretary of State in the Italian Foreign Office, Fulvio Suvich, visited Vienna to demand an elimination of the political parties and constitutional reforms after the Italian model, and above all the destruction of Social Democracy and of 'red' Vienna.[11] Simultaneously the Tyrolese Heimwehren marched into Innsbruck where they submitted their demands to the provincial government. These aimed at 'the quickest possible transformation of our whole state in the . . . direction of a framework of Estates, and above all the end of representation by parties and classes and the immediate establishment of an independent authoritarian leadership'. All public institutions were to be transformed according to the 'will of the patriotic population'; all offices were to be purged from those opposed to these changes; the officials responsible for public security were to be assisted by Heimwehr leaders; the administration of certain towns was to be entrusted to special commissars. In addition, the newspapers announced that the Heimwehren demanded the dissolution of the Social Democratic and Christian Social parties, the resignation of their deputies from all official posts, and the transformation of the Tyrolese government in the same manner, while the Landeshauptmann was to be assisted in future by a committee dominated by the Heimwehren and the Tyrolese Peasant League. Landeshauptmann Dr Stumpf agreed to the setting up of this consultative committee, but pointed out to the Heimwehr leaders that its competence and the transformation of the government were questions which had to be settled by the Diet. In his opinion, the Heimwehr leaders were not at all clear how their demands were to be carried out, and were opposed to the summoning of the Diet because its deputies profited from the existing system and could not be expected to give up their seats or to consent to the removal of the party representatives. The Landeshauptmann also emphasized that he would not go along with any extra-constitutional measures nor agree to the establishment of a counter-government with an authoritarian character.[12]

A few days later the Heimwehr leaders of Upper Austria put forward very similar demands to Landeshauptmann Dr Schlegel and asked 'with justified impatience' that the obstacles to the policy of the chancellor be removed. Government commissars were to be appointed for the towns of Linz and Steyr who were to be approved by the Heimwehr leaders; the same was to be done in all communes where 'the administration is endangered politically or economically'; all offices and schools were to be purged 'of enemies of the state'; the property taxes were to be lowered, especially for woods. The last was perhaps a demand in the interest of the aristocratic Heimwehr leaders. In the discussion with Dr Schlegel the leaders pointed to the 'discouragement and bitterness' caused by the lack of progress in the chancellor's reform programme: they were not using threats, but otherwise the population would go over to the National Socialists. The Landeshauptmann replied that he was elected by the Diet and had sworn an oath to the President of the Republic: they could not expect from him that he would break it. When the Heimwehr leaders argued that these times of emergency permitted to cast aside 'such scruples', Dr Schlegel declared: 'A German man does not break his word, certainly not when he has invoked God as a witness.' He then informed the members of the Land government accordingly. His hand was strengthened by a joint declaration of the Peasant League and the Grossdeutsche who emphasized their determined opposition to any attempt to seize power such as they saw in the Heimwehr demands. They also pointed out that 'only a very small, unimportant part of the population' was behind them and that the Heimwehr tended to identify the terms 'hostility to the state and opposition': a tendency against which they must sharply protest. At Braunau the representatives of the Peasant League informed the Bezirkshauptmann that many of their younger members sympathized with the National Socialists; they would be unable to arrest this trend 'if Austria really embarked on a fascist course'.[13] But a few days later Dr Schlegel resigned as Landeshauptmann of Upper Austria: he had always been in favour of reaching a compromise with the Social Democrats and critical of the Heimwehr and especially of Prince Starhemberg.[14]

That this demarche was by no means a spontaneous action by local Heimwehr leaders was shown by the fact that exactly the same demands were put to Landeshauptmann Rehrl at Salzburg, two days after they were raised in Upper Austria. After a delay, caused by the absence of Rehrl, the Salzburg government was enlarged by two representatives of the local Heimwehren, but Rehrl remained as Landeshauptmann. It was very misleading when the Heimwehren claimed that they had achieved their 'aim of transforming the state on the basis of Estates',[15] for whatever the Heimwehren were they were certainly not an Estate. What occurred was in reality an attempt by the Heimwehren to recover lost ground and to increase their pressure on the Dollfuss government. If it was 'almost another Putsch',[16] then that Putsch failed like the earlier one in Styria; and no similar attempt was made at the centre, in Vienna.

Only a few days after these 'actions' of the Heimwehren in several Austrian Länder, one of their earliest aims was finally achieved: the elimination of Social Democracy. The Republican Defence Corps was dissolved by the Dollfuss government in March 1933 but it continued its activities 'underground'. On 12 February 1934 the police conducted a search for arms in the Social Democratic headquarters at Linz; the search was resisted by the members of the Republican Defence Corps. Its local leader gave the signal for taking up the fight against the government which was done in the whole town, and soon spread to Vienna and some industrial centres. But there was no fighting at all in the more rural Länder, Burgenland, Carinthia, Salzburg, Tyrol and Vorarlberg, and even where fighting broke out there was no general strike to support the Republican Defence Corps. The vastly superior forces of army, police, gendarmerie and Heimwehren were able to break all resistance within a few days by the ruthless use of military force, especially against the council department blocks in Vienna which were bombarded into surrender.[17] As the German military attaché put it, the February rising offered to the regime 'the possibility fully to deploy its apparatus of power and to destroy one of its enemies. At first sight it seemed that the Heimwehr was going to emerge as the final victor. But soon it turned out that this purely military organization lacked the constructive political heads. The chancellor and . . . the Christian Social forces again gained the upper hand.'[18]

The destruction of Social Democracy did not win any adherents to the regime, for the party soon created a well functioning underground organization, while many of its disappointed followers became Communists or National Socialists.[19] A leading National Socialist indeed claimed that 'Austro-Marxism was irrevocably destroyed', but the claim was somewhat premature. His estimate that the battle was now only one between 'the reactionary government circle' and the National Socialists was equally unjustified.[20]

On 1 May 1934, only ten weeks after this victory over the Social Democrats, the new Constitution was promulgated by the government. It abolished all elected institutions and concentrated power in the executive. There was to be a Federal Council of 59 members who were to be delegated by various other councils and could only accept or reject government bills without a debate. There were to be councils of culture, the economy, the Länder, and the state; their members were to be nominated and only had advisory functions. The President was no longer to be elected by the people but by the Austrian mayors. The basis of the whole edifice was to be the Estates, but they had not yet been formed, and the 'democracy of Estates' which was envisaged never came into being. Seven occupational Estates were planned: for industry, trade and communication, small enterprises, banks and insurance, the professions, agriculture, and the public services: but only the last two were ever organized, probably because the government reckoned on receiving support from them. The aim was the creation of a corporative state, similar to that existing in Italy, but this was not achieved. Only the members of the preliminary advisory bodies were nominated in November; as the Estates did not yet exist, they were unable to delegate anyone for this purpose.[21]

It was further planned to organize the Estates vertically so that each subgroup or guild would include employers as well as employees (both white- and blue-collar workers). The aim was to overcome the division between these categories and 'to coordinate these beginnings into a whole, a well-ordered system' of Estates.[22] These plans clearly showed the influence of Othmar Spann and others who had invented systems of Estates, but the plans remained on paper. The state, it was officially claimed, would

> not be a state in which the one enjoys much, and the other little, but a state in which the Estates are called upon to participate with equal rights in legislation, and partly too in administration, in which the state will only intervene to create a just balance between the Estates. And the Estates will no longer be divided into employers and employees, but will sit together at the same table, promoting the common weal, no longer enemies, but . . . fighting for a common goal.[23]

The reality, however, was very different from this idealized picture of social harmony, of a society with equal rights and equal shares, in which the wolf would lie down with the lambs. No attempt was made to realize this Utopia.

It has been pointed out that the ideology of the Estates included 'all elements of a fascist ideology' and that the Austrian regime attempted to imitate its Italian model and its German rival by its methods, its propaganda and its means of suppression.[24] Obviously, there were strong influences, especially those of Italian Fascism, but there also were very marked differences. As has been emphasized, in Austria there was no broad mass movement and no seizure of power by a fascist party. Dollfuss was the constitutional chancellor and used the means of power at his disposal to effect a coup d'état from above which established a dictatorship.[24] This dictatorship was supported by the Christian Social Party – its parliamentary deputies even voted for the constitution of 1 May 1934 – by the Catholic Church and the bureaucracy as well as sections of the bourgeoisie and the nobility, in other words by the old ruling circles which were defending their established positions against the threats from the left and the right. The Heimwehren and the Christian Social Party provided the support which the regime could muster, but played no prominent role in its establishment. The attempt to create in the 'Fatherland Front' a more uniform mass basis on the model of a fascist party was unsuccessful. The regime never overcame the disunity and disparate character of the elements which supported it. In spite of the ideological trappings it was much more akin to a traditional right-wing dictatorship than a modern fascist one. Nor was there any significant social change in the sense that the old ruling elites were replaced by new ones – as happened to some extent in Germany and Italy. All these factors make it very doubtful whether the Austrian regime can be classified as 'fascist'.

The 'Fatherland Front' was created in 1933 as the political instrument of Dollfuss to underpin the regime. It was organized on the basis of the Leadership Principle, with Dollfuss as the Leader. Within it he alone had complete power to issue orders, and all its functionaries and members were obliged 'to unconditional obedience' and to carry out the orders emanating from above. The Leader's deputy and all other officers were appointed by the Leader or one of the sub-leaders. It was a strictly hierarchical and centralist organization[25] but, significantly, it had no programme. The Front leader for Carinthia later described how he was invited to see Dollfuss in the leading hotel of Klagenfurt. Dollfuss welcomed him with the words: 'You are the right man for the Fatherland Front! ' He was immediately appointed Landesleiter for Carinthia, and then, armed with a National Socialist (!) booklet of instructions, travelled up and down the country and appointed everywhere groups of district and local leaders on the basis of Estates (which did not yet exist): one representative each of the peasants, workers, and entrepreneurs.[26] It was improvization on the grand scale. In the autumn of 1933 the father of the Austrian authoritarian constitution, Dr Robert Hecht, a senior civil servant, wrote in an official memorandum that one should not over-estimate the political importance of the Fatherland Front, for it would never become a primary and revolutionary popular movement and would never lose the character of an Austrian club 'with its specifically Viennese coffee-house character'. In his opinion, the State of the Estates too did not correspond to any definite ideas of the population and was 'in reality nothing . . . but an empty word'.[27]

That the Fatherland Front did not consider itself a political party and that Austria was not a one-party state was officially pointed out in 1934, thus once more emphasizing the difference separating it from the Italian and German ruling parties. The Front, the statement continued, only demanded 'loyalty to an independent, Christian, German Austria based on Estates'; this loyalty was the only condition of joining, otherwise there was 'full freedom of conscience'. The tasks of the Front were separate from those of the state, the Länder and the communes. Co-operation between the Front and the state organs was guaranteed through the persons of its leaders who were at the same time the leaders of the state. But the officers of the Front were not entitled to intervene in any way in the work of the public authorities. All that they could do was to draw the attention of the authorities to justified complaints or petitions of individual members with which the authorities should deal quickly; while in Germany the officials of the National Socialist Party allegedly had greater rights than the administrative authorities, a factor which could easily lead to an abuse of power.[28]

If the Fatherland Front to a large extent absorbed the Christian Social Party which eventually dissolved itself, its relationship to the para-military organization of the Heimwehren was by no means clear. On the side of the latter there was strong suspicion of an organization upon which they obviously looked as a rival in the struggle for power. In September 1933 a solution was adopted by the Heimwehr leaders who met in Vienna to discuss the issue. They decided, as the leaders of political parties were now removed from the government and its course was clarified, to join the Fatherland Front collectively as an organiza- tion and to dissolve the Heimatblock, their parliamentary representa- tion. In October Starhemberg was appointed deputy leader of the Front under Dollfuss to express this new-found unity. At a public celebration of the Heimwehren he declared that, through the formation of the Front, all party organizations had become redundant. But he and the other speakers, Vice-Chancellor Fey and Dr Steidle, made it clear that the Heimwehren had not given up their aim of establishing a fascist government in Austria. In any case, the Heimwehren now held positions of vital importance in the government as well as the Fatherland Front. But two leaders of the Christian Social Party immediately countered the Heimwehr claims by stating that their party now as before was entitled to play a leading role.[29] When asked by a journalist whether, as he was appointed deputy leader of the Front, the chancellor was now the leader of the Heimwehren, Starhemberg went out of his way to declare that he himself was, and would remain, the Heimwehr leader and as such remained 'completely independent', but that his new appointment marked 'a further step towards . . . a special fascist con- ception of the state in Austria'.[30]

Several reports from the year 1935 confirmed that the Fatherland Front had made little progress in winning loyal adherents to the new regime but had collected numerous opportunists and passive members. In April a confidential government agent wrote that unfortunately all his worst fears about the Front were justified:

> Exactly as one makes the mistake in militant Catholic circles to want to conduct power politics with the newly baptized, thus the Fatherland Front commits the mistake to be overjoyed by the recruitment of as many members as possible. Instead of assembling few but wholeheartedly Austrian forces and leading them into battle for Austria . . . one creates many members who are

not even loyal and form an unreliable gang. With these people one cannot even conduct a local election without friction, not to speak of crystallizing a political will. . . .[31]

This opinion was echoed by the director of security for Salzburg who wrote that the expectations with regard to the Fatherland Front had so far not been fulfilled; apart from organizing occasional meetings and demonstrations it was a collecting centre for members who wore the badge and paid their contributions, who joined for opportunist reasons and were not interested in its ideas or tasks.[32]

In October the head of the propaganda service of the Fatherland Front sharply criticized the 'organizational chaos' which the people could not disentangle. The Fatherland Front, the para-military and professional organizations were all talking about the 'rejuvenation of Austria', but were competing in recruiting members, and there was no question of a unified will; the younger generation, whether it was 'red' or 'brown' in inclination, was not influenced by official propaganda. In his opinion, the different professional and workers' organizations were developing into economic interest parties, and instead of the four old ones there would soon be seven or eight if the Fatherland Front did not put a stop to it; its propaganda sections had the ungrateful task of mediating between the separate aspirations of the different member associations, or rather those of the little subleaders, and dissipated their energies in continuous efforts at reconciliation.[33] In short, there was disunity and diffusion, competition and rivalry, in an organization which allegedly was built on the Leadership Principle. The Fatherland Front combined many different organizations and tendencies under one roof, but the roof itself was not held up by any firm foundations.

The Heimwehren first adopted a hostile attitude towards the Front in which they saw a continuation of the Christian Social Party, and an obstacle to the establishment of 'Austrian Fascism'. In September 1933 — a few weeks before he was appointed deputy leader of the Front — Starhemberg went so far as to issue an order prohibiting his men to wear the Front badge, to make propaganda for it, or even to participate in uniform in any Front meeting.[34] In 1934, after Dollfuss's death, Starhemberg was appointed Leader of the Fatherland Front; but even then he remained strongly opposed to the incorporation of the Heimwehren in the Front, and his men too rendered determined resistance to this plan. At a meeting of the Heimwehr leaders he allegedly declared: 'If you look with distrust at the Fatherland Front, I share your distrust! ' The Heimwehren would not dissolve themselves in a general para-military formation, but demanded the leadership.[35] According to a well informed observer, the policy of the Heimwehr leaders did not succeed within the Fatherland Front because they consistently aimed at establishing their own hegemony and did not want any co-operation; there was no trust between them and the government.[36]

Locally too, there was much friction between the Heimwehren and the members of other 'patriotic' organizations. From Traun in Upper Austria it was reported in 1935 that the Heimwehr men did not seek better relations with the members of the Front and the other para-military associations but were inveighing against them.[37] Mutual hostility was also reported from other places in Upper Austria, partly caused by the fact that there the Heimwehr largely consisted of former National Socialists.[38] In 1935 a confidential agent reported that not only in Upper Austria, but also in Carinthia and Salzburg whole sections of the Heimwehren, in refuting attacks by former Christian Social politicians, adopted a strongly anti-clerical and 'nationalist' line, and that in some districts they aimed at a reconciliation with the National Socialists to overcome the 'clerical' course of the government.[39] From Salzburg too it was reported that the Heimwehren, out of rivalry with the other para-military associations, were trying to recruit members from 'nationalist' circles, and even from the National Socialists.[40]

In March 1935 the Upper Austrian Heimwehren launched a public attack upon clericalism and 'black' influences in politics, as well as upon the revival of party influence in the state and the Fatherland Front. The Upper Austrian Director of Security, Peter Count Revertera, declared that the Heimwehr had fought successfully against Liberalism and Socialism: they would not suffer any clerical intervention in politics. Another Heimwehr leader exclaimed that attempts to curtail Heimwehr influence must be countered; this could not be allowed to continue and their enemies should beware. This attack was immediately taken up in Salzburg where the Heimwehr leader exclaimed that the most incredible things happened under the cloak of the different militant organizations and the party spirit was being reborn: 'We have been silent for long, but this must end. Pus must be cut and burnt out of the flesh and cannot be covered by a plaster. From the body politic too pus must be removed if need be with brutality (thunderous applause).' This was repeated when he declared that only the will of their leader, Prince Starhemberg, was valid for them. The meeting ended with a vow of loyalty to the Salzburg leader who was called upon to use his fists to intervene and to 'remain hard': the harder he acted, the more strongly would he be supported by his men.[41]

In the Tyrol too, the activities of the Heimwehren were directed against remaining Christian Social influences in the government. There it was the Landesrat Dr Gamper who aroused their wrath and whom they wanted to replace by one of their own leaders. In March 1934 they decided to withdraw their own two representatives from the local advisory council until Gamper resigned, and both declined government posts for the same reason.[42] In December the Tyrolese leader Steidle wrote to another Heimwehr leader from Trieste, where he had been sent as the Austrian consul, that nowhere were relations between the Heimwehren and the other militant formations so bad as in the Tyrol; the Landeshauptmann Dr Stumpf was getting senile and was completely in the hands of the ill-famed Dr Gamper who was a sworn enemy of the Heimwehr and doing as he pleased in the government.[43] The removal of Steidle from the scene did not result in an improvement of the relations of the Heimwehren with the other organizations. In 1936 there was strong opposition in Innsbruck to his successor as Heimwehr leader, the engineer Andreas Gerber, who was attacked because he neglected the movement and had no time for it on account of his government position.[44]

In September the assembled Heimwehr leaders criticized the Fatherland Front because many of its members were hostile to Fascism and it was thus unable to become 'the bearer of Fascism' or of the state; if Starhemberg had worked as hard as certain leaders in Italy or Germany the Heimwehren would have become the bearers of the state, but now they were losing one position after the other; 'we are wedged in between two great fascist states and we want to close the gap between north and south to strengthen the bulwark against the spread of Bolshevism'. The police reported that the Heimwehr leaders would continue their agitation against the Fatherland Front; their support came mainly from the larger towns, and especially from Innsbruck.[45] According to another police report, the movement was split between the adherents of Starhemberg and those of Steidle and Major Fey; the latter wanted to remove Gerber and recall Steidle who was also to become Starhemberg's successor as the Austrian leader; there were differences between republicans and monarchists within the Heimwehren; and in general there was a marked lack of interest among the members.[46] In Innsbruck many Heimwehr men who supported Starhemberg were decidedly anti-clerical and used an official celebration to shout not only 'Heil Starhemberg', but also 'Down with the black government' and 'Down with the black party'.[47]

The Heimwehren were particularly hostile to another para-military formation, the *Ostmärkische Sturmscharen,* which were founded in the early 1930s by the Christian Social leader Dr Schuschnigg to balance the Heimwehr influence and continued to exist within the Fatherland Front. There was not only strong competition between the two formations, but the Heimwehren tended to look at the Sturmscharen as a party guard of the former Christian Social Party. In some places, the Heimwehren even tried to prevent the foundation of a local Sturmschar by force. In others the authorities intervened to prevent such foundations.[48] From one place in Upper Austria the police reported in 1934 that the followers of the Sturmscharen were as hostile to the Heimwehren as they were towards the National Socialists.[49] And from another that in many places serious conflicts existed between the different 'patriotic' associations. 'If this rivalry continues a battle will break out sooner or later between the different patriotic formations which . . . would cause a colossal disaster.'[50] From Kufstein the local authority wrote that the foundation of Sturmscharen had to be prohibited in a number of communes because the founders and their backers were National Socialists.[51]

The government attempted to stop the rivalry by issuing an order early in 1935 that no new groups of the para-military formations were to be founded in places where other local groups already existed. But, according to the Heimwehren, the Sturmscharen of Lower Austria did not take any notice of the decree; therefore the Heimwehren took the law into their own hands and forbade any propaganda or recruitment by the Stumscharen in Lower Austria. In Gloggnitz they went further and removed and destroyed a Sturmschar poster with the chancellor's picture and declared the local Sturmscharen dissolved. The government tried to mediate between the warring leaders, but the chief of staff of the Heimwehren, Seeger, declared that any arbitration by the secretary of state was not binding for him; while the Inspector General of the para-military formations, Major-General Hanno Königsbrun, pointed out that he had long ordered the foundation of rival local groups to be stopped, but none of them had taken any notice.[52] On the basis of the same decree the local Heimwehr refused to permit a meeting of the Sturmschar in Ferlach in Carinthia, and then announced a meeting of their own, whereupon the police prohibited both meetings.[53] In Vienna it came to a veritable battle between the rival organizations in

April 1935 at a meeting which was addressed by the former Christian
Social deputy Kunschak. He was interrupted by the Heimwehr men
with shouts of 'Heil Fey' and 'Long live Fascism', and finally the rivals
attacked each other with chairs, beer glasses, sticks and truncheons.[54]
At the end of 1933 the ministry of defence put the strength of the
Sturmscharen at about 15,000, compared with 40 to 50,000 for the
Heimwehren, while in April 1934 the generally well-informed German
military attaché gave their strength as 22,000 compared with 60 to
65,000 for the Heimwehren.[55]

There was yet another, smaller para-military organization within the
Fatherland Front, the *Freiheitsbund,* which was the militant formation
of the official trade unions and was supported by the union wing of the
former Christian Social Party. On account of the bad economic situation, the low social status of the workers and the continuing severe
unemployment, the Freiheitsbund in 1935-36 adopted an oppositional
position to the government. It tended to look at the Heimwehren as a
guard protecting the employers, and it also became strongly anti-
semitic. Its Viennese leaders, following in the footsteps of Dr Lueger,
believed that the social question could not be solved without tackling
the Jewish problem. This did not happen without German prodding and
German financial support. In March 1936 the Freiheitsbund distributed
300,000 leaflets in Vienna with the headline: 'Jews, buy only from
your co-religionists' – an operation that was considered a great success
by the German ambassador von Papen.[56] In May Papen wrote to Hitler
suggesting further support for the Freiheitsbund so that it would be
able to 'continue the fight against Jewry', and stressing his intimate
connections with the leader of the Freiheitsbund. In 1936 its May Day
demonstration led to violent clashes with Heimwehr men who shouted
'Nazi dogs in disguise' and 'Black Marxists', in addition to their usual
'Heil Starhemberg! '[57] That these attacks were not unjustified is
proved by the fact that the Freiheitsbund leader went so far as to ask
Papen for names agreeable to the German government in case the
Austrian government were to include ministers from the so-called
National Opposition – a development expected to take place in the
summer of 1936.[58]

From what has been said it becomes clear that the Fatherland Front
was not a fascist party, but a curious conglomeration of professional
and para-military organizations which disagreed on fundamental issues,
for example the Heimwehren with the Christian Social successor
groups, and spent a good deal of their energies in in-fighting and

manoeuvring for position. The Dollfuss government survived because it was able to balance the forces of the extreme right — the National Socialists — against those of the left. But, as the German military attaché reported in April 1934, 'the situation of the government remained weak and endangered. Wedged in between National Socialism and Marxism, it enjoyed no support among the broad masses of the people. Within its own camp the fascist forces of the Heimwehren struggled with the democratic Christian Social forces....'[59] But neither of these two camps was in itself united and the labels 'fascist' and 'democratic' hid several conflicting tendencies. Nor was the regime strong enough to destroy the opposition of the left or of the right. Both parties were driven underground but were able to retain the loyalty of their followers and to carry on propaganda on a large scale. Yet neither was strong enough to overthrow the regime, and the attempt made by the National Socialists in July 1934 failed completely.

The regime was able to survive because it enjoyed foreign support, especially from Italy, and that of the Catholic Church, and because it was upheld by the forces of the executive, the army, the police and above all the bureaucracy. These were the forces which had carried the Habsburg Monarchy through many a severe crisis. In certain ways indeed the Dollfuss regime seemed a curious revival of much older tendencies, only that there was no longer an Emperor to whom the masses were attached by strong bonds of loyalty. After Dollfuss's death Steidle wrote to Starhemberg from his observation post at Trieste: 'Immediately after the chancellor's death I could observe how the high bureaucracy of all shades was on the march to brake any impetus and to channel the whole affair into the usual bureaucratic course where as we know everything stagnates....'[60] He could have made the same remark about the preceding year. It was no accident that the Dollfuss government found the legal basis for its rule in Habsburg war-time legislation, which had never been abrogated. Without a ruling party and without enthusiastic mass support, it was and remained a bureaucratic authoritarian regime. Many contemporaries and some later observers noticed the similarities between it and the fascist dictatorships to the north and south of Austria. To the historian it seems that the Dollfuss regime was above all a strange revival of the neo-absolutism of the 1850s when the defeated revolutionaries and all opponents of the absolute monarchy were held down by the repressive measures of the bureaucracy and the forces of the executive. These forces survived the defeat of 1918 and the dissolution of the Habsburg Monarchy: in the

1930s — freed from parliamentary fetters — they came again into their own.

NOTES

1. Grete Klingenstein, 'Bemerkungen zum Problem des Faschismus in Österreich', *Österreich in Geschichte und Literatur,* XIV, Folge 1, 11. Huemer, 'Sektionschef Dr Robert Hecht . . .', II, 271, emphasizes the strength of Dollfuss's religious motives.

2. Zöllner, *Geschichte Österreichs,* 511-12; Huemer, op. cit., 254-55.

3. Huemer, op. cit., 257, quoting Leopold Kunschak, *Österreich 1918-1934* (Vienna, 1934) 176.

4. Huemer, op. cit., 262-64; Zöllner, op. cit., 512.

5. *Wiener Zeitung,* 16 May 1933; *Reichspost,* 12 September 1933: quoted by Huemer, op. cit., 346, 413.

6. Zöllner, op. cit., 515. Cp. above, pp. 167ff. for the ideology of the Estates, and p. 173 for the attitude of Landeshauptmann Ender.

7. Kerekes, *Abenddämmerung einer Demokratie,* 156-59; Zöllner, op. cit., 513.

8. Kerekes, op. cit., 159; Jedlicka, 'The Austrian Heimwehr', *Journal of Contemporary History,* I (1) 143.

9. Botschaftsrat Smend to *Auswärt. Amt,* Rome, 21 September 1933: *Akten zur deutschen auswärtigen Politik,* series C, I (2) (Göttingen, 1971) 818.

10. Notes by Hüffer, Berlin, 5 April 1934: Auswärt. Amt, Abt. II, 6111H, E452764-5; Jürgen Gehl, *Austria, Germany and the Anschluss* (London, 1963) 56, 72-73.

11. Goldinger, *Geschichte der Republik Österreich,* 189.

12. *Innsbrucker Zeitung,* 2 February 1934; official note, Innsbruck, 1 February, Dr Stumpf to Chancellor, Innsbruck 3 February 1934: Tiroler Landesarchiv, Präsidialakten 1934, 479 III 10; Goldinger, op. cit., 192.

13. Notes on discussions of Dr Schlegel with Heimwehr leaders on 6 February and meeting of Land government on 7 February 1934: Oberösterreich. Landesarchiv, II 1432-1931, and MS. by Dr H. Slapnicka on Heimwehren, ibid.; resolution of 10 February 1934: ibid., Politische Akten, Nr. 3 (Braunau).

14. Report by German Consul at Linz, in German Legation to Auswärt. Amt, Vienna, 24 February 1934: Auswärt. Amt, Abt. II, 6112H, E454228.

15. Thus *Heimatschutz in Österreich* (Vienna, 1934) 228-30.

16. Thus Goldinger, op. cit., 192, who says that a similar ultimatum was put forward in Styria.

17. Karl R. Stadler, *Opfer verlorener Zeiten* (Vienna, 1974) 25, 36-43.

18. Reports nos. 7 and 10 by Lieutenant-General Wolfgang Muff, Vienna, 22

March and 17 April 1934: Deutsche Botschaft Wien, Geheimakten 1934, 4938 part 7, E269658, E269688.

19. Thus the Sicherheitsdirektor for Upper Austria already on 24 March 1934: Verwaltungsarchiv Wien, Bundeskanzleramt, 22/gen., box 4884.

20. Notes by Gilbert in der Maur, Vienna, 16 February 1934: *Akten zur deutschen auswärtigen Politik,* series C, II (2) (Göttingen, 1973) 488.

21. Goldinger, op. cit., 199-200; and 'Der geschichtliche Ablauf der Ereignisse in Österreich', in H. Benedikt (ed.), *Geschichte der Republik Österreich* (Vienna, 1954) 222; Huemer, op. cit., 585-89; Zöllner, op. cit., 515.

22. Thus 'Rednerbrief Nr. 1', November 1934, issued by the Vaterländische Front: Burgenländ. Landesarchiv, Zeitgeschichtl. Sammlung.

23. Thus MS. 'Burgenländische Landesschützen', s.d., ibid., A/VIII-3.

24. Gerhard Botz, 'Die historische Erscheinungsform des Faschismus', *Beiträge zur historischen Sozialkunde,* IV (3) (1974) 60.

25. 'Bundes-Organisations-Statut', drafted by Landesleiter Engelbert Dworak, s.d.: Haus-, Hof- u. Staatsarchiv, Liasse Österreich 2/26, fasz. 316, p. 3.

26. Irmgard Bärnthaler, *Die Vaterländische Front* (Vienna-Frankfurt-Zürich, 1971) 23, 109.

27. Huemer, op. cit., 430, 437.

28. *Informationsdienst der Vaterländischen Front,* Nr. 43, 3 November 1934, 4-8.

29. Prinz zu Erbach to Auswärt. Amt, Vienna, 29 September 1933: Bundesarchiv Koblenz, Reichskanzlei, R 43 II/1476; Kerekes, *Abenddämmerung einer Demokratie,* 159-60.

30. Bärnthaler, op. cit., 35-36.

31. Report by 'Martin' or 'Florian', forwarded to *Bundeskanzleramt* on 14 April 1935 by T. Hornbostel: Verwaltungsarchiv Wien, Bundeskanzleramt, 22/gen., box 4913.

32. Sicherheitsdirektor for Salzburg to Bundeskanzleramt, Salzburg, 3 May 1935: ibid.

33. Confidential report by Hans Becker to Bundeskanzleramt, 23 October 1935: ibid., box 4938.

34. Bärnthaler, op. cit., 34.

35. Ibid., 78, 93-94, quoting the *Arbeiter-Zeitung* of 5 May 1935.

36. Thus the leader of the Peasant League, Vinzenz Schumy, in his unpublished MS. on the Heimwehren, p. 161: Institut für Zeitgeschichte, Vienna. According to him (p. 144) the Heimwehren felt that their leader ought to be the head of the government.

37. Report by Bezirksgendarmeriekommando Linz, 2 April 1935: Oberösterr. Landesarchiv, Politische Akten, Nr. 26 (Linz-Land).

38. Police reports from Unterweissenbach, Schönau and Königswiesen, 26 September, 26 October 1934: ibid., Freistadt, Politischer Nachrichtendienst.

39. Report by 'Martin' or 'Florian' of April 1935: Verwaltungsarchiv Wien, Bundeskanzleramt, 22/gen., box 4913.

40. Report by Director of Security for Salzburg, 3 May 1935: ibid.

41. *Prager Presse,* 28 March 1935; *Salzburger Volksblatt,* 1 April 1935.

42. Generaldirektion für die öffentl. Sicherheit, Vienna, 20-21 March 1934: Verwaltungsarchiv Wien, Bundeskanzleramt, 22/gen., box 4888; *Heimatschutz in Österreich* (Vienna, 1934) 269-70.

43. Steidle to Revertera, 6 December 1934: Herrschaftsarchiv Helfenberg, box 102 a.

44. Report by Bundespolizeidirektion Innsbruck, s.d.: Verwaltungsarchiv Wien, Bundeskanzleramt, 22/gen., box 4965.

45. Report by Sicherheitsdirektor Dr Mörl, Innsbruck, 2 October 1936: ibid., box 4969.

46. Report by Bundespolizeidirektion Innsbruck, s.d. (autumn 1936): ibid., box 4969.

47. Report by Sicherheitsdirektor for Tyrol, 20 November 1934: Tiroler Landesarchiv, Präsidialakten 1934, 194 prs XII 57.

48. Police reports from Sierning and Steyr, 24 December 1934 and 2 May 1935: Oberösterreich. Landesarchiv, Politische Akten, Nr. 46 and 48.

49. Police report from Königswiesen, 26 October 1934: ibid., Politische Akten, Freistadt, Politischer Nachrichtendienst 1934-38.

50. Police report from Kefermarkt, 11 February 1935: ibid.

51. Report by Bezirkshauptmannschaft Kufstein, 3 February 1935: Tiroler Landesarchiv, Präsidialakten 1935, 62 prs XII 57.

52. Reports of 21 and 23 March 1935: Verwaltungsarchiv Wien, Bundeskanzleramt, 22/gen., box 4927.

53. Generaldirektion für die öffentl. Sicherheit, 16 December 1934: ibid., box 4907.

54. Report by the same, 16 April 1935: ibid.

55. Report on Regierungstreue Verbände by Ministry of Defence, 12 December 1933: ibid., Bundeskanzleramt, 22/gen., box 4879; Lt.-General Muff to Reichswehrministerium, Vienna, 9 April 1934: Botschaft Wien, Geheimakten 1934, 4938 part 7, E269667, secret.

56. Papen to Hitler, Vienna, 20 March 1936: Botschaft Wien, Geheimakten 1935-38, 4939 part 1, E272277-79; *Documents on German Foreign Policy,* series C, V (Washington, 1966) 225-27, no. 172.

57. Papen to Hitler, Vienna, 12 May 1936: ibid., no. 319, pp. 531-33.

58. Ibid., 531; *Der Hochverratsprozess gegen Dr. Guido Schmidt vor dem Wiener Volksgericht* (Vienna, 1947) 403-4 (Papen to Hitler, Vienna, 21 April 1936: Botschaft Wien, Geheimakten 1935-38, 4939 part 1, E272293).

59. Report no. 10, Vienna, 17 April 1934, by Lt.-General Muff: Deutsche Botschaft Wien, Geheimakten 1934, 4938 part 7, E269657.

60. Steidle to Starhemberg, Trieste, 5 December 1934 (copy): Herrschaftsarchiv Helfenberg, box 102a.

12

THE REVOLT AGAINST DOLLFUSS

In June 1933 the National Socialist Party and its subordinate organizations were dissolved by the Austrian government and any activity for them became an offence. Even earlier open warfare erupted between the Hitler and the Dollfuss governments, and the former imposed a special tax of 1,000 marks on Germans visiting Austria: a ruinous measure for the vital tourist industry of Austria which considerably aggravated the economic crisis. Many Austrian National Socialists, especially members of the SA, fled to Bavaria where they were organized and trained in special camps close to the frontier as an 'Austrian Legion'. The leadership of the Austrian party under Habicht was established in Munich, in close proximity to the headquarters of the German party. Within Austria, the National Socialists not only distributed leaflets and papers, burnt fireworks and painted swastikas in more or less inaccessible places, but they also used high explosives to good effect and committed innumerable acts of sabotage. The overstretched police forces were reinforced by men from the para-military formations, but even so they were unable to cope with this massed activity, especially when it occurred in remote villages and on mountain heights.

The punishments inflicted by the authorities were not very severe, nor were the conditions of imprisonment of those caught in spreading National Socialist propaganda particularly rigorous. From Kufstein the local Heimwehr leader wrote in June 1933 that the district judge allowed forty to fifty National Socialists to visit their arrested comrades in their cells and to confer with them, a laxity due to the fact that several officials sympathized with National Socialism.[1] Another arrested Tyrolese National Socialist, according to Dr Steidle, was allowed to walk outside the prison and to receive food parcels from the local party members: conditions which he described as a 'jolly imprisonment'.[2] In August he added that those arrested not only received quantities of food, but also tobacco and drink, so that some of them found that they had never lived so well as in prison, and the imprisonment became 'a farce'.[3]

Illegal National Socialist leaflets were printed in Munich and smuggled into Austria in large quantities. One of them, signed by Habicht, Proksch and the SA leader Reschny, announced that the underground organization was ready to take up the fight against the government which would be conducted 'with brutal harshness to victory', until Austria was liberated and Greater Germany established: the government had broken the law by prohibiting the National Socialist press and meetings and forced this fight upon the National Socialists.[4] Another illegal leaflet of 1933 made great play with the pronouncements of Archbishop Gröber of Freiburg and other Catholic dignitaries in favour of the Hitler government, which had defeated Bolshevism, destroyed the marxist atheist movement in Germany and freed the German people from the plague of anti-religious propaganda, 'from rubbish and dirt': this, it was claimed, was the true voice of 'the leaders of the German Catholic Church' which accepted Adolf Hitler as their Leader.[5]

Nor was anti-Semitism forgotten. A leaflet from the same source boldly declared that no one could be 'certain of his freedom in Dollfuss Austria because the Jews rule in the country! In former times the native population confined the alien Hebrews to ghettos. Today the Jews, all-powerful in Austria, confine the native people to concentration camps.' A Rumanian Jew had allegedly demanded in a newspaper article the imprisonment of National Socialists in concentration camps and so the 'authoritarian' Dollfuss government, which was 'dominated by the Jew Hecht', quickly empowered the authorities to limit the freedom of movement of people suspected of being hostile to the state; thus any 'dirty Polish Jew' could denounce anyone he disliked and have him sent to a concentration camp.[6] In innumerable stickers the Dollfuss government was accused of a breach of the constitution and of 'national treason'. Another leaflet asked the workers whether the government served their interests or those of 'the Jewish finance capitalists and the owners of the large estates'; would the parliament of the Estates represent the workers' interests, or those of their exploiters? In any election the fat bureaucrats, capitalists and Jews would have a thousand or more votes to one of a workman. Therefore the National Socialists were fighting 'against the authoritarian Jew state' and demanded an immediate general election on the basis of the general and equal franchise.[7] For the winter of 1933-34 the Gauleiter of Upper Austria issued an order to all party members to look after those who did not have enough food or coal — a 'work of Christian brotherly love' from which every suffering National Socialist must benefit.[8]

An underground newspaper pointed out with some justification that the government had proclaimed 'a State of Estates', but that there were no Estates; nor could they be created quickly by the appointment of Christian Social functionaries as leaders of Estates. The present Austrian state did 'not grow organically' and was rejected by the majority of the people. Its programme was based on the Korneuburg demands of the Heimwehren, but their leaders had no concrete idea what a 'State of Estates' was, and their programme was a plagiarism of that of the National Socialists. It was completely wrong when Heimwehr speakers claimed that there was hardly any difference between the Korneuburg programme and the National Socialist one.[9] Another paper, playing on the differences between the Heimwehr leaders, claimed that they were trying to ingratiate themselves with the National Socialists 'so that they would not be called to account by them when they seized power'.[10] One of the principal National Socialist arguments, however, was and remained anti-Semitism. A leading Social Democrat who was imprisoned together with National Socialists wrote to his wife: 'The real plague [here in prison] are the National Socialists. . . . Most of them are terrible anti-semitic rowdies whose only argument is "The Jew". . . .'[11] Not that Jews were all that prominent under the Dollfuss regime, but it always was a popular line.

That anti-Semitism and German nationalism were of decisive importance in the success of National Socialist propaganda emerges from a number of contemporary sources. Prince Starhemberg found that anti-Semitism provided 'the most dangerous breach' in the Austrian defences: 'Everywhere one suspected Jewish influences and, although not a single Jew occupied an important post in the Fatherland Front, the Viennese citizens talked in their coffee houses full of horror about the Judaization of this organization, [and claimed] that the Nazis were right after all, and that order must be created in Austria with regard to the Jews. . . .'[12] On the local level a police official in Upper Austria considered 'the various Jewish credit institutes as the country's plague', for they were responsible for the foreclosure of so many peasant farms, and Jewish lawyers were getting court orders to enforce the payment of interest.[13]

In 1936 the Directorate of Public Security stated 'that eighty per cent of the National Socialist followers identified National Socialism with anti-Semitism, which is increasing among all social groups, or with a nationalist point of view and national thinking'; thus a clever propaganda found it easy 'to work for National Socialism by emphasizing nationalism'. Anti-semitic propaganda was particularly effective among tradesmen and shopkeepers and 'other social groups', while National Socialist militarism was enthusiastically welcomed by ex-servicemen, former officers and small officials. The working class, 'systematically educated in the marxist ideology', on the other hand, and the peasants, except in certain frontier districts, were much less affected by National Socialist propaganda.[14] These points were partly confirmed in a German report from the end of 1933. The 'national movement', it said, above all influenced the youth, but also university graduates and civil servants, very few of whom wore the badge of the Fatherland Front. The movement was also strong among tradesmen and farmers; the German radio made a 'powerful impression'. The exaggerated reports about arrests and purges in the Reich had little effect by way of counter-propaganda, for there such measures were 'at least taken by a decidedly national government under the sign of nationalism', but in Austria by a government supported by France, Czechoslovakia and Italy 'against the national movement'. The report further claimed that about 75 per cent of the gendarmerie sympathized with National Socialism, while from the army all suspects were discharged, in Salzburg alone nine officers; in spite of this many younger officers were in favour of National Socialism.[15]

It is fairly certain that the strength of the National Socialist Party did not suffer from its dissolution and the 'persecution' by the authorities. According to its own figures the party had 68,500 members at the time of the dissolution, and was able to recruit another 21,000 during the following fourteen months, more than half of them in

Vienna and Lower Austria. Of the other Länder, only Styria and Carinthia showed large increases, of 4,300 and 3,800 members, respectively. In Tyrol, Vorarlberg, Upper Austria and Salzburg they were comparatively small, less than a thousand in each case.[16] Perhaps the growth of the party was slowed down by the measures of the government but it certainly continued. Few other figures are available. For the Tyrol Dr Steidle, the Director of Security, in 1933 gave a total strength of the SA of 1,370 men plus 500 in the reserve, and another 100 for the SS, armed with 850 rifles and 22 machine guns.[17] In general the authorities were badly informed about National Socialist strength and tended to over-estimate it considerably. Early in 1935 the Director of Security for Upper Austria gave the figure of 20,000 party members 'according to a count of May 1934', while the real figure — according to the party statistics — was barely more than 2,000,[18] a colossal discrepancy. For the town of Steyr alone the police estimated 3,000 party members in 1934,[19] a figure that was considerably higher than party membership in the whole of Upper Austria.

Differences of opinion developed inside the party and its affiliated organizations about the tactics to be pursued, and these were enhanced by contradictory orders from the party leaders who had found refuge in Germany. At the end of 1933 the ministry of defence reported that there was growing friction between the SA and the party propaganda sections because the SA was exclusively occupied with sabotage and terror and thus had no time for propaganda and not even for military training.[20] Differences also appeared in the negotiations with various members of the Austrian government because the SA leaders negotiated separately from the party. A party negotiator was told that the SA leaders were much more willing to make concessions. A party officer who negotiated on behalf of Habicht with a member of the government found out that the SA leader Reschny had contacts with a different member: 'The success thus was naturally negative [sic] for both sides and the result was a weakening of the authority and the impetus of the movement.' In the writer's opinion the whole thing was 'a game of see-saw' between the leaders of the party and those of the SA.[21]

In July 1934 a leader of the Viennese SA wrote to his superior officer that the party, SA and SS had repeatedly received contradictory orders from Germany: this 'has not only caused time and again a terrible confusion, but has also brought about the most dangerous of all evils: doubts whether the leaders themselves are certain about the goal. . .'. In his opinion, the unity of the movement was only assured if the three organizations 'finally settle their differences'. He then pointed to the 'chasm' that separated the SA from the party and the SS during the weeks before the 30 June 1934 (the purge of the SA in Germany) and continued: 'The lamentable state of affairs that these three groups march separately instead of unitedly causes in the end, to the incredible delight of our enemies, a clear weakening of each of the three organizations mentioned and for the movement as such virtually a disaster. . . .' He also criticized the drinking habits of the SA leaders: 'But if a leader cannot help getting drunk occasionally, at least he must hold his tongue! If he cannot manage that, he must resign as an SA leader! ' The internal party system of surveillance must be prevented from developing into a Russian Cheka. It could only reckon with the co-operation of the SA men if they no longer saw it as 'a spy organization directed against themselves which only sees things that are suspicious, presumes the worst and makes itself hated'.[22] The 'chasm' separating the SA from the SS was to become visible only a few days later, on the day when Dollfuss was murdered by an SS unit.

That the party organization itself was far from united and much less efficient than was usually assumed is shown by a letter found by the Carinthian police on a party officer in the summer of 1933. The unnamed writer vigorously complained about the miserable failure of the organization after its dissolution: 'The Austrian on the average is incapable as an organizer. In the organizational field he needs Prussian help! . . . Without the Prussian power of organization there will always be chaos at decisive moments.' In detail, the countryside was standing firm, but in the three towns of Villach, Klagenfurt and St Veit 'there is disintegration of incredible dimensions'. It was indispensable to resume contact with the Carinthian Gauleiter Hans vom Kothen who had established himself across the frontier in Yugoslavia; but this was not done and even sabotaged, so that he was virtually out of touch with those responsible for the Gau, and only had links to a few local activists in the countryside. Party officers were also sabotaging his contacts with leaders of the Peasant League and the Styrian Heimwehr which co-operated with the National Socialists. 'Everybody wants to lead and to issue orders. . . . Camarilla A fights against Camarilla B, Klagenfurt fights against Villach, etc.'[23]

Opposition to the terrorist tactics employed by the party at the orders of its Munich headquarters came from Dr Riehl who wrote to Hitler and other German leaders and suggested a reconciliation with Dollfuss and co-operation between the German and Austrian governments. This aroused the fury of the 'Inspector General' Habicht against whose policy Riehl's criticism was directed. In August 1933 Riehl was once more expelled from the party 'because he conducted traitorous negotiations with the government by which he wanted to secure for himself the post of minister of justice' and because he was afraid to shed blood and to use force.[24] In April 1934 Riehl addressed a small conference of National Socialists and Völkische in his office. To avoid ruining the völkisch element in Austria it was necessary in his opinion to separate from Habicht and his clique and to act; to gain political influence the Fatherland Front should be replenished with National Socialist and völkisch groups; but 'in any case Hitler must be recognized as the highest Leader of all Germans' and the original National Socialist programme must be preserved. Several National Socialists present, however, stressed that a co-operation with the Dollfuss government was only possible with Hitler's consent.[25] In July Riehl wrote to Dollfuss that his followers had united with the Schulz group. The recent acts of terror in Austria and the events of 30 June 1934 in Germany (the blood purge of the SA and leading politicians) obliged him to start 'constructive work'. He desired, in agreement with the policy of the late Chancellor Seipel, to co-operate with the government and hoped that the latter would permit him to hold a public meeting.[26]

Riehl was not the only prominent party member expelled by Habicht as a 'traitor'. Early in 1934 he also expelled the engineer and peasant leader Anton Reinthaller, who had joined the party in 1928, because he was in opposition to Habicht's course, negotiated with the Dollfuss government (like so many other National Socialists) and formed within the Austrian party 'a separate movement which aimed at detaching it from the Reich' and making it an independent organization.[27] Another expelled National Socialist wrote from Salzburg in June that during the past year they had a taste 'how they think outside of the treatment and conquest of Austria and how we would be treated if Habicht and comrades became the masters in Austria. . .'. As the Fatherland Front was the only functioning organization, the only way would be to work inside it; many had already gone over to it or to the Heimwehren because they did not want to remain passive or 'to participate in the Macedonian Cheka methods' of the party. For the writer such a decision was particularly difficult because he was one of the oldest party members who had spoken in numerous meetings for the union of Austria with Germany.[28]

The National Socialists were particularly strong in the two Länder of

Carinthia and Styria, a fact connected with their strong pro-German national traditions and the völkisch and grossdeutsch tendencies among the Heimwehren. When the leading Carinthian National Socialists were arrested in June 1933 there were strong protests from the Carinthian chamber of agriculture, the organization of doctors and representatives of trade and enterprise, the professions, etc. It was alleged that the arrests were carried out 'without any cause', that 'the confidence of the population in the objectivity of the security organs and the administration as well as respect for the authorities' were undermined by the arrests. Mayors and local councillors had been arrested who were 'the leading and most respected props of the commune', and teachers before the eyes of their pupils so that their authority suffered. 'By these arbitrary measures political unrest has been created among the people and those involved have suffered serious economic damage.'[29] About the same time the National Socialists negotiated with representatives of the Carinthian Slovenes and promised them territorial concessions if their deputies voted in the Diet against the annulment of the National Socialist mandates. Their new slogan was: 'no assimilation of the national minorities!' Meanwhile they were busy establishing their control over the associations of the *Kärntner Heimatdienst,* which had carried the national struggle of the early 1920s to success.[30] In January 1934 a Carinthian party official in Munich reported to his Gauleiter that the general mood was 'really excellent' and that there had never been that many National Socialists; but more funds were essential and more importance must be attached to the 'terror groups' he was organizing: 'now we must really begin to incite people, to work them up'.[31]

In April, as the German Consul at Klagenfurt reported, the whole audience at a concert given by 'national' young teachers sang spontaneously the *Horst Wessel Song,* the German National Socialist battle hymn; he added that the jury regularly acquitted National Socialists accused of distributing forbidden leaflets or of using high explosives.[32] In June a meeting of the Carinthian singers at St Veit became the occasion for large National Socialist demonstrations with which the police were unable to cope. According to a confidential government agent, 'a spirit of sabotage, irony and malicious joy is permeating the whole of Carinthia', and opposition to the government was very strong. National Socialist propaganda material was arriving en masse via Holland, and no one at the post office noticed anything; equally inefficient were the gendarmerie and the security organs, and when searches were conducted nothing was ever found.[33] In the following month a report from Klagenfurt confirmed that the National Socialists were very strong, that two valleys in Upper Carinthia were 'entirely Nazi', that the members of the Peasant League had gone over to them, and that the organs of the executive did not have the energy to cope with the situation, partly because they believed that the regime could not last much longer.[34]

In Styria things were not very different. Here the National Socialists closely co-operated with the Heimwehren which had gone over to them, and both possessed 'a very good and well organized political and militant apparatus'. They paid special attention to propaganda among the members of the executive; especially the gendarmerie and young officers and NCOs of the army were influenced by them. Their attitude to the Dollfuss government remained bitterly hostile, but there was opposition to the 'terror groups' organized from Munich without consultation with the local National Socialists.[35] For the district of Mürzzuschlag the director of security estimated that 40 per cent of the population sympathized with them, and another third or so with the Social Democrats.[36]

In March 1934 the Director of Security for Upper Austria estimated that in the towns and market towns up to 80 per cent of the population sympathized with the National Socialists, but that the figure was much lower among the peasantry; after the defeat of the February rising the more radical among the Social Democrats willingly accepted National Socialist or Communist propaganda.[37] Certain small towns were dominated by the National Socialists. At Braunau – Hitler's birthplace – there was one of them in nearly every house, and 'all together they see in Hitler a Messiah'.[38] The district of Ried on the Inn was another National Socialist stronghold. At Mettmach the members of the Peasant League allied with the National Socialists so that they were able to boycott and supervise shopkeepers and others loyal to the government and threatened the local Heimwehr leader that they would refuse help to him when he needed it.[39]

From Grünau near Gmunden the police reported in April 1934 that 'the brown wave' was not abating, that people were awaiting 'the final struggle which would come soon and bring victory', that the National Socialists were using the local Turnverein to train their SA.[40] In Traunkirchen and Vorchdorf in the same district the police found that many peasants sympathized with National Socialism: many were indebted and believed any fairy tale about Germany where the peasants allegedly paid no taxes and economic conditions were improving rapidly.[41] At Goisern there was a different problem: the Protestant peasants, many of whom had once followed the socialists, became National Socialists out of fear of Catholicism.[42] At Bad Ischl it was estimated that at least 40 per cent of the population were party members, above all many business people, a section of the intelligentsia, and many workers, who were the most radical group.[43] In July 1934 the General Directorate of Security noted that of all the districts of Upper Austria only the Mühlviertel was loyal to the government; in many other districts the National Socialists were extremely active and had organized church boycotts in some mountain valleys; in Steyr the funeral of a nationalist Turner was attended by 2,400 people in spite of pouring rain, among them very many workers.[44]

From Vorarlberg the Director of Security reported early in 1934 that National Socialist influence was particularly strong in the villages close to the German frontier where the peasants had to deliver their milk to Germany. Many villagers and innkeepers were impoverished because there were no German tourists on account of the 1,000 mark fee for a visa and therefore sympathized with the National Socialists; the towns of Dornbirn and Lustenau were the principal centres of their propaganda.[45] In Dornbirn this was supported by local industrialists against whom the police did not intervene; nor was anything done against disturbances of the peace, so that those loyal to the government began to waver and to fear for their safety.[46] From Gaschurn near Bludenz the police reported that in particular the innkeepers and tradesmen were active National Socialists.[47] At Bregenz some party members decided to lure a National Socialist refugee, who had returned from Lindau in Bavaria and was suspected of having committed thefts there, back to Germany. He was to be taken by boat across Lake Constance, but the conspirators when they landed on the Austrian side encountered a Heimwehr patrol and in the struggle which ensued a Heimwehr man was killed.[48]

Very special conditions existed in the village of Riezlern in the Walsertal which politically belonged to Austria, but economically to Germany, so that the 1,000 mark fee did not apply there and German tourists had a virtual monopoly. There the Austrian gendarmes were usually greeted with 'Heil Hitler', the local bookshop displayed National Socialist literature in its window, songs offensive to Dollfuss were sung in the taverns, and the authority of the police was openly flouted. While the majority of the natives remained passive, about 85 workers employed on drainage work took up the challenge, and in September 1933 an open battle for which the men were armed with poles and beer bottles was only prevented with difficulty by the gendarmes. On New Year's Eve the German tourists more or less took over: a large swastika consisting of hundreds of torches was lit, a swastika flag was hoisted on a local inn, the crowd intoned the *Horst Wessel Song,* and the police patrols were molested to such an extent that they had to be withdrawn. Equally molested was anyone who looked Jewish, and in one inn the guests demanded that the Jews present must leave. As Riezlern had no rail link with Austria no arrests could be carried out, and the police feared that any measures taken against the disturbers of the peace would only aggravate the situation. When one man was stopped on suspicion of having painted swastikas the Germans present immediately appeared in front of the police station and demonstratively demanded his release.[49] But elsewhere too the police were confronted with impossible tasks. One inspector was informed that a swastika had been cut into the pelt of a sheep on a mountain alp, but when he got there he found that it was only a cross and was hardly visible any more. Yet he considered it quite feasible that whoever was responsible had tried to cut a swastika and was prevented from completing the work by someone appearing on the scene. He reported that he would continue his efforts to find the culprit so that the 'deed' could be punished.[50]

In the Burgenland the social-democratic mayor of Zuberbach was sentenced to eight days' imprisonment because he had shouted 'Heil Hitler' when drunk. But the sentence could not be enforced because only two cells existed at the Bezirkshauptmannschaft of Oberwart, one of which was reserved for gypsies, and the other for petty criminals, and both were overcrowded. Altogether more than 400 days of arrest had still to be served by several people, and fines could not be collected either, although 'priority' was given to political offenders.[51]

In Bavaria meanwhile the SA men who fled from Austria were trained in the camp at Lechfeld and formed into units of the 'Austrian Legion'; its 10,000 or more men were waiting for the signal to cross the frontier. What was envisaged was an uprising of the Austrian National Socialists which they would have to support. They were told that there was a dictatorship of the Heimwehren and that in general the political development in Austria corresponded to that in Germany: first Dollfuss had ruled with parliament, as Brüning had done in Germany; then without parliament, like Papen in Germany; while Dollfuss plus the

Heimwehr dictatorship corresponded to the German Schleicher government; this would be followed by the seizure of power, which would not pass as quietly as it had in Germany.[52] Significantly, the Austrian SS men were trained separately at the concentration camp of Dachau, allegedly by German army officers.[53] At the end of 1933 the General Directorate of Public Security reported that leading Austrian National Socialists were opposed to an early invasion of Austria by the Austrian Legion because in Austria the SA was insufficiently trained, too much occupied with terror actions and had lost too many men by arrest or flight; it was also doubted whether the population would react favourably to an invasion.[54] At Aibling in Bavaria the Austrian SA organized a demonstration against the Catholic clergy with a poster showing a clergyman waving to small children surmounted by 'Paragraph 175', the provision in the penal code against homosexuality. When the police prohibited the showing of the poster the SA men surrounded the town hall threatening to kill 'the black dog'. Then they continued their demonstration into nearby Rosenheim under the old Schönerer slogan 'Break with Rome! ' and 'Down with the clergy!'[55]

The Austrian authorities repeatedly received warnings that the invasion from Bavaria was imminent, that the Austrian Legion was concentrated at the frontier, that a Putsch was planned in Austria; but nothing happened. In May 1934 a leading Austrian National Socialist, Dr Otto Wächter, who represented Habicht in Austria, visited the Auswärtige Amt in Berlin and expressed his fears that, if martial law was proclaimed it would be difficult to hold back the population (!) and to prevent attempts at a rising. Such attempts he considered particularly dangerous and he apparently held the view 'that if such actions could not be avoided an organized rising was preferable'; he was especially worried about the situation in Carinthia.[56] At the beginning of July the Director of Security for Styria received confidential information that the Austrian National Socialists would use the occasion of the impending journey of Chancellor Dollfuss to Italy to murder him and to attempt a Putsch; the organs of the executive and the paramilitary associations would be attacked and eliminated, and there would be a desperate attempt to seize power by force. This report was circulated to all local authorities, but apparently it was not acted upon.[57] There were more warnings, some even from SA leaders.

It is possible that this information was based on news of a meeting held by Habicht at Zürich on 25 June, which was attended by several leading Austrian National Socialists, among them Dr Wächter, Dr

Rudolf Weydenhammer, and the leader of the SS 'Standard' 89 in Vienna, SS *Sturmbannführer* Fridolin Glass. The latter since the previous year had prepared plans to arrest the president and the members of the cabinet; he declared at the meeting that his plan could still be carried out although the situation was deteriorating from day to day, but that it could not be shelved any longer. His unit to a large extent consisted of unemployed workers and soldiers discharged from the army for National Socialist activities; it had received 'splendid military training' and was 'totally reliable'.[58] The men were particularly radical and on bad terms with the SA. At the meeting in Zürich Wächter enquired whether he should establish contact with the Viennese SA but was told by Habicht that they would receive their orders from their leader in Munich, Reschny. Glass promised that units of the army, in particular the 2nd and 3rd brigades in Vienna, would participate, and it was decided to go ahead with the plan. The last, decisive meeting before the Putsch was held in Habicht's flat in Munich, and among those present were Reschny, the Vienna Gauleiter Frauenfeld, Glass, Weydenhammer, and a Major Egert from the intelligence section of the Austrian ministry of defence. According to Weydenhammer, Hitler was informed by Habicht and was opposed to 'a little Putsch', but in favour of a general rising against the Dollfuss regime. He left the details to Habicht, but Habicht was in Munich, and in practice Glass more or less independently organized the undertaking in Vienna. Habicht established the necessary contacts with Vienna and with Rome and conducted negotiations 'with the appropriate offices', while Weydenhammer procured the arms and uniforms required for the coup in Vienna.[59]

At lunch time on 25 July about 150 men of the SS unit, who had donned army uniforms in a near-by gym hall, occupied the Austrian chancery without meeting any resistance. They intended to arrest the members of the cabinet, but its meeting had already ended, and in the building they found only Dollfuss. He tried to escape by a side-door leading to the archives but was shot in the attempt. The SS men also occupied the building of the Austrian broadcasting company and announced that the government had resigned and that the former Landeshauptmann of Styria, Dr Rintelen, who had conveniently arrived in Vienna from his post in Rome, would form a new government. It is difficult to explain how these two well-guarded government buildings could have been so easily taken over in spite of all the previous warnings. The minister of justice, Dr Kurt Schuschnigg, formed the new government. Negotiations were carried on with the Putschists in the chancery to whom a safe conduct was offered. But when it became known that Dollfuss was dead the government did not feel tied by this promise: they were arrested and tried, and seven participants were eventually executed.

The failure of the Putsch in Vienna was above all due to the fact that no army unit supported it and that the SA did not co-operate with the SS. Dr Wächter indeed found the local SA leaders assembled in the Hotel St James. When asked where the SA was their leader pretended that he had not been told about any action. When Wächter informed him about the situation he ordered the SA of Vienna and Lower Austria to be mobilized and promised that they would march to the city centre within an hour, but later he cancelled the order. Two days after he issued another order in which he described the action as a private affair of the SS 'Standard' 89 for which the SA bore no responsibility.[60] An order by a member of the government to mobilize the Viennese Heimwehr units against the National Socialists was sabotaged by the deputy mayor of Vienna and local Heimwehr leader, Major Lahr, who sympathized with the National Socialists.[61] In Vienna, the friction between SA and SS was no doubt very much increased by the German purge of 30 June 1934 when the SA leaders were killed by the SS: this was the revenge of the Austrian SA for the murder of Röhm and many others.[62]

Nor did the SS support the SA when the latter rose in several Austrian Länder on receiving the prearranged signal over the radio occupied by the Putschists in Vienna. The rising occurred in parts of Upper Austria and Salzburg and above all in Carinthia and Styria where it was at least partially successful. The Burgenland, Lower Austria, Tyrol and Vorarlberg were not affected. The army and gendarmerie were reinforced by Heimwehr units and, thanks to their better armaments and discipline, were successful within a few days in defeating the revolt. There was no mutiny among the armed forces, although Starhemberg later asserted that many senior officers were at first waiting how things would go and what kind of new government would come into power.[63] Even officers who were National Socialists carried out the orders they received and some of them were killed in the fighting. In Styria alone, 88 men were killed and 164 wounded.[64]

By far the heaviest fighting occurred in Styria where the National Socialists were supported by the Heimwehren commanded by Kammerhofer and Meyszner. Their units were indeed the first which obeyed the radio signal from Vienna and took over large parts of Styria.[65] Everywhere a leading part was played by the local intelligentsia, teachers, lawyers and doctors. The public buildings of Radkersburg in the south were occupied without any resistance, and several other towns of southern Styria were similarly taken over by the insurgents. In northern Styria the district of Leoben was the scene of severe fighting; at Troifach about 80 per cent of the population sympathized with the rising and put out flags from their houses; at Donawitz and elsewhere the workers of the *Alpine Montan* came out on strike. In eastern Styria the brunt of the fight against the rebels was borne by Heimwehr units loyal to the government which defeated the SA in the area of Ilz without help from the army. But around Leoben and in the south infantry units and even artillery were used to break the resistance and the fighting lasted for several days until the rebels were defeated and dispersed; many fled across the frontier into Yugoslavia.[66]

At Preding the National Socialists occupied the post office and the police station and took away the weapons. At St Florian they seized the rifles of the loyal Heimwehr unit and then marched to Stainz which was occupied by rebel forces, but finally they surrendered to an army unit.[67] The rebels, however, failed to take Graz, the capital of Styria, which was held by a strong garrison and loyal Heimwehr forces. According to a report from Austria, forwarded to the German Foreign Office, there were many thousands of youngsters willing to fight, but they did not possess enough weapons and far too little ammunition. The fate of the rising was sealed because the organs of the executive remained loyal and carried out their orders, while there was 'total confusion' on the side of the SA.[68] Another report attributed the ill-success in Styria to the lack of any information from Carinthia, the negative attitude of the Munich radio station, and the failure to attack at Bruck on the Mur and in the Mürz valley to the north-east of it.[69]

In Carinthia, curiously enough, the rising did not start on 25 July but only on the 26th, when the authorities were much better prepared. Yet by the 27th Upper Carinthia and the towns of St Veit, Lavamünd, Oberdrauburg, Feldkirchen, Völkermarkt and Bleiburg were in the hands of the insurgents who appointed new officials in the district towns occupied by them.[70] They also proclaimed martial law, took hostages, and arrested political opponents. At Ettendorf and elsewhere the gendarmes handed over their arms because they thought that resistance was hopeless.[71] The Social Democrats in some places were invited to join the revolt but declined. From the surrendering gendarmes and old Heimwehr depots the rebels received arms, but these were insufficient and there was, as in Styria, a serious shortage of ammunition.[72] Above all, they failed to take the more important towns, Klagenfurt, Villach and Spittal. They probably did not have the military training required for operations on such a scale and they lost vital hours. When they finally made the attempt on Klagenfurt it was badly organized and easily repulsed.

The National Socialist plan — if indeed there was an overall plan — was to surround Klagenfurt and to concentrate their units from Upper and Lower Carinthia against the capital.[73] In the villages and small towns of the neighbourhood the men were mobilized on the 26th by motor cyclists and told to assemble at certain places where they could cross the Drau river. Many of them were unarmed, and some rifles and guns with ammunition were handed out to them. They then crossed the Drau by ferry (which the authorities had failed to immobilize) and waited in the woods around Klagenfurt during the night; but that was the end of the affair, for in the morning they were told to return home. Most of them then threw their weapons away. Later the gendarmes collected not only rifles but also machine guns with ammunition. At Pörtschach near Klagenfurt the SA men were only ordered to assemble in a near-by wood to await further orders there, but were then sent home again; it seems that their local leader simply did not receive any further instructions.[74] A report from Austria forwarded to the German Foreign Office soon after mentioned 'confusion, mistakes in the organization, difficulties of the command, too little military training and lack of ammunition (at St Veit)' as the reasons which allowed the army to reconquer the lost districts. The principal causes of the confusion were that 'the leaders started with the conviction that the situation was hopeless' and that from Munich the whole action was called off. 'It is not surprising that in these circumstances the greatest bitterness reigns in Carinthia and that the attitude of Munich is classified as "criminal". . . . Can you understand the bitterness which fills the best of us?'[75]

The fighting in Carinthia lasted until 29 July, several days longer than in Styria. The insurgents first offered to hand over their arms if they received a free pardon, but then the majority fled into the mountains or into Yugoslavia.[76] From the west units of the Tyrolese Heimwehren marched into Upper Carinthia and reoccupied Oberdrauburg, Greifenburg, and the area around Spittal on the Drau. As there was no uprising in the Tyrol the 5,000 men called up from the para-military associations were available for service elsewhere in Austria. The Tyrolese Heimwehren also reported that the Carinthian rebels were badly armed, with old rifles or hunting guns, and that they mainly consisted of youngsters and subleaders of the former Styrian Heimwehr.[77] In Salzburg too the SA men were mobilized. They occupied the heights around Seekirchen but failed to take it, and were finally dispersed by three companies of Viennese Heimwehr which were sent from Salzburg to Seekirchen. Other Viennese Heimwehr units assisted the gendarmerie in the neighbourhood of Salzburg.[78] The service rendered by such volunteer units was uniformly praised in the official reports, as was that of the army units engaged in the fighting. It is indeed very surprising that there was no sign of disaffection or any unwillingness to obey orders.

In Bavaria the 'Austrian Legion' was mobilized near the frontier ready for the invasion. Some of its units indeed crossed the frontier at Kollerschlag to the north of the Danube, but were repulsed by the Austrians. In the opinion of the Austrian authorities the full-scale invasion did not take place because Italian troops were concentrated at the Brenner frontier.[79] In Austria there was deep depression among the National Socialists after the failure of the revolt. In Upper Austria all illegal activity came to an end for the time being.[80] In the Tyrol responsible party officials declared that they were unwilling to permit a continuation of the previous state of affairs when the leaders who remained in Austria were not consulted by Munich; they would resist energetically if the Munich practices were not changed. Similar opinions were voiced in Carinthia and Styria, and everywhere the word of a 'crime against Austria' could be heard.[81] Yet this mood did not last very long. To the Austrian National Socialists those executed after the uprising remained martyrs 'who died on the gallows for Germany's honour and freedom, ignominiously murdered by a government that has broken the constitution, perjured itself and committed treason against the nation'; they were confident that the day of justice and vengeance would come.[82] That day came within eight months of the announcement just quoted.

The rising of July 1934 differed radically from the Munich Putsch eleven years earlier. The latter was undertaken to force the Bavarian government under von Kahr to make common cause with the rebels and to proclaim the 'national revolution'; no attempt was made to seize power by military force. On 9 November 1923 there was a mass demonstration in the streets of Munich which was dispersed by a salvo from the rifles of the Bavarian police, and that was the end. The Austrian revolt was indeed the only attempt ever made by any National Socialist organization to overthrow the existing government by military means, and it failed miserably: to a large extent on account of disunity and inefficiency among the National Socialists, the friction between SA and SS, between the Munich party leaders and those who remained in Austria. In general the revolt was badly prepared and undertaken with insufficient and ill-trained forces which had little chance against the highly superior ones of the army, the gendarmerie and the Heimwehren. Only if these forces had disintegrated would the rising have been a serious threat to the regime. As it was the government emerged considerably strengthened from its successes over the Social Democrats and the National Socialists of February and July 1934. It now had a chance of winning over the disaffected sections of the population and of making an attempt at reconciliation. The policy of the Austrian government, however, remained at first implacably hostile to both the Socialists and the National Socialists, that is to the majority of the population.

NOTES

1. Andreas Huber to Steidle, Kufstein, 15 June 1933: Tiroler Landesarchiv, Präsidialakten 1933, 181 XII 59.

2. Steidle to Ministry of Justice, Innsbruck, 10 July 1933: ibid. Steidle was Director of Security for the Tyrol.

3. Steidle to president of the local court, 1 August 1933: ibid.

4. Leaflet of 5 July 1933: Verwaltungsarchiv Wien, Bundeskanzleramt, 22/gen., box 4877.

5. Leaflet signed by the Tyrolese Gauleiter Franz Hofer, s.d.: Tiroler Landesarchiv, Präsidialakten 1933, 181 XII 59.

6. Leaflet signed by the same: Vorarlberger Landesarchiv, Bezirkshauptmannschaft Bregenz, Nr. 3875, 1933.

7. Illegal leaflets, s.d.: Verwaltungsarchiv Wien, Bundeskanzleramt, 22/gen., box 4886.

8. Leaflet signed by Andreas Bolek, Passau, 11 December 1933: ibid.

9. *Der rote Adler, Kampfblatt der N.S.D.A.P. für Tirol und Vorarlberg,* 3. Jahrgang, Folge 20, 14 May 1934: Vorarlberger Landesarchiv, Bezirkshauptmannschaft Feldkirch, 1934.

10. *Der Rote Adler,* 3. Jahrgang, Folge 6, 5 February 1934: ibid.

11. Stadler, *Opfer verlorener Zeiten,* 96: letter of Theodor Grill to his wife s.d. (1934).

12. 'Aufzeichnungen des Fürsten Ernst Rüdiger Starhemberg bis zum Jahre 1938 verfasst während des zweiten Weltkrieges in London', 186: Institut für Zeitgeschichte, Vienna.

13. Report by Revierinspektor Kohout, Neumarkt, 27 March 1934: Oberösterreich. Landesarchiv, Freistadt, Politischer Nachrichtendienst 1934-38.

14. 'Information über den gegenwärtigen Stand der nationalsozialistischen Bewegung in Österreich', 4 April 1936: Haus-, Hof- u. Staatsarchiv, Liasse Österreich 2/21, fasz. 468.

15. Report by Dr Gabert from Salzburg, 31 December 1933: Bundesarchiv Koblenz, Nachlass Otto Gessler, Nr. 24.

16. 'Zusammenstellung bis 19. Nov. 38': ibid., Sammlung Schumacher, Nr. 303.

17. Report by Steidle, Innsbruck, 11 September 1933: Tiroler Landesarchiv, Präsidialakten 1933, 181 XII 59.

18. Sicherheitsdirektor for Upper Austria, Linz, 12 February 1935: Oberösterreich. Landesarchiv, Politische Akten, Nr. 18. The correct figure by 4 August 1934 was 2,034 party members for Upper Austria.

19. Police report from Steyr, 14 June 1934: Verwaltungsarchiv Wien, Bundeskanzleramt, 22/gen., box 4888.

20. Report by Ministry of Defence, Vienna, 12 December 1933: Verwaltungsarchiv Wien, Bundeskanzleramt, 22/gen., box 4879.

21. Standartenführer Otto Wächter to Himmler, Vienna, 31 May 1938: Berlin Document Center, SS Personalakten.

22. The leader of the SA *Untergruppe Wien* to *Brigadeführer* T. in Munich, Vienna, 23 July 1934: Verwaltungsarchiv Wien, Bundeskanzleramt, 22/gen., box 4894.

23. Report by Dr Domenig (?), 26 June 1933: Bezirkshauptmannschaft Klagenfurt, JI 1934, 121-257.

24. Brandstötter, op. cit., 301-9; *Gaurundschreiben* Nr. 5 of Gauleitung Salzburg, September 1933: Verwaltungsarchiv Wien, Bundeskanzleramt, 22/gen., box 4879.

25. Police report of 28 April 1934: ibid., box 4887.

26. Riehl to Dollfuss, Vienna, 2 July 1934: ibid., box 4895.

27. Habicht to NSDAP *Flüchtlingswerk,* Wittenberg, 25 March 1937: Berlin Document Center, Partei-Kanzlei Korrespondenz.

28. Letter by anon. former National Socialist to Riehl (?), Salzburg, 4 June 1934: Verwaltungsarchiv Wien, Bundeskanzleramt, 22/gen., box 4891.

29. Protests by doctors' organization, chamber of agriculture, etc., Villach and Klagenfurt, 16-19 June 1933: Kärntner Landesarchiv, Präs, 9-2/1411, fasz. 904.

30. Reports by 'Martin' and Dr Moebius, 7 September, 23 December 1933: Haus-, Hof- u. Staatsarchiv, Nachlass Hornbostel, fasz. 247; *Freie Stimmen,* Klagenfurt, 30 December 1933.

31. Otto Trumbl to Gauleiter vom Kothen in Berlin, Munich, 30-31 January 1934: Bundesarchiv Koblenz, NS 26, vorl. 143 (Gau Kärnten). The writer as well as the recipient were safely installed in Germany.

32. German Consul at Klagenfurt to Auswärt. Amt, 14 May 1934: Auswärt. Amt, Abt. II, Akten betr. Nationalsozialismus, 6112H, E453408.

33. Report by 'Martin', Klagenfurt, 16 June 1934: Haus-, Hof- u. Staatsarchiv, Liasse Österreich 2/21, fasz. 303.

34. Unsigned report from Klagenfurt, 21 July 1934: Verwaltungsarchiv Wien, Bundeskanzleramt, 22/gen., box 4898.

35. Information by Generaldirektion für die öffentl. Sicherheit, July 1934: ibid., box 4891.

36. Report by Sicherheitsdirektor for Styria, Graz, 3 March 1934: ibid., box 4883.

37. Report by Sicherheitsdirektor for Upper Austria, Linz, 24 March 1934: ibid., box 4884.

38. The same to Bezirkshauptmann of Braunau, 9 September 1933: Oberösterr. Landesarchiv, Politische Akten, Nr. 1 (Braunau).

39. Official note, Ried, 3 October 1933: ibid., Nr. 30.

40. Police reports, Grünau, 10 April, 11 May 1934: ibid., Nr. 11.

41. Police reports, Vorchdorf, 9 May, and Traunkirchen, 8 June 1934: ibid.

42. Police reports, Goisern, 9 April, 8 May, 23 July 1934: ibid.

43. Police report, Bad Ischl, 9 May 1934: ibid. All the above places are in the district of Gmunden (Salzkammergut).

44. Information by Generaldirektion für die öffentl. Sicherheit, July 1934: ibid., Politische Akten, Nr. 6.

45. Report by Sicherheitsdirektor for Vorarlberg, Bregenz, 2 March 1934: Verwaltungsarchiv Wien, Bundeskanzleramt, 22/gen., box 4883.

46. Anon. letter from Dornbirn, 18 January 1934: Vorarlb. Landesarchiv, Präsidialakten 544, 1933.

47. Police reports, Gaschurn, 21 and 26 July 1933: ibid.

48. Report by Bezirkshauptmannschaft Bregenz, 16 November 1933: ibid., Bezirkshauptmannschaft Bregenz, Nr. 384, 1936.

49. Police reports, Riezlern, 25-26 September 1933, 1 January, 10 February 1934: ibid., Bezirkshauptmannschaft Bregenz, Nr. 170, 1871, 1934.

50. Police report, Mellau, 26 September 1933: ibid., Nr. 3625, 1933.

51. Report by Bezirkshauptmannschaft Oberwart, 13 December 1933: Burgenländ. Landesarchiv, Landesamtsdirektion, 243-1933.

52. Report by Bundespolizeikommissariat Innsbruck, 5 October 1933: Verwaltungsarchiv Wien, Bundeskanzleramt, 22/gen., box 4878. Information by Generaldirektion für die öffentl. Sicherheit, 23 March 1936: ibid., box 4961.

53. Report of 22 January 1935: Botschaft Wien, Geheimakten 1935-38, 4939 part 1, E271826.

54. Report by Generaldirektion für die öffentl. Sicherheit, Vienna, 21 December 1933: Oberösterreich. Landesarchiv, Politische Akten, Nr. 1.

55. Report by Reichsstatthalter of Bavaria, Munich, 31 August 1935: Botschaft Wien, Geheimakten 1935-38, 4938 part 9, E271296-97.

56. Notes by Councillor of Legation von Renthe-Fink, Berlin, 29 May 1934: *Akten zur deutschen auswärtigen Politik,* series C, II (1) no. 469, 833.

57. Communication by Sicherheitsdirektor for Styria, Graz, 5 July 1934, and by Sicherheitsdirektor for Upper Austria, Linz, 10 July: Vorarlb. Landesarchiv, Bezirkshauptmannschaft Bregenz, Nr. 3250, 1934; Oberösterreich. Landesarchiv, Politische Akten, Nr. 1.

58. Thus a National Socialist account: Wladimir von Hartlieb, *Parole: Das Reich* (Vienna and Leipzig, 1939) 222.

59. The above according to letter by Wächter to NSDAP *Oberstes Parteigericht,* Vienna, 28 May 1938: Berlin Document Center, SS Personalakten; and the report by Weydenhammer of 1964: Zeugenschrifttum Nr. 1928, Institut für Zeitgeschichte, Munich, with notes made by Dr Auerbach on 14 February 1964. The account by Gehl, *Austria, Germany and the Anschluss* (London, 1963) 96-97, is different.

60. Thus report by Wächter of January 1937: *Die Erhebung der österreichischen Nationalsozialisten im Juli 1934 (Akten der historischen Kommission des Reichsführers SS)* (Vienna-Frankfurt-Zürich, 1965) 133.

61. Letter by Lahr to an NSDAP office, s.d.: Berlin Document Center.

62. Cp. the conclusion reached by the SS committee of enquiry: *Die Erhebung der österreichischen Nationalsozialisten . . .,* 133.

63. 'Aufzeichnungen des Fürsten Ernst Rüdiger Starhemberg bis zum Jahre 1938 verfasst während des zweiten Weltkrieges in London', MS. p. 105.

64. Pauley, *Hahnenschwanz und Hakenkreuz,* 190; his figures corrected after report by Landesgendarmeriekommando for Styria, 18 August 1934: Verwaltungsarchiv Wien, Bundeskanzleramt, 22/gen., box 4904a.

65. NSDAP Landesleitung Österreich to NSDAP Reichsleitung, Berlin, 23 January 1935: Bundesarchiv Koblenz, Sammlung Schumacher, Nr. 277.

66. Reports by Landesgendarmeriekommando for Styria, 18 August 1934, and Generaldirektion für die öffentl. Sicherheit, 27 December 1934: Verwaltungsarchiv Wien, Bundeskanzleramt, 22/gen., box 4904a.

67. Many similar detailed reports are ibid., box 4903.

68. Anon. report, Vienna, 31 July 1934: *Akten zur deutschen auswärtigen Politik,* series C, III (1) (Göttingen, 1973) no. 143, 276-8.

69. Anon. report, late August 1934: Auswärt. Amt, Akten betr. Nationalsozialismus, Bd. 2, 6114 H, E454325-26.

70. Anon. report, Vienna, 31 July 1934: *Akten zur deutschen auswärtigen Politik,* series C, III (1) 278.

71. Report on Carinthia by Generaldirektion für die öffentl. Sicherheit, s.d.: Verwaltungsarchiv Wien, Bundeskanzleramt, 22/gen., box 4902.

72. Anon. report from Vienna, 31 July 1934, loc. cit.

73. Thus a rebel broadcast of 27 July 1934: Verwaltungsarchiv Wien, Bundeskanzleramt, 22/gen., box 4898.

74. Very detailed police reports of 26, 30 July, 2, 11 August 1934: Bezirkshauptmannschaft Klagenfurt, 1934 J 1-300, JI 1934 1-120, JI 1935 1-100, 1935 J 1-300.

75. Anon. report from Vienna, 31 July 1934: loc. cit.

76. Situation reports from Carinthia, 28 and 29 July 1934: Verwaltungsarchiv Wien, Bundeskanzleramt, 22/gen., box 4898.

77. Report by Sicherheitsdirektor for Tyrol, Innsbruck, 8 August 1934, and supplement 4: ibid., box 4904a.

78. Report by Generaldirektion für die öffentl. Sicherheit on events at Seekirchen, 27 April 1935: ibid., box 4922a. The boxes 4902-4 and 4922 a-b contain very detailed reports of the events of July 1934.

79. Information by Generaldirektion für die öffentl. Sicherheit, 23 March 1936: ibid., box 4961; Zöllner, op. cit., 517.

80. Confidential information by Sicherheitsdirektor for Upper Austria, Linz, 3 October 1934: Oberösterr. Landesarchiv, Politische Akten, Nr. 1.

81. Anon. report, of late August 1934: Auswärt. Amt, Akten betr. National-sozialismus, Band 2, 6114H, E454327.

82. Thus the National Socialist underground paper *Österreichischer Beobachter* of July 1937: Oberösterr. Landesarchiv, Politische Akten, Nr. 11 (Eferding).

13

AUSTRIA UNDER SCHUSCHNIGG

Dollfuss's successor as head of the Austrian government was Dr
Kurt von Schuschnigg who had been minister of justice under
Dollfuss and, like him, a prominent leader of the Christian Social
Party. The policy of the government remained unchanged. Externally, it relied on the support of Mussolini, but it had to take
into account the slow rapprochement between Italy and Germany,
which became more rapid with the outbreak of the Abyssinian
conflict in 1935, and the growing military might of Hitler's
Germany. Hitler's great successes – the plebiscite in the Saar, the
reintroduction of conscription, the reoccupation of the Rhineland,
rearmament and the decline of unemployment – were bound to
have strong repercussions in Austria whose economic recovery was
extremely slow. It was only too easy to assume that all economic troubles could be solved if better relations were established
with the mighty neighbour to the north to whom Austria was
tied by so many bonds. Then German tourists would once more
stream into Austria, and Austria would find a ready market for
her timber and agrarian produce. German successes also reflected
on the Austrian National Socialists who had suffered a severe defeat in July 1934, but whose recovery – with German help –

was only a question of time.

Internally, Schuschnigg continued to steer a middle course between the Scylla of Socialism and the Charybdis of National
Socialism; but this meant that the basis of his support remained
small. There was at first no serious attempt to bring about a
reconciliation with any of the opponents of the government; and
continuing friction among its supporters and the final dissolution
of all para-military associations further narrowed the base which
upheld the shaky structure of the regime. While Hitler and Mussolini, flushed with success, undoubtedly enjoyed growing mass
support this decisive factor was sadly lacking in Austria. The
government's policy was humdrum, hesitant and cautious and
lacked the drive of the fascist regimes.

These facts were admitted even in the naturally careful reports of
the official organizations. At the end of 1934 the leaders of the
'Fatherland Front' of Vorarlberg drew up a detailed survey of the
political and economic conditions in their district in which they
stressed time and again that the mood of the population was 'very
depressed', largely for economic reasons: unemployment, low agrarian
prices, difficulties of selling, absence of German tourists, and the
general malaise. In addition, the supporters of the government complained, at least in some places, that its enemies, the capitalists, etc.
were not tackled more energetically, that the workers were too much
exploited, that the left-wing opponents were punished much more
harshly than 'the brown terrorists', and that the officials and white-
collar workers were better paid than the farmers. Perhaps most
significant was the complaint that so many of the opponents of the
government were still employed in the factories and other enterprises
while so many members of the Fatherland Front were unemployed:
clearly membership was seen as a kind of guarantee of obtaining work
at the expense of non-members. That such grievances were incorporated
into the report without comment shows that even senior officials of the
Fatherland Front looked at it as a kind of social insurance scheme,
rather than as a political organization rallying the convinced adherents
of the regime. How strongly economic motives conditioned the political
loyalties is also attested by the chance remark: 'We are certainly good
Austrians, but we want to live and to exist and we have the right to do
so. . . .'[1] The Director of Security for Vorarlberg attributed the
National Socialist sympathies 'in certain circles' directly to 'the heavy
burden of debts, the high rate of interest (Breaking of the Shackles of

Interest!) and the impossibility of earning money caused by the total absence of tourists'.[2]

A similar attitude towards the Fatherland Front emerges from the files of the Front Gauleiter of the Upper Austrian district of Freistadt which contain many applications for jobs by unemployed 'loyalists' and other attempts to interest the local leaders in a variety of private requests.[3] The Bezirkshauptmann of Eferding, also in Upper Austria, reported to his superiors that many joined the Fatherland Front 'not out of love of the fatherland, but for other reasons', and indicated these by the brief note: 'in general members of the Fatherland Front are preferred in the allocation of work'. No wonder that there were 5,304 members in October 1935 in his district, about 24 per cent of the total population including children.[4] In the district of Freistadt the membership was a little higher, nearly 26 per cent of the entire population, and in the town of Freistadt itself it amounted to exactly 50 per cent in the spring of 1936. But the Upper Austrian Landesleitung of the Front aimed at a figure of about half the total population everywhere and initiated an enquiry in all places, where a minimum of one-third of the population had not been enrolled why the figure was so low.[5] For the district around Linz the police were able to report that by the autumn of 1935 45-50 per cent of the adult population had joined the Front; but some months before they had to admit that 'the sympathies for the government do not grow. Some police stations report that many people only outwardly show their patriotic attitude to draw advantages from it, but their innermost conviction is different', and this applied especially to those who depended on others.[6] In the Burgenland the membership of the Fatherland Front in June 1935 amounted to only 23 per cent of the total population, but by April 1937 it had increased to more than 38 per cent.[7] This increase may partly be explained by the manifold social services of the Front, such as distribution of food parcels, allocation of milk, 'winter help', protection of mothers: non-political activities to which few people could object.[8]

In November 1936 the General Directorate of Public Security stated that the Front lacked 'an activist group', that this had unfortunate results, that its officials were unable to counter effectively the fear of communism created by National Socialist propaganda, and that in Styria in particular any organizational and propagandist activity of the Front was woefully lacking. In Vorarlberg there was a mood of crisis among its local leaders which brought about the removal of local officials – a mood caused by the alleged lack of political effort on the side of the Front's leaders.[9] Shortly after, the police reported from the Styrian town of Bruck that there was a general fatigue and lack of interest in loyalist circles; 'it seems as if no one were willing to serve the Fatherland Front out of inner conviction, true love or joy. A certain depressed mood prevails.'[10] Twelve months later it was reported from the same district that people only joined the Front for economic reasons or if they were forced to do so.[11] A local police station found that people participated in the Front's activities so as not to suffer any damage or to gain an advantage; there was 'no unity, no cohesion'.[12]

There were very similar reports from the Tyrol. According to the Innsbruck police, the Tyrolese leaders of the Fatherland Front were 'totally lacking in forceful drive and organizational activity', hence unable to remedy a situation which the police considered dangerous.[13] In 1937 the Bezirkshauptmann of Innsbruck found life in the local Front groups sluggish;[14] and his colleague at Reutte reported that the Front was showing no signs of any external activity. When a meeting was held in Reutte it was very badly attended; the participants either held official positions or were functionaries of the Front. In the debate the only questions asked were about the membership dues, and no topical issue was touched upon.[15]

The question might well be asked what use was this amorphous mass organization which possessed no drive and showed such few signs of activity from the point of view of the government. One thing is certain: it was unable to arouse any enthusiasm, even among the supporters of the regime. The German National Socialist Party as well as the Russian Bolshevik Party claimed that they represented the elite of the nation, but an organization which aimed at including half the *total* population could not possibly possess an elite character. The Austrian government obviously felt the need to underpin its structure by a mass organization, but did the Fatherland Front really shore up the Austrian state to any significant extent? Its slogan was 'Austria', but most Austrians considered themselves Germans. The Front possessed no distinctive ideology for the idea of the 'State of the Estates' was much too nebulous and vague to attract large numbers; and it did not even possess a programme. At the first national 'roll-call' of the Front in January 1936 Prince Starhemberg, who had become the leader of the Front after Dollfuss's death, announced that such a programme would be published, but this never happened.[16] He also discussed at length the question of the restoration of the monarchy – an issue that was likely not to unite, but to divide the members of the Front. Schuschnigg only became the deputy leader of the Front, and the resultant dualism proved another source of weakness. Schuschnigg aimed at the incorporation of the Heimwehren in the Fatherland Front: a policy strenuously resisted by the Heimwehr leaders.[17] The latter also distrusted the political Catholicism of Schuschnigg and his adherents, and equally the strong influence of the bureaucracy which continued to govern Austria as it had done in the past. In their opinion, the bureaucrats only caused stagnation and prevented any 'dynamic' developments.[18]

At the end of 1935 the Papal Nuncio in Vienna, Cardinal Sibilia, reported to Rome that the Schuschnigg government had at most 30 per cent of the population behind it. This he considered sufficient to consolidate the regime and then systematically to broaden the basis of the government, but this was prevented by the 'totalitarian aims' of the Heimwehren whose following had become very small. In several conversations the chancellor told the Nuncio that the Heimwehr leaders were demanding changes in the government and in particular the post of the minister of defence for one of themselves — a demand which Schuschnigg was determined to reject. His aim, he told the Nuncio, was the formation of a militia and its subordination to the army, whose leaders were good Catholics: this aim he would pursue 'with inflexible energy'.[19] The Heimwehren were not to be permitted to gain any influence on the army, but on the contrary, through their incorporation in a militia, were to be made subordinate to the army. According to another well-informed observer, the Heimwehr leaders strenuously attempted to establish their hegemony and did not know how to cooperate with their partners in the government and in the Fatherland Front.[20] In such circumstances, a conflict could hardly be avoided.

Meanwhile Starhemberg kept his options open. He continued his contacts with German officials, in particular Hitler's new ambassador in Vienna, Franz von Papen. In a conversation at the beginning of 1936 Starhemberg expressed his admiration for Hitler, 'the first statesman who has recognized the danger of a bolshevik-freemason united front for the whole world and fights against it without making any concession', and expressed his opposition to political Catholicism in Austria.[21] In March Starhemberg reported to Papen on his visit to Mussolini whom he had told that it was essential 'to form a front of the authoritarian states against the common offensive of Bolshevism and Jewish democracy'. Mussolini warmly welcomed this proposal and emphasized the need of a new constellation of powers in Europe after the end of the Abyssinian conflict. Starhemberg suggested to the Italians that three representatives of the three governments should meet privately at Easter so as to establish what united the three regimes and to what extent they could co-operate to achieve their great aims; and Mussolini expressed the hope that Germany would accept. Starhemberg also supported the proposal, as he informed Papen, because he did not want his followers to continue an alliance with democrats and Christian Social partisans with whom he had nothing in common but the preservation of the independence of Austria.[22]

In his offensive against the Heimwehr influence Schuschnigg in April 1936 reintroduced general conscription: a measure bound to weaken the position of Starhemberg and to strengthen that of the army leaders. Papen considered this only a first step towards the dissolution of the para-military associations and the elimination of the Heimwehren.[23] It is thus not surprising that the new law met with a cool reception from them, while many government supporters expressed the wish that all para-military formations would disappear.[24] At the end of April Starhemberg counter-attacked and proclaimed that the most important task was the fight against Bolshevism; this necessitated a close co-operation with Fascism and if possible also with the National Socialists and could only be carried out through a separation 'from the saboteurs of the authoritarian government, the democrats within the government camp'; he would resist any attempt to disarm the Heimwehr and would rather die than give in.[25] In Vienna members of the Heimwehren and the Freiheitsbund – another para-military group within the Fatherland Front – openly clashed at a demonstration of the latter headed by Schuschnigg himself at the beginning of May.[26] For the chancellor this open defiance may have been the last straw, for a few days later he dismissed Starhemberg from his posts of vice-chancellor and leader of the Fatherland Front: a step which caused renewed hostility on the side of the Heimwehren.[27] But, in spite of Starhemberg's previous declamation, there was no resistance.

To add insult to injury Starhemberg was entrusted with the patronage of the Mothers' Aid Work of the Fatherland Front: a bitter humiliation in the opinion of the Upper Austrian Heimwehr paper, *Neue Zeit*. But for the time being he remained the leader of the Heimwehr, and his deputy leader, Baar-Baarenfels, was promoted vice-chancellor in Starhemberg's place. The former was also to have the command of the new militia which Schuschnigg was determined to create to replace the para-military formations as a further step in the dismantling of Heimwehr influence. According to its own paper, the mood among the Heimwehr men was such that the leaders had to assert all their authority to prevent any rash actions.[28] But all that seems to have materialized in the way of opposition were some painted slogans 'Heil Starhemberg' and 'Heil Mussolini' and an illegal leaflet widely distributed in Styria which attacked clericalism, vilified Schuschnigg as a traitor and glorified Starhemberg and his activities.[29] The Heimwehr leaders proved as irresolute as they had been on earlier occasions. Within the Fatherland Front they tried to unite the 'anti-democratic forces' and to continue the fight against the Freiheitsbund. They also discussed a plan to induce President Miklas to resign so that he could be succeeded by Starhemberg, and thus they hoped to regain some of the ground which they had lost.[30] But once again all their plans were frustrated by lack of interest and friction within their own ranks, in particular between the followers of Starhemberg and those of Major Fey, the Viennese leader, which finally caused a complete breach between them.[31]

The conflict broke out openly in October 1936. Within the Heim-wehren increasing opposition developed to Starhemberg's ineffective leadership. The leaders in Carinthia and the Tyrol demanded that he should resign. In September Fey was re-elected as the leader for Vienna and used his position to bring about the downfall of Starhemberg. The latter replied by decreeing the expulsion of Fey and the vice-mayor of Vienna, Major Lahr; but Fey defied him and declared that only his orders were valid for the Viennese Heimwehr formations.[32] According to Lahr, the whole move was undertaken to bring about an under-standing with the National Socialists, to lead 'the Heimwehr finally into the national camp'.[33] In any case, the whole affair gave to the chan-cellor the opportunity for which he had waited, to deprive the Heim-wehr leaders of all political influence. On 10 October the government decreed all para-military formations dissolved and the militia of the Fatherland Front the only legal military formation apart from the army.[34] This meant the end of the Heimwehr as a legal, uniformed force, and set the seal on its decline during the previous years. Starhem-berg announced at a meeting of his followers that a 'loyal co-operation with the government' was no longer possible and called upon the Heimwehr members of the government to resign from it;[35] but these were empty gestures which produced no result. From Schuschnigg he demanded to be readmitted to the government and to be appointed the leader of the new militia, but Schuschnigg felt strong enough to reject these demands.[36] On the face of it he had gained a victory. But at the same time he deprived himself of the support of a militant formation which, in spite of its decline and disunity, still possessed a substantial following:[37] a support which the regime could ill afford to lose.

Until 1938 the dissolved Heimwehr continued to exist in the form of an association of former members which called itself *Alt-Heimatschutz*. This inherited the strong personal conflicts so characteristic of the organization in its better days. Many former Heimwehr leaders held Starhemberg responsible for the debacle and had only bad things to say about him.[38] The friction between the followers of Starhemberg and Fey continued, while Starhemberg himself remained silent and finally left Austria, to pose abroad as an inveterate opponent of National Socialism. Occasionally the police found illegal leaflets spread by former Heimwehr men which repeated the old slogans, expressed their absolute fidelity to the oath of Korneuburg, attacked democracy and the parties, and especially the clericals and 'blacks' who occupied the lucrative posts. One leaflet classified Chancellor Schuschnigg as a traitor, a Judas in the pay of the clericals, a man who betrayed the inheritance of Dollfuss.[39] But, deprived of its uniforms and its influence in the government, the Heimwehren virtually disappeared, and many disappointed members joined the National Socialists.

Nor did the Front Militia founded in 1936 to absorb the para-military formations ever flourish. It was too artificial a creation and never aroused any enthusiasm among its members. There are numerous local reports in the Austrian archives complaining about the slow progress in the formation of the militia, the lack of interest, the small numbers recruited (often balanced by resignations), the negative attitude adopted by the members of the dissolved para-military organizations, etc. Even where local militia groups were founded they showed few signs of activity.[40] One Bezirkshauptmann expressly commented that the militia was totally lacking the drive and enthusiasm which had animated the para-military formations; where local groups existed it required all the influence of the commandant to keep them together.[41] In Upper Austria, the old friction between the Heimwehren and the other para-military formations was transplanted into the new militia.[42] In May 1937 even an official government report admitted that 'some districts' reported more resignations from the militia than new members.[43] The Fatherland Front to which the militia belonged at least had a mass membership, but the militia itself remained small, inactive and stillborn.

On the face of it Schuschnigg's victory over the Heimwehren resembled that of Hitler over the SA of June 1934. In both cases, the ambitions of the leaders of a para-military organization proved incompatible with the aims and policy of an authoritarian regime. Yet there was an enormous difference. Hitler, by killing the SA-leaders and depriving the SA of all political power, assured himself of the loyalty of the army and the approval of the large majority of his supporters who heartily disliked the ambitions and behaviour of the SA leaders. Schuschnigg, by defeating the Heimwehr aspirations, may have won the approval of the army leaders who were probably only too glad to see a rival influence eliminated.[44] But in the political field he did not gain any support and only further narrowed the small base on which the system rested. Nor were the Social Democrats or the National Socialists in any way reconciled by the emasculation of the Heimwehr. Their main enemy remained the authoritarian regime, not the defunct paramilitary formations from which the National Socialists had recruited so many of their followers. It was a Pyrrhic victory while that of Hitler was a very real one. If Schuschnigg relied on the continuing support of Mussolini that too was a miscalculation.

There can be little doubt either that Dr Schuschnigg, himself a pupil of the Jesuits and an ardent Catholic, relied on the support of the Vatican and the Catholic hierarchy — a highly important factor in a strongly Catholic country. The many attacks on the 'clericals' and 'blacks' in Heimwehr propaganda must have been one of the reasons which made the chancellor turn against his former allies. He conferred frequently with the Papal Nuncio, and the latter reported to Rome in December 1935 that Schuschnigg 'assessed the situation absolutely correctly and clearly recognized the dangers emanating from the "totalitarian tendencies" of the Heimatschutz. . . .'[45] It is quite clear from the report that the Nuncio strongly approved of Schuschnigg's policy and that Schuschnigg sought to gain this backing. Twelve months later a German intelligence report, which discussed the growing strength of the monarchists and their attempts to gain stronger influence in the government, stated that Schuschnigg was pursuing a via media between the 'national' and the legitimist camps and therefore was attacked by both; 'but as long as he is supported by the Vatican and especially by the Italians all the current speculations about a reshuffle of the Austrian cabinet are pointless. . . .'[46] Another German report, however, considered that the clergy's support for the regime met with much criticism, 'in spite of all the loyalty to the Catholic Church. . . . This disapproval is so strong that in certain circumstances it may develop into a danger for the Church itself. . . .'[47] But it seems likely that the report, coming from a National Socialist source, exaggerated this tendency. In any case, the Austrian hierarchy was by no means united in its political attitude. In 1937 the leader of the Austrian National Socialists, Josef Leopold, informed his subordinates that Cardinal Archbishop Innitzer as well as Bishops Alois Hudal and Ferdinand Pawlikowski (Graz) were in favour of a 'reconciliation with us', while Bishop Johannes Gföllner of Linz and Archbishop Sigismund Waitz of Salzburg were opposed to it: a split inside the Church that reached down to the last vicarage.[48]

According to the same report, Leopold instructed his comrades 'to be entirely reticent in church affairs' and to let the clergy themselves sort out their own differences. But such reticence was not always practised by the National Socialists. In 1934 they successfully organized boycotts of religious services in some areas of Upper Austria — a fact admitted even by the authorities.[49] In later years the authorities several times expressed their apprehension that the National Socialists were reviving the old slogan of Schönerer 'Break with Rome!' to embarass the government. They admitted that Leopold prohibited any such propaganda, but maintained that it had nevertheless been launched, especially by the Austrian SS.[50] According to information which reached the Vienna police, underground National Socialist propaganda also encouraged the people to leave the Church and to convert to Protestantism — another revival of Schönerer's policy. These conversions allegedly reached such proportions, especially in Salzburg and Styria, that they caused widespread antagonism among the population.[51] In Austria any such propaganda was likely to backfire, a fact which explains Leopold's caution with regard to anti-catholic propaganda. From the National Socialist point of view it was highly preferable to try and loosen the ties between the Church and the Austrian regime and to play on the differences within the hierarchy with regard to the 'national' issue. This policy was to pay ample dividends in 1938 when Cardinal Innitzer welcomed the Anschluss and the Austrian bishops issued a proclamation praising 'the outstanding achievements of National Socialism in the fields of völkisch and economic reconstruction and of social policy'.[52] To the National Socialists the support of the Church was as valuable as it had been to Dollfuss and Schuschnigg.

If there can be no doubt about the pro-catholic trend in Schuschnigg's policy his attitude towards another vital issue, that of the restoration of the monarchy, was extremely cautious. In contrast with Dollfuss, the Germans considered him a legitimist.[53] Yet his policy was not a monarchist one, because he was afraid of Germany's reaction and did not want to antagonize Austria's neighbours to the north and south.[54] Austria had a small, but active and growing monarchist movement; and the restoration of the Habsburgs might effectively have buried any possibility of the Anschluss. The National Socialists were well aware of this and regularly broke up monarchist meetings. After a meeting at Linz in 1937 in honour of the 25th birthday of the Archduke Otto, which was attended by many active and former army officers as well as the local authorities, the National Socialists distributed a leaflet 'To the German people of Linz!' as a 'last warning': 'We will not suffer Habsburg! Habsburg is anti-German! . . . Habsburg is treason! Defend yourselves! Do not suffer a monarchist Putsch! *Never again Habsburg!* ' During the meeting itself the National Socialists present tried to drown the Habsburg anthem by singing *Deutschland über Alles* and threw chairs and tables from the gallery into the hall; after a free fight they were finally evicted.[55]

It is very difficult to say what proportion of the Austrians would have welcomed the restoration of the monarchy or would have voted in favour if the question had ever been submitted to a plebiscite. What is certain is that the Social Democrats on the left and the National Socialists on the right were implacably opposed to it. A German report of 1933 stated somewhat surprisingly: 'A large part of the Austrian population, especially in circles of the peasantry, has become monarchist in recent days. It would be possible to strengthen the monarchist idea even further in these days were it not compromised by the cooperation and the applause of the Jews, for the entire population is more strongly anti-semitic than it is legitimist.' If the two ideas were ever combined, the restoration would have a real chance in Austria which it could never obtain in any other way.[56] Three years later Papen believed that the only alternative to a rapprochement with Germany was the restoration: 'The mass of the peasants in the Alpine lands who previously were loyal monarchists only too easily adopt the slogan "Things must get better whatever may happen." In so far as the clergy in these rural districts have any influence among the peasants they work to a hundred per cent in the service of legitimist propaganda.' For this development Papen held the religious struggle in Germany largely responsible.[57] Apart from many peasants and the clergy, there can be no doubt that many middle-aged people, especially civil servants and army officers, were monarchists.

Legitimism was comparatively strong in the Tyrol. The Innsbruck police estimated in 1934 that the monarchist organization, the *Reichsbund der Österreicher,* had as many as 6,000 members; but the birthday celebration in honour of the Archduke Otto was only attended by about 350 people.[58] In the following year the same occasion in Linz attracted 'numerous participants', among them representatives of the police and gendarmerie and of all para-military associations.[59] The Burgenland in the east of Austria in 1934 reported 'a quick growth of legitimism'.[60] In the spring of 1936 official situation reports mentioned that the monarchist movement was making considerable progress in Salzburg and in Styria.[61] In the same year about 300 people attended the obligatory birthday celebration in honour of Otto of Habsburg in Klagenfurt, and as many as 1,200 a similar meeting in Villach in Carinthia, among them many workers. The meeting was preceded by a special conference with former trade union officials who declared that they could only join the Reichsbund if they received more detailed information about the movement's aims with regard to the working class; their legitimate aspirations still met with the greatest difficulties, while the National Socialists found shelter in the 'national' sports clubs.[62] From Wiener Neustadt too the police reported that many workers, among them 'numerous Communists and revolutionary Socialists', attended a monarchist meeting.[63]

At the beginning of 1937 the police stated that the Reichsbund der Österreicher had recently recruited many new members; most of its followers were civil servants and former officers; it had some among the working class, but few among the young; a restoration would form the 'best bulwark against the advance of German National Socialism and of Russian Bolshevism'.[64] When a memorial mass was celebrated in honour of the former Emperor Charles in Vienna's cathedral in the spring of 1937 it was attended by members of the government and of the imperial family as well as about 4,000 people. Afterwards several hundred people shouted 'Long live Austria-Hungary! ' and 'We want the Emperor!'[65] In the autumn the German embassy also reported that the legitimist movement, after an earlier stagnation, now showed great activity, not only in Vienna, but also in the provinces. In Vienna two meetings were held on 4 October 1937. The first was attended by more than a thousand and was so overcrowded that the police had to close the doors at 7.30 p.m. Although all available rooms in the same restaurant were used for parallel meetings many people had to be sent away. The other meeting was equally crowded out.[66] A legitimist festival in the Tyrol in June 1936 was graced by the presence of the Field-Marshal Archduke Eugen and the Archduchess Adelheid. It took place 'under the aegis of the traditional and direct union between the Tyrolese people and its ancestral dynasty and was not darkened by any false tone or disturbance'. Units of the army, the old army, the Heimwehr, the riflemen, etc. participated in the march past, and a chapel in honour of the former Emperor Charles was consecrated at Lienz in the presence of representatives of the authorities.[67]

By the beginning of 1938 the strength of the *Reichsbund* had increased to such an extent that it was able to embark on its most ambitious venture: the holding of simultaneous mass meetings in all parts of Austria under the slogan 'We desire the independence of Austria! ' On 11 January - only a few weeks before the occupation of Austria by the German army – forty meetings were held, nine of them in Vienna, ten in other Lower Austrian towns, and the remainder in the Burgenland, Carinthia, Styria, Tyrol and Vorarlberg. The majority of the rallies were crowded out, especially those in Vienna where the doors had to be closed by the police long before the announced start of the meeting. According to the police about 10,000 people attended in Vienna, and another 10,500 to 10,800 in the provinces, among them 2,000 in Graz and over 2,000 in Deutsch-Kreuz. None of the others reached an audience of more than 900. Among the audiences all age groups were represented, but the majority were middle-aged or elderly, and there were many women. Among those present were also many National Socialists, and at Mödling near Vienna they were the large majority. At two of the Viennese meetings and at Graz they tried to disrupt the proceedings, and in the resulting free fights beer mugs and chairs were freely used as weapons by both sides; but all meetings were brought to a successful conclusion in spite of the disturbances.[68] This, however, was the last effort of the Reichsbund on any scale. It had grown into a comparatively large organization, able to attract about 20,000 people, but it was not yet a mass movement. Whether it could ever have become one, able to compete with the National Socialists, must remain an open question. To some extent it was a difference of generations, for National Socialism was particularly attractive to many of the young, and the same was true of the underground socialist movement. It was virtually impossible to create an activist mass movement based on the support of the middle-aged.

Already in 1933 a shrewd German observer noticed that the

monarchist movement in Austria would only have a real chance if it adopted anti-Semitism.[69] Perhaps Archduke Otto also realized this, or he tried to take some wind out of the National Socialist sails. In any case, when he granted an 'audience' to some of his loyal adherents at Vaduz in Liechtenstein in December 1937 he stated that certain radical measures against the Jews must be adopted in Austria; their influence on the press should be combated and in economic affairs it should be curtailed. But he added that a dividing line should be drawn between the old established Jews whose attitude to the state was positive and other sections which were less respectable. Above all, the social question must be solved, and sufficient old age and widows' pensions must be introduced for the benefit of the workers. In this form Otto's views on the foremost issues of the day were reported by one of the participants to the members of the Reichsbund at Steyr in Upper Austria.[70] What Otto does not seem to have realized is that most of those who desired 'radical measures' against the Jews and to 'solve the social question' were not looking to him for a solution, but rather across the frontier where another Austrian was pursuing a similar programme with considerable success.

During these years anti-Semitism indeed remained a major force in Austrian politics. In 1935 a German visitor reported many discussions of the Jewish question: people were saying that the Jews exercised strong influence on the government, that they secured positions for themselves by joining the Fatherland Front, that they occupied the best posts in public and private enterprises, and that they had bribed Starhemberg.[71] In the same year a play written by the local priest was enacted at Rinn in the Tyrol which claimed that 'the blessed child Andreas from Rinn' was the victim of a ritual murder according to the local legend. After an official intervention the text of the play was tuned down, and in that form it was permitted to continue.[72] In 1936 the *Tiroler Bauernzeitung* published as a proof of the 'Jewishness' of Vienna the fact that of 166 Viennese cinemas 120 were allegedly in Jewish hands. Another article in the same paper accused the Jews of fomenting revolution 'in innumerable cases' and as proof pointed to the example of the Spanish civil war! [73] In 1936 the General Directorate of Public Security noted that 'social anti-Semitism was continuously growing' and might easily develop into a 'racial anti-Semitism'.[74]

The National Socialists systematically spread anti-semitic propaganda, and — as the authorities had to admit — it 'found a ready echo among the population'.[75] In November 1937 their underground paper,

Österreichischer Beobachter, instructed all party groups to check on the customers of Jewish shops and department stores and to publish their or their wives' names in a 'Jewish pillory list'. This was not an empty threat, for some weeks later the paper printed seven names of 'Aryan' customers seen in Jewish shops at Linz, two such names for Wels, and one for Bad Hall, and announced that a special list would follow for the Jewish Palmers shops where 'many ladies and gentlemen of the better classes' had been observed.[76] When a young National Socialist died of appendicitis the same paper accused a Jewish doctor of having murdered him and demanded that his practice be closed and a criminal investigation be started against him.[77] Papen too reported to Hitler from Vienna that he was successfully fanning 'the basic anti-semitic attitude'.[78]

The activities of the Anti-Semitic League, which had existed for many years, were naturally supported by the underground National Socialists. Their Upper Austrian Gauleitung in 1937 instructed the party members to support the League meetings and to report any remarks critical of National Socialism to the Gauleitung: the latter maintained close relations with the leaders of the Anti-Semitic League and could achieve that any such 'infringements' would cease.[79] A meeting of the League in Graz in February 1937 was attended by about 500 people; the hall was so crowded that many more were refused admission by the police. Among the audience civil servants, business-men, white-collar workers and students were particularly prominent. The principal speaker, Karl Peter, leader of the League, attacked the Fatherland Front for not doing anything against the Jews: it would know itself why not. 'The Anti-Semitic League will create order in Austria . . . with the Jews! For the Anti-Semitic League is not a club but a movement of the people! For 75 per cent of the Austrians are anti-Semites! ' He classified the Jews as an alien body the removal of which was necessary in the interest of a healthy state. His speech was received with such phrenetic applause that he was often unable to continue. Another speaker quoted from the 'Protocols of the Elders of Zion' and accused the Jews of supporting 'World Bolshevism': 'if the Jewish rule is not broken the liberation of our fatherland is not possible'. He did not say what 'fatherland' he meant, but the reporter commented: 'perhaps he meant Austria'.[80]

The anti-semitic tendencies were strongly reinforced by the collapse of the Phönix Insurance Company in 1936 on account of faulty speculations. As there were Jews among the managers and as a leading official of the ministry of the interior, whose task was the supervision of the company, committed suicide an assiduous propaganda could magnify the affair into a corruption scandal: a convenient stick to beat the government and to accuse it of shady dealings with the Jews. According to several local reports, the affair caused much bad blood and severe depression in circles otherwise loyal to the government and severely damaged the confidence in it. Many declared that, if such corruption had been characteristic of the former democratic state, they could not understand its recurrence under the authoritarian regime.[81] According to Papen, the Phönix affair considerably increased the anti-semitic tendencies among the Catholic workers and strengthened their apprehensions that the government was not motivated by 'social' considerations and that the workers' interests were neglected by the new corporations.[82] There was little that the government could do to counter this propaganda, helped as it was by the German radio and by German funds.

Yet, from the point of view of the government, the most serious obstacle was the continuing economic crisis, the severe unemployment which receded only very slowly, the depressed prices of the agrarian products and the difficulty of finding buyers for them. That this situation had strong political repercussions emerges even from the guarded language of the official reports. Thus the survey for March 1935 stated bluntly: 'Among the peace-loving population a certain indifference vis-à-vis the political developments and the loyalist movement is gaining ground, partly even embitterment and hopelessness. Thus the advance of the Fatherland Front is meeting with great difficulties. . . .'[83] In the same year a report on a ministerial visit to Carinthia mentioned the 'negative attitude of the population', caused by 'the very bad economic situation'; 'the distress among the peasants is particularly great'.[84] The Director of Security for Vorarlberg predicted: 'In view of the ever growing impoverishment of the peasants in the mountain districts, which is above all caused by the absence of tourists owing to the closing of the German frontier, it is to be feared that the number of National Socialists . . . will continue to increase further.'[85] In 1936 the Upper Austrian Security Director reported: 'The mood of the population in respect of the Austrian ideas seems to have become more indifferent. This is caused by the dissatisfaction of the peasants with insufficient sales and low prices and of the workers with continuing unemployment. . . .'[86] And at the end of the year the official survey for November 1936 repeated: 'On account of the prevailing distress a certain fatigue is noticeable among the local leaders of the Fatherland Front. . . .'[87]

Many local reports stress the results of the economic depression, the misery which it brought to wide circles of the population. From Edelschrott in Styria the police reported in 1934 that because of their economic difficulties the local peasants were opposed to all political parties and the majority did not believe that there would be any improvement; therefore it was impossible to form a local group of the Fatherland Front.[88] From Kufstein the Bezirkshauptmann reported in November 1935 that the number of unemployed had increased compared with the previous year. In one small place near Kufstein it was established that of 3,500 inhabitants nearly half were in need of support by the Winter Help scheme; but after discussions with the local priest and the police it was possible to eliminate about a hundred from the list and to reduce it to about 1,600 names! [89] Early in 1936 the Bezirkshauptmann of Imst in Tyrol expressed his apprehension that the cuts in the federal budget would have a negative influence on the employment situation and enable the local National Socialists to create dissatisfaction among the workers by pointing to the alleged economic boom in the Third Reich; in his district the number of unemployed was still the same as in 1934.[90] At the beginning of 1937 the Bezirkshauptmann of Graz reported that the local enterprises did not have sufficient orders, hence had to dismiss workers or introduce shorter working hours. He attributed the lack of orders to the inability of 'wide circles of the population' to buy things and to the severe unemployment which had slightly grown. In one village a quarter of the total population had to receive public support; the Winter Help alleviated the worst distress but did not bring effective help to the victims of the crisis.[91] In November the same Bezirkshauptmann repeated that unemployment had increased further and was particularly severe in two communes near Graz where almost 50 per cent of the population were unemployed.[92]

There is no doubt that the prevailing anti-Semitism and economic misery among large sections of the population provided the National Socialists with their most effective weapons against the Austrian regime. In both cases, they were able to point to the effective measures taken by the Hitler government to combat these 'dangers' and to contrast the conditions in Austria unfavourably with those in Germany. In the circumstances, the Austrian government found itself in a position that was difficult to defend, while German propaganda found it easy to establish a link between the two issues. As Papen informed Hitler in

1936, 'in the last few months the leading personalities of both organizations [the official trade unions and the Freiheitsbund, both parts of the Fatherland Front] have become convinced that the social question cannot be solved without solving the Jewish problem. . .'[93]

NOTES

1. Report by Landesleitung Vorarlberg of the Fatherland Front, based on the monthly reports for November and December 1934, s.d.: Vorarlberger Landesarchiv, Bezirkshauptmannschaft Bregenz, Nr. 169, 1935.

2. Sicherheitsdirektor for Vorarlberg to Bundeskanzleramt, Bregenz, 2 February 1934: Verwaltungsarchiv Wien, Bundeskanzleramt, 22/gen., box 4883. The words in brackets refer to the well known National Socialist slogan.

3. Two bundles 'Vaterländische Front 1934-38' in Oberösterreich. Landesarchiv, Freistadt.

4. Report by Bezirkshauptmann of Eferding, 28 October 1935: ibid., Politische Akten, Nr. 10.

5. Landesleitung of Fatherland Front to Bezirksleitung Freistadt, 11 May 1936: ibid., Politische Akten, Freistadt, Vaterländ. Front.

6. Reports by Bezirksgendarmeriekommando Linz, 2 July, 29 November 1935: ibid., Politische Akten, Nr. 26.

7. Burgenländ. Landesarchiv, Zeitgeschichtl. Sammlung, A/VIII-3, IV 1-2.

8. Ibid., A/VIII-3, XI 1-3, files for the local groups at Donnerskirchen, Loretto and St Georgen.

9. Generaldirektion für die öffentl. Sicherheit, Vienna, 30 November 1936: Haus-, Hof- u. Staatsarchiv, Nachlass Hornbostel, Fasz. 250.

10. Report by Gendarmeriepostenkommando Bruck, 30 December 1936: Steiermärk. Landesarchiv, Bezirkshauptmannschaft Bruck 1936, Gruppe Vrst.

11. Report by Bezirkshauptmann of Bruck, 30 November 1937: ibid., 1937, Gruppe Vrst. 1-2.

12. Report by Gendarmeriepostenkommando Breitenau, 27 October 1937: ibid.

13. Report by Bundespolizeidirektion Innsbruck, s.d.: Verwaltungsarchiv Wien, Bundeskanzleramt, 22/gen., box 4969.

14. Report by Bezirkshauptmann of Innsbruck, 1 May 1937: Tiroler Landesarchiv, Präsidialakten 1937, 29 prs. XII 57.

15. Reports of Bezirkshauptmann of Reutte, 6 April and 6 July 1937: ibid.

16. Bärnthaler, *Vaterländische Front*, 66, 109.

17. Ibid., 66, 78.

18. Thus Steidle to Starhemberg, Trieste, 5 December 1934: Herrschaftsarchiv Helfenberg, box 102 a.

19. Sibilia's report of 5 December 1935 quoted in Botschaft Wien, Geheimakten 1935-38, 4939 part 1, E272758-60: Papen's private papers.

20. MS. by Vinzenz Schumy, p. 161: Institut für Zeitgeschichte, Vienna.

21. Papen to Hitler, Vienna, 10 January 1936: Botschaft Wien, Geheimakten 1935-38, 4939 part 1, E272200.

22. Papen to Hitler, Vienna, 13 March 1936: *Documents on German Foreign Policy,* Series C, V (Washington, 1966) no. 90, 125.

23. Papen to Hitler, 21 April 1936: Botschaft Wien, Geheimakten 1935-38, 4939 part 1, E272293.

24. Sicherheitsdirektor for Upper Austria to Bundeskanzleramt, Linz, 15 April 1936: Verwaltungsarchiv Wien, Bundeskanzleramt, 22/gen., box 4962.

25. Papen to Hitler, 29 April 1936: Bundesarchiv Koblenz, Reichskanzlei, R 43 II/1473.

26. Wandruszka, in H. Benedikt (ed.), *Geschichte der Republik Österreich,* 368. For the Freiheitsbund, see above, p. 244.

27. Bärnthaler, op. cit., 111, 113. Cp. Kurt Schuschnigg, *Im Kampf gegen Hitler* (Vienna-Munich-Zürich, 1969) 176-77, for a different version.

28. *The Times,* 18 May; *Thurgauer Zeitung,* 18 May 1936.

29. Reports by Generaldirektion für die öffentl. Sicherheit, 17 and 20 May 1936: Verwaltungsarchiv Wien, Bundeskanzleramt, 22/gen., box 4942.

30. Thus a confidential German report: Auswärt. Amt, Österreich 1A, Polit. Lageberichte der Geheimen Staatspolizei u. SA, Bd. 1, 2971H., D578760.

31. Report by Bundespolizeidirektion Innsbruck, s.d.: Verwaltungsarchiv Wien, Bundeskanzleramt, 22/gen., box 4969 (ca. Oct. 1936).

32. Report by Bundespolizeidirektion Innsbruck, s.d., ibid.; *Bohemia,* Prague, 6 and 8 October 1936.

33. Thus Lahr in an undated letter to a National Socialist office: Berlin Document Center.

34. *Prager Abendzeitung,* 10 October 1936; report by Lieutenant-General Muff, Vienna, 12 October 1936: Botschaft Wien, Geheimakten 1935-38, 4938 part 10, E271619-20.

35. Papen to Hitler, Vienna, 12 October 1936: ibid., 4939 part 1, E272467; undated report about the meeting: Bundesarchiv Koblenz, Nachlass Seyss-Inquart, Sondermappe II, Nr. 7.

36. Thus Papen to Hitler, Vienna, 12 October 1936, loc. cit.

37. Gehl, *Austria, Germany and the Anschluss,* 143-44.

38. Thus a circular of the Verband Alt-Heimatschutz in Lower Austria, 21 September 1937: Verwaltungsarchiv Wien, Bundeskanzleramt, 22/gen., box 4975; Wandruszka, op. cit., 368.

39. Leaflets in Burgenländ. Landesarchiv, Zeitgeschichtl. Sammlung, A/VIII-14, III-3; Steiermärk. Landesarchiv, Bezirkshauptmannschaft Voitsberg, 1936, Gruppe 14 Vo-Z.

40. Reports of 31 August, 30 September, 30 November 1937: ibid., Bezirkshauptmannschaft Graz, 1936, Gruppe 14; Bezirkshauptmannschaft Bruck, 1937, Gruppe Vrst. 1-2.

41. Report by Bezirkshauptmann of Imst, 5 May 1937: Tiroler Landesarchiv, Präsidialakten 1937, 29 prs. XII 57.

42. The Upper Austrian leader of the Front Militia to Dr Felix Reitter, Linz,

12 August 1936: Oberösterreich. Landesarchiv, Politische Akten, Nr. 58 (Schutzkorps).

43. 'Lagebericht über den Monat Mai 1937', Vienna, 25 June 1937: Haus-, Hof- u. Staatsarchiv, Nachlass Hornbostel, fasz. 252.

44. That, in any case, was the opinion of the German military attaché who had close connections to leading Austrian officers: report by Lt.-Gen. Muff, Vienna, 21 October 1936: Botschaft Wien, Geheimakten 1935-38, 4938 part 10, E271629.

45. Report of 5 December 1935, quoted in Botschaft Wien, Geheimakten 1935-38, 4939 part 1, E272759. There is no reason to doubt its veracity.

46. Report of 10 December 1936: Auswärt. Amt, Österreich 1A, Akten betr. Politische Lageberichte, Bd. 2, 2971H, D579043.

47. Dr W. Förster, mayor of Bautzen, to the German Foreign Minister, July 1935: Auswärt. Amt, Akten betr. Nationalsozialismus, Österreich Bd. 3, 6111 H, E453187.

48. Report of 16 April 1937: Haus-, Hof- u. Staatsarchiv, Liasse Österreich 2/21, fasz. 308.

49. Reports by Generaldirektion für die öffentl. Sicherheit, July 1934, and Gendarmeriepostenkommando Grünau, 11 September 1934: Oberösterreich. Landesarchiv, Politische Akten, Nr. 6 and Nr. 11.

50. Reports of 30 December 1936 and 27 January 1937: Verwaltungsarchiv Wien, Bundeskanzleramt, 22/gen., box 4975 and 4913.

51. Police Directorate Vienna to Bundeskanzleramt, 27 July 1937: Haus-, Hof- u. Staatsarchiv, Liasse Österreich 2/21, fasz. 308.

52. Quoted by Bracher, *Die deutsche Diktatur,* 337-38. Even the use of the word völkisch implied an adaptation to National Socialist usage.

53. The German envoy Rieth to Auswärt. Amt, Vienna, 18 April 1934: Botschaft Wien, Habsburger Frage, K 1066, K274803.

54. Schuschnigg, op. cit., 181-82.

55. German Consul at Linz to German embassy in Vienna, 30 November 1937: ibid., K275157; report of 28 November 1937: Verwaltungsarchiv Wien, Bundeskanzleramt, 22/gen., box 4984.

56. Report of 11 October 1933: Auswärt Amt, Akten betr. Nationalsozialismus, Österreich, Bd. 1, 6111H, E452563.

57. Papen to Hitler, 17 June 1936: Botschaft Wien, Geheimakten 1935-38, 4939 part 1, E272376.

58. Police report, Innsbruck, 13 December 1934: Verwaltungsarchiv Wien, Bundeskanzleramt, 22/gen., box 4901.

59. Report of 24 November 1935: ibid., box 4907.

60. 'Lagebericht 2. Hälfte April 1934': ibid., box 4884.

61. Reports of 25 June and 27 July 1936: ibid., box 4913.

62. Police reports of 21 November and 15 December 1936: ibid., boxes 4945, 4987.

63. Police report of 22 February 1937: ibid., box 4987.

64. Report by Bundespolizeidirektion Vienna, 26 January 1937: ibid.

65. Report by Generaldirektion für die öffentl. Sicherheit, 4 April 1937: ibid., box 4984.

66. Freiherr v. Stein to Auswärt. Amt, Vienna, 14 October 1937: Botschaft Wien, Habsburger Frage, K 1066, K275116-17.

67. Sicherheitsdirektor for Tyrol to Bundeskanzleramt, Innsbruck, 1 July 1936: Verwaltungsarchiv Wien, Bundeskanzleramt, 22/gen., box 4945.

68. Report by Generaldirektion für die öffentl. Sicherheit, 12 January 1938: ibid., box 5011; the detailed figures of attendance at each meeting outside Vienna: ibid., box 5013 (the additions are mine). A report by Lt.-Gen. Muff of 14 January: Botschaft Wien, Geheimakten 1935-38, 4938 part 10, E271730, and Botschaft Wien, Habsburgerfrage, K 1066, K275188.

69. See above, p. 281.

70. Police report, Steyr, 24 January 1938: Verwaltungsarchiv Wien, Bundeskanzleramt, 22/gen., box 5013.

71. The mayor of Bautzen to the German foreign minister in July 1935: Auswärt. Amt, Akten betr. Nationalsozialismus, Österreich, Bd. 3, 6111 H, E453186.

72. Union of Austrian Jews to minister of the interior, Vienna, 19 December 1935: Verwaltungsarchiv Wien, Bundeskanzleramt, 22/gen., box 4957, also quoting anti-semitic remarks from a pamphlet published by the 'Reichsbund der katholischen deutschen Jugend Österreichs'.

73. *Tiroler Bauernzeitung,* 7 May and 3 September 1936: copies ibid., box 4939.

74. Report by Generaldirektion für die öffentl. Sicherheit, 30 November 1936: Haus-, Hof- u. Staatsarchiv, Nachlass Hornbostel, fasz. 250.

75. Report by the same, 2 March 1937: ibid., fasz. 252.

76. *Österreichischer Beobachter,* second November and first December issues 1937: copies in Burgenländ. Landesarchiv, Zeitgeschichtl. Sammlung, A/VIII-10, X.

77. *Österreichischer Beobachter,* Folge 10, March 1937: copy ibid., A/VIII-14, III-1.

78. Papen to Hitler, Vienna, 20 March 1936: *Documents on German Foreign Policy,* series C, V, no. 172, 227.

79. Police report, Linz, 19 February 1937: Oberösterreich. Landesarchiv, Politische Akten, Nr. 9: copy of 'Gau-Weisungsblatt Nr. 11'.

80. Reports about the meeting of 18 February and 14 April 1937: Verwaltungsarchiv Wien, Bundeskanzleramt, 22/gen., box 5016.

81. Reports, Vienna, 24 April, Linz, 29 April, Ried, 1 May, Freistadt, May 1936: ibid., box 4913; Oberösterreich. Landesarchiv, Politische Akten, Nr. 27, 33, Freistadt − Politischer Nachrichtendienst 1934-38. Cp. Starhemberg's comment in his 'Aufzeichnungen . . . verfasst während des zweiten Weltkrieges in London', 187, Institut für Zeitgeschichte, Vienna.

82. Papen to Hitler, Vienna, 12 January 1937: *Akten zur deutschen auswärtigen Politik,* series D, I (Baden-Baden, 1950) no. 196, 303.

83. 'Lagebericht über den Monat März 1935', 25 April 1935: Verwaltungsarchiv Wien, Bundeskanzleramt, 22/gen., box 4913.

84. 'Dienstreise des Staatssekretärs für Sicherheitswesen nach Steiermark und Kärnten . . .', s.d.: ibid., box 4932.

85. Report by Sicherheitsdirektor for Vorarlberg, Bregenz, 2 March 1934: ibid., box 4883.

86. Report by Sicherheitsdirektor for Upper Austria, Linz, 7 April 1936: ibid., box 4962. The report refers to the Innviertel close to the German frontier.

87. 'Lagebericht über den Monat November 1936', 30 December 1936: ibid., box 4913.

88. Report by Gendarmerie, 7 March 1934: Steiermärk. Landesarchiv, Bezirkshauptmannschaft Voitsberg, 1934, Gruppe 14, L-R.

89. Report of 2 November 1935: Tiroler Landesarchiv, Präsidialakten 1935, 62 prs. XII 57.

90. Report from Imst, 5 February 1936: ibid., Präsidialakten 1937, 434 XII 57.

91. Report from Graz, 1 February 1937: Steiermärk. Landesarchiv, Bezirkshauptmannschaft Graz 1936, Gruppe 14.

92. Report from Graz, 2 November 1937: ibid.

93. Papen to Hitler, Vienna, 20 March 1936: *Documents on German Foreign Policy*, series C, V, no. 172, 227: Botschaft Wien, Geheimakten 1935-38, 4939 part 1, E272279.

14

THE UNDERGROUND NATIONAL SOCIALIST PARTY

The defeat of the revolt of July 1934 caused deep depression among the National Socialists and sharpened the divisions within their ranks. A few days after the defeat Hitler, anxious to avoid any complications in foreign affairs, and especially any difficulties with Italy, ordered the Austrian Landesleitung, which was established in Munich and carried the responsibility for the uprising, to be dissolved. This applied, at least officially, also to the party organization in Austria and its subordinate organizations. A leader of the Austrian SS, Rodenbücher, a German citizen, was charged with the execution of this order.[1] Some weeks later Hess, Hitler's deputy, repeated that the German party was forbidden to maintain contacts with the Austrian National Socialists in any form, and that this also applied to the Austrian leaders who had found refuge in Germany. To eliminate any misunderstanding Hess added that the order was not a formality but had to be carried out; any infringement would be severely punished.[2] The German minister who had played a somewhat doubtful role in Vienna on the day of the coup was recalled. In his place Franz von Papen was sent as Hitler's special ambassador to calm the Austrian fears by his diplomatic skill and his conservative Catholicism. In reality he did his best to rally pro-German national sentiments in Austria and to fish in troubled waters. To the

German nationalists in Austria Papen became the symbol of the growing strength of the Third Reich; his voluminous reports to Hitler show
that he fully understood the task with which he was entrusted.

For the moment, however, the Austrian National Socialists were
thrown back on their own resources. Hitherto all their activities had
been directed and financed from Munich. At the beginning of
September 1934 the German military attaché reported from Vienna:

> It is now noticeable in a most disagreeable manner that no coordinating
> leadership was established within Austria as a result of the illegality of the
> party and of an exaggerated Leadership Principle, a leadership able to control
> the whole organization of the party and its military formations.... Now
> circles willing to negotiate with the government are hostile to others opposed
> to any compromise; a moderate faction stands against a radical one. Followers
> are rallying around different leaders. The conflict between the political organi-
> zation of the party, the SA and the SS erupts openly....[3]

A report by the Director of Security for Upper Austria spoke of two
groupings among the National Socialists: one adhered to the view that
the seizure of power was only possible through a Putsch or uprising, the
other favoured an 'evolutionary' way: the party members should join
the Fatherland Front and bring about the disintegration of the loyalist
organizations and para-military formations from within 'in a peaceful
fashion'.[4] Some National Socialists openly expressed their abhorrence
not only of the Dollfuss murder, but also of the terrorist and sabotage
actions ordered by the Austrian leaders from Munich, especially by
Habicht.[5] Hitler was able to blame Habicht for the Austrian debacle
and to decline all responsibility.[6]

One of the critics of the Munich leaders who was willing to negotiate
with the Schuschnigg government was – as might have been exptected
– Dr Walter Riehl. In an interview with a foreign journalist in October
he expressed his conviction that Schuschnigg too wanted a reconciliation for reasons of foreign policy and because he was supported 'only
be a weak third of the population'; the Austrian Völkische would
concur if they were granted freedom of political movement, an
amnesty, etc. Schuschnigg received Riehl and Anton Reinthaller who
had opposed Habicht's policy in the past, and had therefore been
expelled by him from the party together with Riehl.[7] In a circular to
his political friends Riehl emphasized that he would do his utmost to
bring about the much desired internal peace on the basis of his own
programme. He desired the 'national elements' to join the Fatherland
Front en masse if they were given influential posts in it as well as in the

public administration. His further conditions were: friendly relations with Germany, introduction of general conscription and unification of all para-military formations in a militia which National Socialists too could join, and the foundation of 'Aryan' groups of the Fatherland Front in Vienna because the Völkische must decline to sit together with Jews.[8] It may have been this last condition, or it may have been doubts about the following of Riehl and Reinthaller which caused the failure of the negotiations, for as we have seen the demands about conscription and the militia were fully acceptable to Schuschnigg.

By the beginning of 1935, in any case, the fronts hardened. The new leadership of the Austrian National Socialists in Vienna was opposed to a compromise on the lines suggested by Riehl and drew a sharp line between him and the loyal adherents of Hitler.[9] Yet, according to a 'reliable' report received by the German embassy in Vienna, there were still two groups, one in favour of reconciliation and the other of an aggressive policy, and both had their supporters in the German government: the former Göring and Hess, the latter Goebbels.[10] From these two reports it seems certain that meanwhile the German authorities had resumed their interference in Austrian affairs and were once more issuing directives to the Austrian National Socialists. In Vienna, a new 'leader' emerged in the person of Dr Hermann Neubacher, the director general of an engineering firm and a school friend of Reinthaller. When Neubacher was interrogated by the police in February 1935 he declared that he was opposed to the policy of Habicht and the Austrian émigrés and in favour of a reconciliation; he hoped that the Fatherland Front would be transformed and in its new form would allow the National Socialists to exercise the influence which was their due.[11] According to the General Directorate of Public Security, the systematic reorganization of the underground party started in September 1934 and was more or less complete by November; but the relations between the party, the SA and SS were 'not good' and an internal party document considered those between the SA and SS 'very bad'.[12] This was partly confirmed by an intercepted order of the party in Styria of November 1935 which admitted friction on two grounds: the co-ordination of party and SA and the distribution of the available funds. To eliminate the existing friction the Gauleitung decreed that, because of the special conditions prevailing in Austria, the Austrian Landesleiter of the party was entitled to issue orders and instructions to the SA and that the Austrian SA was subordinate to him.[13]

The most sober picture of internal rivalries among the party leaders was drawn, rather surprisingly, by the German military attaché in Vienna who obviously exercised functions very different from his official one. According to him, Dr Neubacher from the outset experienced great difficulties as Landesleiter because many lower leaders distrusted and rejected him as a newcomer to the party. But when the former Gauleiter of Lower Austria, Leopold, was released by the authorities and demanded the post of Landesleiter for himself as the most senior Gauleiter Neubacher's position became untenable. The other Gauleiter then arranged a compromise by which Leopold became the Landesleiter and Neubacher his assistant. But soon they came to realize that Leopold did not possess the necessary political qualifications and 'that his political sergeant methods constituted a danger in the long run'. They called a conference to decide the issue, but before it could take place both Leopold and Neubacher were arrested. Immediately afterwards a 'will' allegedly written by Leopold appeared in which he nominated the former officer and deputy Franz Schattenfroh as his successor and, in case the latter was unable to act, appointed a directory. But several Gauleiter of the Alpine lands doubted that this will was genuine and disputed Leopold's right to regulate the succession on his own authority. They therefore decided at a meeting at which all Gaue except Vienna and Lower Austria were represented to shelve the issue of the Landesleiter until Leopold's release; meanwhile the party was to be led by a Gauleiter collective under the chairmanship of the Carinthian one. Thus the majority of the Gauleiter were in opposition to the directory appointed by Leopold, and the latter was itself rent by disagreement. Then Schattenfroh was released. He insisted that he was the rightful Landesleiter owing to his nomination by Leopold and 'saw in the Gauleiter collective just a group of rebels against the hallowed party discipline'. He tried to assert his absolute authority against these 'dissidents' from the Leadership Principle and treated them accordingly. All this caused a severe crisis in party affairs which the writer compared with the election of a duke by the Germanic tribes or the appointment of a dictator by the Roman Senate.[14] It was a revival of earlier struggles among the various Gauleiter and showed that the party was as disunited as it had ever been.

In spite of all disunity the party was soon able to regain its former influence, although not entirely through its own efforts. In March 1936 the General Directorate of Public Security admitted that the movement received 'a strong impetus' from Hitler's occupation of the Rhineland and the subsequent plebiscite in Germany, successes which also impressed loyalist circles.[15] In April the same authority stated that National Socialist propaganda identified national ideas and national convictions with National Socialism, hence found it easy to win adherents by emphasizing the national component. Among the peasants, this propaganda met with little resistance, especially among those in the mountainous areas whose situation was very bad. The former Grossdeutsche had lost nearly all their followers to the National Socialist Party and were condemned to complete passivity. It would be entirely wrong to assume, the report continued, that the party and its leaders would ever accept a compromise solution, for their ideology was dogmatically fixed and unchangeable, and no deviation from its principles was possible. Furthermore, 'the embitterment and the thirst for vengeance as well as the belief in the National Socialist idea is too strong to allow any satisfactory outcome' — satisfactory in the sense of a compromise with the Austrian authorities. According to this report, the leaders of the underground party largely came from the unemployed intelligentsia, especially the students who at the end of their studies saw no possibility of finding any job. Apart from them, among the most active supporters of the party were the many unemployed white-collar workers and the numerous small shopkeepers and craftsmen whose enterprises had collapsed; many former officers hoped to regain their positions after a National Socialist victory; numerous small officials strongly sympathized with National Socialism for 'national' reasons and because they hoped to obtain some party post in one of the many affiliated organizations. The last two groups were strongly attracted by National Socialist militarism, while craftsmen, shopkeepers and other social groups were particularly prone to fall for anti-semitic propaganda.[16]

These findings were to some extent confirmed by local reports. Thus the Bezirkshauptmann of Lienz in Tyrol stated early in 1936 that circles of the intelligentsia still adhered 'steadfastly' to National Socialism, but that this was less true of the peasantry. One village was still strongly National Socialist because there the most prosperous farmers called the tune who — before the rise of National Socialism — had been grossdeutsch in their views.[17] From Liezen in Styria the Bezirkshauptmann wrote that many officials were strongly critical of the government, especially its measures of economy; the majority of the middle-class population had always been 'national' in their views and thus sympathized with the National Socialists until the July revolt; the middle class as well as the peasantry desired above all an understanding with Germany which would improve the economic situation; the working class on the other hand was never much influenced by the NSDAP and was now almost entirely opposed to it.[18]

In Styria sympathies with National Socialism and the Third Reich continued to be very strong. In June 1936 the General Directorate of Public Security even spoke of 'the open and hidden terror of the National Socialists' which was particularly strong in Styria; the loyalist circles were intimidated by it and became 'despondent'.[19] In 1935-36 many agricultural labourers and peasant sons went to Germany in search of work. When they returned they were well clad, had saved some money and were full of enthusiasm for Germany where things were 'considerably better than they were in Austria'.[20] In Carinthia, the districts which had played a leading part in the July rising continued in their negative attitude towards the government; an official visitor noted that there the majority were hostile and sullen.[21] From the district of Völkermarkt the Bezirkshauptmann reported in 1935 that National Socialist propaganda, under the influence of Klagenfurt intellectuals, was especially directed against Italy; they called for a boycott of Italian fruit and vegetables, and they revived memories of Italian enmity in the world war and of the seizure of the South Tyrol 'at the most unnecessary occasions', so as to attack the pro-Italian policy of the Austrian government; across the Yugoslav border National Socialist circles in Slovenia engaged in exactly the same campaign against Italy; the economic and agrarian policies of the Third Reich were pictured in the most glowing colours, and economic co-operation with Germany as the solution of all economic difficulties for the frontier areas.[22] Virulent anti-Italian propaganda by word of mouth and violent attacks on the government's pro-Italian policy were also reported from other parts of Austria.[23]

In the Tyrol National Socialist sympathies were particularly strong in the many sports clubs 'in which extreme nationalist tendencies have been carefully cultivated for decades'. When a German swimmer gave the Hitler salute at a swimming display in Innsbruck in 1935 the majority of the spectators applauded enthusiastically.[24] In Vorarlberg the leader of the underground organization was the manager of a hotel at Dornbirn; the party members met regularly every other week in certain inns at Dornbirn and were briefed on the political situation. They paid the small sum of 50 *groschen* a month, and the cell leaders paid the money over to the treasurer. Large contributions were given by well situated National Socialists and those in need of support received help from this fund. The leading manufacturers of Dornbirn, well known for their National Socialist sympathies, were regular guests in the same hotel where the party's leader worked as a manager, and thus contacts could be easily maintained and propaganda material and money be distributed from there. In Bregenz a firm making furs served as the party headquarters.[25] In the small Burgenland in the east the underground party claimed in 1936 that they had not only preserved their strength of 1933, but founded many new local groups and recruited 'thousands' of new members, as they proudly informed the Director of Security.[26] But no figures are available for the strength of the party during these years, and a recruitment on this scale seems very unlikely.

In Upper Austria, the Director of Security, Peter Count Revertera, maintained friendly relations with prominent members of the 'national opposition'. In a conversation with Papen in August 1935 he emphasized his efforts to secure for the opposition 'a possibility to exist', but it must first separate visibly from the German party.[27] In November Revertera had a discussion with the 'moderate' National Socialist Reinthaller and told him that his efforts at bringing about a reconciliation would be continued; there would be a partial amnesty for National Socialists at Christmas and he would try to make it as comprehensive as possible.[28] Two weeks later he received Franz Langoth, who had once been a prominent Grossdeutscher and then moved ever closer to the National Socialists. To this visitor Revertera expressed his regret that he had to carry out so many arrests; this was not only disagreeable but also disturbed his other plans; the illegal National Socialist leaflets were incredibly stupid and achieved no purpose.[29] Earlier in 1935 Revertera gained a momentary success in that a number of local National Socialist leaders surrendered voluntarily to the police and signed an undertaking not to engage in any underground activities in future. But, as he admitted ruefully to Langoth, after their release they did not keep their promise, hence they would have to be rearrested.[29] Local police reports from Upper Austria estimated that the National Socialists and their sympathizers counted about 14-15 percent of the population.[30] But this may have been an underestimate.

In spite of their claims to the contrary, it does not seem that the National Socialist underground organization made much progress in 1935-36; it was too much hampered by internal conflicts and by the many arrests of activists. Nor did the government succeed in broadening its narrow base. But this stalemate was dramatically altered in favour of

the National Socialists by the modus vivendi concluded, thanks to
Papen's efforts, between the Austrian and German governments on 11
July 1936. The agreement as such dealt with diplomatic relations. It
recognized the political independence of Austria and resulted in a
cautious rapprochement of the two countries. German tourists were
again allowed into Austria, a circumstance of considerable economic
importance. But the agreement also contained a secret 'clause ix' in
which the Austrian chancellor promised 'a far reaching political
amnesty' for all arrested National Socialists including the émigrés. Even
more important, he undertook to let 'representatives of the so-called
"national opposition in Austria" partake in political responsibility';
they would have the task of promoting 'the internal pacification of the
national opposition and its participation in Austrian politics'; the representatives were to be selected by the Austrian chancellor from men
enjoying his confidence.[31] Thus 'the national opposition' was granted
quasi-official status, and its leaders were provided with a lever as they
or the German government could always insist that the terms of the
secret clause were not carried out. It was entirely wrong if the Fatherland Front claimed that Austria had made no concessions, that the
agreement fully recognized the Austrian point of view with regard to
independence, that Hitler had given up a point of his programme, and
that the 'extreme Nationalist Socialists suffered a defeat'.[32] It was
equally an illusion to believe that the agreement 'recognized Austria's
existence as an independent German state and secured its frontiers'.[33]

Bewilderment, however, reigned among the underground National
Socialists, many of whom felt that the German government had made
too many concessions. The official communication of the Landesleitung of the Austrian NSDAP spoke of 'depression, even discouragement' in the party ranks and went out of its way to assure the party
faithful that Hitler 'knows what it necessary and will always do the
right thing. ... We Austrian National Socialists feel it in our blood
[*sic*]: Adolf Hitler will not desert us, he will never forget us. Whoever
doubts this does not belong to us....' The announcement also confirmed that the party's aim, 'the conquest of power in this state',
remained unchanged; the members were to carry out the orders of the
leaders and to maintain 'iron discipline in any situation'.[34] The 'depression' caused by this 'worthless peace' was also expressed by a party
activist in Vienna: if the opportunists and fellow-travellers who had
never made any sacrifice were enthusiastic about the agreement, one
could only smile about their shortsightedness; in his opinion, the

agreement constituted 'a clear victory of the obstinate Schuschnigg who has made no concession and as before will brutally suppress with his black friends every national aspiration. . . What remains is a certain embitterment in the heart and a bad taste on the tongue, for . . . on the instructions from the Reich we have conducted a guerrilla war that has demanded many sacrifices and has deprived many of everything. With what success? . . .'[35]

Similar criticisms were at first voiced by the functionaries of various German organizations in Vienna, especially directed against Papen, the architect of the agreement. Leopold, the Landesleiter of the Austrian National Socialists, called on him and reproached him bitterly. But after a discussion between Papen and three of the German officials their attitude changed completely. They now pictured the agreement 'as the greatest stroke of Hitler's genius' and hinted that there were clauses 'which in the end would bring about a complete capitulation of the Austrian government', that in truth it was the latter which had fallen into a trap. The German National Socialist Rittgen accompanied by an Austrian comrade then toured the provinces to establish the reaction of the party members and to allay any dissatisfaction. With a wink the German functionaries assured any doubter that nothing had changed, not even in their relations with the Austrian National Socialists.[36] At Gmunden in Upper Austria the 'moderate' National Socialists declared their satisfaction with the agreement, but others, especially the youngsters, were indignant, and some even railed against Hitler.[37] A similar division was observed at Bruck in Styria, 'but the large majority of the National Socialists is full of confidence and sees in the agreement the beginning of a political solution favourable to National Socialism. . .'.[38] At the end of July the National Socialists used the opportunity of an Olympic relay race through Vienna to organize noisy mass demonstrations.[39]

If the National Socialists were divided in their attitude to the agreement of 11 July 1936, the same applied to the supporters of the regime and the Fatherland Front. In the opinion of the General Directorate of Public Security it weakened the will to resist the advance of National Socialism. It also made people more receptive to National Socialist propaganda which pictured Bolshevism as the only danger and Hitler as its only real enemy. Thus even loyalist circles began to favour an alliance of the Fatherland Front and the National Socialists against the communist danger, a view even shared by members of the clergy.[40] From Gmunden in Upper Austria the Bezirkshauptmann reported strong indignation among the loyalists against the agreement, and partly even despondency.[41] In another small place of Upper Austria, however, the police found that the majority including the Heimwehr members, greatly welcomed the agreement, while the peasants hoped that it would bring more favourable sales and better prices; most enthusiastic were the National Socialists who saw in it the first step towards their final seizure of power.[42] At Innsbruck, loyalist circles were apprehensive whether the government would in future be able to keep the National Socialists down and whether the whole fight against them had not been in vain.[43] It seems clear from these scattered reports that the will to oppose National Socialism which had never been very strong was further weakened in consequence of the agreement, while it considerably increased the self-confidence of the National Socialists and their determination to wring further concessions from the government.

Equally determined to use the lever provided by the secret clause was Hitler's special envoy in Vienna, von Papen. In November 1936 he proudly reported to Berlin that, 'under the pressure of my continuous representations concerning an internal transformation of the government in the sense of 11 July', certain changes had been effected in the government. The representatives of the Heimwehr were removed (the Heimwehren themselves had been dissolved in the previous month) and were replaced by three men who were not National Socialists but were considered 'national' in their convictions. As Papen put it: 'Even if the new cabinet does not contain any National Socialists, the move to a decidedly national policy indicates a gratifying progress and will accelerate the consolidation of the policy of 11 July.'[44] Even before, the Austrian government had been far from united; from now on the partisans of a pro-German course among the ministers were always ready to plead for further concessions to the 'national opposition'. They were the real Trojan horse within the gates.

Another considerable change resulted from the political amnesty which the government carried out according to the terms of the agreement of 11 July. During the preceding period so many of the leading functionaries of the party, the SA and SS had been arrested that the organization was led by 'political corporals', as the party itself had to admit. After July the more experienced officials, among them the Landesleiter Leopold, most of the Gauleiter and higher leaders of the SA and SS, were released and resumed their functions in the illegal party apparatus which was reorganized and strengthened. These men felt like martyrs and were determined not to make any concession to the hated regime. Their efforts were supported by the German National Socialist Party. Their aim was not internal 'pacification', but the total defeat of the Schuschnigg government and the seizure of power by the NSDAP.[45]

Leopold immediately established contact with Papen and, at first rather critical of the agreement, enquired how Papen envisaged the future of the party in Austria. After a visit to Germany he also approached Schuschnigg to whom he presented himself as the leader of the 'national opposition': as Schuschnigg wanted to negotiate with the opposition Leopold declared his readiness to do so. But he assured his own followers that no part of the party programme would be sacrificed and that only the tactics would become more elastic, so as 'to reply in kind to the Jesuitic methods of fighting'.[46] At first Leopold confirmed some of the younger men who had led the party in his absence in their offices and only reserved to himself the last decision in important questions. But in September 1936 he removed several from their posts and once more appointed Schattenfroh as his deputy. But the latter's choice aroused strong opposition in the party, above all because he was married to a Jewess — 'an obvious infraction of the principles of the party programme'. According to the notes of a German diplomat the dissatisfaction therefore affected not only the younger party leaders but 'also the broad mass of the movement'[47]

During the remaining months of 1936 the National Socialists were lying rather low. The acts of sabotage were not resumed, and even the visible propaganda subsided. According to information reaching the Austrian police this was done on instructions from the German party according to which contact was to be maintained with the party members and work to proceed quietly. These tactics were attributed to the difficulties of German foreign policy and the hope of winning over the population to National Socialist ideas by peaceful methods, tactics which would achieve success in the long run. Allegedly Leopold, on direct instructions from Berlin, attempted to induce the party to adopt more pacific methods, but this met with resistance by activist students and workers who were in favour of more radical actions.[48] In Upper Austria, the Gauleitung went so far as to forbid any propaganda for the Anschluss and the slogan 'One nation, one Reich', for 'Adolf Hitler has recognized by a treaty the independence of Austria and affirmed it. He will know why.'[49] From Innsbruck the police reported early in 1937 that the local SA hardly showed any sign of activity; skiing excursions were taking the place of roll-calls and drill; the mood among the men was depressed, and they were convinced that all their doings were valueless. Few of them put in an appearance when called out, but the internal reports always claimed that there was a complete turnout.[50] From Freistadt in Upper Austria it was stated that there was less National Socialist propaganda among the peasants who were more satisfied with the higher prices for cattle and corn.[51] In December 1936 a German visitor wrote of the 'catastrophic situation of the National Socialists in Carinthia' who — like those in Austria in general. — were hard hit by unemployment and government persecution. 'In the Reich the masses were won over to the idea of National Socialism, but in Austria only the intellectuals, in Carinthia the intellectuals and the peasants.' It was essential to win over the workers of Vienna and the larger towns and this could be done 'to a certain extent in spite of the prohibition of the party', otherwise Bolshevism would triumph with the help of the Czechs.[52]

In the early months of 1937, however, the National Socialist tactics became more aggressive, perhaps because Hitler felt now certain of Mussolini's support. When Schuschnigg paid a state visit to Venice in April 1937 Mussolini, while still assuring him of his loyalty to Austria, stressed that Austria must meet the German demands according to the agreement of July 1936.[53] As the underground National Socialist paper put it:

> A second illusion disappeared at Venice: the view that the 11th July is purely a matter of foreign policy. On the contrary, the largest part of the diplomatic talks in the Palazzo Corner was taken up by a discussion of Austrian home affairs. . . . The Duce demanded in the name of Italy and the German Reich: the fulfilment of article ixb of the declaration of 11 July 1936 . . . which provides for the participation of the so-called national opposition in political responsibility and the formulation of the political will. . . . Today Hitler and Mussolini are the guarantors of the equality of rights of the National Socialists in Austria.[54]

A few weeks before. when the German Foreign Minister von Neurath visited Vienna, the National Socialists organized monster demonstrations in his honour for which their followers were brought to Vienna from many places in Lower Austria. As these were ovations to honour the representative of a 'friendly state' the police could not interfere; but the Fatherland Front organized counter-demonstrations.[55]

From the beginning of 1937 negotiations between representatives of the government and of the 'national opposition' took place which aimed at legalizing the opposition under the guise of a German Social

League, but Schuschnigg in the end rejected the project. In early February, the National Socialist representatives were advised by von Papen and by General Glaise-Horstenau, a 'national' member of the Austrian cabinet to form a committee to discuss with the authorities the further progress of 'pacification', and this was then done with the approval of Leopold. It had seven members three of whom were active National Socialists; three others represented the government, and the seventh was the vice-chancellor of Vienna University, Professor Oswald Menghin, whose 'national' sympathies were well known. This so-called Committee of Seven henceforth led a legal existence and occupied an office in the Teinfaltstrasse. It also co-operated closely with Leopold and the underground National Socialist Party. The committee decided to adopt a cautious line and agreed to postpone the foundation of a legal political association rather than demand what the government would refuse to grant. Two of the members were received by Schuschnigg and assured him that they 'took notice' of the independence of Austria 'out of realistic considerations', as well as of the Constitution and the law about the Fatherland Front. The same assurance was given to the chancellor by Leopold. But internally he emphasized that there was a vital difference between 'take notice of' and 'recognize', which would have meant to 'consider as unchangeable': the whole did not amount to a conclusion of peace, 'but was only the first step that could lead to a discussion of a preliminary peace', provided that both sides loyally adhered to this line.[56]

In spite of all these clever formulae strong opposition developed inside the party, especially in Vienna itself. Many party officials considered the 'pacification course' too heavy a strain on the party and 'in the long run intolerable': how could their Landesleiter negotiate with a regime against which the party was fighting to the death, a regime which incarcerated hundreds and thousands of party members?[57] In March the Vienna Gauleiter and his officials formally renounced their obedience to Leopold whose policy they considered a 'betrayal of National Socialist principles', for in their opinion he had recognized the independence of Austria and the Fatherland Front. In Leopold's eyes this was open 'mutiny' and he replied by removing the Gauleiter and his subordinate officials from their posts, as well as all those lower down in the party hierarchy who supported the deposed Gauleiter.[58] As the new Gauleiter of Vienna Leopold appointed Dr Leopold Tavs, a member of the Committee of Seven, who thus could happily combine his 'legal' function with his leadership of the underground party — both from the same office in the Teinfaltstrasse. He succeeded in quelling the 'mutiny' inside the party within a few days.[59]

An even more severe crisis erupted for very similar reasons in Styria. Especially leaders of the SA sharply attacked Leopold's policy. The attacks also affected the organization of the Styrian party and caused, in National Socialist opinion, 'an almost complete paralysis and splintering of all the forces'. The year 1937 was 'marked by insubordination and mutiny, denunciations with subsequent arrests, complete failure of propaganda, internal conflicts and political aimlessness. . . .'[60] In Upper Austria, Reinthaller continued his efforts to persuade National Socialists to join the Fatherland Front, efforts which he claimed were approved by Leopold. But the National Socialist Gauleitung of Upper Austria opposed his activities and ordered the party members not to join the Front unless they were forced to do so for economic reasons. It also accused Reinthaller of continuously exceeding the instructions given by Leopold.[61]

Reinthaller co-operated with another 'moderate' National Socialist, Dr Arthur Seyss-Inquart, a well known Viennese lawyer who was appointed a member of the State Council by Schuschnigg with the special task 'of investigating how to bring about the cooperation of groups which hitherto have stood aside in the formulation of the political will with the Fatherland Front *[sic]* and of submitting suitable suggestions'.[62] In other words, Riehl's old scheme of inducing the 'national opposition' to join the Front was once more under discussion under this abstruse formula, but opposition to such a policy among the National Socialists proved as strong as ever.[63] In the eyes of the Austrian authorities, Seyss-Inquart was 'a hundred per cent loyal to the National Socialists. His aim is the same as that of the Austrian NSDAP, only his tactics are different. Dr Seyss is a bridge between Leopold and the chancellor. . . .'[64] Seyss-Inquart and another man 'with decidedly national views' were put in charge of the so-called *Volkspolitische Referat* of the Fatherland Front which was to promote the internal pacification between the Front and the 'national opposition'. One Front speaker went out of his way to assure his listeners that both men 'stood a hundred per cent on the basis of Austria and have made the programme of the Fatherland Front and of its leaders entirely their own'.[65] But this was an illusion – as was the expectation that by small concessions such as these a reconciliation with the National Socialists could be achieved.

Yet the activities of Seyss-Inquart and his collaborators resulted in renewed friction among the National Socialists. At a meeting in Mondsee in Upper Austria Leopold declared in the presence of a special envoy of Hitler that Seyss-Inquart's collaborators were rejected by the party and only had contacts 'with traitors, scoundrels and knaves'. According to another version, Leopold with these epithets directly aimed at Seyss's collaborators, especially Odilo Globotschnigg, Dr Mühlmann and Dr Rainer (all National Socialists). After the meeting Seyss-Inquart wrote to Hitler's representative Dr Keppler to establish which was the correct version 'because my further attitude must depend on that'.[66] According to the General Directorate of Public Security, the leaders of the underground party not only rejected these endeavours but actively opposed them. The Directorate further reported that there were severe conflicts between the Austrian Landesleitung and the provincial party organizations, that the resulting disorganization was particularly noticeable in Vienna, Salzburg and Tyrol where many members refused to pay their dues, and that the contributions to the illegal party sent from Berlin failed to arrive in July and August 1937.[67] In October the party announced that one of Seyss's collaborators, Odilo Globotschnigg, was expelled for anti-party activities.[68]

At the end of September 1937 Dr Keppler, Hitler's special envoy for Austrian affairs, described to Bormann his difficulties with Landesleiter Leopold. Bormann who knew of these difficulties recommended that Keppler should demand 'asbolute discipline' from Leopold and should threaten him with removal from his post if he did not obey orders (i.e. orders from Germany). Hitler, in conversations with Leopold, had emphasized that he attached little value to the party and its organizations and instructed Leopold to find a new platform for his work, in clubs, societies and if need be in the Fatherland Front and to agitate there 'for a real German policy'.[69] In another conversation with Bormann four weeks later Keppler described the battle within the Austrian party: one group favoured the evolutionary way, the other wanted to work illegally by revolutionary methods; in view of the danger of a split the second group had won the upper hand. Bormann, however, held that the party should adopt the evolutionary way: 'there is no other possibility because of Hitler's wishes'.[70] In his fight against Keppler and Seyss-Inquart Leopold went so far as to forbid all party members to have any political contact with either of them. Reinthaller was deprived of all his party functions because he declined to sign a declaration to that effect. In internal conversations Leopold remarked that 'a certain comrade Keppler' wanted to direct policy in Austria, but that he would not suffer the imposition of a Habicht no. 2 (who had once directed Austrian party affairs on behalf of Hitler).[71] It thus seems certain that in 1937 Hitler – clearly disgusted with Austrian party squabbles and the mediocre Austrian leaders – had no clear plan for Austria. But it is also clear that the Austrian National Socialists, harrassed by the police and deeply disunited, depended on German instructions and German contributions.

Resistance to Leopold's 'soft' policy was particularly strong among radical groups of the SA and the SS. They had their own chains of command and refused to accept orders from Leopold.[72] In Lower Austria the SS issued an order in 1936 that members were forbidden to discuss SS matters even with members of the party: 'We do not babble but we act. We do not talk much about the seizure of power but we prepare it!'[73] In the Burgenland, the party Gauleiter during an absence of three months entrusted the local SS leader with the leadership of the Gau. When he returned he found that the SS leader meanwhile had studiously tried to make the whole party dependent on the SS so that heated arguments ensued between the two men. Then the Gauleiter rescinded certain orders issued during his absence and entrusted the SS with new tasks. But the SS leader instructed his men that all such tasks were internal SS matters and that the party officials had no right to give any orders in such matters. He also remarked: 'If the Gauleiter thinks he can get rid of me like the others he is deceiving himself. . . .' The Gauleiter therefore insisted that the party leaders should be entitled to exercise supervision over the SA, the SS, the Hitler Youth and similar organizations, otherwise there would never be unity within the movement during the underground period, and the whole movement would remain hamstrung.[74] Leopold in his turn complained to Himmler that the Austrian SS leader, Dr Ernst Kaltenbrunner, accused him of saying that Hitler was surrounded by a camarilla which prevented him from obtaining a clear picture of affairs in Austria. Leopold demanded an investigation by the SS, 'because in these circumstances no one can demand that I should cooperate with the present SS leadership in Austria'.[75] But apparently no such investigation took place.

The National Socialists were particularly strong and self-confident in Carinthia and in Styria. The authorities were well aware of this situation; in 1937 they were informed from a reliable source that the movement was steadily growing in both areas and that certain districts must be considered 'lost'.[76] In September 1936 the police of Mariazell

in Styria reported that the local National Socialists were more opti-
mistic than ever and that a large part of the population remained 'in the
national camp': thus the situation had deteriorated.[77] In April 1937
the Bezirkshauptmann of Bruck noticed a greater confidence and expectation of victory among the National Socialists. This he attributed
to the 'pacification' policy of the government and the discussions of
Schuschnigg and Mussolini in Venice which, the National Socialists
hoped, would result in their joining the Fatherland Front and later the
government.[78] A meeting of the craftsmen and artisans at Voitsberg in
March 1937 resulted in many interruptions such as 'Down with the
Jews! ' and 'Chuck them out! ' and proved to the reporter the
extremist views held by many of the participants.[79]

In the Carinthian village of Bodensdorf Hitler's birthday was openly
celebrated in April 1937. A beginning was made the previous evening
by the ringing of the bells of the Protestant church. Then swastika fires
were lit, and National Socialist leaflets openly distributed. On the day
itself the servants went about in Sunday dress and were invited to
dinner by the wealthier farmers.[80] In Styria the SA was strong and well
organized in three brigades. The 5th brigade centered on Graz in 1937
consisted of eight *Standarten* with about 7,700 men; the 9th brigade
centered on Leoben, had nine Standarten and was considered a model
brigade from the point of view of military preparedness.[81] In Carinthia,
however, the SA was much weaker; the police estimated its total
strength at less than 3,000 men.[82] The total SA strength in the Tyrol
was thought to be only about 1,700 men.[83]

Not only the strength of the SA, but also that of the party varied
considerably from district to district. In Carinthia and Styria (both had
non-German minorities) 'national' feeling had always been strong, in
particular since the days of the fighting against the Yugoslavs in
1918-19. In both, too, the SA was considerably strengthened by its
combination with the Heimwehren in the early 1930s and showed its
mettle in the rising of July 1934. In the Tyrol, on the other hand, the
strong Catholicism of the people and Hitler's renunciation of the South
Tyrol seem to have been barriers which slowed down the progress of
the National Socialists. There the party as late as November 1938 had
only 4,104 members compared with 19,611 in Carinthia and 26,808 in
Styria. But Upper Austria had fewer members still, namely 2,212 − a
surprisingly low figure.[84] These discrepancies become even more
striking if one takes the size of the population into account. Upper
Austria in 1938 had 13.35 per cent of the Austrian population, but

only 1.8 per cent of the party members. Tyrol and Vorarlberg together had 7.47 of the population, but only 3.2 of the party members, and Salzburg 3.64 and 1.3 per cent respectively. Styria, on the other hand, with 15 per cent of the total population had 21.1 per cent of the party members, and Carinthia — with only 6 per cent of the population — as many as 15.4 of the party members. Only in Lower Austria and Vienna did the figures roughly correspond; together they had about 54.5 per cent of the population and 57.2 of the party members.[85] The uneven strength of National Socialist influence in the different parts of the country and among the different social groups had its parallel in Germany in the years before 1933,[86] but the discrepancies were particularly marked in Austria. The greatest and the most persistent obstacle in the path of the National Socialists, however, was their internal disunity, the violent conflicts between the different party leaders which marred the party's development from the outset.

Yet the government and the forces behind it were equally disunited and its supporters were less than enthusiastic in the defence of Austria. From this point of view Göring was quite right when he explained to an Austrian visitor in November 1937 that the Anschluss was inevitable: 'for resistance can only be contemplated by a country which is united from the head of the government down to the last peasant and is determined to render resistance. But this was not the case in Austria, for the Austrian army would never . . . raise its arms in earnest against its old ally, and at least one third of the Austrian people stood firmly behind the new German Reich. . . .'[87]

NOTES

1. Hitler's order of 3 August quoted in note by Hüffer, Berlin, 7 August 1934: Auswärt. Amt, Akten betr. Nationalsozialismus, Österreich, Bd. 2, 6111H, E452910-11.

2. Hess to Frauenfeld, Munich, 21 August 1934: ibid., 6111H, E452942.

3. Report by Lt.-Gen. Muff: Auswärt. Amt, Militär-Attaché Wien, Bd. 2, 5705H, E414377-78.

4. Report by Sicherheitsdirektor for Upper Austria, Linz, 3 October 1934: Oberösterreich. Landesarchiv, Politische Akten, Nr. 1.

5. The Austrian Consul in Cologne to Bundeskanzleramt, 26 August 1934: Verwaltungsarchiv Wien, Bundeskanzleramt, 22/gen., box 4896.

6. Habicht's disgrace is indicated by the fact that – after a decent interval – he was appointed to the minor post of mayor of Wittenberg in Saxony and dit not receive any position in Austria.

7. Informationsdienst der Vaterländischen Front, Nr. 41, Vienna, 19 October 1934; Habicht's letter of 25 March 1937 about the expulsions: Berlin Document Center, Partei-Kanzlei Korrespondenz.

8. Brandstötter, 'Dr. Walter Riehl . . .' (Ph.D. thesis, Vienna, 1969) 325-27.

9. Information received by the Bundeskanzleramt, Vienna, 10 January 1935: Verwaltungsarchiv Wien, Bundeskanzleramt, 22/gen., box 4920.

10. Report from Berlin, 22 January 1935: Botschaft Wien, Geheimakten 1935-38 4939 part 1, E271824.

11. Report by Bundespolizeidirektion Vienna, 6 February 1935: Verwaltungsarchiv Wien, Bundeskanzleramt, 22/gen., box 4919.

12. Report by Generaldirektion für die öffentl. Sicherheit, 11 February 1935: ibid., box 4914.

13. Order by Kreisleitung Mittelsteiermark of the NSDAP, Graz, 18 November 1935: ibid., box 4939: copy.

14. Report by Lt.-Gen. Muff, Vienna, 28 August 1935, secret: Auswärt. Amt, Akten betr. Nationalsozialismus, Österreich, Bd. 3 6111H, E453231-36.

15. 'Lagebericht über den Monat März 1936', 24 April 1936: Verwaltungsarchiv Wien, Bundeskanzleramt, 22/gen., box 4913. Already the report for January mentioned 'the strong revival of National Socialist activity': ibid.

16. Extracts from a 22-page report by Generaldirektion für die öffentl. Sicherheit, 4 April 1936 (pp. 2-4, 6, 9, 12-15): Haus-, Hof- u. Staatsarchiv, Liasse Österreich 2/21, fasz. 468.

17. Report, Lienz, 22 January 1936: Tiroler Landesarchiv, Präsidialakten 1937, 434 XII 57.

18. Report, Liezen, 30 June 1936: Steiermärk. Landesarchiv, Bezirkshauptmannschaft Liezen, Vrst. 1935-36.

19. Report by Generaldirektion für die öffentl. Sicherheit, 25 June 1936: Verwaltungsarchiv Wien, Bundeskanzleramt, 22/gen., box 4913.

20. Police report, Stallhofen, 30 December 1936: Steiermärk. Landesarchiv, Bezirkshauptmannschaft Voitsberg, 1936, Gruppe 14 Gi-La.

21. 'Dienstreise des Staatssekretärs für Sicherheitswesen nach Steiermark und Kärnten. . . .': Verwaltungsarchiv, Bundeskanzleramt, 22/gen., box 4932.

22. Report by Sicherheitsdirektor for Carinthia, Klagenfurt, 25 March 1935: ibid., box 4923.

23. Report by the Bundeskommissar für Heimatdienst, Vienna, 30 January 1935: Haus-, Hof- u. Staatsarchiv, Liasse Österreich, 2/21, fasz. 305.

24. Report by Sicherheitsdirektor for Tyrol, Innsbruck, 9 September 1935: Verwaltungsarchiv, Bundeskanzleramt, 22/gen., box 4925.

25. Reports by Bezirkshauptmann of Bregenz, 20 June, 9 July 1935: Vorarlberger Landesarchiv, Bezirkshauptmannschaft Bregenz, Nr. 1138 (1935).

26. The NSDAP Gauleiter for Burgenland to the Sicherheitsdirektor, 18 March 1936: Burgenländ. Landesarchiv, Zeitgeschichtl. Sammlung, A/VIII-10, VIII/5.

27. Papen to Hitler, Vienna, 12 August 1935: Botschaft Wien, Geheimakten 1935-38, 4939 part 1, E272101. In Upper Austria, Revertera was a prominent aristocrat and Heimwehr leader.

28. Langoth to Papen, Linz, 21 November 1935: Botschaft Wien, Geheimakten 1935-38, 4938 part 8, E270124-25.

29. Langoth, *Kampf um Österreich* (Wels, 1951) 193. In the Third Reich L. was rewarded for his services by an honorary rank in the SS and the post of mayor of Hitler's favourite city, Linz.

30. Police reports, Eferding, 29 July, and Linz, 29 November 1935: Oberösterreich. Landesarchiv, Politische Akten, Nr. 10 and Nr. 26.

31. The text of the secret clause or 'Gentleman Agreement' [*sic*] in Schuschnigg. op. cit., 189-90; Haus-, Hof- u. Staatsarchiv, Liasse Österreich 1/12, fasc. 466; and *Der Hochverratsprozess gegen Dr. Guido Schmidt vor dem Wiener Volksgericht,* 481-82. There is nothing in the text about the admission of National Socialists to the Fatherland Front (as asserted by Bracher, *Die Deutsche Diktatur,* 336).

32. Thus comment of a Front Bezirksführer on 22 July 1936: Oberösterreich. Landesarchiv, Politische Akten, Freistadt, Vaterländische Front.

33. Thus the Heimwehr paper *Die neue Zeit,* Linz, 27 January 1937, in a leader.

34. Weisungsblatt of the Austrian NSDAP Landesleitung, 13 July 1936: Haus-, Hof- u. Staatsarchiv, Liasse Österreich 2/21, fasz. 306.

35. 'Otto' to Dr Lohmann, Vienna, 13 July 1936: Verwaltungsarchiv Wien, Nachlass Lohmann, box 6.

36. Unsigned note, Vienna, 17 July 1936: Haus-, Hof- u. Staatsarchiv, Liasse Österreich 1/12, fasz. 466.

37. Unsigned note, Gmunden, 26 July 1936: Oberösterreich. Landesarchiv, Politische Akten, Nr. 12.

38. Report by Bezirkshauptmann of Bruck, 31 August 1936: Steiermärk. Landesarchiv, Bezirkshauptmannschaft Bruck 1936, Gruppe Vrst.

39. Report by Bundespolizeidirektion Vienna, s.d.: Polizeiarchiv Wien, Staatspolizeiliche Agenden 1933, NSDAP.

40. 'Lagebericht über den Monat August 1936', Vienna, 24 September 1936: Verwaltungsarchiv Wien, Bundeskanzleramt, 22/gen., box 4913.

41. Report, Gmunden, 5 August 1936: Oberösterreich. Landesarchiv, Politische Akten, Nr. 12.

42. Police report, Sandl, 20 July 1936: ibid., Politische Akten (Reservat) 1936-38.

43. The Sicherheitsdirektor for Tyrol to Bundeskanzleramt, Innsbruck, 5 August 1936: Verwaltungsarchiv, Bundeskanzleramt, 22/gen., box 4968.

44. Papen to Hitler, 3 November 1936: Botschaft Wien, Geheimakten 1935-38, 4939 part 2, E272484.

45. Report by Bundespolizeidirektion Vienna, s.d. (1937): Polizeiarchiv Wien, Staatspolizeiliche Agenden 1933: NSDAP.

46. Report on a discussion between Leopold and the Viennese party leaders, 16 April 1937: Haus-, Hof- u. Staatsarchiv, Liasse Österreich 2/21, fasz. 308.

47. Notes by Councillor of Legation Altenburg, Auswärt. Amt, 22 September 1936: *Akten zur deutschen auswärtigen Politik,* series D, I, no. 165, 248.

48. Police reports, Vienna, 30 December 1936 and 27 January 1937: Verwaltungsarchiv Wien, Bundeskanzleramt 22/gen., box 4913.

49. 'Gau-Weisungsblatt Nr. 11' of Upper Austrian NSDAP: Oberösterreich. Landesarchiv, Politische Akten, Nr. 9.

50. Report by Polizeidirektor of Innsbruck, 23 January 1937: Verwaltungsarchiv Bundeskanzleramt, 22/gen., box 4979.

51 Report by Bezirkshauptmann of Freistadt, 3 January 1937: Oberösterreich. Landesarchiv, Freistadt, Politischer Nachrichtendienst 1934-38.

52. Oberrechnungsrat Max Freese to Himmler, Stuttgart, 4 December 1936: Institut für Zeitgeschichte, Munich, Akten des Reichsführers SS, Fa 199/45. His information was based on conversations with the Deputy Gauleiter of Carinthia, Longin.

53. Bullock *Hitler* (edn. 1973), 362.

54. *Österreichischer Beobachter*, Folge 17, 1 April 1937: copy in Burgenländ. Landesarchiv Zeitgeschichtl. Sammlung, A/VIII-14, X.

55. 'Amtlicher Informationsdienst', Vienna, 5 March 1937: Haus-, Hof- u. Staatsarchiv, Liasse Österreich 2/3, fasz. 285.

56. 'Bericht II über die Zeit vom 24.I. bis 14.II.' (1937), signed by Gilbert in der Maur, a member of the Committee: Burgenländ. Landesarchiv, Zeitgeschichtl. Sammlung, A/VIII-10, VIII/5.

57. 'Standort, am 17.II.1937' (a document seized by the police on 21 April at the Teinfaltstr.): Verwaltungsarchiv Wien, Bundeskanzleramt, 22/gen., box 5000.

58. 'Kurzinformation über Gau Wien der NSDAP Hitlerbewegung', s.d., ibid. (another document seized there by the police).

59. Report by Generaldirektion für die öffentl. Sicherheit, Vienna, 30 May 1937: Haus-, Hof- u. Staatsarchiv, Nachlass Hornbostel, fasz. 251; report by Bundespolizeidirektion Vienna, s.d.: Polizeiarchiv Wien, Staatspolizeiliche Agenden 1933: NSDAP.

60. 'Die Ereignisse vom Feber und März 1938 in Graz . . .', MS. in Nachlass Lohmann, Box 7, Verwaltungsarchiv Wien.

61 Reinthaller to Seyss-Inquart, Attersee, 2 November 1937: Bundesarchiv Koblenz, Nachlass Seyss-Inquart, Sondermappe 2.

62. *Österreichischer Beobachter*, October 1937: Burgenländ. Landesarchiv, Zeitgeschichtl. Sammlung A/VIII-10, varia X/1.

63. Cp. above, pp. 294-95.

64. Confidential note, Vienna, 22 June 1937: Verwaltungsarchiv Wien, Bundeskanzleramt, 22/gen., box 5001.

65. Report on meeting of the Fatherland Front at Hietzing on 9 July 1937: Bundesarchiv Koblenz, Nachlass Seyss-Inquart, Sondermappe 1.

66. Seyss-Inquart to Dr Keppler, Salzburg, 18 August 1937: *Akten zur deutschen auswärt. Politik*, series D, I, no. 248, 371-72.

67. 'Lagebericht über den Monat August 1937': Auswärt. Amt, Akten betr. Politische Lageberichte der Geheimen Staatspolizei, Bd. 3, 2971H, D579309.

68. *Österreichischer Beobachter*, 1. Novemberfolge 1937: Oberösterr. Landesarchiv, Politische Akten, Nr. 11. In the Third Reich G. became one of the most notorious high SS officials.

69. Notes about conversation Bormann-Keppler on 30 September 1937: *Akten zur deutschen auswärt. Politik*, series D, I, no. 255, 379.

70. Notes on conversation Bormann-Keppler on 2 November 1937: ibid., no. 287, 392.

71. Notes by Keppler (?), 4 October 1937: ibid., no. 257, 381. For Habicht see above p. 203.

72. Confidential note, Vienna, 30 December 1936: Verwaltungsarchiv, Wien, Bundeskanzleramt, 22/gen., box 4975.

73. Order of SS Standarte 9, 1 October 1936: Haus-, Hof- u. Staatsarchiv, Liasse Österreich 2/21, fasz. 306.

74. 'Bericht über die Stellung der SS im Gau', 31 January 1937: Burgenländ. Landesarchiv, Zeitgeschichtl. Sammlung, A/VIII-10, varia X/1.

75. Leopold to Himmler, Krems, 4 December 1937: Berlin Document Center, Partei-Kanzlei Korrespondenz.

76. Note, s.d.: Haus-, Hof- u. Staatsarchiv, Nachlass Hornbostel, fasz. 252.

77. Police report, Mariazell, 14 September 1936: Steiermärk. Landesarchiv, Bezirkshauptmannschaft Bruck 1936, Gruppe 14, K-N.

78. Report by Bezirkshauptmann of Bruck, 30 April 1937: ibid. 1937, Gruppe Vrst. 1-2.

79. Report by Bezirkshauptmann of Voitsberg, 31 March 1937: ibid., Bezirks-hauptmannschaft Voitsberg 1938, Gruppe 14 L-O.

80. Report of October 1937: Bundesarchiv Koblenz, Nachlass Seyss-Inquart, Nr. 26.

81. Report by Sicherheitsdirektor for Styria, Graz, 9 April 1937: Verwaltungsarchiv Wien, Bundeskanzleramt, 22/gen., box 4993.

82. Report by Sicherheitsdirektor for Carinthia, Klagenfurt, 26 March 1937: ibid.

83. Report by Bundespolizeidirektion Innsbruck, 25 March 1937: ibid.

84. The total party membership on 21 November 1938 was given as 127,056 in *Finanz- und Parteiverwaltung – Mitgliedschaftswesen* to Reichsamtsleiter Meiler, Vienna, 14 December 1938: Bundesarchiv Koblenz, Sammlung Schumacher, Nr. 303.

85. The percentages are counted from the above letter, the population figures are given in *Encyclopaedia Britannica,* Vol. II (1949 edn.) 744.

86. For the geographical distribution of National Socialist influence in Germany according to the elections from 1924 to 1932, see the table in K. D. Bracher, *Die Auflösung der Weimarer Republik* (Stuttgart-Düsseldorf, 1955) 647. There were differences, but they were not all that marked in the 1930s.

87. Peter Count Revertera to Schuschnigg, Vienna, 20 November 1937: *Der Hochverratsprozess gegen Dr. Guido Schmidt vor dem Wiener Volksgericht* (Vienna, 1947) 295. Göring received Revertera on 17 November.

15

THE 'ANSCHLUSS'

At the beginning of 1938 it did not seem that the internal political situation in Austria had substantially changed. The National Socialists were still an underground party and were still harrassed by the police. Their following had not grown to any considerable extent, and they were still deeply disunited about the tactics to be pursued against the government. But it is also true that the latter's position had been slowly eroded by its willingness to make small concessions, be that the admission of ministers of 'national' persuasion to the government, or the institution of the *Volkspolitische Referat* within the Fatherland Front under so-called 'moderate' National Socialists, or by the policy of 'internal pacification' in general. From the National Socialist point of view, there was good reason to think that concessions such as these would be followed by similar steps, that sooner or later the 'national opposition' would become a legal party and then be able to gain the upper hand. Such 'salami tactics' could be followed almost indefinitely and were more than likely to bring final victory. All that was required was patience, and some united effort by the Austrian National Socialists in the pursuit of their goal.

We have seen that in November 1937 Hitler and Bormann still favoured such an 'evolutionary way'[1] Three months later no change was noticeable in this policy. As Keppler, Hitler's special envoy for Austrian affairs, wrote to Ribbentrop early in February:

> Circles of the Austrian government which are well inclined towards us have repeatedly pointed out to me that Schuschnigg is in no position to let the few National Socialists *[sic]* who are openly members of the government leave; in my opinion the aim of any possible action must be to gain such a position in the government that it will become impossible for the chancellor to allow the departure of these gentlemen. When this aim is achieved we can prevail more and more if our policy is relatively adroit. . . .

But, he added, the carrying out of such a policy was made 'extraordinarily difficult' by the disunity and opposition of the Austrian Landesleitung; all his patient endeavours to induce Landesleiter Leopold to toe 'the right line' had been in vain, and he and Göring were of the opinion that Leopold must be removed.[2] A few days later Keppler enlarged on this. Although Hitler himself had repeatedly declared that the party's efforts should be transferred 'to the legal sector' and that less should be done 'on the illegal side', Leopold was still opposing this policy and continued his fight against Keppler and the work of Dr Seyss-Inquart, in spite of a promise given in Göring's presence that he would change his attitude. During the past week Leopold had once more organized large demonstrations which had resulted in mass arrests.[3]

The plans of the leading Austrian National Socialists went further than this step-by-step programme. At the beginning of 1938 they drafted an 'Action Programme 1938'. It started from the bold premise (for which there was no evidence): 'Schuschnigg does not want to fulfil the agreement of 11 July 1936; therefore its fulfilment is to be enforced without or against Schuschnigg.' As to the European situation, there was a shrewd analysis: Italy depended on Germany's friendship; France was in the middle of a severe internal crisis and incapable of mounting an attack outside its frontiers; in Russia there was chaos (meaning Stalin's purges); as to Britain, it was tied in the Far East, India and the Mediterranean, had done nothing to oppose Hitler's occupation of the Rhineland 'although the Rhine is England's frontier', and would much less march 'for the Danube'. 'Therefore the German Reich [has] freedom of action.' It should request 'the integral fulfilment of the agreement of 11 July 1936 through a limited démarche addressed to the Austrian government'. After consultation with the Italian government it could be further demanded that the Austrian government should resign and a chancellor be appointed 'who is capable and willing to fulfil inter-state treaties'. If the Austrian government did not accept the demands, the German air force and armoured divisions were to be moved to the frontier; Italy and Yugoslavia should take similar measures. The transitional Austrian government was to grant complete toleration to the NSDAP and to hold a free plebiscite; the cabinet list was to be agreed upon in consultation 'with the leader of the national opposition', presumably meaning Leopold. Until the carrying out of the plebiscite, every authority on the provincial and local levels was to be shared between the National Socialists and others, in each case under a chairman who was to be a National Socialist. In the opinion of the police, the programme with its detailed knowledge of the foreign and internal political situation was probably 'the result of repeated and thorough discussions within a circle of leaders'; but the arrested Vienna Gauleiter Dr Tavs claimed that he had drafted it alone shortly before his arrest.[4] It is remarkable to what extent this plan was followed during the months of February and March 1938.

On 11 February Schuschnigg travelled to Berchtesgaden to meet Hitler — a meeting arranged at the suggestion of Papen. There Schuschnigg was presented with Hitler's demands: the ban on the National Socialist Party was to be lifted, there was to be a general amnesty for arrested National Socialists, and more of their sympathizers were to receive government posts; Seyss-Inquart was to become minister of the interior, responsible for security and police matters; and control over the Austrian army was to pass to General Glaise-Horstenau who was one of the 'national' representatives admitted to the cabinet after July 1936. The fulfilment of these demands would have given the Austrian Nationalist Socialists the decisive positions to achieve full power, and it could be foreseen that the Fatherland Front would quickly disintegrate under a concerted attack mounted by its opponents. But, threatened by German military preparations, Schuschnigg felt unable to resist and accepted the conditions of the ultimatum.[5] Yet even this success was insufficient to eliminate the conflicts within the Austrian party and the friction between its leaders and the German authorities. Leopold indeed was persuaded by them to go to Germany for the time being, and a new Austrian Landesleiter was appointed, a Major Klausner. But the Vienna Gauleiter Tavs ordered his men to break all the windows of the German embassy, and one of Leopold's underlings declared that even Hitler had nothing to say in Austrian affairs. There was also continuing violent opposition to the new minister of the interior, the 'traitor' Seyss-Inquart.[6] The wrath of the faithful was understandable in the circumstances, for he was now a minister under the hated Schuschnigg and they were still in the wilderness.

On 21 February Leopold met Hitler and Göring in Berlin and complained that he had not been informed in advance about the meeting at Berchtesgaden. Hitler in his turn sharply criticized Leopold's activities in Austria after the meeting as well as his opposition to 'the policy of the Führer'. Leopold was ordered to abstain from any intervention in Austrian affairs: Hitler would take care of him and entrust him with a different task. Four other Austrian National Socialists received orders to come to Germany. Then Hitler received Major Klausner and gave him detailed instructions 'how the Party in Austria should be led'; its underground tactics must be transferred 'to the field of legality' following the example of Gauleiter Bürckel in the Saar some years ago; as he had combined all suitable elements in a 'German Front' from which later the Party was organized, a similar route must be followed in Austria.[7] Five days later Hitler saw the five 'exiled' Austrian leaders (Leopold, Schattenfroh, Tavs, In der Maur and Rüdiger) and informed them that 'the Austrian question could never be solved through a revolution'; he had to abandon this way for Germany after 1923, and for Austria too no such possibility existed. The five were to remain in Germany and to look round the country.[8] Clearly Hitler had no further use for them.

In Vienna the members of the Austrian government who had 'national' sympathies favoured the acceptance of the German conditions, but those who had belonged to the Christian Social Party were opposed to the appointment of Seyss-Inquart as minister of the interior. Opposition became so strong that Schuschnigg even threatened to resign. Only when news of German military measures near the frontier reached Vienna did 'the resistance of the ultra-black circles collapse'. At a simultaneous meeting of the functionaries of the Fatherland Front the mood was very depressed, and some of the critics told Schuschnigg in no uncertain terms 'that this sad development for Austria would not have occurred to such an extent if Starhemberg were still a member of the government'.

In Upper Austria news of the acceptance of the German conditions and of the changes in the government caused a 'mood of victory' among the 'moderate' National Socialists, but disappointment and refusal to acquiesce among the more radical elements, as Count Revertera, the Director of Security, noted on 17 February.[9] On the previous day the new Austrian government announced an amnesty for all National Socialists, including those condemned for the murder of Chancellor Dollfuss.[10]

On 19 February, as Count Revertera reported to Vienna, he met the leaders 'of the national camp' to discuss 'all eventualities' and to avoid any demonstration following upon a speech by Hitler and they promised to co-operate with him. In the evening the rival groups walked through Linz and greeted their political friends with 'Heil Hitler! ' or 'Heil Austria! ' as the case might be. No friction developed, and any more ebullient National Socialist demonstrations were prevented by their own security organs, especially the SS, who ordered their followers to keep quiet and to move on: a sign how strict the discipline was in the National Socialist ranks.[11] Two days later the functionaries of the Fatherland Front met in Linz and declared their willingness to co-operate 'with all those national forces which are prepared to accept the premises of the National Front'. The local representative of its *Volkspolitische Referat* stated solemnly that from that day onwards all underground work in Upper Austria would cease and that no illegal activity outside the Front would be allowed. On the same day the leaders of the Upper Austrian National Socialists also met and decided that under no circumstances would they depart from the 'legal and evolutionary way'. They expressly rejected any revolutionary method and promised Revertera that they would see to the preservation of law and order and would strictly carry out the instructions of the authorities.[12] Once more Revertera found cause to admire the well functioning organization of the National Socialists which, in his opinion 'put to shame . . . this unfortunate irremovable stain of the Fatherland Front'.[13] On 23 February he noted that the Fatherland Front was 'breaking down all along the line; everybody is coming to me for advice and instructions, from the National Socialists to the Communists: a queer state of affairs'.[14]

Meanwhile, however, things had taken a very different course in Graz and Styria where the National Socialists were much stronger and much less inclined to accept any compromise. There active preparations for a takeover were made by the 'National Socialist Soldiers' Ring' – a secret organization in the army and the police. In Graz this comprised about a quarter of the garrison and the police and included a special *Verfügungstruppe* composed of civilians. On 19 February groups of the latter walked through the city and greeted each other demonstratively with 'Heil Hitler!' The policemen – many of them members of the

Soldiers' Ring – did not interefere. In the afternoon the director of
police issued the order to dissolve any National Socialist demonstrations and to confiscate their flags and torches. The inspector in charge
replied that the order could not be carried out, sabotaged all further
orders to prevent the demonstrations, and instructed his subordinates
to do nothing against the National Socialists. Thus the SA of Graz
could assemble their men and start the first open demonstration against
the Austrian regime. In view of the prevailing mood among the policemen nothing could be done to prevent this.[15] According to an official
report, about 8,000 people took part in a torchlight procession which
was preceded by swastika flags. One of them was hoisted on the town
hall, together with a picture of Hitler, but these were removed by the
police. Smaller demonstrations took place in eleven other towns of
Styria, the number of participants varying from 70 to about 3,000. But
on the following day there were many more: over 10,000 in Graz and
about 35,000 in twenty-six other towns of Styria. In some of them
soldiers participated, in others officials of the Fatherland Front. On
that day similar demonstrations were organized in Carinthia and Tyrol,
but with much smaller attendances: only 3,000 in Innsbruck and only
1,400 in Klagenfurt, but 4,000 in Villach, and 2,000 in Spittal in
Carinthia.[16]

On 24 February Schuschnigg attempted to rally his followers by a
speech which was transmitted to all major towns. At Voitsberg in Styria
about 500 of them listened to it in a hall; but the National Socialists
assembled nearly four times that number from the whole area. Their
adherents wore swastika badges, their torchlight processesion was preceded by a band, not only *Deutschland über Alles* but also the *Horst
Wessel Song* was played and sung, and there was a march past at which
the leaders took the salute. The authorities noticed among the participants many judges, lawyers, teachers, doctors and employees of the
public corporations, apart from shopkeepers, workers and peasants, in
short they came 'from all sections of the population'.[17] In Graz alone,
on the 27th, the para-military formations of the SA were reported as
10,000 strong. They showed an 'enthusiastic attitude' towards the army
and the reinforcements which had been ordered to Graz but did not
take any action, perhaps because they were no longer reliable.[18]

On 21 February the new minister of the interior, Dr Seyss-Inquart,
tried to prohibit the wearing of swastika emblems and party uniforms
as well as the showing of the swastika flag; the Hitler salute was only
permitted if used as a 'private' greeting, but not vis-à-vis any authority

or in any office. The government emphasized that Hitler had recognized the Austrian Constitution according to which there were no political parties and party emblems were not allowed to be worn.[19] As late as 1 March the ministry of the interior repeated that the Hitler salute was permitted only if it was used by individuals and 'not in a demonstrative fashion'. It was decreed that Austrian citizens were forbidden to hoist the swastika flag and that the General Directorate of Public Security reserved to itself the right to decide 'in each concrete case . . . to what extent the swastika alone can be used as a symbol of National Socialist *Weltanschauung*'.[20] On 8 March the ministry ordered all party uniforms and swastika emblems to be confiscated and all public demonstrations not sanctioned by the authorities to cease.[21] Yet all such attempts to stem the tide were bound to fail. In many places the police and other authorities were unable or unwilling to enforce the decrees which only proved that the wheels of the Austrian bureaucracy were still turning. On 7 March Keppler, reporting on his recent visit to Vienna, was full of optimism: ' "Heil Hitler! " and the Hitler salute are tolerated. . . . Already metal swastikas while not officially permitted are worn everywhere. . . .'[22]

In Graz meanwhile developments had taken an ever more radical turn. Many soldiers and policemen fraternized with the National Socialists. The commanding general estimated that 'at least 70 per cent of the civil servants of all categories' were National Socialists, and many more of the officials employed by the municipality, many of whom had once been Social Democrats.[23] Clearly, there were very many anxious to jump on the band waggon while there was still time. Keppler in turn mentioned an estimate of about 80 per cent of the Graz population espousing the cause of National Socialism. He considered it necessary to curb the movement to some extent 'so as to obtain more and more concessions from Schuschnigg'. On 1 March Seyss-Inquart himself went to Graz to prevent excesses and to pacify the National Socialists, for it was feared that otherwise the movement would assume ever more extremist forms. He negotiated with the local authorities and he used the SA and SS formations to 'restore order'. Finally they were permitted to stage yet another torchlight parade, this time in honour of the new minister.[24] Vis-à-vis Schuschnigg Seyss-Inquart emphasized that law and order could only be preserved if 'the old organizations and leaders were used for this purpose on account of the discipline which they maintained', and thus was able to achieve what in practice amounted to their legalization. As Keppler reported to Berlin, 'I believe that the party is once more in good fighting trim and with its inherent discipline can be used in the political game. . . .' He was confident that Seyss-Inquart would succeed in creating the legal preconditions necessary for the party organization.[25]

In Upper Austria the provincial government met on 1 March and the Landeshauptmann suggested that 'militant detachments should be formed from the Fatherland Front' which were to prevent any excesses by the National Socialists. The comment of the Director of Security was: 'and therefore the Heimwehren have been dissolved? ' He also noted that 'it is symptomatic of the complete confusion in the Fatherland Front' that only now the lists of the district and Gau leaders were gone through to establish who was 'reliable'. In the evening he was visited by three of the 'national' leaders who told him that their followers were getting 'excited'.[26] On 2 March a public demonstration of the National Socialists announced for the 6th was prohibited by the authorities, but their leaders declared that they would demonstrate in spite of this. In the opinion of the Director of Security the result could be an uprising. The Landeshauptmann asked him whether he ought to resign, but was persuaded not to do so, and equally to desist from his plan of creating 'militant detachments' of the Fatherland Front because such a project could not be carried out in practice. The Director of Security considered it essential to make certain concessions to the 'national' elements so as to gain time: 'The present situation is extremely unfavourable for us and, if the national elements really desire it and if they are backed by the Reich, the independence of Austria could be terminated today.'[27]

This picture from Linz is confirmed by police reports from some smaller places in Upper Austria. From Weng near Braunau it was stated on 7 March that the National Socialists now included about 70 per cent of the population and had gained considerably since 12 February. The Fatherland Front had officially 618 members, but it now turned out that many of them in reality belonged to the 'national' camp.[28] From Ried the police reported on 9 March that 'almost every person in the street visibly wears a swastika' and that the population showed 'an extraordinary readiness to greet by lifting the right hand'; the 'national population' seemed to suffer from 'a swastika psychosis', while the loyalists avoided to be seen in public; they were intimidated and depressed.[29] On the previous day Schuschnigg had decided to hold a plebiscite whether the Austrian people desired to live in a free and independent Austria; but the news did little to cheer his supporters, and only served to arouse Hitler's fury.[30]

In Linz, in Graz, in Innsbruck and elsewhere in Austria the National Socialists took over even before the German army marched into the country. In the evening of the 11 March the house of the Tyrolese government was occupied by SS men and large National Socialist demonstrations took place in many towns. On the central square at Linz the SA and SS paraded in uniform; the 'Heil Hitler' shouts and other slogans were repeated by a vast crowd (about 15 to 20,000 according to the police). Then the Gauleiter of Upper Austria announced that the Schuschnigg government had resigned and that a new government would be formed by Dr Seyss-Inquart. The units of the SA and SS were instructed to co-operate with the police. Some hours later an SS unit of 125 men appeared in front of the police headquarters. Their leader informed the director of police that, in the name of the new chancellor, the SS were taking over and were putting themselves at the disposal of the authorities; no files were to be destroyed, and the offices were guarded by SS men. All public buildings were likewise occupied by para-military units in the name of the new chancellor. The director of police admonished his men to serve the new government loyally and to co-operate with the National Socialist formations.[31] On the following day Hitler made his triumphal entry into Linz, the town where he spent so many years of his youth — the Anschluss was finally accomplished. The victory owed much to the efforts of the Austrian National Socialists, but even more to German pressure and the military might of the Third Reich.

NOTES

1. See above, p. 307.
2. Keppler to Ribbentrop, 7 February 1938: _Akten zur deutschen auswärtigen Politik,_ series D, I, no. 285, 411.
3. Same to same, 10 February 1938: ibid., no. 289, 415.
4. Text of the Action Programme with police comments in: Bundespolizeidirektion Vienna to Staatsanwaltschaft Vienna, 28 January 1938: Verwaltungsarchiv Wien, Bundeskanzleramt, 22/gen., box 5022.
5. For details see Bullock, _Hitler_ (1973 edn.) 422-25; Schuschnigg, op. cit., 237-39.
6. Report by Dr Veesenmayer, 18 February 1938: _Akten zur deutschen auswärtigen Politik,_ series D, I, no. 313, 440.
7. Ibid., no. 318, 443.
8. Ibid., no. 328, 450.
9. Notes by Revertera, Thursday, 17 February 1938: Herrschaftsarchiv Helfenberg, box 102a.
10. Bullock, op. cit., 426.
11. Revertera to Generaldirektion für die öffentl. Sicherheit, Linz, 21 February 1938: Herrschaftsarchiv Helfenberg, box 102a.
12. Same to same, Linz, 22 February 1938: ibid.
13. Notes by Revertera, 22 February 1938, ibid.
14. Notes by Revertera, 23 February 1938, ibid.
15. 'Die Ereignisse vom Feber und März 1938 in Graz', MS. in Nachlass Lohmann, box 7, Verwaltungsarchiv Wien.
16. 'Situationsberichte' of 20 and 21 February 1938: ibid., Bundeskanzleramt, 22/gen., box 5011.
17. Reports from Voitsberg, 25 February, 1 March 1938: Steiermärk. Landesarchiv, Bezirkshauptmannschaft Voitsberg 1938, Gruppe 14 L-O. The two songs were the official German anthems.
18. Report by the general commanding at Graz to the ministry of defence, forwarded to Berlin by Lt.-Gen. Muff, 27 February 1938: Botschaft Wien, Geheimakten 1935-38, 4938 part 10, E271754.
19. Telephone communication to Freistadt by Upper Austrian Sicherheitsdirektion, 20 February 1938: Oberösterreich. Landesarchiv, Politische Akten, Freistadt, 1934-38.
20. Generaldirektion für die öffentl. Sicherheit to all Sicherheitsdirektoren, 1 March 1938: Vorarlberger Landesarchiv, Bezirkshauptmannschaft Bregenz 1938, Nr. 603.
21. Same to same, 8 March 1938, 'strictly confidential': ibid.
22. Keppler's report on his visit to Vienna from 3 to 6 March 1938: quoted by Schuschnigg, _Im Kampf gegen Hitler,_ 293.
23. Report by the commanding general to the defence ministry, 27 February 1938, sent to Berlin by Lt.-Gen. Muff: Botschaft Wien, Geheimakten 1935-38, 4938 part 10, E271754.
24. Report by Keppler on his visit to Vienna, 3 to 6 March 1938, quoted by Schuschnigg, op. cit., 293; _Basler Nachrichten,_ 2 March 1938.

25. Report by Keppler on his visit to Vienna, quoted by Schuschnigg, op. cit., 293-94.

26. Notes by Revertera, Tuesday, 1 March 1938: Herrschaftsarchiv Helfenberg, box 102a.

27. Notes by Revertera, Wednesday, 2 March 1938: ibid.

28. Police report, Weng, 7 March 1938: Oberösterreich. Landesarchiv, Politische Akten, Nr. 10 (Braunau).

29. Police report, Ried, 9 March 1938: ibid., Nr. 36 (Ried).

30. Bullock, op. cit., 426.

31. Report by Bundespolizeidirektion Linz, 11 March 1938: Verwaltungsarchiv Wien, Bundeskanzleramt, 22/gen., box 5026.

FASCISM IN AUSTRIA AND IN GERMANY

There are, clearly, very striking parallels between the development of fascist or semi-fascist movements in Austria and in Germany. It was not only that the same language was spoken in both countries so that political influences could easily penetrate from the one into the other. Politically it was much more important that, until 1938, most Austrians felt that they were Germans, that there was only German but no Austrian nationalism. Schuschnigg reports that on 11 March 1938 a member of his own government exclaimed: 'I am ashamed to be a German.'[1] After the revolution of 1918 all Austrian political parties favoured the Anschluss because they considered the small 'German Austria' not viable. It was only natural that the weak Austrian republic should seek to join the much stronger neighbour with whom it had been linked in one form or the other until 1866. The grossdeutsch tradition was very much alive in Austria, especially among the Social Democrats and on the political right, where a Grossdeutsch Party was founded in 1919. Only the leaders of the Christian Social Party were more hesitant towards the idea of the Anschluss because they disliked North German Protestantism and the 'red' influences of the early months of the German Republic; but even they always stressed that they were Germans and that their policy followed a German course. At the beginning of March 1938 even Dr Schuschnigg assured Hitler's emissary Keppler of his 'unconditional loyalty to German nationhood *(Volksdeutschtum)*, to a common policy in which he would never disappoint us'. Keppler was asked to study Schuschnigg's 'great works for Germanization, especially in the Burgenland'.[2]

German nationalism was particularly strong among the Burschenschaften and in other student corporations whose former members played such a prominent part in the political and economic life of the country thanks to the network of contacts which existed in favour of the 'old boys'. Ever since the days when Georg von Schönerer joined hands with them, the Burschenschaften, the Turnerschaften, and many other clubs and associations propagated a völkisch and anti-semitic ideology – indeed to a greater extent than did similar organizations in Germany. Many of them early on adopted the 'Aryan' principle, which excluded not only Jews but all who were not of purely German 'racial' origin. The greater strength of this ideology in Austria before 1914 can perhaps be explained by the somewhat different conditions which existed in the Habsburg Monarchy: many Austrian Germans really felt threatened by a tide of Pan-Slavism; they were only a minority in the Austrian part of the Habsburg Monarchy, very much on the defensive when faced by Czech or Southern Slav demands; the Viennese Jews really occupied important economic and cultural positions, and their influence was much stronger than that of the Jews in Germany. The German Empire of 1871 also had a substantial Slav minority in its Polish provinces, but they were a minority which posed no threat to the Germans and they could not possibly bring about the disintegration of the monarchy which seemed so imminent in the case of Austria.

There was another fear which affected in particular 'the small man' in Vienna and other towns: the fear of rapid economic change, of the advance of capitalism and big enterprise which threatened the very existence of many independent craftsmen and shopkeepers. These fears were dramatically confirmed by the 'Black Friday' of May 1873, the crash of the Viennese stock exchange, which caused the collapse of many banks and industrial enterprises and created a severe economic crisis. As so many banks were in Jewish hands, it also led to a growth of anti-Semitism, encouraged by the Catholic Church and the nascent Christian Social Party. In Germany, too, the decades before 1914 saw the rapid growth of anti-Semitism, Pan-Germanism and a strident and aggressive nationalism fostered by the Pan-German League and many similar associations. But in neither case is it possible to speak of a 'fascist' or even 'proto-fascist' movement. All we can say is that organizations such as the Pan-German League or Schönerer's party in Austria prepared the ground on which fascist movements could develop after the collapse of the two Empires, that the principal components of their ideologies were taken over by new mass movements in the years after 1918, that many of the later fascist leaders took their first political steps in these pre-war organizations.

For it needed the great catastrophe of 1918, the collapse of a world which had seemed so safe and secure, the 'shame' of the defeat and the threat of 'red' revolution, the near-starvation of the post-war years and the progressive inflation of the currency to create the conditions under which fascist movements could develop. Indeed, in Austria the early Heimwehren were founded almost immediately after the revolution of 1918, to counter the threat emanating from 'red' Vienna, from a government which for the first time included socialist ministers, from a new army which showed strong traces of socialist influence. Some of the new ministers, too, were Jews, and many eastern Jews sought refuge in Vienna in the troubled period of 1918-19: facts which aroused strong opposition among the 'natives' and caused a vast growth of anti-Semitism, which became far stronger than it had been in the pre-war period. The loss of the war could then be attributed, not to the fact that Germany and Austria were so much weaker than their enemies, but to 'traitors' who were socialists or Jews. Thus the new Front Soldiers' Association claimed that the collapse was brought about 'in a traitorous fashion', but that its own members 'had *victoriously* withstood the onslaught of superior hostile forces and as a reward were exposed to the most spiteful calumnies and meanest defamations by Jewish shirkers' and had to encounter the hostile attitude of the authorities.[3]

In Bavaria as well as in Hungary the year 1919 saw the establishment of short-lived Soviet republics which were led almost exclusively by Jewish intellectuals. The danger that Bolshevik revolution might spread to Vienna seemed very real for a short time. The Soviet republics and the Bolshevik danger created a trauma which was not dispersed by the suppression of these republics carried out in 1919 by 'white' troops. On the contrary, the danger which had already passed proved one of the primary motors in the rise of the early fascist movements. In both Bavaria and Hungary strong right-wing governments were established in the early 1920s; they helped and protected these movements which sprouted like mushrooms in this reactionary atmosphere and enjoyed the help of the army. In Austria, it was above all the support from Bavaria as well as from several provincial governments which facilitated the rise of the early Heimwehren. Indeed, at that time there were strong tendencies to create a Catholic conservative and anti-Bolshevik 'axis' from Munich to Budapest to oppose Berlin and the allegedly 'marxist' governments of Germany: schemes fostered in particular by Colonel Bauer and other völkisch officers. These plans were buried after 1923 when some stability and order returned to Central Europe, but the tendencies survived as well as the organizations which propagated such ideas.

The small Reichswehr and the much smaller Austrian army of the 1920s could not provide employment for the numerous professional officers and NCOs of the former imperial armies. Their days of glory were gone, and they were left to eke out their meagre pensions as best they could. But many could find a new field of activity in the numerous para-military associations, such as the Heimwehren or the Stahlhelm, where they could drill the men for new deeds of glory and could once more occupy honoured and elevated positions. They were permanently alienated and disgruntled and refused to accept the new republican order which was drab and civilian and did not accord to the officer the position which he considered his due. Together with former front soldiers they formed the cadres of the early fascist formations.[4] These provided the uniforms, the flags and the military bands behind which the men could parade every Sunday. They were soon joined by many youngsters who, because of their age, had been unable to take part in 'the days of glory' and were now eager to fight 'the internal enemy', be that the Marxists or the Jews. The well disciplined and uniformed Free Corps and para-military associations were essential for the development of the fascist movements. In them, the ideology of the Leader was first developed – the Leader whom the men could worship, who outdid them in deeds of valour, as the commander of a patrol or leader of an attack had done in the Great War. Thus out of the military defeat there arose a new militant spirit, not so much directed against the external enemy but against the 'traitors' and 'reds' at home.

Neither Austria nor Germany possessed a strong democratic tradition. The parliaments of the pre-war period played but a modest role, and in particular that of the Austrian Reichsrat was stultified by obstruction tactics and the never ending quarrels of national factions. When democracy was established in 1918 this was due to the military collapse, not to a strong popular movement in favour of democratic government. Only the Social Democratic workers pressed for the necessary constitutional changes, but to many members of the middle and upper classes democracy was an alien growth. They looked askance at the new order which deprived them of their leading social positions and which they held responsible for their economic misery. To them, democracy was 'un-German', an invention of the hated French: hence the many attempts at the creation of a new 'German' order, based on Estates or professional associations. Meanwhile in both countries countless teachers did their level best to educate the youth of the country in a spirit of hostility to anything democratic, of revenge against the hated foe, of veneration for anything 'German'.[5] Many of these people were not fascists, but the atmosphere created by them was the breeding ground of fascism. As early as November 1919 the Police Directorate of Vienna reported that 'there is a general cry for a strong government which would rally all forces to attend to the needs of the people and promote the interests of the *whole* working popula-tion . . .'[6] – a clear implication that in their opinion the government of the day did not have these interests at heart. And ten years later there was a police report: 'What the population desires is a strong executive and state power which renders superfluous and makes impossible all *[sic]* other organizations.'[7] In Austria in the later 1920s, there was indeed the threat of civil war, brought about by the endless parades and rival demonstrations of the para-military organizations. The threat which the Heimwehren allegedly had been created to eliminate became much more real because of their provocative militant activities, which the Social Democrats countered by similar activities of their own.

The red scare was strongly revived by the fire of the Palace of Justice and the street riots in Vienna in 1927. The economic crisis of the 1930s seemed to bring a renewed Bolshevik danger, at least in Germany, for the Austrian Communists remained very weak. But again the danger was more imaginary than real, for millions of Communist votes did not mean that the Communists were in a position to overthrow the govern-ment, a government supported by a strong army and police. Yet there was a real danger feared by countless members of the middle classes, that of proletarization. Thousands and thousands of employees and white-collar workers lost their jobs; thousands and thousands of students saw no hope of ever obtaining a post; thousands and thousands of officials had their salaries cut; unemployment increased by leaps and bounds. Everywhere the victims of the crisis provided the fascist move-ments with a mass following. To only too many, the elimination of

Jewish competition or of the department stores seemed to offer the only possible solution. To the victims of the crisis in Austria the much flaunted recovery in the Third Reich appeared to prove that only the Anschluss would bring economic salvation.

As the peasants were particularly hard hit by the economic crisis the German National Socialists in the early 1930s were able to make rapid progress in the countryside where whole provinces − Schleswig-Holstein, Lower Saxony, Pomerania, East Prussia − fell under their spell. In Austria, too, the deep agrarian crisis, aggravated by the German economic measures against Austria and the disappearance of German tourists, enabled the National Socialists to win over large sections of the peasantry, especially in Styria and Carinthia, where the majority of the Heimwehr members and leaders went over to them. In Germany as well as in Austria, on the other hand, the National Socialists were much less successful among the urban working class. In both countries the two traditionally strongest parties, the Social Democrats and the Catholic parties, were much better able to withstand the National Socialist onslaught than the parties of the right. Indeed, in Austria the many right-wing and völkisch organizations and sports clubs provided the ideal recruiting ground for the National Socialists whose rise was enormously facilitated by their existence. In Germany, too, they succeeded in recruiting the majority of the Völkische in the course of the 1920s. As the large majority of the Völkische came from the middle and lower middle classes, this strongly influenced the social composition of the National Socialist Party.

From the same social groups also came the leaders of the Heimwehren as well as of the National Socialists. Very prominent among them were former officers and men with an academic or semi-academic background who had belonged to a Burschenschaft or a Free Corps, who could put the 'Dr' title in front of their names, or at least the title of 'Ing.', indicating a trained engineer who had not attended a university but only a technical college. Prominent among the leaders were also lawyers, teachers and minor officials. In Austria, to a larger extent than in Germany, the 'intelligentsia' of all kinds called the tune in the fascist organizations; their völkisch and anti-semitic background and their rampant nationalism predestined them for this role. In these movements they could issue orders and occupy positions of authority and influence which only too often were denied them in real life. Many of them had in their younger days been followers of Schönerer; many had belonged to a Burschenschaft. Some of them came from parts of the Monarchy which now belonged to Czechoslovakia or Yugoslavia, hence they had an additional grievance against the new order. Among the leaders of the Heimwehr, but not of the National Socialists, some came from very old aristocratic families who still considered themselves the 'natural' leaders of 'their' peasants. Yet in the person of Prince Starhemberg the old and the new elements were combined, for he had fought with the German Free Corps against the Poles in Upper Silesia and had been a leader of Oberland before he became the Heimwehr leader.

Characteristic of the Austrian fascist movements – much more than of the German ones – were their never-ending rivalries and internal conflicts and splits. The whole history of the Heimwehren was marred by personal and political friction among the leaders which prevented the movement from becoming unified, indeed prevented it from gaining political success. Even the attempt to impose a fascist ideology on the Heimwehr proved a failure and only caused new conflicts. The Heimwehren had many leaders, but no Leader. In the foreign field, some looked towards Italy and others towards Germany. Neither the lawyers Dr Pfrimer and Dr Steidle, nor the young Starhemberg possessed sufficient drive and charisma to unite the rival factions. In the end Chancellor Schuschnigg found it surprisingly easy to dissolve the Heimwehren and to deprive their leaders of all influence. But what was so characteristic of the Heimwehren also applied to the other major fascist movement, the Austrian National Socialists. They too suffered from constant in-fighting and the rivalries of the various Gauleiter who behaved like the rulers of feudal domains where they would brook no interference from outside. The National Socialist movement never produced a leader recognized in the whole of Austria, and the 'sergeant' methods employed by some party leaders to enforce their control only antagonized others. Equally unsuccessful were the attempts to impose control from outside through German emissaries or plenipotentiaries who tried to introduce 'Prussian' methods of command. This inherent weakness of the Austrian right would probably have condemned it to political impotence if it had not been for constant Italian or German support. It is indeed a strange irony of history that the only Austrian who became a charismatic Leader on the right left Austria as a disgruntled young man and rose to fame and a position of undisputed leadership not in Austria, but in Germany. It was he who finally imposed a German system and German rule upon the country, to the disgust of many Austrian National Socialists. Thus the story of the

Austrian fascist movements is really a story of their failure to achieve power by their own efforts.

It must remain an open question why the Austrian National Socialists in 1926 so willingly accepted Hitler as their Leader. But at least subconsciously they may have been aware that the Austrian party itself would not produce a man whose claim to leadership could be recognized by the different factions. Their most experienced leader, Dr Riehl, had been expelled earlier and clearly was unacceptable to many. The party in Austria was still very small, and Hitler was not only an Austrian, but the leader of a much larger party who had gone to prison (a rather lenient confinement) for his attempt in Munich to start the 'national revolution'. To his Austrian admirers, he was a martyr and a hero. At Passau, Hitler's oratory and supreme self-confidence carried the day. His Austrian followers clearly hoped that Hitler's prestige and authority would do away with the internal rivalries and the in-fighting, but these hopes were not fulfilled. Faction fights and Gauleiter rivalries continued until the party was dissolved by the authorities and punctuated its history during the five years of underground work. They only served to reinforce Hitler's contempt for the Austrian party leaders and his determination to impose his will on the Austrian party, exactly as he had imposed his will on the German party and on Germany as a whole. In Germany, in March 1933 when Hitler was already chancellor, the National Socialists polled almost 44 percent of the total vote. It seems extremely unlikely that their Austrian comrades would have polled that much if there had been a free election in March 1938.

After March 1938 the very name of Austria disappeared; even Lower Austria and Upper Austria were renamed 'Lower Danube' and 'Upper Danube' to eradicate any memory of Austria as a separate entity. Austria was divided into seven Gaue and these were treated like any Gau in Germany. At Passau in 1926 Hitler had proclaimed that the differences separating Austria from Bavaria were no greater than those between Bavaria and any other part of Germany, and on this principle he acted twelve years later. His attempt to destroy any Austrian national traits or separateness, however, produced exactly the opposite result: a rebirth of Austrian patriotism. When the Second World War came to an end the large majority of the Austrians felt that they were Austrians, and not Germans. And the united Germany which had been so attractive to so many Austrians had ceased to exist.

NOTES

1. Schuschnigg, *Im Kampf gegen Hitler*, 25.

2. Report by Keppler on conversation with Schuschnigg on 5 March 1938: *Akten zur deutschen auswärtigen Politik,* series D, I, no. 334, 457.

3. Resolution adopted by a mass meeting in Vienna in July 1920: Oberösterreich. Landesarchiv, Archiv der k.k. Statthalterei, Präsidium, 6 J 1, Nr. 274. My italics.

4. Similar points are made by Fritz Fellner, 'The Background of Austrian Fascism', in P. F. Sugar (ed.), *Native Fascism in the Successor States 1918-45* (Santa Barbara, 1971) 21.

5. Fellner, loc. cit., 20.

6. Police report, Vienna, 17 November 1919: Verwaltungsarchiv Wien, Bundeskanzleramt, 22/gen., box 4860. Italics in original.

7. Police report, Jennersdorf, 27 August 1929: Burgenländ. Landesarchiv, Landesregierungsarchiv, III-16/1929.

BIBLIOGRAPHY

A. UNPUBLISHED SOURCES

Berlin Document Center

Nationalsozialistische Kartei: Alfred Eduard Frauenfeld, Theo Habicht, Hugo Jury, Josef Leopold, Hermann Reschny, Heinrich Suske.
Akten des Obersten Parteigerichts: letters by Reichsamtsleiter Meiler and Alfred Proksch.
Parteikanzlei-Korrespondenz: letters by Major Lahr, Walther Oberhaidacher.
SS Personal Akten: Anton Reinthaller, Dr Otto Wächter.

Bundesarchiv Koblenz

Reichskanzlei, Akten betreffend Österreich R 43 I/105-112, R 43 II/1473-1479.
Hauptarchiv der NSDAP, NS 26/54, vorl. 143, vorl. 642, vorl. 647-649.
Sammlung Schumacher, Nr. 277, 302, 303, 305 I and II.
Nachlass Max Bauer, Nr. 30a and b.
Nachlass Otto Gessler, Nr. 24.
Nachlass Arthur Seyss-Inquart, Sondermappe I and II, Nr. 6, 7, 25, 26.
Nachlass Hans Steinacher, Nr. 45, 47.

Foreign Office Library

Auswärtiges Amt, Akten betreffend Heimwehr-Organisationen in Österreich, 6080H.

Akten betreffend Nationalsozialismus, Österreich, Band 1-3, 6111H.
Akten betreffend Nationalsozialismus – Terrorakte, 6112H.
Akten betreffend Nationalsozialismus, Österreich – Einigungsverhandlungen, Band 1-2 6114H.
Militarattaché Wien, Band 1-3, 5705H.
Politische Abteilung, Österreich 1A, Akten betreffend Politische Lageberichte der Geheimen Staatspolizei und der SA, Band 1-3, 2971H.
Botschaft Wien, Geheimakten 1930, 1931, 1932, 1933, 1934, 1935-38, 4938 part 3-10, 4939 part 1.
Botschaft Wien, Habsburger-Frage, K 1066.

Institut für Zeitgeschichte, Munich

Akten des Reichsführers SS, Fa 199/45.
Hauptarchiv der NSDAP, Microfilm MA 731.
Lebenslauf Hanns Rauter, 2108/57.
Zeugenschrifttum 1928, Dr Rudolf Weydenhammer.

Institut für Zeitgeschichte, Vienna

Lebenserinnerungen des Fürsten Ernst Rüdiger von Starhemberg von ihm selbst verfasst im Winter 1938-39 in Saint Gervais.
Aufzeichnungen des Fürsten Ernst Rüdiger Starhemberg bis zum Jahre 1938 verfasst während des zweiten Weltkrieges in London.
Vinzenz Schumy, Manuscript on Heimwehren, written in 1938, revised about 1960.

Haus-, Hof- und Staatsarchiv, Vienna

Liasse Österreich, 2/3, Faszikel 275, 276, 277, 285.
Liasse Österreich, 2/21, Faszikel 302, 303, 305, 306, 308, 468.
Liasse Österreich, 2/26, Faszikel 316.
Liasse Österreich, 19 Faszikel 401.
Liasse Österreich, 1/12, Faszikel 466, 467.
Nachlass Theodor Hornbostel, Faszikel 246-252.

Polizeiarchiv, Vienna

Nachlass Theodor Reimer, box 7.
Nachlass Johann Schober, box 2a and b, 8, 27/4, 28, 31, 32, 33/1, 34, 37, 38/1, 46/1, 49, 50, 74, 87, 92, Politische Informationen 1919.
Box 1929/1, file 'Freikorps Oberland 1929-1932'.
Staatspolizeiliche Agenden 1933, NSDAP.

Verwaltungsarchiv, Vienna

Bundeskanzleramt, 15/gen., box 2418.
Bundeskanzleramt, 22/gen., box 4860 to 5026.
Polizeidirektion Wien, Berichte 1919, Berichte 1920.
Grossdeutsche Volkspartei, box 1 to 30.
Verhandlungsschriften der 'Grossdeutschen Vereinigung' 1919-1920.

Nationalsozialistische Parteistellen, box 5, 6, 12, 13, 19, 20.
Nachlass Walter Lohmann, box 6, 7, 10.

Burgenländisches Landesarchiv, Eisenstadt

Landesregierungsarchiv, 4-11/1924, V-8/1925, III-6/1926, III-16/1927,
   III-3/1928, III-16/1929, III-31/1930, L-16/1931.
Landesamtsdirektion – 243 – 1933: Nationalsozialistische Partei.
Landesamtsdirektion – 245 – 1933: Sicherheitspolizeiliche Berichte.
Landesamtsdirektion – 19 – 1934 Sicherheitspolizeiliche Berichte.
Burgenländische Vereinsakten, A/IV-14.
Zeitgeschichtliche Sammlung, A/VIII-3,
   III 1-2, IV 1-2, VIII-3, XI 1-3,
   A/VIII-10, VIII/5, Varia X/1 and X,
   A/VIII-14, III-1, III-2 and III-3.

Herrschaftsarchiv Helfenberg

Box 102a.
Vortrag Peter Graf Revertera, 9 March 1961, on Heimwehr.

Kärntner Landesarchiv, Klagenfurt

Präs. 7-12/8356, 1922, Faszikel 653.
Präs. 17-1/237 1923, Faszikel 678.
Präs. 7-1/1038, 1923, Faszikel 672.
Präs. Lo-2/3490, 1923, Faszikel 675.
Präs. 9-2/1411, 1928, Faszikel 904.
Präs. 7-6/450, 1932, Faszikel 941.

Klagenfurt, Bezirkshauptmannschaft

J 1-300, 1934.
JI 1934, 121-257.
JI 1934, 1-120.
JI 1935, 1-100.
J 1-300, 1935.

Oberösterreichisches Landesarchiv, Linz

Archiv der k.k. Statthalterei, Präsidium, 6 J 1, Nr. 274.
Archiv der Landesregierung, Nr. 7.
Politische Akten, Nr 1 to 81.
Politische Akten Freistadt, Reservat 1934-35, 1936-38.
Politische Akten, Freistadt, Schutzkorps und sonstige politische Akten.
Politische Akten, Freistadt, Politischer Nachrichtendienst 1934-38.
Politische Akten, Freistadt, Vaterländische Front 1934-38.
Politische Akten, Freistadt, Politische Akten 1934-38.
Nachlass Theodor Berger, Nr. 26, 27, 31.
Nachlass Landeshauptmann Dr Schlegel, Nr. 1, Faszikel 2.
Dr Harry Slapnicka, Manuscript on 'Heimwehren und Schutzbund in Oberöster-
   reich'.

Steiermärkisches Landesarchiv, Graz

Präsidialakten, E. 91, 1921-1925, Polizeiberichte.
Akten der k.k. steiermärkischen Statthalterei – Präsidium, E. 91, 1918 and 1919-1920.
Präsidialakten 1919, 443 J 204 and 289 J 204.
Landesamtsdirektion 1926, 384 V 1.
Landesamtsdirektion 1928, 384 W 26.
Landesamtsdirektion 1932, 384 He 2: Heimatschutzverband.
Landesamtsdirektion 1932, 384 Mo 1: Monarchisten.
Landesamtsdirektion 1932, 384 A 114.
Bezirkshauptmannschaft Graz, 1927, Gruppe 14.
Bezirkshauptmannschaft Graz, 1929, Gruppe 14.
Bezirkshauptmannschaft Graz, 1934, Gruppe 14.
Bezirkshauptmannschaft Graz, 1936, Gruppe 14.
Bezirkshauptmannschaft Bruck an der Mur, 1928-29, Gruppe Vst.
Bezirkshauptmannschaft Bruck an der Mur, 1931, Gruppe Vst.
Bezirkshauptmannschaft Bruck an der Mur, 1933, Gruppe Vst. 1.
Bezirkshauptmannschaft Bruck an der Mur, 1934, Gruppe Vst. A-C.
Bezirkshuaptmannschaft Bruck an der Mur, 1934, Gruppe 14.
Bezirkshauptmannschaft Bruck an der Mur, 1936, Gruppe Vrst.
Bezirkshauptmannschaft Bruck an der Mur, 1936, Gruppe 14.
Bezirkshauptmannschaft Bruck an der Mur, 1937, Gruppe Vrst. 1-2.
Bezirkshauptmannschaft Bruck an der Mur, 1938, Gruppe Vrst.
Bezirkshauptmannschaft Liezen, 1927, Gruppe 14.
Bezirkshauptmannschaft Liezen, 1935-36, Gruppe Vrst.
Bezirkshauptmannschaft Liezen, 1936, Gruppe 14 S-W and V-Z.
Bezirkshauptmannschaft Voitsberg, 1927, Gruppe 14.
Bezirkshauptmannschaft Voitsberg, 1931, Gruppe 14.
Bezirkshauptmannschaft Voitsberg, 1933, Gruppe 14 A-O.
Bezirkshauptmannschaft Voitsberg, 1934, Gruppe 14 L-R.
Bezirkshauptmannschaft Voitsberg, 1935, Gruppe 14 A-M.
Bezirkshauptmannschaft Voitsberg, 1936, Gruppe 14 Gi-La and Vo-Z.
Bezirkshauptmannschaft Voitsberg, 1937, Gruppe 14 V-Z.
Bezirkshauptmannschaft Voitsberg, 1938, Gruppe 14 L-O.

Tiroler Landesarchiv, Innsbruck

Präsidialakten 1919, XII 76 e.
Präsidialakten 1921, XII 76 e.
Präsidialakten 1922, II 11 g: 'Festschiessen der Heimatwehren November 1920'.
Präsidialakten 1922, 165 II 11 g.
Präsidialakten 1929, 1709 XII 57.
Präsidialakten 1930, 956 III 10.
Präsidialakten 1932, 303 III 10: 'Bildung der Heimatwehren in Tirol'.
Präsidialakten 1933, 675 III 10.
Präsidialakten 1933, 181 XII 59.
Präsidialakten 1933, 1851 I 6.
Präsidialakten 1934, prs XII 57 and 479 III 10.

Präsidialakten 1935, 62 prs XII 57.
Präsidialakten 1937, 434 XII 57 and prs XII 57.
Nachlass Michael Mayr, V/20: Tiroler Ständerat.

Vorarlberger Landesarchiv, Bregenz

Landesregierung, Präsidialakten 900, 1928.
Präsidialakten 488, 1931.
Präsidialakten 232, 1932.
Präsidialakten 252, 1933.
Präsidialakten 1093, 1933.
Präsidialakten 544, 1933.
Präsidialakten 757, 1933.
Präsidialakten 321, 1934.
Präsidialakten 484, 1934.
Bezirkshauptmannschaft Bregenz, Nr. 613, 1931.
    Nr. 1380, 1934.
    Nr. 3625, 1933.
    Nr. 3875, 1933.
    Nr. 170, 1934.
    Nr. 1871, 1934.
    Nr. 403, 1934.
    Nr. 3250, 1934.
    Nr. 1138, 1935.
    Nr. 169, 1935.
    Nr. 384, 1936.
    Nr. 174, 1938.
    Nr. 603, 1938.

B. PUBLISHED SOURCES

Akten zur deutschen auswärtigen Politik 1918-1945, Serie C, Band I(1), I(2) (Göttingen, 1971).
Akten zur deutschen auswärtigen Politik 1918-1945, Serie C, Band II(1) (Göttingen, 1973).
Akten zur deutschen auswärtigen Politik 1918-1945, Serie C, Band III(1) (Göttingen, 1973).
Akten zur deutschen auswärtigen Politik 1918-1945, Serie D, Band I (Baden-Baden, 1950).
Documents on German Foreign Policy, Series C, vol. IV (Washington, 1962).
Documents on German Foreign Policy, Series C, vol. V (Washington, 1966).
Erhebung der österreichischen Nationalsozialisten im Juli 1934 (Akten der Historischen Kommission des Reichsführers SS) (Vienna-Frankfurt-Zürich, 1965).
Hochverratsprozess gegen Dr. Guido Schmidt vor dem Wiener Volksgericht – Die gerichtlichen Protokolle mit den Zeugenaussagen, unveröffentlichten Doku-

menten, sämtlichen Geheimbriefen und Geheimakten (Vienna, 1947).

Kerekes, L. (ed.), 'Akten zu den geheimen Verbindungen zwischen der Bethlen-Regierung und der österreichischen Heimwehrbewegung', *Acta Historica*, XI (Budapest, 1965) 299-339.

Nemes, D. (ed.), ' "Die österreichische Aktion" der Bethlen-Regierung', *Acta Historica*, XI (Budapest, 1965) 187-258.

Österreichischer Beobachter, 1-3. Jahrgang 1936-38.

Panther, Der, Steirische Heimatschutzzeitung, 1-4. Jahrgang, 1930-33.

Rote Adler, Der, 3. Jahrgang 1934.

C. SECONDARY AUTHORITIES

Anon., '50 Jahre Burgenland – Die ersten Jahre des Burgenlandes', *Burgenländisches Leben*, 22. Jahrgang, Nr. 11-12 (Nov.-Dec. 1971).

Ardelt, Rudolf, G., *Zwischen Demokratie und Faschismus – Deutschnationales Gedankengut in Österreich 1919-1930* (Vienna-Salzburg, 1972).

Bärnthaler, Irmgard, *Die Vaterländische Front – Geschichte und Organisation* (Vienna-Frankfurt-Zürich, 1971).

Berg, Friedrich, *Die weisse Pest – Beiträge zur völkischen Bewegung in Österreich* (Vienna, 1926).

Billroth, Theodor, *Über das Lehren und Lernen der medicinischen Wissenschaften an den Universitäten der deutschen Nation* (Vienna, 1876).

Botz, Gerhard, 'Die historische Erscheinungsform des Faschismus', *Beiträge zur historischen Sozialkunde*, IV(3) (July-Sept. 1974), 56-62.

Bracher, Karl Dietrich, *Die Deutsche Diktatur* (Cologne, 1969).

Brandstötter, Rudolf, 'Dr Walter Riehl und die Geschichte der nationalsozialistischen Bewegung in Österreich' (Ph.D. thesis, Vienna, 1969) MS.

Bullock, Alan, *Hitler – A Study in Tyranny* (London, 1973 edn).

Carsten, F. L., *Revolution in Central Europe 1918-1919* (London, 1972).

Ciller, A., *Vorläufer des Nationalsozialismus* (Vienna, 1932).

Fellner, Fritz, 'The Background of Austrian Fascism', in Peter F. Sugar (ed.), *Native Fascism in the Successor States 1918-1945* (Santa Barbara, 1971) 15-23

Gedye, G. E. R., *Fallen Bastions – The Central European Tragedy* (London, 1939).

Gehl, Jürgen, *Austria, Germany and the Anschluss, 1931-1938* (London, 1963).

Goldinger, Walter, 'Der geschichtliche Ablauf der Ereignisse in Österreich von 1918 bis 1945', in Heinrich Benedikt (ed.), *Geschichte der Republik Österreich* (Vienna, 1954) 15-288.

––, *Geschichte der Republik Österreich* (Vienna, 1962).

Haag, John, 'Knights of the Spirit – the Kameradschaftsbund', *Journal of Contemporary History*, VIII(3) (July 1973) 133-53.

Hartlieb, Wladimir von, *Parole: Das Reich* (Vienna-Leipzig, 1939).

Heer, Friedrich, 'Freud, the Viennese Jew', in Jonathan Miller (ed.), *Freud – The Man, his World, his Influence* (London, 1972) 1-20.

Heimatschutz in Österreich (Vienna, 1934).

Huemer, Peter, 'Sektionschef Dr Robert Hecht und die Entstehung der ständisch-autoritären Verfassung in Österreich' (Ph.D. thesis, Vienna, 1968) MS.

Hofmann, Josef, *Der Pfrimer-Putsch – Der steirische Heimwehrprozess des Jahres 1931* (Vienna-Graz, 1965).

Jedlicka, Ludwig, 'The Austrian Heimwehr', *Journal of Contemporary History*, I(1) (Jan. 1966) 127-44.

Kann, Robert A., *Das Nationalitätenproblem der Habsburger Monarchie* (Graz-Cologne, 1964).

Kerekes, Lajos, 'Italien, Ungarn und die österreichische Heimwehrbewegung 1928-1931', *Österreich in Geschichte und Literatur*, IX (1965) 1-13.

––, *Abenddämmerung einer Demokratie – Mussolini, Gömbös und die Heimwehr* (Vienna-Frankfurt-Zürich, 1966).

Klemperer, Klemens von, *Ignaz Seipel – Christian Statesman in a Time of Crisis* (Princeton, 1972).

Klingenstein, Grete, 'Bemerkungen zum Problem des Faschismus in Österreich', *Österreich in Geschichte und Literatur*, XIV(1) (1970) 1-13.

Langoth, Franz, *Kampf um Österreich – Erinnerungen eines Politikers* (Wels, 1951).

Nusser, Horst G. W., *Konservative Wehrverbände in Bayern, Preussen und Österreich 1918-1933* (Munich, 1973).

Pauley, Bruce F., *Hahnenschwanz und Hakenkreuz – Der Steirische Heimatschutz und der österreichische Nationalsozialismus* (Vienna, 1972).

Pichl, Eduard, *Georg Schönerer*, 6 vols (Oldenburg, 1938).

Pulzer, Peter G. J., *The Rise of Political Anti-Semitism in Germany and Austria* (New York-London, 1964).

––, 'The Development of Political Antisemitism in Austria', in Josef Fraenkel (ed.), *The Jews of Austria* (London, 1967) 429-43.

Rape, Ludger, 'Die österreichische Heimwehr und ihre Beziehungen zur bayerischen Rechten zwischen 1920 und 1923' (Ph.D. thesis, Vienna, 1968) MS.

Rintelen, Anton, *Erinnerungen an Österreichs Weg* (Munich, 1941).

Rosar, Wolfgang, *Deutsche Gemeinschaft – Seyss-Inquart und der Anschluss* (Vienna-Frankfurt-Zürich, 1971).

Rosenkranz, Herbert, 'The Anschluss and the Tragedy of Austrian Jewry', in Josef Fraenkel (ed.), *The Jews of Austria* (London, 1967) 479-526.

Schneller, Martin, *Zwischen Romantik und Faschismus – Der Beitrag Othmar Spanns zum Konservativismus der Weimarer Republik* (Stuttgart, 1970).

Schuschnigg, Kurt, *Im Kampf gegen Hitler – Die Überwindung der Anschlussidee* (Vienna-Munich-Zürich, 1969).

Schweiger, Franz, 'Geschichte der niederösterreichischen Heimwehr von 1928 bis 1930' (Ph.D. thesis, Vienna, 1964) MS. 2 vols.

Spann, Othmar, *Der wahre Staat – Vorlesungen über Abbruch und Neubau der Gesellschaft gehalten im Sommersemester 1920 an der Universität Wien* (Leipzig, 1921).

Stadler, Karl R., *Opfer verlorener Zeiten – Die Geschichte der Schutzbund-Emigration 1934* (Vienna, 1974).

Staudinger, Anton, 'Christlichsoziale Partei und Errichtung des "Autoritären Ständestaates" in Österreich', *Vom Justizpalast zum Heldenplatz* (Vienna, 1975) 65-81.

Van Arkel, Dirk, 'Antisemitism in Austria' (Leiden, 1966) MS.

Wandruszka, Adam, 'Österreichs politische Struktur', in Heinrich Benedikt (ed.), *Geschichte der Republik Österreich* (Vienna, 1954) 289-485.

Warren, John Christopher Peter, 'The Political Career and Influence of Georg Ritter von Schönerer', (Ph.D. thesis, London, 1963) MS.

Whiteside, Andrew, G., 'Nationaler Sozialismus in Österreich vor 1918', *Vierteljahrshefte für Zeitgeschichte*, IX (1961) 333-59.

— —, *Austrian National Socialism before 1918* (The Hague, 1962).

— —, 'Austria', in: Hans Rogger and Eugen Weber (eds.), *The European Right – A Historical Profile* (Berkeley and Los Angeles, 1966) 308-63.

— —, *The Socialism of Fools – Georg Ritter von Schönerer and Austrian Pan-Germanism* (Berkeley-Los Angeles-London, 1975).

Zöllner, Erich, *Geschichte Österreichs* (Vienna, 1961).

FRANCIS L. CARSTEN is Masaryk Professor of Central European History at the University of London. He is the Editor of the *Slavonic and East European Review,* and the author of various publications including *The Origins of Prussia* (1959), *Princes and Parliaments in Germany* (1959), *The Reichswehr and Politics 1918-1933* (1966), *The Rise of Fascism* (1967) and *Revolution in Central Europe 1918-1919* (1972).

E7